Dublin

"All you've got to do is decide to go and the hardest part is over.

So go!"

Fionn Davenport

Contents

(left) **The Spire p137** Marvel at the famous landmark on O'Connell St.

....

(above) **Fusiliers' Arch p69** Relax in St Stephen's Green park

....

(right) **Grafton St p52** Enjoy buskers' music

....

North of the Liffey p126

Temple Bar p98

Docklands & the Grand Canal p145

Kilmainham & the Liberties p110

Grafton Street & Around p52

Merrion Square & Around p84

The Southside p151

Welcome to Dublin

A small capital with a huge reputation, Dublin's mix of heritage and hedonism will not disappoint. All you have to do is show up.

Layers of History

Dublin has been in the news since the 9th century, and while traces of its Viking past have been largely washed away, the city is a living museum of its history since then, with medieval castles and cathedrals on display alongside the architectural splendours of its 18th-century heyday, when Dublin was the most handsome Georgian city of the British Empire and a fine reflection of the aspirations of its most privileged citizens. How power was wrested from their hands is another story, and you'll learn that one in its museums and on its walking tours.

Personality Goes a Long Way

Dubliners will admit theirs isn't the prettiest city, but will remind you that pretty things are as easy to like as they are to forget...before showing you the showstopper Georgian bits to prove that Dublin has a fine line in sophisticated elegance. True love is demonstrated with brutal unsentimentality round here, but they'll go soft at the knees when talking about the character and personality of the 'greatest city in the world, if you ignore all the others'. Garrulous, amiable and witty, Dubliners at their ease are the greatest hosts of all, a charismatic bunch with compelling soul and sociability.

A Few Scoops

Even in these times of green juices and heart-monitoring apps, the pub remains the alpha and omega of social interaction in Dublin. The city's relationship with alcohol is complex and conflicted, but at its very best, a night out in the pub is the perfect social lubricant and one of the highlights of a visit to Dublin. Every Dubliner has their favourite haunt, from the never-changing traditional pub to whatever new opening is bringing in the beautiful people. With more than 1000 of them spread about the city, you'll be spoilt for choice.

All the World is Dublin

For as long as it's been around, Dublin has looked beyond Irish shores for inspiration. Once the second city of the (British) empire, Dublin has always maintained a pretty cosmopolitan outlook and in the last two decades has conspicuously embraced diversity and multiculturalism. You'll hear languages and eat foods from all four corners of the globe, and while it used to be said that 'real' Dubs had to be born within the canals like their parents and grandparents before them, these days you're just as likely to meet a Dub whose parents were born in Warsaw, Lagos, Cairo or Beijing.

Why I Love Dublin

By Fionn Davenport, Writer

Dublin's had a rough ride the last decade or so, but it has retained the quintessence of its true self: affable, easygoing and never forgetting to take the rough with the smooth with a kind of grumpy dignity. I love how small and intimate the city is, how I can go for an amble through town and always meet someone I know or strike up a conversation with a stranger. Forget Paris: Dublin is the flâneur capital of Europe, for it still puts a premium on the art of slowing down enough to take in the world around you.

For more about our writers, see p256

Top: Long Room, Trinity College (p54)

Dublin's
Top 10

A Dublin Pub (p35)

1 'A good puzzle would be to cross Dublin without passing a pub', mused Leopold Bloom in James Joyce's *Ulysses*. A conundrum, given there's at least one on every street, but the answer is simple: go into each one you find. A hundred years later, the centre of all social life in Dublin remains the bar. There are more than 1000, from traditional boozers, such as John Mulligan's, to the trendiest watering holes. It's where you'll meet Dubliners at their convivial, easygoing best and get a sense of what makes this city tick. BELOW LEFT: LONG HALL (P75)

🍷 *Drinking & Nightlife*

Trinity College (p54)

2 Since its foundation in 1592, Trinity College has become one of the world's most famous universities; it's the alma mater of Swift, Wilde and Beckett; it's where you'll find the most beautiful library in the whole country and the home of the world's most famous illuminated Gospel, the *Book of Kells*. Its 16 hectares are an oasis of aesthetic elegance, its cobbled quadrangles lined with handsome neoclassical buildings that lend an air of magisterial calm to the campus, evident as soon as you walk through Front Arch.

◉ *Grafton St & Around*

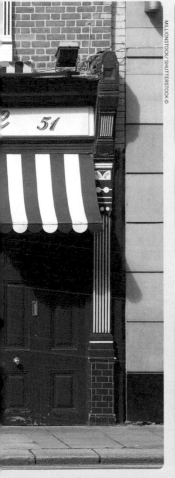

MILLIONSTOCK / SHUTTERSTOCK ©

GIMAS / SHUTTERSTOCK ©

National Museum of Ireland *(p86; p133)*

3 The artefacts of a nation are to be found in this eminent institution, which opened in 1890 with a fine collection of coins, medals and 'significant Irish antiquities'. The collection has grown significantly since then, and now numbers in excess of four million objects split across three separate museum buildings, including prehistoric archaeological finds and Celtic and medieval treasures, an extensive folklore collection, and the stuffed beasts and skeletons of the natural history section.

◉ *Merrion Square & Around; North of the Liffey*

Dublin City Gallery – the Hugh Lane *(p128)*

4 Hanging on the walls of a magnificent Georgian pile is arguably the city's finest collection of modern and contemporary art, which runs the gamut from Impressionist masterpieces (Degas, Monet, Manet et al) to Irish artists such as Dorothy Cross and Sean Scully. The gallery's extra-special treat is Dublin-born Francis Bacon's actual London studio, brought over piece by piece and painstakingly reassembled in all its glorious mess – you can't step inside it but you can observe exactly how the artist lived and worked, down to the minute details.

◉ *North of the Liffey*

Kilmainham Gaol *(p118)*

5 Ireland's struggle for independence was a bloody and tempestuous journey, and this forbidding prison on the western edge of the city played a role in it for nearly 150 years, as the forced temporary home of many a rebel and revolutionary. Unoccupied since 1924, it is now a museum with an enthralling exhibit on the history of Irish nationalism. The guided tour of its grim cells and corridors is highly memorable and it finishes in the yard where the leaders of the failed 1916 Easter Rising were executed.

◉ *Kilmainham & the Liberties*

Dining Scene *(p31)*

6 It was unthinkable less than two decades ago, but Dublin's foodie scene is now one of the city's major highlights. There are restaurants to suit every taste and budget, but the most exciting ones are the places – such as Richmond, 101 Talbot and Chapter One – that have led the way in defining Modern Irish cuisine, a catholic style that uses the basic ingredients and recipes of Irish cuisine and infuses them with influences from virtually every other cuisine in the world. BELOW: RESTAURANT PATRICK GUILBAUD (P96)

✕ *Eating*

Guinness Storehouse *(p112)*

7 One of the world's most famous beer brands is Guinness, as inextricably linked with Dublin as James Joyce and... no, we can't think of anything else. An old fermentation plant in the St James's Gate Brewery has been converted into a seven-storey museum devoted to the beer, the company's history, how the beer is made and how it became the brand it is today. The top floor is an atrium bar, where you put the theory to the test and drink a pint; just below it is an excellent spot for lunch.

⊙ *Kilmainham & the Liberties*

6

8

St Stephen's Green *(p64)*

8 Dublin is blessed with green spaces, but none is so popular or so beloved by its citizens as St Stephen's Green, its main entrance through an arch at the southern end of Grafton St. When the sun burns through the cloud cover, virtually every blade of grass is occupied, by students, lovers and workers on a break. Many a business meeting is conducted along its pathways, which run by flower gardens, playgrounds and old Victorian bandstands.

⊙ *Grafton St & Around*

Chester Beatty Library *(p62)*

9 Alfred Chester Beatty was a mining magnate with exceedingly good taste, and the fruit of his aesthetic sensibility is gathered in this remarkable museum. Books, manuscripts and scrolls were his particular love, and his collection includes one of the world's finest gatherings of Qu'rans (pictured right), the finest collection of Chinese jade books in existence, and some of the earliest biblical parchments ever found. The remainder of the collection is fleshed out with tablets, paintings, furniture and other beautiful objets d'art.

◉ *Grafton St & Around*

LONELY PLANET/GETTY IMAGES ©

National Gallery *(p90)*

10 The state's art collection is an impressive one, a history of art spread across six centuries and 54 separate galleries, which have just reopened after a major refurbishment. The marquee names include Goya, Caravaggio and Van Gogh, but no less impressive are the paintings by luminaries such as Orpen, Reynolds and Van Dongen. Don't miss the paintings by Jack B Yeats, or the seasonal exhibit of watercolours by JMW Turner; as you find your way there, you'll pass the odd Rembrandt, Velázquez and Vermeer.

◉ *Merrion Square & Around*

What's New

National Gallery

A four-year, €30-million revamp of the country's most important art gallery was finally completed in 2017, with the Dargan and Milltown wings gleaming once again with state-of-the-art security and heating systems and new galleries never before open to the public. The long-awaited reopening was the occasion for a major exhibition of work by Vermeer and others. (p90)

Irish Family History Centre

Explore your family history on an extensive database at the new Irish Family History Centre and get a 15-minute consultation with a genealogist on how best to track your ancestry. (p147)

Whiskey Distilleries

Teeling led the way a couple of years ago, but the Liberties is set to get two more distilleries in the next few years: the Pearse Lyons Distillery opened in 2017 and will be followed by the Dublin Liberties Distillery sometime in 2019.

Luas Link

After years of traffic obstruction and roadworks, the new Luas link opened in late 2017, bridging the red and green lines with a new track running from the top of O'Connell St to St Stephen's Green. (p218)

Burgers, Food Trucks & Odd Cafes

Dublin's dining scene continues to spread its wings with the arrival of food trucks and a cafe in a converted tram called the Tram Cafe. In 2017 burgers were king with the likes of Bunsen and Wow Burger offering some pretty tasty ones. (p70, p105, p138)

Green Mile Tours

Donal Fallon's superb one-hour themed walking tours of the city offer funny and educational insights into this most interesting city. (p83)

Conrad Redux

A major restyling of the Conrad (p182) has positioned it firmly as a five-star hotel to rival the city's very best, while the in-house Coburg Brasserie is a wonderful midrange option for lunch or dinner. (p95)

Greenhouse

Arguably Dublin's most exciting culinary adventure is to be had in the Greenhouse, courtesy of the newly minted Michelin-starred cuisine of chef Mickael Viljanen. (p75)

AdventureRooms

What better way of testing your puzzle-solving skills and having fun in the process than a session in the new AdventureRooms? (p144)

For more recommendations and reviews, see **lonelyplanet.com/ireland/dublin**

Need to Know

For more information, see Survival Guide (p215)

Currency
Euro (€)

Language
English

Visas
Not required for citizens of Australia, New Zealand, the USA or Canada, or citizens of European nations that belong to the European Economic Area (EEA).

Money
ATMs are widespread. Credit cards (with PIN) are accepted at most restaurants, hotels and shops.

Mobile Phones
All European and Australasian phones work in Dublin; some North American (non-GSM) phones don't. Check with your provider. Prepaid SIM cards cost from €10.

Time
Western European Time (UTC/GMT November to March; plus one hour April to October)

Tourist Information
Dublin Visitor Centre (Map p238; www.visitdublin.com; 25 Suffolk St; h9am-5.30pm Mon-Sat, 10.30am-3pm Sun; gall city centre) General visitor information on Dublin and Ireland, as well as accommodation and booking service.

Daily Costs

Budget:
Less than €150
➡ Dorm bed: €14–25

➡ Cheap meal in cafe or pub: €15–25

➡ Bus ticket: up to €2.70

➡ Some museums: free

➡ Pint: €5.50–7

Midrange: €150–250
➡ Budget hotel double: €90–150

➡ Midrange hotel or townhouse double: €150–250

➡ Lunch or dinner in midrange restaurant: €30–40

➡ Guided tours and admission to paid attractions: €20

Top end:
More than €250
➡ Double in top-end hotel: from €250

➡ Dinner in top-end restaurant: €60–120

Advance Planning
One month before Book accommodation, especially in summer. Book tickets for bigger live gigs, especially touring musicians and comedians.

Two weeks before Secure accommodation in low season. Book weekend performances for main theatres, and Friday or Saturday night reservations at top-end restaurants.

Three days before Book weekend tables at the trendiest or most popular restaurants.

Useful Websites
➡ **Dublin Tourism** (www.visitdublin.com) Official website of Dublin Tourism.

➡ **Dublintown** (www.dublintown.ie) Comprehensive list of events and goings on.

➡ **Failte Ireland** (www.discoverireland.ie) Official tourist-board website.

➡ **Lonely Planet** (www.lonelyplanet.com/dublin) Destination information, hotel bookings, traveller forums and more.

➡ **Lovin Dublin** (www.lovindublin.com) Honest, sometimes scathing, reviews of bars, restaurants and other Dublin-related activities.

➡ **Old Dublin Town** (www.olddublintown.com) In a city in flux, this haphazard-looking website is an excellent resource.

WHEN TO GO

Weather is at its best from June to August, and September can be warm and sunny. November to February are cold, but dry; May sees rain and sun.

Dublin

°C/°F Temp · Rainfall inches/mm

Arriving in Dublin

Dublin Airport Buses to the city centre run every 10 to 15 minutes between 6am and midnight; taxis (€25) take around 45 minutes.

Dublin Port terminal Buses (adult/child €3/1.50, 20 minutes) are timed to coincide with arrivals and departures.

Busáras All Bus Eireann services arrive at Busáras; private operators have arrival points in different parts of the city.

Heuston and Connolly Stations Main-line trains from all over Ireland arrive at Heuston Station (for all destinations south and west of Dublin, including Wexford, Waterford, Cork, Limerick and Galway) or Connolly Station (all destinations northwest and north of Dublin, including Sligo and all trains from Northern Ireland).

For much more on **arrival** see p216

Getting Around

Walking Dublin's city centre is compact, flat and eminently walkable – it's less than 2km from one end of the city centre to the other.

Bicycle The city's rent-and-ride Dublinbikes scheme is the ideal way to cover ground quickly.

Bus Useful for getting to the west side of the city and the suburbs.

Luas A three-line light-rail transport system that links the city centre with the southern suburbs.

Taxi Easily recognised by light-green-and-blue 'Taxi' signs on the doors, they can be hailed or picked up at ranks in the city centre.

DART Suburban rail network that runs along the eastern edge of the city along Dublin Bay.

For much more on **getting around** see p218

Sleeping

The surge in tourist numbers and the relative lack of beds means hotel prices are higher than they were during the Celtic Tiger years. There are good midrange options north of the Liffey, but the biggest spread of accommodation is south of the river, from midrange Georgian townhouses to the city's top hotels. Budget travellers rely on the selection of decent hostels.

For much more on **sleeping** see p176

Top Itineraries

Day One

Grafton Street & Around (p52)

Start with a stroll through the grounds of **Trinity College**, visiting the **Long Room** and the **Book of Kells** before ambling up **Grafton St** to **St Stephen's Green**. For more beautiful books and artefacts, drop into the **Chester Beatty Library**. On your way, you can do a spot of retailing in **Powerscourt Townhouse Shopping Centre** or the many boutiques west of Grafton St.

 Lunch The lunch bento at Yamamori (p74) is both great value and delicious.

Merrion Square & Around (p84)

Pick your heavyweight institution, or visit all three: the **National Museum of Ireland – Archaeology** (if only for the Ardagh Chalice and Tara Brooch), the **National Gallery** (be sure to check out the Jack B Yeats room) and the **Museum of Natural History**, which the kids will surely enjoy.

Dinner Etto (p95) is one of the best Italian restaurants in town.

Temple Bar (p98)

Dublin's one-time party zone still likes to have a good time, and is definitely at its most animated in the evenings, where you have the choice of a **traditional music session**, some decent clubbing at **Mother** (Saturdays only) or just straight up drinking at any of the district's many **pubs**.

Day Two

Kilmainham & the Liberties (p110)

Begin with a little penance at either (or both) of Dublin's medieval cathedrals, **St Patrick's** and **Christ Church**, before pursuing pleasure at Dublin's most popular tourist attraction, the **Guinness Storehouse**; make sure to sample the almost perfect Guinness you get at the end of the visit.

 Lunch Fumbally (p120) has great soups, sandwiches and coffee.

Kilmainham & the Liberties (p110)

Go further west to Kilmainham, visiting first the fine collection at the **Irish Museum of Modern Art** (don't forget to visit the gardens too) before going out the back entrance and stepping into **Kilmainham Gaol**, the tour of which offers one of the most illuminating and interesting insights into Ireland's struggle for independence. If the weather is good, a stroll in the **War Memorial Gardens** is also recommended.

 Dinner Super seafood at Fish Shop (p139), in Stoneybatter.

North of the Liffey (p126)

Walshe's of Stoneybatter is a superb traditional bar, full of interesting locals and hipster blow-ins looking for a 'real' Dublin experience. Alternatively, you could take in a play at either the **Gate** or Ireland's national theatre, the **Abbey**. Use the Luas to get you from Stoneybatter (get on at the Museum stop) to Abbey St.

National Botanic Gardens (p142)

St Patrick's Cathedral (p116)

Day Three

North of the Liffey (p126)

 After walking the length of **O'Connell St**, and pausing to inspect the bullet holes in the **General Post Office**, explore the collection of the **Dublin City Museum – the Hugh Lane**, including Francis Bacon's reconstructed studio. The **Old Jameson Distillery**, to the west in Smithfield, is the place to learn about (and taste) Irish whiskey.

 Lunch Get a healthy sandwich or salad at the welcoming Third Space (p138).

North of the Liffey (p126)

The collection of the **National Museum of Ireland – Decorative Arts & History** is excellent, but you'll be distracted by the stunning 18th-century barracks that is its home. The nearby **Arbour Hill Cemetery** is where the executed leaders of the 1916 Easter Rising are buried, while further west again is the broad expanse of **Phoenix Park**, the largest city park in Europe.

Dinner Chapter One (p141) is ideal for a special occasion. Book ahead.

Grafton Street & Around (p52)

The biggest choice of nightlife is in the streets around **Grafton St**. There are traditional pubs, trendy new bars and music venues. You can drink, talk and dance the night away, or go see a show at the **Gaiety Theatre**. Whatever you choose, everything is easily reached in what is a pretty compact district.

Day Four

North of the Liffey (p126)

 You'll get a particularly interesting insight into the vagaries of Irish history with a visit to **Glasnevin Cemetery**, the final resting place of so many Irish notables – but be sure to take the brilliant tour. The **National Botanic Gardens** are just around the corner, and well worth an amble. Sporting fans will enjoy the tour of **Croke Park**, Ireland's biggest stadium and the HQ of the Gaelic Athletic Association.

Lunch Oxmantown (p138) in Stoneybatter has a great range of lunch options.

Howth (p167)

Hop on a DART and head northwards to the suburb of **Howth**, a nice fishing village at the foot of a bulbous headland overlooking Dublin Bay. There are great walks around the headland itself, but if you prefer something a little more sedate, there's a fine selection of pubs in the village and some excellent seafood restaurants along the pier. There's also a terrific **farmers market** at weekends.

Dinner Make your way to Ranelagh with advance booking for the Butcher Grill (p153)

Southside (p151)

A visit to **O'Donoghue's** on Merrion Row is guaranteed to be memorable. It's a beautiful traditional bar that is always full of revellers, and there's a good chance there'll be a trad music session on.

If You Like...

Traditional Pubs

Kehoe's Beautiful traditional pub with elegant Victorian bar beloved of locals and visitors alike. (p75)

John Mulligan's This historic place has featured in films and is synonymous with the quiet, ticking-clock style of the Dublin pub. (p149)

Fallon's Great neighbourhood bar at the edge of the Liberties frequented by locals and hipsters in the know. (p122)

John Kavanagh's It's worth the trek to the north Dublin suburb of Glasnevin for this traditional classic. (p141)

Stag's Head The most picturesque of Dublin's traditional bars hasn't changed a jot since it was remodelled in 1895. (p75)

Toner's Flagstone floors and an old-style bar make this a favourite boozer for the local business crowd, who come here to unwind. (p96)

Old Royal Oak Traditional pub in the western suburb of Kilmainham beloved of aficionados of the classic pub experience. (p122)

Walshe's Wonderful local pub frequented by old men in flat caps and young arty types in...flat caps. (p141)

Traditional Music

Cobblestone The best pub in Dublin to hear good traditional music, both old-style and contemporary. (p141)

O'Donoghue's Folk music's unofficial HQ during the 1960s,

CSFOTOIMAGES/GETTY IMAGES ©

Jeanie Johnston (p147)

O'Donoghue's still hosts regular sessions of traditional music. (p97)

Ha'Penny Bridge Inn A regular session of ballads, folk and traditional music takes place on Sunday nights in the upstairs room. (p108)

Devitt's Thursday to Saturday open sessions in which anyone can play – so long as you're really, really good at playing traditional music. (p79)

Oliver St John Gogarty Sessions here may be strictly for tourists, but they're performed by some really excellent musicians. (p106)

Irish History

Kilmainham Gaol Ireland's troubled and bloody struggle for independence is revealed in a visit to this historic jail. (p118)

Glasnevin Cemetery Almost everyone who was anyone in the last two centuries of Irish history is interred at this cemetery. (p142)

1916 Rebellion Walking Tour A detailed and informative walking tour of all the sites and stories associated with the Easter Rising. (p220)

Epic Ireland This interactive museum explores the story of emigration and the diaspora. (p147)

Irish Family History Centre The ideal place to begin – or further – your exploration of your own Irish family history. (p147)

Jeanie Johnston An exact replica of a 19th-century Famine ship that sailed across the Atlantic. (p147)

Admiring Art

Irish Museum of Modern Art Art from the 20th and 21st centuries on its walls, amid elegant surroundings and beautiful gardens. (p118)

Dublin City Gallery – the Hugh Lane Impressionist masterpieces and Francis Bacon's actual studio, reconstructed piece by exacting piece. (p128)

National Gallery Home of the Irish State's art collection, including a Caravaggio and a whole room dedicated to Jack B Yeats. (p90)

Royal Hibernian Academy (RHA) Gallagher Gallery Privately run gallery where installations, sound pieces and other treats complement the contemporary paintings. (p94)

Museum Meanders

National Museum of Ireland – Archaeology The country's most important cultural institution, with sacred historical treasures. (p86)

Chester Beatty Library Breathtaking collection of sacred books and objets d'art from the Middle East and Asia. (p62)

Little Museum of Dublin This museum tells the story of Dublin in the 20th century through photographs and objects. (p64)

For more top Dublin spots, see the following:
➡ Eating (p31)
➡ Drinking & Nightlife (p3)
➡ Entertainment (p40)
➡ Shopping (p43)
➡ Sports & Activities (p45)

Museum of Natural History The Dead Zoo's collection has hardly changed since 1857. (p92)

National Print Museum Sounds dull, but is anything but – and if you've any interest in the printed word then it's a memorable visit. (p153)

Live Gigs

Workman's Club A great spot for left-of-centre stuff, from electronica to alt rock and beardy folk music. (p107)

Whelan's The spiritual home of the singer-songwriter, this terrifically intimate venue allows you to get up close and personal . (p79)

Vicar Street A midsized venue that generally hosts soul, folk and foreign music. (p123)

3 Arena The place to see your favourite touring international superstar, along with 23,000 others. (p150)

Wigwam First-class DJs do their thing in the basement bar. (p143)

Button Factory A good mix of live music and DJs at this Temple Bar venue. (p108)

Markets & Shopping

Powerscourt Townhouse Shopping Centre The city's most elegant shopping centre, selling everything from hand-crafted leather bags to hats by Irish designers. (p81)

George's St Arcade Beneath the arches of this Victorian arcade you'll find everything from secondhand LPs to patchouli oil. (p81)

Temple Bar Food Market The best gourmet food market in town is the place to sample all kinds of goodies. (p108)

Ulysses Rare Books Rare books, maps and first editions are found in this beautiful bookshop, which specialises in Irish titles. (p80)

Irish Design Shop Irish crafts from jewellery to kitchenware that make for an excellent local memento or gift. (p80)

Article Imaginative and elegant collection of homewares and gift ideas, from egg cups to posters. (p80)

Eating Out

Chapter One Michelin-starred and beloved by its regulars, this is one of the best restaurants in town. (p141)

Banyi Japanese Dining If you want authentic Japanese cuisine, look no further than this sensational restaurant in Temple Bar. (p105)

Greenhouse One Michelin star hardly does justice to the superb Scandi-Irish cuisine of this wonderful restaurant. (p75)

Coburg Brasserie Exquisite fare in a hotel restaurant with elegant, contemporary art-deco features. (p95)

Etto Superb, modern interpretations of Italian fare. (p95)

Fish Shop The best seafood restaurant in town works only with the freshest catch. (p139)

Restaurant Patrick Guilbaud For the ultimate splash-out meal, this is arguably the best restaurant in Ireland. (p96)

Literary Locations

Marsh's Library Founded in 1701, Ireland's oldest library is home to more than 25,000 books and manuscripts dating back to the 1400s. (p118)

Old Library Trinity College is home to the world's most famous illuminated Gospels and the breathtaking Long Room library. (p64)

Dublin Writers Museum Dublin's literary heritage explored through writers' personal possessions, scribblings and memorabilia. (p136)

Bloomsday Edwardian gear is de rigueur on 16 June if you want to celebrate Dublin's unique tribute to James Joyce. (p204)

James Joyce Cultural Centre A fascinating flavour of Joyce's Edwardian heyday intermingled with some excellent films on the author's life and work. (p134)

Green Spaces

St Stephen's Green The city's favourite sun trap, with every blade of its manicured lawns occupied by lounge lizards and lunchers. (p64)

Merrion Square Perfectly raked paths meander by beautifully maintained lawns and flower beds. (p91)

Phoenix Park Dublin's biggest park, home to deer, the zoo, the president and the US ambassador. (p129)

Iveagh Gardens Delightful, slightly dishevelled gardens hidden behind St Stephen's Green. (p68)

War Memorial Gardens The best-kept open secret in town are these magnificent gardens by the Liffey. (p119)

Herbert Park This extensive park is one of the most popular green lungs south of the Liffey. (p153)

Georgian Buildings

Leinster House Richard Cassels built this home for the Duke of Leinster; it's now the home of the Irish parliament. (p92)

Charlemont House Lord Charlemont's city dwelling, now the Dublin City Gallery – the Hugh Lane, was one of the city's finest Georgian homes. (p128)

Powerscourt Townhouse Shopping Centre Once home to the third Viscount Powerscourt, Robert Mack's beautiful building is now a popular shopping centre. (p81)

Four Courts The home of the highest courts in the land is the joint effort of Thomas Cooley and James Gandon. (p135)

Custom House James Gandon announced his arrival in Dublin with this architectural stunner. (p147)

Bank of Ireland Now a bank, this was designed by Edward Lovett Pearce for the Irish parliament. (p66)

(Top) Leinster House (p92)
(Bottom) Temple Bar Food Market (p108)

SPECTRUMBLUE/SHUTTERSTOCK ©

SEAMICK PHOTO/SHUTTERSTOCK ©

PLAN YOUR TRIP IF YOU LIKE...

Free Stuff

Bank of Ireland The world's first purpose-built parliament building; free to enter the surviving House of Lords. (p66)

Irish Museum of Modern Art Contemporary Irish and international art is housed in the elegant, airy expanse of the Royal Hospital Kilmainham. (p118)

National Museum of Ireland – Archaeology The primary repository of the nation's archaeological treasures. (p86)

National Gallery Home to 15,000 paintings and sculpture, including a wonderful Carravagio. (p90)

National Museum of Ireland – Decorative Arts & History The building, formerly the world's largest military barracks, is as impressive as the collection it houses. (p133)

Trinity College No trip to Dublin is complete without a wander through the grounds of Trinity. (p54)

Forty Foot Pool An open-air, seawater bathing pool. (p174)

Glasnevin Cemetery The final resting place for many names from Irish history. (p142)

Phoenix Park This huge park houses the president, the American ambassador, the zoo and a herd of fallow deer. (p129)

Chester Beatty Library The city's foremost small museum is a treasure trove of ancient books and other gorgeous objets d'art. (p62)

Science Gallery Tap into your inner nerd and discover how interesting it all is...for absolutely nothing. (p66)

Month By Month

TOP EVENTS

St Patrick's Festival, March

Forbidden Fruit, June

Taste of Dublin, June

Culture Night, September

Dublin Fringe Festival, September

January

It's cold and often wet, and the city is slowly getting over the Christmas break.

New Year's Eve Celebrations

Experience the birth of another year with a cheer among thousands of revellers at Dublin's iconic Christ Church Cathedral.

February

Bad weather makes February the perfect month for indoor activities. Some museums launch new exhibits.

Audi Dublin International Film Festival

Most of Dublin's cinemas participate in the city's film festival (www.diff. com), a two-week showcase for new films by Irish and international directors, which features local flicks, arty international films and advance releases of mainstream movies.

☆ Six Nations Rugby

Ireland plays its three home matches at the Aviva Stadium in the southern suburb of Ballsbridge. The season (www.irishrugby.ie) runs from February to April.

March

This month is all about one festival. Weather is uncertain; it is often warmer but really cold spells are also common.

St Patrick's Festival

The mother of all Irish festivals (www.stpatricks festival.ie), where hundreds of thousands gather to 'honour' St Patrick on city streets and in venues throughout the centre over four days around 17 March.

April

The weather is getting better, the flowers are beginning to bloom and the festival season begins anew.

☆ Irish Grand National

Dublin loves horse racing, and the race that's loved the most is the Grand National (www.fairyhouse. ie), the showcase of the national hunt season that takes place at Fairyhouse in County Meath, 25km northwest of the city centre, on Easter Monday.

May

The May bank holiday (on the first Monday) sees the first of the busy summer weekends as Dubliners take to the roads to enjoy the budding good weather.

✨ International Literature Festival Dublin

A four-day literature festival (p205) held in mid-May, attracting Irish and international writers to its readings, performances and talks.

✨ Bloom in the Park

Ireland's largest gardening expo (www.bloominthepark.com) sees more than 90,000 visitors coming to Phoenix Park over one weekend at the beginning of the month to eat food, listen to music and, yes, test their green thumbs.

International Dublin Gay Theatre Festival

A fortnight at the beginning of May (www.gaytheatre.ie) devoted exclusively to gay theatre – plays by gay writers past and present that have a gay or gay-related theme.

June

The bank holiday at the beginning of the month sees the city spoilt for choice as to what to do. There's a bunch of festivals to choose from in the good weather.

✨ Bloomsday

Edwardian dress and breakfast of 'the inner organs of beasts and fowls' are but two of the elements of the Dublin festival (p204) celebrating 16 June, the day on which James Joyce's *Ulysses* takes place; the real highlight is retracing Leopold Bloom's steps.

🍴 Taste of Dublin

The city's best restaurateurs share their secrets and their dishes with each other and the public at the wonderful Taste of Dublin (www.tasteofdublin.ie) in the Iveagh Gardens, which takes place over a long weekend in June and features talks, demonstrations, lessons, and some extraordinary grub.

☆ Forbidden Fruit

An alternative-music festival (www.forbiddenfruit.ie) in the grounds of the Irish Museum of Modern Art over the first weekend in June.

🏃 Women's Mini-Marathon

A 10km charity run (www.vhiwomensminimarathon.ie) on the second Sunday of the month that attracts up to 50,000 participants – including some poorly disguised men.

July

There's something on every weekend, including the biggest music festival of the year.

☆ Dublin Horse Show

The international horsey set trot down to the Royal Dublin Society (RDS) for the social highlight of the year (www.dublinhorseshow.com). Particularly popular is the Aga Khan Cup, an international-class competition packed with often heart-stopping excitement in which eight nations participate.

☆ Longitude

A mini-Glastonbury in Dublin's Marlay Park, Longitude (www.longitude.ie) packs them in over three days in mid-July for a feast of EDM, nu-folk, rock and pop.

☆ Street Performance World Championships

The world's best street performers (www.cityspectacular.com) test their skills over two July weekends in Merrion Square – from jugglers to sword-swallowers.

August

Schools are closed, the sun is shining (or not!) and Dublin is in holiday mood. It's the busiest time of the year for visitors.

🏃 Liffey Swim

Five hundred lunatics swim 2.5km from Rory O'More Bridge to the Custom House in late August (www.leinsteropensea.ie) – one can't but admire their steel will.

September

Summer may be over, but September weather can be surprisingly good, so you can often enjoy the dwindling crowds amid an Indian summer.

☆ All-Ireland Finals

The climax of the year for fans of Gaelic games as the season's most successful county teams battle it out for the All-Ireland championships in hurling and football, on the first and third Sundays in September, respectively.

☆ Culture Night

For one night in September (www.culturenight. ie), there's free entry to museums, churches, galleries and historic homes throughout the city. These places host performances, workshops and talks.

☆ Dublin Fringe Festival

This excellent theatre showcase (www.fringefest.com) precedes the main theatre festival with 700 performers and 100 events – ranging from cutting edge to crap – and takes place over three weeks. It's held in the Famous Spiegeltent.

🍷 Irish Craft Beer Festival

The RDS hosts the country's largest celebration of craft beer (www.irishcraft beerfestival.ie), with plenty of music, cuisine and, of course, 200-plus craft beers.

🏃 Great Dublin Bike Ride

More than 5000 cyclists in shimmering lycra gather for the Great Dublin Bike Ride (www.greatdublinbikeride. ie), a 60km- or 100km ride around the city for charity.

October

The weather starts to turn cold, so it's time to move the fun indoors again. The calendar is still packed with activities and distractions, especially over the last weekend of the month.

(Top) Fire breather at the Street Performance World Championships
(Bottom) Temple Bar (p106), St Patrick's Festival

AITORMMFOTO/GETTY IMAGES ©

AITORMMFOTO/GETTY IMAGES ©

☆ Dublin Theatre Festival

This two-week festival (p79) at the beginning of the month is Europe's oldest theatre festival and showcases the best of Irish and international productions at various locations around town.

🏃 Dublin City Marathon

If you fancy a 42km running tour through the streets of Dublin on the last Monday of October (www.sseairtricitydublinmarathon.ie), you'll have to register at least three months in advance. The winner crosses the finishing line on O'Connell St at around 10.30am.

☆ Hard Working Class Heroes

The only showcase (www.hwch.net) in town for unsigned Irish acts, this three-day music festival features 100 bands and musicians playing at venues on and around Camden St on the south side of the city.

🎆 Samhain (Hallowe'en)

Tens of thousands take to the city streets on 31 October for a night-time parade, fireworks, street theatre, drinking and music in this traditional pagan festival celebrating the dead, end of the harvest and Celtic new year.

November

There's less going on in November. It's too cold for outdoor activities, and everyone is getting ready for Christmas.

🎆 Metropolis

A fairly new addition to the Dublin calendar is this wonderful multidisciplinary festival (www.metropolisfestival.ie) that takes place over three days at the RDS – music, art and talks.

December

Christmas in Dublin is a big deal, with everyone looking forward to at least a week's holiday.

🏃 Christmas Dip at the Forty Foot

At 11am on Christmas Day, a group of very brave swimmers jump into the icy waters at the Forty Foot, just below the Martello Tower in the southern suburb of Sandycove, for a 20m swim to the rocks and back.

☆ Leopardstown Races

Blow your dough and your post-Christmas crankiness at this historic and hugely popular racing festival at one of Europe's loveliest courses (www.leopardstown.com). Races run from 26 to 30 December.

With Kids

Kid-friendly? You bet. Dublin loves the little 'uns, and will enthusiastically 'ooh' and 'aah' at the cuteness of your progeny. But alas such admiration hasn't fully translated into child services such as widespread and accessible baby-changing facilities.

Hands-On Museums

If your kids are between three and 14, spend an afternoon at Ark Children's Cultural Centre (p103), which runs activities aimed at stimulating participants' interests in science, the environment and the arts – but be sure to book well in advance.

Only five minutes' walk from the Stillorgan stop on the Luas is **Imaginosity** (www.imaginosity.ie; The Plaza, Beacon South Quarter, Sandyford; adult/child €8/7; ⊙9.30am-5.30pm Tue-Fri, 10am-6pm Sat & Sun, 1.30-5.30pm Mon; ⊠Sandyford), the country's only designated interactive museum for kids. Over the course of two hours they can learn, have fun and get distracted by the museum's exhibits and activities.

There are loads of ways to discover Dublin's Viking past, but Dublinia (p103), the city's Viking and medieval museum, has interactive exhibits that are specifically designed to appeal to younger visitors.

Hop on to Dublin Zoo

A recommended mobile option is a **hop-on, hop-off open-top bus tour** (Map p249, F5; www.citysightseeingdublin.ie; 14 Upper O'Connell St; adult/student €19/17; ⊠all city centre, ⊠Abbey), which helps you get your bearings and lets the kids enjoy a bit of Dublin from the top deck. You can use the bus to get to Dublin Zoo (p129), where you can hop aboard the zoo train and visit the animals. There are roughly 400 animals from 100 different species across eight different habitats, which range from an Asian jungle to a family farm, where kids get to meet the inhabitants up close.

Make a Splash

Kids of all ages will love a Viking Splash Tour (p83), where you board an amphibious vehicle, put on a plastic Viking hat and roar at passersby as you do a tour of the city before landing in the water at the Grand Canal basin.

The AquaZone at the National Aquatic Centre (p47) in Blanchardstown has water roller coasters, wave and surf machines, a leisure pool and all types of flumes to keep the kids happy.

VICTOR WALSH PHOTOGRAPHY/GETTY IMAGES ©

Tiger, Dublin Zoo (p129)

Viking Splash Tours (p83)

Only in Ireland

Across the river from Dublinia is the National Leprechaun Museum (p136), which despite its high-sounding name is really just a romper room for kids with a little bit of Irish folklore thrown in for good measure. The optical-illusion tunnel (which makes you appear smaller to those at the other end), the room full of oversized furniture, the wishing wells and, invariably, the pot of gold are especially appealing for little ones.

Doll & Teddy-Bear Hospital

On the 2nd floor of the Powerscourt Townhouse Shopping Centre is the Dolls Store (p81), which sells all kinds of dolls and doll houses, but should your little one's doll or teddy get 'ill', this is also the home of Ireland's only doll and teddy-bear hospital.

Wide, Open Spaces

While it's always good to have a specific activity in mind, don't forget Dublin's parks – from St Stephen's Green (p64) to Merrion Square (p91), from Herbert Park (p153) to Phoenix Park (p129), the city has plenty of green spaces for the kids to run wild in.

NEED TO KNOW

Transport Children under five travel free on all public transport.

Pubs Unaccompanied minors are not allowed in pubs; accompanied children can remain until 9pm (10pm May to September).

Babysitting Agencies including **Belgrave Agency** (☎01-280 9341; www. nanny.ie; 55 Mulgrave St, Dun Laoghaire; per hr €12 plus agency booking fee €25 & 23% VAT, per hr after 6pm €20 plus VAT) provide professional nannies for €12 to €20 per hour, plus taxi fare.

Resources Parents with young children should check out www.eumom. com; an excellent site about family-friendly accommodation is www. babygoes2.com.

Like a Local

Dublin is, depending on your perspective, a small city or a very large village, which makes it at once easy to navigate but difficult to understand. Spend enough time here and you'll realise exactly what we mean.

O'Donoghue's (p97)

'Slagging'

Dubliners are, for the most part, an informal and easygoing lot who don't stand on excessive ceremony and generally prefer not to make too much of a fuss. Which doesn't mean that they don't abide by certain rules, or that there isn't a preferred way of doing things in the city. But the transgressions of the unknowing are both forgiven and often enjoyed – the accidental faux pas is a great source of entertainment in a city that has made 'slagging', or teasing, a veritable art form. Indeed, slagging is a far more reliable indicator of the strength of friendship than virtually any kind of compliment: a fast, self-deprecating wit and an ability to take a joke in good spirits will win you plenty of friends. Mind you, even slagging has its hidden codes, and is only acceptable among friends: it wouldn't do at all to follow an introduction by making fun of their shoes!

Dublin Accents

Even in a small city like Dublin there is a lot of variation, ranging from suburban dialects that sound faintly American to working-class 'Dublinese' that is nearly incomprehensible to outsiders.

Dartspeak

Aka the D4 accent (after the posh southside postal district). Reminiscent of Home Counties British English and American English and is distinctive for its distorted vowels ('Dort' instead of 'DART'), liberal use of 'like' (pronounced 'loike') and 'right' (pronounced 'roysh') as well as use of upspeak, where every sentence ends with an upwards inflection, like a question.

'Inner City' Accent

Synonymous with working-class Dubliners, the most impenetrable of Dublin dialects, marked by cramped vowels and words that run into each other, coupled with the liberal insertion of extra consonants ('world' pronounced as 'wordled'). It is stigmatised as the uneducated accent of the city's poorer quarters, but of all the city's accents it is the closest to the earliest days of modern English.

ANDREW MONTGOMERY/LONELY PLANET ©

Suburban Accent

The easiest accent to understand, this is also the accent of the overwhelming majority of the city's middle-class population. It is self-consciously clear and enunciated, and has its origins in the efforts of post-independence educators to foster a well-spoken accent that was deliberately 'unBritish', instead filtering its clear diction and pronunciation through an Irish voice.

Dubliners & Sport

Dubliners can tell a lot about each other from their preferred sport and favourite teams.

Gaelic Football

Generally the preserve of the middle-class suburbs of the northside and southwest, where most of the city's clubs are located. True fans will support not just 'the Dubs' but their local club too; the county championship is a highly competitive affair. The game is also popular in the working-class areas of the north inner city, where supporting Dublin is an expression of local pride.

Football

The most popular game in Dublin has support throughout the city, primarily in working-class and middle-class neighbourhoods, where it is known as 'football' or, simply, 'ball' (as in 'Did you watch the ball last night?'). Although the Dublin-based teams in the League of Ireland have trenchant support, your average football fan in Dublin is also a die-hard supporter of a team in the English Premier League, usually one of Manchester United, Liverpool or Arsenal, but also Aston Villa (particularly among fans born in the late 1970s and early 1980s, who came of age when Dublin legend Paul McGrath played for them) and, latterly, Manchester City and Chelsea (mostly young fans born since the millennium). Generally speaking, Dubliners who refer to the game as 'soccer' are doing so derisively.

Rugby

The traditional game of the city's elite – love and knowledge of rugby was a telltale indicator of privilege and elevated social status. The most exclusive schools in the city favour rugby over other sports, and to be a

> **NEED TO KNOW**
> **Dinner time** At home, Dubliners dine early, between 6pm and 7pm; when they go out, they eat later, usually after 7pm.
>
> **Rounds** If someone buys you a drink, you always need to return the favour – or at least offer to.
>
> **Drinking water** Don't bother with bottled water in restaurants; Dublin's tap water is perfectly safe, free and generally excellent.

Blackrock boy (an exclusive boys school in the southern suburb of the same name) is code for privileged youngster whose greatest ambition is to line out for Ireland while taking a law or medical degree. The advent of professionalism, Ireland's repeated successes at international level and the Celtic Tiger changed all that, however, transforming rugby from an elitist pursuit to a more general expression of national pride (flavoured by the social aspirations that accompanied the disposable wealth of the Celtic Tiger years). The girls' equivalent is hockey, which is played at the most exclusive schools. But, like most sport played by girls in Dublin, it's generally out of the limelight.

The Rounds System

The rounds system – the simple custom where someone buys you a drink and you buy one back – is the bedrock of Irish pub culture. It's summed up in the Irish saying: 'It's impossible for two men to go to a pub for one drink'. Nothing will hasten your fall from social grace here like the failure to uphold this pub law. The Irish are extremely generous and one thing they can't abide is tight-fistedness.

Another golden rule about the system is that the next round starts when the first person has finished (or preferably just about to finish) their drink. It doesn't matter if you're only halfway through your pint, if it's your round, get them in.

Your greatest challenge will probably be trying to keep up with your fellow drinkers, who may keep buying you drinks in every round even when you've still got a clatter of unfinished pints in front of you and you're sliding face first down the bar.

For Free

Dublin has a reputation for being expensive and there's no doubt you can haemorrhage cash without too much effort. But the good news is you can see and experience much of what's great about Dublin without having to spend a cent.

Museums

The nation's cultural and historical legacy is yours to enjoy at no cost.

National Museum of Ireland

All three Dublin branches of the National Museum – Archaeology (p86), Decorative Arts & History (p133) and Natural History (p92) – are free of charge, and you're welcome to wander in and explore its myriad treasures and fascinating exhibits at your leisure.

National Gallery (p90)

The State's proud collection of art, from the Middle Ages up to the modern age, is well represented on the walls of the National Gallery.

Dublin City Gallery – the Hugh Lane (p128)

This extraordinary collection of modern art (as well as Francis Bacon's studio) are free to peruse.

Irish Museum of Modern Art (p118)

Ireland's foremost collection of contemporary art is available to all at no cost.

Chester Beatty Library (p62)

The city's foremost small museum is a treasure trove of ancient books, illuminated manuscripts, precious scrolls and other gorgeous objets d'art.

Science Gallery (p66)

Tap into your inner nerd and discover how interesting it all is...for absolutely nothing.

Green Spaces

Dublin is blessed with green spaces, all but one of which is open to the public.

St Stephen's Green (p64)

The city's most popular park is always packed with folks looking to take advantage of the good weather.

Merrion Square (p91)

The most elegant of Dublin's free parks has beautiful lawns, delicate flower beds and a statue of Oscar Wilde (among others).

Iveagh Gardens (p68)

A little wilder and not as well known as the city's other parks is this bit of countryside smack in the middle of the city.

Phoenix Park (p129)

The largest non-wildlife enclosed park in Europe is huge – big enough to house the president, the American ambassador, the zoo, a herd of fallow deer and more green space than you could ever need.

Herbert Park (p153)

Jog, run, walk or play tennis – it's all yours to enjoy.

Grand Canal (p145)

It's green in big chunks, and a walk along its banks is one of the more bucolic activities you can engage in in the city centre.

No Cost Tours

Áras an Uachtaráin (p129) Guided tours of the presidential residence are free.
Glasnevin Cemetery (p142) Excellent free guided tours of the country's most famous resting place.

Antipasto, Dublin market

Eating

The choice of restaurants in Dublin has never been better. Every cuisine and every trend – from doughnuts on the run to kale with absolutely everything – is catered for, as the city seeks to satisfy the discerning taste buds of its diners.

NEED TO KNOW

Opening Hours

Cafes 8am to 5pm Monday to Saturday

Restaurants Noon to 10pm (or midnight); food service generally ends around 9pm. Top-end restaurants often close between 3pm and 6pm; restaurants serving brunch open around 10am.

Booking Tables

You'll need to reserve a table for most city-centre restaurants Thursday to Saturday, and all week for the trendy spots. Most restaurants operate multiple sittings, which means 'Yes, you can have a table at 7pm, but we'll need it back by 9pm'. A recent trend is to adopt a no-reservations policy in favour of a get-on-the-list, get-in-line policy where you leave your number and wait for your table over a drink in a nearby pub.

Tipping

It's industry standard these days to tip between 10% and 12% of the bill, unless the waiter has dumped the dinner in your lap and given you the finger, while the gratuity for exceptional service is only limited by your generosity and/or level of inebriation. If you're really unhappy, don't be afraid to leave absolutely nothing, though it will very rarely come to that.

Price Ranges

The following price ranges refer to a main course:

€ less than €15

€€ €15–28

€€€ more than €28

Local Specialities

It's a wonder the Irish retain their good humour amid the perpetual potato-baiting they endure. But, despite the stereotyping, potatoes are still paramount here and you'll see lots of them on Dublin menus. The mashed potato dishes colcannon and champ (with cabbage and spring onion respectively) are two of the tastiest recipes you'll find.

Most meals are meat-based, with beef, lamb and pork common options. The most Dublin of dishes is coddle, a working-class

Winding Stair (p140) restaurant

concoction of bacon rashers, sausages, onions, potato and plenty of black pepper. More easily available is the national edible icon: Irish stew, the slow-simmered one-pot wonder of lamb, potatoes, onions, parsley and thyme (note, no carrots).

The most famous Irish bread, and one of the signature tastes of Ireland, is soda bread. Irish flour is soft and doesn't take well to yeast as a raising agent, so Irish bakers of the 19th century leavened their bread with bicarbonate of soda. Combined with buttermilk, it makes a superbly light-textured and tasty bread, and is often on the breakfast menus at B&Bs. Scones, tarts and biscuits are specialities too.

Veggie Bites

Vegetarians are finding it increasingly easier in Dublin as the capital has veered away from the belief that food isn't food until your incisors have ripped flesh from bone, and towards an understanding that healthy eating leads to, well, longer lives.

There's a selection of general restaurants that cater to vegetarians beyond the token dish of mixed greens and pulses – places such as M&L (p138), Yamamori (p74) and Chameleon (p105). The Wednesday night dinner at the Fumbally (p120) always includes a tasty vegetarian option, while Assassination Custard (p69) strikes an even balance between meat and vegetarian dishes.

Solidly vegetarian places include Blazing Salads (p71), with organic breads, Californian-style salads and pizza; Cornucopia (p71), Dublin's best-known vegetarian restaurant, serving wholesome salads, sandwiches and a selection of hot main courses; and Govinda's (p72), an authentic beans-and-pulses place run by the Hare Krishna.

Organic & Farmers Markets

For more info on local markets, check out www.irishfarmersmarkets.ie, www.irishvillagemarkets.com or local county council sites such as www.dlrcoco.ie/markets.

Dublin Food Co-op (p123) Eco friendly and organic market that is especially popular on Saturday.

➡ **Harcourt Street Food Market** (Map p242 www.irishfarmersmarkets.ie; Park Pl, Station Bldgs, Upper Hatch St; ⊗noon-2pm Thu; 🖾all city centre, 🖳Harcourt) Organic produce used to make products representing cuisines from all over the world.

➡ **CHQ Farmers' Market** (p148) Local producers hawking everything from chocolate to homemade sauce.

➡ **People's Park Market** (🖉087 957 3647; People's Park, Dun Laoghaire; ⊗11am-4pm Sun; 🖳Dun Laoghaire) Seafood, meat and locally sourced veg.

When to Eat

➡ **Breakfast** Usually eaten before 9am, although hotels and B&Bs will serve until 11am Monday to Friday, and to noon at weekends. Many cafes serve an all-day breakfast.

➡ **Lunch** Usually a sandwich or a light meal between 12.30pm and 2pm. On weekends Dubliners have a big meal (called dinner) between 2pm and 4pm.

➡ **Tea** No, not the drink, but the evening meal – also confusingly called dinner. A Dubliner's main daily meal, usually eaten around 6.30pm.

Eating by Neighbourhood

➡ **Grafton Street & Around** (p69) The best choice of restaurants and cafes in all price brackets.

➡ **Merrion Square & Around** (p95) Sandwich bars and Michelin-starred gourmet experiences, but little in-between.

➡ **Temple Bar** (p104) A fine selection of food-as-fuel eateries and ethnic cuisine, including the best Japanese restaurant in town.

➡ **Kilmainham & the Liberties** (p120) A relative latecomer to the foodie scene, but catching up with a handful of excellent choices.

➡ **North of the Liffey** (p138) A fine selection of cafes, midrange restaurants and ethnic cuisine that is just getting better all the time.

➡ **Docklands** (p148) A handful of vaguely trendy restaurants.

➡ **Southside** (p153) Some excellent dining for weekend gourmands.

Self-Catering

Dublin's choice of artisan street and covered markets continues to improve. If you're looking to self-cater, there are some excellent options, especially south of the river, including Fallon & Byrne (p71), the Dublin Food Co-op (p123) in Newmarket and the Temple Bar Food Market (p108) – not to mention a fine selection of cheesemongers and bakeries. North of the river, the traditional Moore Street Market (p144) is the city's most famous, where the colour of the produce is matched by the language of the dentally challenged spruikers.

Lonely Planet's Top Choices

Chapter One (p141) Sublime cuisine, fabulous service and a wonderfully relaxed atmosphere.

Coburg Brasserie (p95) Best midrange hotel dining in town.

Greenhouse (p75) The most exciting new restaurant for years – and Michelin-starred.

Banyi Japanese Dining (p105) Superb Japanese cuisine – including the city's best sushi.

Best to Linger

Simon's Place (p71) Grab a sandwich and stare out at the world through the windows.

Third Space (p139) Perpetual refills, great music…is that the time?

L Mulligan Grocer (p140) When you're done eating, stay for the beer.

Best Asian

Yamamori (p74) Tasty Japanese classics north and south of the Liffey.

Musashi Noodles & Sushi Bar (p140) Lovely atmosphere, tasty food.

Banyi Japanese Dining (p105) Hands down the best sushi in town.

Saba (p74) Thai and Vietnamese classics in a handsome dark-wood room.

Best Italian

Bottega Toffoli (p71) Tiny, tucked-away cafe serving mouth-watering food – on request – from the chef's family recipe book.

Paulie's Pizza (p148) Excellent, authentic pizza.

Honest to Goodness (p71) Superb city-centre pizza out of a stone oven.

La Dolce Vita (p106) Excellent antipasti dishes to be washed down with lashings of good wine.

Best Quick Bites

Honest to Goodness (p71) Tasty sandwiches and hot stuff to go.

Assassination Custard (p69) Great sandwiches on the fly.

Soup Dragon (p139) Get in line for the city's best liquid lunches.

Lemon (p71) Crêpes both savoury and sweet like you'd get in France.

Oxmantown (p138) Breakfast and sandwiches to go.

Best Irish Cuisine

Chapter One (p141) Nobody knew Irish cuisine could taste this good!

101 Talbot (p140) A stalwart with an always excellent menu.

Workshop Gastropub (p148) The standard bearer for pub grub in Dublin.

Winding Stair (p140) Classic Irish dishes given an elegant twist.

Union8 (p122) Beautifully pre-sented modern Irish cuisine.

Best Afternoon Tea

Merrion (p181) The most deca-dent petit fours.

Shelbourne (p182) A timeless experience.

Westbury (p181) Afternoon tea with a view of Grafton St.

Best by Budget

€

Fumbally (p120) Great warehouse space with filling sandwiches and good coffee.

M&L (p138) The most authentic Chinese restaurant in town.

Gerry's (p70) Traditional greasy spoon with a proper greasy breakfast.

Oxmantown (p138) Great sandwiches and breakfasts.

Cotto (p138) Lovely flavours of the Mediterranean.

€€

Coburg Brasserie (p95) French-influenced, mostly seafood brasserie.

Pichet (p72) Modern French cuisine done to perfection.

Banyi Japanese Dining (p105) The best Japanese food in town.

Fish Shop (p139) Exquisitely fresh seafood at this tiny restaurant.

Juniors Deli & Cafe (p148) New York–style Italian restaurant.

€€€

Chapter One (p141) The food is sublime, the atmosphere is wonderfully relaxed.

L'Ecrivain (p96) Excellent cuisine à *la française*.

Restaurant Patrick Guilbaud (p96) Perhaps the best restau-rant in Ireland, where everything is just right.

Greenhouse (p75) Michelin-starred and marvellous: Irish meets Scandinavian.

Temple Bar district (p98)

🍷 Drinking & Nightlife

If there's one constant about life in Dublin, it's that Dubliners will always take a drink. Come hell or high water, the city's pubs will never be short of customers, and we suspect that exploring a variety of Dublin's legendary pubs and bars ranks pretty high on the list of reasons you're here.

NEED TO KNOW

Opening Hours

Last orders are at 11.30pm Monday to Thursday, 12.30am Friday and Saturday and 11pm Sunday, with 30 minutes' drinking-up time each night. However, many central pubs have secured late licences to serve until 1.30am or even 2.30am (usually pubs that double up as dance clubs).

Made to Measure

➡ When drinking beer the usual measure is a 'pint' (568mL).

➡ Half a pint is called a 'glass'.

➡ If you come to Ireland via Britain and drink spirits, watch out: the English measure is a measly 25mL, while in Dublin you get a whopping 35mL, nearly 50% more.

Tipping

The American-style gratuity is not customary in bars. If there's table service, it's polite to give your server the coins in your change (up to €1).

Pubs

The pub – or indeed anywhere people gather to have a drink and a chat – remains the heart of the city's social existence and the broadest window through which you can experience the essence of the city's culture, in all its myriad forms. There are pubs for every taste and sensibility, although the traditional haunts populated by flat-capped pensioners bursting with insightful anecdotes are about as rare as hen's teeth and most Dubliners opt for their favourite among a wide selection of trendy bars, designer boozers and hipster locales. But despair not, for it is not the spit or sawdust that makes a great Dublin pub but the patrons themselves, who provide a reassuring guarantee that Dublin's reputation as the pub capital of the world remains in perfectly safe (if occasionally unsteady!) hands.

O'Donoghue's (p97)

Bars & Clubs

Dubliners like to throw down some dance-floor moves, but for the most part they do it in bars equipped with a late licence, a decent sound system and a space on the floor. It's all changed from even a decade ago, when clubbing was all the rage: these days fewer people pay to simply go dancing, preferring instead the option of dancing in a bar they've been in most of the evening. DJs are an increasingly rare breed, but the ones that thrive usually play it pretty safe; the handful of more creative DJs (including occasional international guests) play in an increasingly restricted number of venues.

The busiest nights are Thursday to Saturday, and most clubs are free if you arrive before 11pm. After that, you'll pay between €5 and €10.

Cafes

Dublin's coffee junkies are everywhere, looking for that perfect barista fix that will kill the cravings until the next one. You can top-up at any of the chains – including that one from Seattle (with multiple branches throughout the city centre) – but we reckon you'll get the best fix at places such as Clement & Pekoe (p76), Brother Hubbard (p139), Wall and Keogh (p77) and Kaph (p77).

(Top) Kehoes (p75)

(Right) Men drinking in Grogan's Castle Lounge (p75)

Drinking & Nightlife

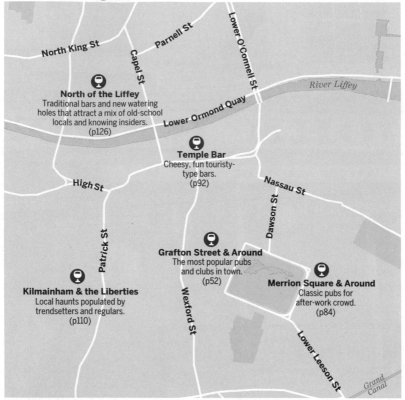

North of the Liffey
Traditional bars and new watering holes that attract a mix of old-school locals and knowing insiders.
(p126)

Temple Bar
Cheesy, fun touristy-type bars.
(p92)

Grafton Street & Around
The most popular pubs and clubs in town.
(p52)

Merrion Square & Around
Classic pubs for after-work crowd.
(p84)

Kilmainham & the Liberties
Local haunts populated by trendsetters and regulars.
(p110)

Drinking & Nightlife by Neighbourhood

→ **Docklands** (p149) Nice mix of older pubs and newer bars popular with sports fans.

→ **Grafton St & Around** (p75) Biggest choice of bars – from contemporary superpub to traditional pub.

→ **Kilmainham & the Liberties** (p122) Old-fashioned boozers where time seems to have stood still.

→ **Merrion Square & Around** (p96) Some beautiful pubs popular with the after-work crowd.

→ **North of the Liffey** (p140) Fine choice of old pubs packed with locals and a growing selection of trendy bars.

→ **Southside** (p155) Contemporary bars catering to affluent locals.

→ **Temple Bar** (p106) Popular choice of contemporary bars and 'traditional' boozers (strangely devoid of locals but full of Spanish tourists).

Lonely Planet's Top Choices

Grogan's Castle Lounge (p75) Favourite haunt of Dublin's writers and painters.

Toner's (p96) Closest thing you'll get to a country pub in the heart of the city.

Kehoe's (p75) Atmospheric pub in the city centre.

Long Hall (p75) One of the city's most beautiful and best-loved pubs.

No Name Bar (p76) Great bar in a restored Victorian townhouse.

John Mulligan's (p149) Established in 1782, this old boozer is still going strong.

Best Pint of Guinness

Kehoe's (p75) Stalwart popular with locals and tourists.

John Mulligan's (p149) Perfect setting for a perfect pint.

Grogan's Castle Lounge (p75) Great because the locals demand it!

Fallon's (p122) Centuries of experience.

Best Choice of Beer

L Mulligan Grocer (p140) A wide range of cask ales.

Porterhouse (p107) Serves its own delicious brews.

Wigwam (p143) Big selection of craft beers.

P.Mac's (p76) Thirty different IPAs as well as established brews.

Best Traditional Pubs

John Mulligan's (p149) The gold standard of traditional.

Long Hall (p75) Stylishly old-fashioned.

Hartigan's (p97) The bare essentials.

Stag's Head (p75) Popular with journalists and students.

Old Royal Oak (p122) A proper neighbourhood pub.

Best Musical Pubs

O'Donoghue's (p97) The unofficial HQ of folk music.

Devitt's (p79) Trad music most nights.

Cobblestone (p141) Best sessions in town.

Auld Dubliner (p107) Traditional sessions for tourists.

Best Local Haunts

Fallon's (p122) The Liberties' favourite bar.

Old Royal Oak (p122) Shh. Strictly for insiders.

John Kavanagh's (p141) A poorly kept secret.

Best New Bars

P.Mac's (p76) Old-style new hipster hang-out.

Opium Rooms (p78) Dublin's version of Hakkasan.

Bow Lane (p72) Elegant bar.

Chelsea Drug Store (p76) Art-deco hang-out.

Best Club Nights

Grand Social (p143) Open, free jazz jam session on Monday.

Opium Rooms (p78) Student night of R&B, hip hop and pop on Tuesday.

Workman's Club (p107) Indie, house and disco in different rooms on Friday.

Mother (p107) Disco, electro and pop on Saturday...not for the faint-hearted.

Whelan's (p79) Indie rock on Thursday.

Best DJ Bars

Whelan's (p79) Classic and contemporary rock.

Dice Bar (p143) Dive bar with an eclectic range, from rock to lounge and dance.

Bernard Shaw (p77) Great DJs playing a mix of tunes.

Workman's Club (p107) Regular line-up of excellent DJs.

Wigwam (p143) Basement bar with rockin' DJs.

Best Terraces

Bruxelles (p79) Drink next to Phil Lynott.

Café en Seine (p78) Elegance and heaters.

Beggar's Bush (p155) Convenient bench seating.

Grogan's Castle Lounge (p75) On-street overspill.

Best Hotel Bars

Central Hotel (p179) The Library Bar is discreet and elegant.

Radisson Blu Royal Hotel (p179) Bangkok-style bar.

Westbury Hotel (p181) I recognise him/her/them!

Marker (p186) The rooftop bar is *the* summer spot to be.

⭐ Entertainment

Believe it or not, there is life beyond the pub. There are comedy clubs and classical concerts, recitals and readings, marionettes and music – lots of music. The other great Dublin treat is the theatre, where you can enjoy a light-hearted musical alongside the more serious stuff by Beckett, Yeats and O'Casey – not to mention a host of new talents.

Theatre

Despite Dublin's rich theatrical heritage, times are tough for the city's thespians. Once upon a time, everybody went to the theatre to see the latest offering by Synge, Yeats or O'Casey. Nowadays a night at the theatre is the preserve of the passionate few, which has resulted in the city's bigger theatres taking a conservative approach to their programming and many fringe companies having to make do with non-theatrical spaces to showcase their skills.

In 2016 the theatrical establishment was taken to task by the #wakingthefeminists pressure group, who led a hugely successful campaign to highlight the institutional discrimination against women in the industry: its 2017 report revealed that there was an inverse relationship between levels of state funding and female representation. The two biggest sinners, the Abbey and the Gate, have made wholesale changes to their programs and staffing to address the imbalance.

As a result, future programs will see the city's bigger theatres strike more of a balance between traditional plays and newer work reflecting the broad range of experiences and perspectives.

Theatre bookings can usually be made by quoting a credit-card number over the phone, then you can collect your tickets just before the performance. Expect to pay anything between €12 and €25 for most shows, with some costing as much as €30. Most plays begin between 8pm and 8.30pm. Check www.irishtheatreonline.com to see what's playing.

Comedy

The Irish have a reputation for hilarity – mostly off-the-cuff, iconoclastic humour – and the funniest of them generally find their way out of Ireland and onto bigger stages. Notable among these are Dara O'Briain, Dylan Moran and Chris O'Dowd, who's a bona-fide star thanks to films such as *Bridesmaids* (2011) and *This Is 40* (2012).

Other big names to look out for include Sharon Horgan, the Irish-born, London-based creator and star of TV sitcoms *Pulling, Catastrophe* and *Divorce,* the latter starring Sarah Jessica Parker. Another big talent is David O'Doherty, who's been a regular festival winner since the early noughties but in 2015–16 toured the world with his hit show *We Are All in the Gutter, but Some of Us Are Looking at David O'Doherty.* Newcomers to the scene include Kildare-born, London-based Aisling Bea, who besides comedy has also starred in crime thriller *The Fall;* and Alison Spittle, who also hosts an excellent eponymous podcast.

Film

Of the five cinemas in the city centre, two (Irish Film Institute and Lighthouse) offer a more offbeat list of foreign releases and art-house films. Save yourself the hassle of queuing and book your tickets online, especially for Sunday-evening screenings of popular first-run films. After drinking sessions on Friday and Saturday nights, most Dubliners have neither the energy nor the cash for more of the same, so it's a trip to the cinema at the end of the weekend. Admission prices are generally €9. If you have a student card, you pay only €6.

Live Music
POPULAR

Dubliners love their live music and are as enthusiastic about supporting local acts as they are about cheering touring international stars – even if the latter command the bigger crowds and ticket prices. You can sometimes buy tickets at the venue itself, but you're probably better off going through an agent. Prices for gigs range dramatically, from as low as €5 for a tiny local act to anywhere up to €90 for the really big international stars. The listings sections of both paper and online resources will have all the gigs.

TRADITIONAL & FOLK
The best place to hear traditional music is in the pub, where the 'session' – improvised or scheduled – is still best attended by foreign visitors who appreciate the form far more than most Dubs and will relish any opportunity to drink and toe-tap to some extraordinary virtuoso performances.

Also worth checking out is the **Temple Bar Trad Festival** (www.templebartrad.com; ⊙Jan; ⬚all city centre), which takes place in the pubs of Temple Bar over the last weekend in January. For online info on sessions, check out www.dublinsessions.ie.

CLASSICAL
Classical music is constantly fighting an uphill battle in Dublin, with inadequate funding, poor management and questionable repertoire all contributing to its limited appeal. Resources are appalling, and there's neither the talent nor the funding to match their European counterparts. But before lambasting Ireland's commitment to classical forms, it's well worth bearing in mind that this country has never had a tradition of classical music or lyric opera – the musical talents round these parts naturally focused their attentions on Ireland's homegrown repertoire of traditional music. And still they managed to produce one of the great lyric tenors of the 20th century, Count John McCormack (1884–1945).

But it's not all doom and gloom. Classical music may be small fry, but it survives thanks to the efforts of a number of (subsidised) orchestras and the Opera Theatre

NEED TO KNOW
Bookings
Theatre, comedy and classical concerts are usually booked directly through the venue. Otherwise you can buy through booking agencies such as Ticketmaster (p79), which sells tickets to every genre of big- and medium-sized show – but be aware that it charges between 9% and 12.5% service charge *per ticket*.

Pre-Theatre Deals
Look out for good-value pre-theatre menus in some restaurants, which will serve dinner before opening curtain and coffee and drinks after the final act.

Opening Hours
➡ Doors for most gigs open at 7pm.
➡ By law, gigs in bigger venues and arenas finish by 11pm.

Newspaper Listings
➡ *The Herald* (www.herald.ie; €1) Thursday edition has a good listings page.
➡ *Hot Press* (www.hotpress.com) Fortnightly music mag; Ireland's answer to *NME* or *Rolling Stone*.
➡ *Irish Times* (www.irishtimes.com; €2) Friday listings pullout called 'The Ticket'.
➡ *Irish Independent* (www.independent.ie; €1.90) 'Night/Day' listings pullout on Friday.

Online Listings
➡ **Entertainment.ie** (www.entertainment.ie) For all events.
➡ **MCD** (www.mcd.ie) Biggest promoter in Ireland.
➡ **Nialler9** (www.nialler9.com) Excellent indie blog with listings.
➡ **Sweebe** (www.sweebe.com) More than 200 venues listed.
➡ **Totally Dublin** (http://totallydublin.ie) Comprehensive listings and reviews.
➡ **What's On In** (www.whatsonin.ie) From markets to gigs and club nights.

Company, which works to keep opera alive. Bookings for all classical gigs can be made either at the venues or through Ticketmaster (p79).

Entertainment by Neighbourhood

→ **Grafton Street & Around** (p79) The entertainment heartland of Dublin has something for everyone.

→ **Merrion Square & Around** (p97) Quiet at night-time except for the pubs, some of which have live music.

→ **Temple Bar** (p107) From clubbing to live traditional music, you'll find a version of it in Temple Bar.

→ **Kilmainham & the Liberties** (p123) The Irish Museum of Modern Art hosts the occasional concert.

→ **North of the Liffey** (p143) Live gigs, traditional music and the city's two most historic theatres dominate the entertainment skyline.

→ **Docklands** (p149) Make your way eastward along the Liffey to Dublin's biggest theatre.

→ **Southside** (p155) Only the very biggest acts play the Aviva Stadium, which holds 40,000.

Bord Gais Energy Theatre (p149)

Lonely Planet's Top Choices

Cobblestone (p141) Best traditional-music sessions in town.

Dublin Fringe Festival (p24) Exciting new theatre.

Gate Theatre (p143) Masterfully presented classics.

Bord Gáis Energy Theatre (p149) Top-class club venue.

Whelan's (p79) For the intimate gig.

Workman's Club (p107) To see the best new bands.

Best Comedy

Ha'Penny Bridge Inn (p108) Local humour hits and misses.

International Bar (p77) Rising crop of Irish talent.

Laughter Lounge (p144) Established names and visiting stars.

Best High Culture

Abbey Theatre (p143) Top names in Irish theatre.

Bloomsday (p23) Making sense of *Ulysses*.

Culture Night (p24) Art, architecture and heritage.

Best Festivals

Dublin Fringe Festival (p24) Best of contemporary theatre.

St Patrick's Festival (p22) A city goes wild.

Temple Bar Trad Festival (p41) One of the best parties of the year.

Taste of Dublin (p23) A weekend of gourmet goodness.

Forbidden Fruit (p23) Excellent alternative-music fest.

Best Theatres

Gate Theatre (p143) Wonderful old classic.

Project Arts Centre (p107) For interesting fringe plays.

Bord Gáis Energy Theatre (p149) The best indoor venue in town.

Best Live-Music Venues

Cobblestone (p141) For traditional music.

3 Arena (p150) Big-name acts only.

Whelan's (p79) Singer-songwriter HQ.

Workman's Club (p107) Who's cool, right now.

Best Busking Spots

Grafton St From hard rock to Japanese *noh*.

Temple Bar Comedy, poetry and earnest guitars.

Henry St Dublin's wannabe hip-hop artists.

Shopping

If it's made in Ireland – or pretty much anywhere else – you can find it in Dublin. Grafton St is home to a range of largely British-owned high-street chain stores; you'll find the best local boutiques in the surrounding streets. On the north side, pedestrianised Henry St has international chain stores, as well as Dublin's best department store, Arnott's.

Traditional Irish Products

Traditional Irish products such as crystal and knitwear remain popular choices, and you can increasingly find innovative modern takes on the classics. But steer clear of the mass-produced junk whose joke value isn't worth the hassle of carting it home on the plane: trust us, there's no such thing as a genuine *shillelagh* (Irish fighting stick) for sale anywhere in town.

Fashion

Men's bespoke tailoring is rather thin on the ground. Designers have tried to instil a sense of classical style in the Dublin male, but the species doesn't seem too interested – any pressed shirt and leather shoe seems to suffice.

Streetwear is very trendy and the most obvious buyers are the city's younger consumers. They spend their Saturdays, days off and lunch hours ambling about Grafton St and its side streets on the south side, or Henry St and its surrounds on the far side of the Liffey.

At the other end of the fashion spectrum, you'll find all the knit and tweed you want at Avoca Handweavers (p80).

Markets

In recent years Dublin has gone gaga for markets. Which is kind of ironic, considering the city's traditional markets, such as Moore St, were ignored by those same folks who now can't get enough of the homemade hummus on sale at the new gourmet spots. It's all so... continental.

Shopping by Neighbourhood

➡ **Grafton Street & Around** (p80) International chains and big stores are on main street, but search boutiques in the warren of surrounding streets.

➡ **Temple Bar** (p108) Tourist-only tat retailers, weird and (sometimes) wonderful individual boutiques, as well as weekend markets.

➡ **North of the Liffey** (p144) High-street chain store and easy-access shopping centres.

Lonely Planet's Top Choices

Avoca Handweavers (p80) Irish knits and handicrafts.

Irish Design Shop (p80) Beautifully crafted jewellery, kitchenware and others.

Ulysses Rare Books (p80) For that rare first edition.

Claddagh Records (p108) Traditional and folk music.

Article (p80) Homewares and gift ideas.

Sheridan's Cheesemongers (p80) A proper cheese shop.

Best Markets

Temple Bar Book Market (p109) Rummage through secondhand books.

Cow's Lane Designer Mart (p109) A real market for hipsters: more than 60 of the best clothing, accessory and craft stalls.

Fitzwilliam Square Market (p96) A small selection of purveyors, but the most beautiful location, in this handsome Georgian park.

Temple Bar Food Market (p108) The city's best open-air food market.

Moore Street Market (p144) Open-air, steadfastly 'Old Dublin' market, with fruit, fish and flowers.

Best Fashion

Louis Copeland (p81) Fabulous suits made to measure, as well as ready-to-wear suits by international designers.

Costume (p82) Exclusive contracts with some of Europe's most innovative designers.

Nowhere (p80) The very latest fashions for young men.

Maven (p82) The latest international fashions for women.

Best Guaranteed Irish

Avoca Handweavers (p80) Our favourite department store in the city has myriad homemade gift ideas.

Irish Design Shop (p80) Wonderful handicrafts carefully sourced.

Barry Doyle Design Jewellers (p80) Exquisite handcrafted jewellery with unique contemporary designs.

Ulysses Rare Books (p80) For that priceless first edition or a beautiful, leather-bound copy of Joyce's *Dubliners*.

Louis Copeland (p81) Dublin's very own top tailor with made-to-measure suits.

Best Homewares

Martin Fennelly Antiques (p123) Fine furniture and furnishings from the Georgian, Victorian and Edwardian eras.

Industry (p82) Scandi-style homewares with an Irish touch.

Article (p80) Beautiful tableware and decorative home accessories made by Irish designers.

Avoca Handweavers (p80) Stylish but homey brand of modern Irish life.

Best Jewellery

Appleby (p81) High-quality silver and gold jewellery.

Loulerie (p80) Beautiful selection of delicate jewellery.

Barry Doyle Design Jewellers (p80) Handmade jewellery exceptional in its beauty and simplicity.

Rhinestones (p82) Fine antique and quirky costume jewellery from the 1920s to 1970s.

Best Museum Shops

Dublin City Gallery – the Hugh Lane (p128) Dig out masterpiece colour-by-number prints, cloth puppets, unusual wooden toys and beautiful art and pop-culture hardbacks.

Irish Museum of Modern Art (p118) Offers a comprehensive selection of coffee-table books on Irish contemporary art.

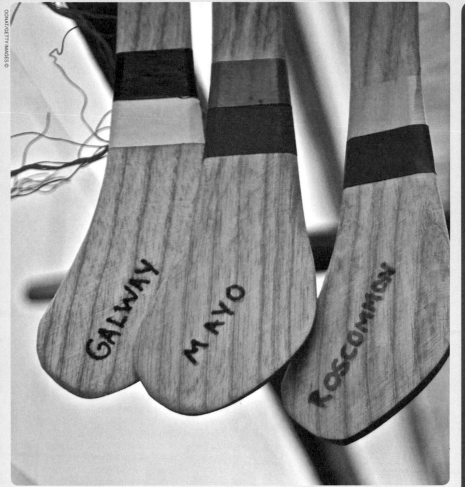

Hurls, used in traditional Gaelic hurling

Sports & Activities

To many Dubliners, sport is a religion. For an ever-increasing number, it's all about faith through good works such as jogging, amateur football, cycling and yoga; for everyone else, observance is enough, especially from the living-room chair or the pub stool.

NEED TO KNOW

Sporting Seasons
➡ **Football** April to October

➡ **Gaelic sports** April to September

➡ **Rugby internationals** February to April

Planning Ahead
➡ **Two months** Tickets for rugby internationals or the latter stages of the Gaelic championship

➡ **One month** Leinster rugby matches in the Champions Cup

➡ **One week** Local football matches and Gaelic league games

Online Resources
➡ **Gaelic Athletic Association** (www.gaa.ie)

➡ **Football Association of Ireland** (www.fai.ie)

➡ **Irish Rugby Football Union** (www.irfu.ie)

➡ **Horse Racing Ireland** (www.goracing.ie)

➡ **Golf Union of Ireland** (www.gui.ie)

➡ **Ladies Gaelic Football Association** (www.ladiesgaelic.ie)

Golf

A round of golf is a highlight of many an Irish visit. Dublin's suburban courses are almost all private clubs, but many of them allow visitors on a pay-to-play basis. Tough times means reduced green fees, especially if you book online beforehand. You'll generally need your own transport if you wish to head to any of the major courses.

The best courses within reach of the city are **Killeen Castle** (www.killeencastle.com; Dunsany, Co Meath; green fee €50-90) in Dunsany, County Meath; **Carton House** (☑01-651 7727; www.cartonhousegolf.com; green fees €75-95), just outside Maynooth in County Kildare; Portmarnock (p175), by the sea in north county Dublin; and **Druid's Glen** (☑01-287 3600; www.druidsglenresort.com; Newtownmountkennedy; green fees €70-90), 45km south of the city in County Wicklow.

Spectator Sport

Sport has a special place in the Irish psyche, probably because it's one of the few times when an overwhelming expression of emotion won't cause those around you to wince or shuffle in discomfort. Sit in a pub while a match is on and watch the punters foam at the mouth as they yell pleasantries at the players on the screen, such as, 'They should pay me for watching you!'.

GAELIC FOOTBALL & HURLING
Gaelic games are at the core of Irishness; they are enmeshed in the fabric of Irish life and hold a unique place in the heart of its culture. Of the two main games, football is by far the most popular – and Dublin (www.dublingaa.ie) is currently the most successful team in Ireland, winning three All-Ireland Senior Championship titles between 2013 and 2016, even though its 26 overall championships trail Kerry's record 37 wins.

The big event in both sports is the All-Ireland championship, a knockout contest that begins in April and ends on the first (for hurling) and third (for football) Sunday in September with the All-Ireland Final, played at a jam-packed **Croke Park** (☑01-836 3222; www.crokepark.ie; Clonliffe Rd; ☐3, 11, 11A, 16, 16A, 123 from O'Connell St), which is also where the Dubs play all of their championship matches. The All-Ireland's poorer cousin is the National Football League (there's also a National Hurling League), which runs from February to mid-April. Dublin plays its league matches at **Parnell Park** (www.dublingaa.ie; Clantarkey Rd, Donnycarney; adult/child €11/8; ☐20A, 20B, 27, 27A, 42, 42B, 43, 103 from Lower Abbey St or Beresford Pl), which is smaller and infinitely less impressive than Croke Park but a great place to see these games up close. Tickets for league games can be easily bought at the ground; tickets for All-Ireland matches get tougher to find the further on the competition is, but those that are available can be bought online (https://gaa.tickets.ie) or at most Centra and SuperValu convenience stores throughout the city centre.

FOOTBALL
Although Dubliners are football (soccer) mad, the five Dublin teams that play in the **League of Ireland** (www.leagueofireland.com) are semi-pro, as the best players are all drawn to the glamour of the English Premier League. The season runs from April to November; tickets are available at all grounds.

The national side plays its home games at the Aviva Stadium (p155); a relatively high pricing structure and the general mediocrity of the team means that home matches don't always sell out. You can buy tickets (€30 to €60) from the **Football Association of Ireland** (FAI; ☏01-676 6864; www.fai.ie).

RUGBY

Rugby is a big deal in certain parts of Dublin – generally the more affluent neighbourhoods of south Dublin – and the successes of both provincial side Leinster and the national team have catapulted rugby to the forefront of sporting obsessions.

Three-time European champions Leinster play home games at the Royal Dublin Society Showgrounds (p155). Tickets for both competitions are available at the Spar opposite the Donnybrook Rugby Ground or online from Leinster Rugby (www.leinsterrugby.ie).

The premier competition is the yearly Six Nations championship, played between February and April by Ireland, England, France, Italy, Scotland and Wales. Home matches are played at the Aviva Stadium (p155); tickets are available from the IRFU.

HORSE & GREYHOUND RACING

Horse racing is a big deal in Dublin, especially when you consider that Irish trainers are among the best in the world and Irish jockeys dominate the field in British racing. There are several racecourses within driving distance of the city centre that host good-quality meetings throughout the year. These include the **Curragh** (☏045-441 205; www.curragh.ie; €15-30; ⊕mid-Apr–Oct), which hosts five classic flat races between May and

September; **Fairyhouse** (☏01-825 6167; www.fairyhouse.ie; Fairyhouse Rd, Ratoath, Co Meath; €15-25; 🚌special from Busáras), home of the Grand National on Easter Monday; and **Leopardstown** (☏01-289 3607; www.leopardstown.com; Foxrock, Dublin 18; tickets from €12.50; 🚌special from Eden Quay, 🚇Sandyford), where the big event is February's Hennessy Gold Cup. The flat racing season runs from March to November, while the National Hunt season – when horses jump over things – is October to April. There are also events in summer.

Traditionally the poor-man's punt, greyhound racing ('the dogs') has been smartened up in recent years and partly turned into a corporate outing. It offers a cheaper alternative to horse racing. Dublin's dog track is Shelbourne Park (p149), in the Docklands, but racing was interrupted for much of the first half of 2017 as dog owners protested the Irish Greyhound Board's decision to sell the city's other dog track in Harold's Cross. Check ahead to see if the fight is been resolved.

Swimming & Water Sports

Dublin might have miles of beachy coastline, but swimming and water sports aren't as big a deal as they might be in, say, a destination where the climate is more conducive to being wet and outdoors. There are boating aficionados (and designated clubs) in the seaside suburbs of Dun Laoghaire, Howth and Malahide, but when it comes to regular old swimming, there's relatively little choice, although one of

these is an international-standard **aquatic centre** (☏01-646 4300; www.nationalaquaticcentre.ie; Snugborough Rd; adult/child & student €7.50/5.50, incl AquaZone €15/13; ⊕6am-10pm Mon-Fri, 9am-8pm Sat & Sun; 🚌38 & 38A from O'Connell St). The relatively new sport of wakeboarding (p150) is also available in the Docklands.

Sports & Activities by Neighbourhood

Kilmainham & the Liberties Jogging and walking in the War Memorial Gardens. (p119)

North of the Liffey Running, football, cycling in Phoenix Park, also cricket and polo. (p129)

Docklands Wakeboarding in the Grand Canal Dock, jogging along the canal. (p146)

Lonely Planet's Top Dublin Sporting Moments

A cheeky intercept try by Brian O'Driscoll results in Leinster beating perennial rivals Munster in front of 80,000 fans during the 2009 Heineken Cup.

Dublin beating Kerry 0-12 to 0-9 in the 2015 All-Ireland Final for their third title in five years, their 25th overall.

Ireland beating England 1-0 in 1988 during the European Championship finals in Stuttgart, the first – and only – time the Irish soccer team has ever beaten England competitively.

The Irish rugby team beating England by a record-margin 43-13 on 24 February 2007 at Croke Park: history and victory wrapped up in one delicious moment.

Boxer Katie Taylor winning Olympic gold at the 2012 games in London.

FAITHIE/SHUTTERSTOCK ©

Explore Dublin

DUBLIN'S
TOP SIGHTS

Neighbourhoods at a Glance

① Grafton St & Around p52

Dublin's most famous street is pedestrianised Grafton St, the bustling heart of the city centre. You'll find the biggest range of pubs, shops and restaurants in the busy hive that surrounds it, a warren of side streets that is almost always full of people. Many of the city's most important sights and museums are here, as is Dublin's best-loved city park, St Stephen's Green (p64).

② Merrion Square & Around p84

Georgian Dublin's apotheosis occurred in the exquisite architecture and elegant spaces of Merrion and Fitzwilliam Sqs. Here you'll find the perfect mix of imposing public buildings, museums, private offices and residences. It's round here that much of moneyed Dublin works and plays, amid the neoclassical beauties thrown up during Dublin's 18th-century prime.

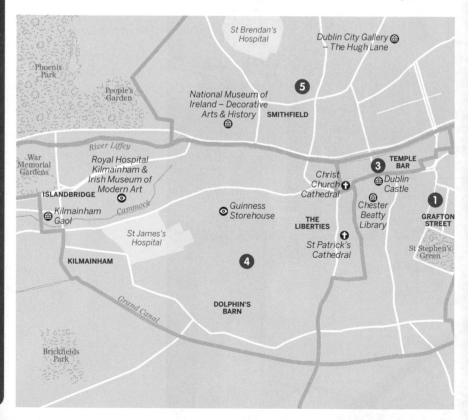

These include the home of the Irish parliament at Leinster House and, immediately surrounding it, the National Gallery, the main branch of the National Museum of Ireland and the Museum of Natural History.

③ Temple Bar p98

Dublin's best-known district is the cobbled playpen of Temple Bar, where mayhem and merriment is standard fare, especially on summer weekends when the pubs are full and the party spills out onto the streets. During daylight hours there are shops and galleries to discover, which at least lend some truth to the area's much-mocked title of 'cultural quarter'.

④ Kilmainham & the Liberties p110

Dublin's oldest and most traditional neighbourhoods, immediately west of the south city centre, have a handful of tourist big

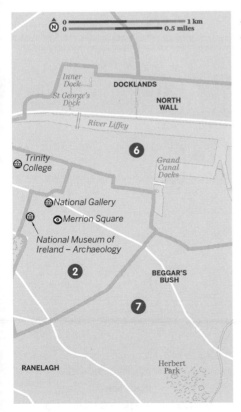

hitters, not least the Guinness Storehouse, Dublin's most-visited museum. Keeping watch over the ancient Liberties is St Patrick's Cathedral, the most important of Dublin's three (!) cathedrals, while further west is the country's premier modern-art museum and a Victorian prison that played a central role in Irish history.

⑤ North of the Liffey p126

Grittier than its more genteel southside counterpart, the area immediately north of the River Liffey offers a fascinating mix of 18th-century grandeur, traditional city life and the multicultural melting pot that is contemporary Dublin. Beyond its widest, most elegant boulevard you'll find art museums and whiskey museums, bustling markets and some of the best ethnic eateries in town. Oh, and Europe's largest enclosed park (p129) – home to the president, the US ambassador and the zoo.

⑥ Docklands & the Grand Canal p145

The gleaming modern blocks of the Docklands were designed as the ultimate expression of the ambitions of the Celtic Tiger, when Dublin was vying for the title of financial capital of Europe. The collapse of 2008 put a curb on those ambitions, but the city's recent revival has reinvigorated the area, especially around Grand Canal Dock, on the south side of the Liffey, east of the city centre. A couple of architectural beauties – most notably a theatre designed by Daniel Libeskind – stand out among the modern apartment and office blocks.

⑦ The Southside p151

The neighbourhoods that border the southern bank of the Grand Canal are less about sights and more about the experience of affluent Dublin – dining, drinking and sporting occasions, both watching and taking part. Here are the city's most desirable neighbourhoods and most precious postcodes: Dublin 4, which includes fancy schmancy Ballsbridge and Donnybrook, home to embassies and local potentates; and Dublin 6, covered by the elegant residential districts of Ranelagh, Rathgar and Rathmines, where the professional classes who still want a slice of city life reside.

Grafton Street & Around

Neighbourhood Top Five

❶ Chester Beatty Library (p62) Basking quietly in the aesthetic glow of the magnificent collection at one of the finest museums in Ireland.

❷ Old Library & Book of Kells (p64) Staring in wonderment at the colourful pages of the *Book of Kells*, the world's most famous illuminated gospel, before visiting the majestic Long Room.

❸ St Stephen's Green (p64) Enjoying a sunny, summer afternoon on the grass, where Dubliners come to rest, romance and remind themselves of what makes life worth living.

❹ Little Museum of Dublin (p64) Exploring the marvellous collection of donated historical objects.

❺ A Night Out (p75) Eating dinner in one of the area's fabulous restaurants followed by a pint or more in a pub, such as Kehoe's.

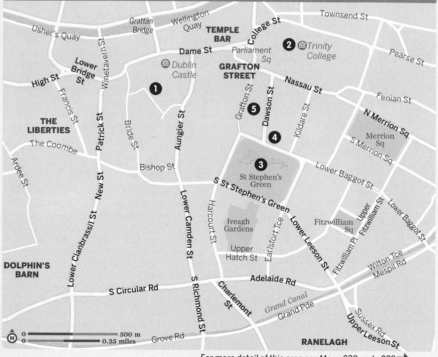

For more detail of this area see Map p238 and p239 ➡

Explore Grafton Street & Around

Grafton St and its surrounding precinct are something of a flexible feast of activities and sights, but it'll take you two days to even begin to do them justice – and much longer if you really want to get to the heart of what this part of the city is all about. The main attraction is Trinity College (p54), whose pleasures and treasures can be explored in no more than a couple of hours; right on its doorstep is Grafton St itself, always worth an amble for a little retail experience or just to take in the sound of one of its buskers.

Just south of Grafton St is the centrepiece of Georgian Dublin, St Stephen's Green (p64), beautifully landscaped and dotted with statuary that provides a veritable who's who of Irish history. But to really get the most out of the neighbourhood, you'll need to get off Grafton St and into the warren of narrow lanes and streets to the west of it – here you'll find a great mix of funky shops and boutiques, some of our favourite eateries, and a handful of the best bars in the city.

Further west again is Dublin Castle (p59) and the Chester Beatty Library (p62), both of which can be explored in half a day. Thankfully, Dublin's compact size means you don't have to stay here to have it all at your doorstep, but if you do, be aware that most of the lodgings are among the priciest in town.

Local Life

→**Hang-Outs** Grogan's Castle Lounge (p75) is the artiest of the city's bohemian pubs; the Stag's Head (p75) is a Victorian classic; sit at the window in fashionable Clement & Pekoe (p76) and watch the fashion parade outside.

→**Retail** Costume (p82) is the place for high-end women's fashions and Nowhere (p81) the men's equivalent; wander the boutiques of the Powerscourt Townhouse (p81) for quirky one-offs and local fashions.

→**Sustenance** Bunsen (p70) is great for a burger and Super Miss Sue (p73) for superb fish, but for sumptuous fare book a table at the Greenhouse (p75).

Getting There & Away

→**Bus** All cross-city buses make their way to – or through, at least – this part of the city.

→**Tram** The Luas Green Line has its terminus at the south end of Grafton St, on the west side of St Stephen's Green.

→**On Foot** Grafton St is in the heart of the city and no more than 500m from all other neighbourhoods (including the western edge of the Docklands).

Lonely Planet's Top Tip

The most interesting shops in town are in the warren of streets between Grafton St and South Great George's St; here you'll also find some of the best lunch deals.

Best Places to Sleep

→ Westbury Hotel (p181)
→ Fitzwilliam Hotel (p181)
→ Radisson Blu Royal Hotel (p179)

For reviews, see p179➡

Best Places to Eat

→ Assassination Custard (p69)
→ Eatyard (p69)
→ Pichet (p72)
→ Greenhouse (p75)
→ Bunsen (p70)

For reviews, see p69➡

Best Shopping

→ Article (p80)
→ Costume (p82)
→ Nowhere (p81)
→ Irish Design Shop (p80)
→ Siopaella (p80)

For reviews, see p80➡

TOP SIGHT
TRINITY COLLEGE

This calm and cordial retreat from the bustle of contemporary Dublin is Ireland's most prestigious university, a collection of elegant Georgian and Victorian buildings, cobbled squares and manicured lawns that is among the most delightful places to wander.

DON'T MISS

- Long Room
- *Book of Kells*
- Science Gallery
- Walking Tour

PRACTICALITIES

- Map p238, F2
- 01-896 1000
- www.tcd.ie
- College Green
- admission free
- 8am-10pm
- all city centre

History
The college was established by Elizabeth I in 1592 on land confiscated from an Augustinian priory in an effort to stop the brain drain of young Protestant Dubliners, who were skipping across to continental Europe for an education and becoming 'infected with popery'. Trinity went on to become one of Europe's most outstanding universities, producing a host of notable graduates – how about Jonathan Swift, Oscar Wilde and Samuel Beckett at the same alumni dinner?

Front Square & Parliament Square
The elegant **Regent House entrance** on College Green is guarded by statues of the writer **Oliver Goldsmith**, 1728–74, and the orator **Edmund Burke**, 1729–97. The railings outside are a popular meeting spot.

Through the entrance, past the Students Union, are Front Sq and Parliament Sq, the latter dominated by the 30m-high **Campanile**, designed by Edward Lanyon and erected from 1852 to 1853 on what was believed to be the centre of the monastery that preceded the college. According to superstition, students who pass beneath it when the bells toll will fail their exams. To the north of the Campanile is a statue of **George Salmon**, the college provost from 1886 to 1904, who fought bitterly to keep women out of the college. He carried out his threat to permit them in 'over his dead body' by dropping dead when the worst happened. To the south of the Campanile is a statue of historian **WEH Lecky** (1838–1903).

Chapel & Dining Hall

North of Parliament Sq is the 1798 **Chapel** (Map p238; 🖉01-896 1260; ☺8.30am-5pm, admission by special permission only), designed by William Chambers and featuring fine plasterwork by Michael Stapleton, Ionic columns and painted-glass windows. It has been open to all denominations since 1972 and is only accessible by organised tour. Next is the **Dining Hall** (Map p238; Parliament Sq, ☺closed to the public), originally built by Richard Cassels in the mid-18th century. The great architect must have had an off day because the vault collapsed twice and the entire structure was dismantled 15 years later. The replacement was completed in 1761 and extensively restored after a fire in 1984.

Library Square

On the far east of Library Sq, the red-brick **Rubrics Building** (Map p238; Trinity College; ☺closed to the public; 🚆all Trinity College) dates from around 1690, making it the oldest building in the college. Extensively altered in an 1894 restoration, it underwent serious structural modification in the 1970s.

If you are following the less-studious-looking throng, you'll find yourself drawn south of Library Sq to the Old Library (p64), home to Trinity's prize possession and biggest crowd-puller, the astonishingly beautiful *Book of Kells*.

Upstairs is the highlight of Thomas Burgh's building, the magnificent 65m Long Room with its barrel-vaulted ceiling. It's lined with shelves containing 200,000 of the library's oldest manuscripts, busts of scholars, a 14th-century harp and an original copy of the Proclamation of the Irish Republic.

Fellows' Square

West of the brutalist, brilliant **Berkeley Library** (Map p238; Fellows' Sq; ☺closed to the public; 🚆all city centre, 🚆College Green), designed by Paul Koralek in 1967, the **Arts & Social Science Building** (☺closed to the public) is home to the Douglas Hyde Gallery (p66), one of the country's leading contemporary galleries. It hosts regularly rotating shows presenting the works of top-class Irish and international artists across a range of media.

Examination Hall

On the way back towards the main entrance, past the Reading Room, is the late 18th-century Palladian **Examination Hall** (Map p238; Trinity College; ☺9am-6pm during exams only; 🚆all city centre), which closely

A CATHOLIC BAN

Trinity was exclusively Protestant until 1793, but even when the university relented and began to admit Catholics, the Catholic Church forbade it; until 1970, any Catholic who enrolled here could consider themselves excommunicated.

A great way to see the grounds is on a walking tour (Authenticity Tours; Map p238; www.tcd.ie/visitors/tours; Trinity College; tours €6, incl Book of Kells €14; ☺10.15am-3.40pm Mon-Sat, to 3.15pm Sun May-Sep, fewer midweek tours Oct & Feb-Apr; 🚆all city centre,🚆College Green), which depart from the College Green entrance.

SWORD & GUNS

For nearly two centuries students weren't allowed through the grounds without a sword – and duels with pistols were not uncommon in the 17th and 18th centuries.

Book a fast-track ticket online to get cheaper and speedier access to the Book of Kells and the Long Room.

Trinity College, Dublin

STEP INTO THE PAST

Ireland's most prestigious university, founded on the order of Queen Elizabeth I in 1592, is an architectural masterpiece, a cordial retreat from the bustle of modern life in the middle of the city. Step through its main entrance and you step back in time, the cobbled stones transporting you to another era, when the elite discussed philosophy and argued passionately in favour of empire.

Standing in Front Square, the 30m-high ❶ **Campanile** is directly in front of you with the ❷ **Dining Hall** to your left. On the far side of the square is the Old Library building, the centrepiece of which is the magnificent ❸ **Long Room**, which was the inspiration for the computer-generated imagery of the Jedi Archive in *Star Wars Episode II: Attack of the Clones*. Here you'll find the university's greatest treasure, the ❹ **Book of Kells**. You'll probably have to queue to see this masterpiece, and then only for a brief visit, but it's very much worth it.

Just beyond the Old Library is the very modern ❺ **Berkeley Library**, which nevertheless fits perfectly into the campus' overall aesthetic: directly in front of it is the distinctive ❻ **Sphere Within a Sphere**, the most elegant of the university's sculptures.

DON'T MISS

➡ Douglas Hyde Gallery, the campus' designated modern-art museum.

➡ A cricket match on the pitch, the most elegant of pastimes.

➡ A pint in the Pavilion Bar, preferably while watching the cricket.

➡ A visit to the Science Gallery, where science is made completely relevant.

Campanile
Trinity College's most iconic bit of masonry was designed in the mid-19th century by Sir Charles Lanyon; the attached sculptures were created by Thomas Kirk.

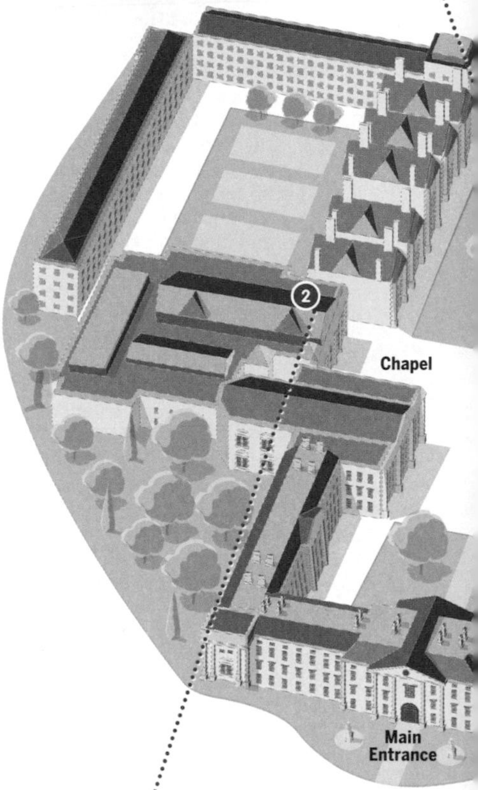

Chapel

Main Entrance

Dining Hall
Richard Cassels' original building was designed to mirror the Examination Hall directly opposite on Front Square: the hall collapsed twice and was rebuilt from scratch in 1761.

Sphere Within a Sphere

Arnaldo Pomodoro's distinctive sculpture has an inner ball that represents the earth and an outer sphere that represents Christianity; there are versions of it in Rome, New York and Tehran.

Berkeley Library

Paul Koralek's brutalist library seems not to fit the general theme of the university, but the more you look at it the more you'll appreciate a building that is a modernist classic.

New Square

Old Library

Library Square

Fellows Square

Parliament Square

Long Room

At 65m long and topped by a barrel-vaulted ceiling, Thomas Burgh's masterpiece is lined with shelves groaning under the weight of 200,000 of the library's oldest books and manuscripts.

Book of Kells

Examine a page (or two) of the world's most famous illuminated book, which was produced by monks on the island of Iona around AD 800 before being brought to Kells, County Meath.

TRINITY COLLEGE

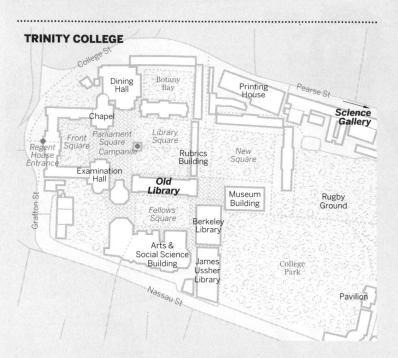

resembles the chapel opposite because it too was the work of William Chambers. It contains an oak chandelier rescued from the Irish parliament (now the Bank of Ireland).

College Park

Towards the eastern end of the complex, College Park is a lovely place to lounge around on a sunny day and occasionally you'll catch a game of cricket, a bizarre sight in Ireland. Keep in mind that **Lincoln Place Gate** is located in the southeast corner of the grounds, providing a handy shortcut to Merrion Sq.

Science Gallery

Although it's part of the campus you'll have to walk along Pearse St to get into Trinity's newest attraction, the Science Gallery (p66). Since opening in 2008, it has proven immensely popular with everyone for its refreshingly lively and informative exploration of the relationship between science, art and the world we live in. Exhibits have touched on a range of fascinating topics including the science of desire and an exploration of the relationship between music and the human body. The ground-floor cafe (p66), bathed in floor-to-ceiling light, is a pretty good spot to take a load off.

TOP SIGHT
DUBLIN CASTLE

If you're looking for a medieval castle straight out of central casting you'll be disappointed; the stronghold of British power here for 700 years is principally an 18th-century creation that is more hotchpotch palace than turreted castle.

History

Only the Record Tower survives from the original Anglo-Norman fortress, which was built in the early 13th century and served as the centre of English colonial administration until 1922.

When Henry VIII's firm-handed representative in Ireland, Lord Deputy Henry Sidney, took charge in 1565, he declared the castle to be 'ruinous, foul, filthy and great decayed' – and he wasn't far wrong. Until then most of the king's deputies in Ireland had been Anglo-Irish lords who preferred living in their own castles than taking up residence at Dublin Castle, and so it fell into disrepair. Sidney oversaw a 13-year building program that saw the construction of a 'a verie faire house for the Lord Deputie or Chief Governor to reside in' as well as a new chapel and the Clock Tower.

Sidney's new castle became the permanent residence of the monarch's chief representative – known at different times as the Justiciar, Chief Lieutenant, Lord Lieutenant or Viceroy – until the construction of the vice-regal lodge in Phoenix Park in 1781 (now Áras an Uachtaráin, the residence of the president).

The new castle reflected the changing status of English power in Ireland – Henry's conquest of the whole island ('beyond the Pale') and his demolition of the old Anglo-Irish hegemony resulted in the castle no longer being a colonial outpost but the seat of English power and the administrative centre for all of Ireland – a new role that brought with it a huge civil service.

DON'T MISS

➡ Chapel Royal
➡ State Apartments
➡ Upper Yard

PRACTICALITIES

➡ Map p242, A2
➡ ☎01-677 7129
➡ www.dublincastle.ie
➡ Dame St
➡ guided tours adult/child €10/4, self-guided tours €7/3
➡ ⊙9.45am-5.45pm, last admission 5.15pm
➡ ▣all city centre

CASTLE CATHOLICS

Until independence, some Catholic Dubliners who were deemed to be too friendly with or sympathetic to the British crown were derisively termed 'Castle Catholics'.

The only way you'll get to see the castle's most interesting bits is by guided tour. The castle is occasionally used for government functions, so parts may be closed to the public.

DID YOU KNOW?

During British rule the castle's social calendar was busiest for the six weeks leading up to St Patrick's Day, with a series of lavish dinners, levées and balls for the city's aristocratic residents – even during the Famine years.

The Irish Parliament met in the Great Hall, which burnt down (along with most of the rest of the castle) in the great fire of 1684 – the Parliament eventually moved in 1731 to what is now the Bank of Ireland building in College Green.

Below ground, the castle dungeons were home to the state's most notorious prisoners, including – most famously – 'Silken' Thomas Fitzgerald, whose defeated challenge to Henry VIII in 1534 kicked off Henry's invasion of Ireland in the first place. Needless to say, the native Irish came to view the castle as the most menacing symbol of their oppressed state.

When it was officially handed over to Michael Collins on behalf of the Irish Free State in 1922, the British viceroy is reported to have rebuked Collins for being seven minutes late. Collins replied, 'We've been waiting 700 years, you can have the seven minutes.' The castle is now used by the Irish government for meetings and functions, and can only be visited on a guided tour.

Chapel Royal

As you walk into the grounds from the main Dame St entrance, there's a good example of extravagant 19th-century Irish architecture: on your left is the Victorian Chapel Royal (occasionally part of the Dublin Castle tours), decorated with more than 90 heads of various Irish personages and saints carved out of Tullamore limestone. The interior is wildly exuberant, with fan vaulting alongside quadripartite vaulting, wooden galleries, stained glass and lots of lively looking sculpted angels.

Upper Yard

The Upper Yard enclosure roughly corresponds with the dimensions of the original medieval castle. On your right is a Figure of Justice with her back turned to the city, reckoned by Dubliners to be an appropriate symbol for British justice. Next to it is the **Bedford Tower**, built in 1761 on the site of the original Norman gate. The Irish Crown Jewels were stolen from the tower in 1907 and never recovered.

Guided Tours

The 70-minute guided tours (departing every 20 to 30 minutes, depending on numbers) are pretty dry, seemingly pitched at tourists more likely to ooh and aah over period furniture than historical anecdotes, but they're included in the entry fee. You get to visit the **State Apartments**, many of which are decorated in dubious taste. There are beautiful chandeliers (ooh!), plush Irish carpets (aah!), splendid rococo ceilings, a Van Dyck portrait and the throne of King George V. You also get

DUBLIN CASTLE

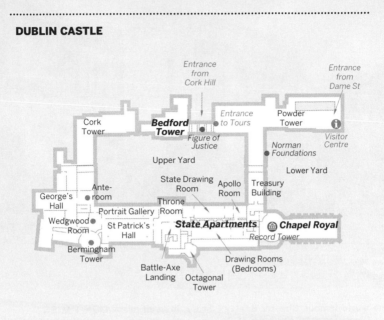

to see **St Patrick's Hall**, where Irish presidents are inaugurated and foreign dignitaries toasted, and the room in which the wounded James Connolly was tied to a chair while convalescing after the 1916 Easter Rising – brought back to health to be executed by firing squad.

The highlight is a visit to the **subterranean excavations** of the old castle, discovered by accident in 1986. They include foundations built by the Vikings (whose long-lasting mortar was made of ox blood, eggshells and horsehair), the hand-polished exterior of the castle walls that prevented attackers from climbing them, the steps leading down to the moat and the trickle of the historic River Poddle, which once filled the moat on its way to join the Liffey.

The Rest of the Castle

Beside the Victorian Chapel Royal is the Norman **Record Tower**, the last intact medieval tower in Dublin. On your right is the Georgian **Treasury Building**, the oldest office block in Dublin, and behind you, yikes, is the uglier-than-sin **Revenue Commissioners Building** of 1960.

 TOP SIGHT
CHESTER BEATTY LIBRARY

The world-famous Chester Beatty Library, housed in the Clock Tower at the back of Dublin Castle, is not just Ireland's best small museum, but one of the best you'll find anywhere in Europe. This extraordinary collection, so lovingly and expertly gathered by New York mining magnate Alfred Chester Beatty, is breathtakingly beautiful and virtually guaranteed to impress.

Alfred Chester Beatty

An avid traveller and collector, Alfred Chester Beatty (1875–1968) was fascinated by different cultures and amassed more than 20,000 manuscripts, rare books, miniature paintings, clay tablets, costumes and any other objets d'art that caught his fancy and could tell him something about the world. Fortunately for Dublin, he also happened to take quite a shine to the city and made it his adopted home. In return, the Irish made him their first honorary citizen in 1957.

Arts of the Book

The collection is spread over two levels. On the ground floor you'll find *Arts of the Book*, a compact but stunning collection of artworks from the Western, Islamic and East Asian worlds. Highlights include the finest collection of Chinese jade books in the world and illuminated European texts featuring exquisite calligraphy that stand up in comparison with the *Book of Kells*. Audiovisual displays explain the process of bookbinding, paper-making and printing.

DON'T MISS

➡ Nara e-hon scrolls (East Asian Collection, Sacred Traditions)

➡ Ibn al-Bawwab Qu'ran (Qu'ran Collection, Sacred Traditions)

➡ New Testament papyri (Western Collection, Sacred Traditions)

PRACTICALITIES

➡ Map p242, A2

➡ 📞01-407 0750

➡ www.cbl.ie

➡ Dublin Castle

➡ admission free

➡ ⏰10am-5pm Mon-Fri, 11am-5pm Sat, 1-5pm Sun year-round, closed Mon Nov-Feb, free tours 1pm Wed, 2pm Sat & 3pm Sun

➡ 🚌all city centre

Sacred Traditions

The 2nd floor is home to *Sacred Traditions*, a wonderful exploration of the world's major religions through decorative and religious art, enlightening text and a cool cultural-pastiche video at the entrance. The collection of Qu'rans dating from the 9th to the 19th centuries (the library has more than 270 of them) is considered by experts to be the best example of illuminated Islamic texts in the world. There are also outstanding examples of ancient papyri, including renowned Egyptian love poems from the 12th century, and some of the earliest illuminated gospels in the world, dating from around AD 200. The collection is rounded off with some exquisite scrolls and artwork from China, Japan, Tibet and Southeast Asia, including the two-volume Japanese *Chogonka Scroll,* painted in the 17th century by Kano Sansetu.

The Building

As if all of this wasn't enough for one visit, the library also hosts temporary exhibits that are usually too good to be missed. Not only are the contents of the museum outstanding, but the layout, design and location are also unparalleled, from the marvellous Silk Road Café (p71) and gift shop to the Zen rooftop terrace and the beautiful landscaped garden out the front. These features alone would make this an absolute Dublin must-do.

THE YOUNG PHILATELIST

Beatty's main collecting activity began in Denver between 1898 and 1905, where he amassed an impressive, prize-winning collection of stamps that chronicled the early postal history of the United States.

The museum hosts a series of free lunchtime talks; check the website for details. The garden atop the building is a slice of serenity in the middle of the city.

INSIDE JOB

Between 1983 and 1989 the library's Islamic curator, Dr David James (1941–2012), stole manuscripts from the collection valued at nearly £500,000. Most of them were recovered with his help, however, he was convicted of theft and served time in prison for the crime.

SIGHTS

TRINITY COLLEGE   HISTORIC BUILDING
See p54.

DUBLIN CASTLE   HISTORIC BUILDING
See p59.

CHESTER BEATTY LIBRARY   MUSEUM
See p62.

★**OLD LIBRARY
& BOOK OF KELLS**   LIBRARY
Map p238 (www.tcd.ie; Library Sq; adult/student/family €11/9.50/22, fast-track €14/12/28; ⊗8.30am-5pm Mon-Sat, 9.30am-5pm Sun May-Sep, 9.30am-5pm Mon-Sat, noon-4.30pm Sun Oct-Apr; 🖳all city centre) Trinity's greatest treasures are found within the Old Library, built by Thomas Burgh between 1712 and 1732. The star of the show is the Book of Kells (p66), a breathtaking, illuminated manuscript of the four Gospels of the New Testament, created around AD 800 by monks on the Scottish island of Iona, but more stunning still is the 65m **Long Room**, the library's main chamber, which houses around 200,000 of the library's oldest volumes.

Other displays include a rare copy of the **Proclamation of the Irish Republic**, read out by Pádraig Pearse at the beginning of the Easter Rising in 1916, as well as the so-called **harp of Brian Ború**, which was definitely not in use when the army of this early Irish hero defeated the Danes at the Battle of Clontarf in 1014. It does, however, date from around 1400, making it one of the oldest harps in Ireland.

Your entry ticket also includes admission to temporary exhibitions on display in the East Pavilion.

The Old Library gets very busy during the summer months, so it's recommended to go online and buy a **fast-track ticket**, which gives timed admission to the exhibition and allows visitors to skip the queue. You'll still get only a fleeting moment with the *Book of Kells,* as the constant flow of viewers is hurried past.

★**ST STEPHEN'S GREEN**   PARK
Map p242 (⊗dawn-dusk; 🖳all city centre, 🚇St Stephen's Green) As you watch the assorted groups of friends, lovers and individuals splaying themselves across the nine elegantly landscaped hectares of Dublin's most popular green lung, St Stephen's Green, consider that those same hectares once formed a common for public whippings, burnings and hangings. These days, the harshest treatment you'll get is the warden chucking you off the grass for playing football or Frisbee.

The buildings around the square date mainly from the mid-18th century, when the green was landscaped and became the centrepiece of Georgian Dublin. The northern side was known as the Beaux Walk and it's still one of Dublin's most esteemed stretches, home to Dublin's original society hotel, the Shelbourne (p182). Nearby is the tiny Huguenot Cemetery (p95), established in 1693 by French Protestant refugees.

Railings and locked gates were erected in 1814, when an annual fee of one guinea was charged to use the green. This private use continued until 1877 when Sir Arthur Edward Guinness pushed an act through parliament opening the green to the public once again. He also financed the central park's gardens and ponds, which date from 1880.

The main entrance to the green today is beneath Fusiliers' Arch (p69), at the top of Grafton St. Modelled to look like a smaller version of the Arch of Titus in Rome, the arch commemorates the 212 soldiers of the Royal Dublin Fusiliers who were killed fighting for the British in the Boer War (1899–1902).

Spread across the green's lawns and walkways are some notable artworks; the most imposing of these is a **monument to Wolfe Tone**, the leader of the abortive 1798 Rising. Occupying the northeastern corner of the green, the vertical slabs serving as a backdrop to the statue have been dubbed 'Tonehenge'. At this entrance is a **memorial** to all those who died in the Potato Famine (1845–51).

On the eastern side of the green is a **children's playground** (⊗dawn-dusk) and to the south there's a fine old **bandstand**, erected to celebrate Queen Victoria's jubilee in 1887. Musical performances often take place here in summer. Near the bandstand is a **bust of James Joyce**.

★**LITTLE MUSEUM OF DUBLIN**   MUSEUM
Map p238 (📞01-661 1000; www.littlemuseum.ie; 15 St Stephen's Green N; adult/student €8/6; ⊗9.30am-5pm Mon-Wed & Fri, to 8pm Thu; 🖳all city centre, 🚇St Stephen's Green) This award-winning museum tells the story of Dublin over the last century via memorabilia, photographs and artefacts donated by the general public. The impressive collection, spread over the rooms of a handsome Georgian house, includes a lectern used by JFK on his

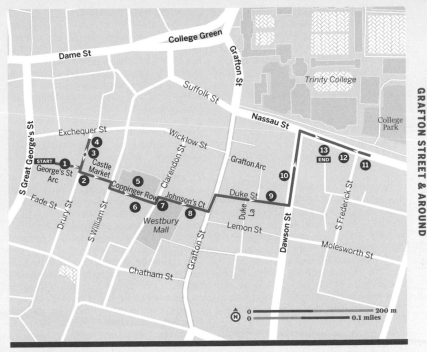

Neighbourhood Walk
A Retail Stroll

START GEORGE'S ST ARCADE
END KNOBS & KNOCKERS
LENGTH 1.1KM; TWO HOURS

Start retail adventure in the **1 George's Street Arcade** (p81), with its range of interesting stalls selling all kinds of alternative wares. In the midst of all this bohemia, take a look at the beautiful pieces in Barry Doyle Design Jewellers and browse the shelves of Stokes Books.

Exit at the Drury St side and cross onto Castle Market, stopping to browse the high-end women's fashions in **2 Costume** (p82) or, if you prefer, go north on Drury St to the gorgeous homewares and handicrafts in **3 Industry** (p82) or, next door, the excellent **4 Irish Design Shop** (p80).

From Castle Market, cross S William St and enter the **5 Powerscourt Townhouse Shopping Centre** (p81), the city's most elegant retail space – inside you'll find cafes and a host of wonderful shops, including Article, for homewares and gifts, and, on the top floor, the Design Centre, a top-end boutique.

Exit the centre on S William St and walk south, taking the first left onto Coppinger Row. The **6 eponymous restaurant** (p73) is a great spot for a little lunch. Continue east and cross Clarendon St. At the corner is **7 Magills** (p81), a proper old-fashioned grocer selling cheeses and cold cuts. On Johnson's Ct itself, the southern side is lined with jewellery shops, including **8 Appleby** (p81); you'll find something sparkly worth coveting in the elegant window.

Take a left on Grafton St and turn right onto Duke St: on your left is **9 Ulysses Rare Books** (p80), the city's most illustrious seller of rare books. The biggest bookshop in town is **10 Hodges Figgis** (p83), around the corner on Dawson St. From here walk down to Nassau St and take a right to **11 Kilkenny Shop** (p82), which has all kinds of locally produced handicrafts, knits, glassware and silverware.

If you still need to pick up some Irish gifts, return to Nassau St, to **12 House of Names** (p82), for coasters with your family's coat of arms, and **13 Knobs & Knockers** (p82), for a replica Georgian door handle!

1963 visit to Ireland and an original copy of the fateful letter given to the Irish envoys to the treaty negotiations of 1921, whose contradictory instructions were at the heart of the split that resulted in the Civil War.

There's a whole room on the 2nd floor devoted to the history of U2, as well as the personal archive of Alfred 'Alfie' Byrne (1882–1956), mayor of Dublin a record 10 times and known as the 'Shaking Hand of Dublin'. Visit is by guided tour, which goes on the hour every hour. The museum also runs the Green Mile walking tour (p83) of St Stephen's Green.

IRISH WHISKEY MUSEUM MUSEUM

Map p238 (☎01-525 0970; www.irishwhiskeymuseum.ie; 119 Grafton St; adult/child classic tours €17/€8.50, premium tours €20, blending experiences €28; ⏱10am-6pm; 🚌all city centre) If you'd like to learn a little more about one of Ireland's most famous tipples, spend an hour here. You'll find out why the Irish call it *uisce beatha* (water of life), how Dublin's whiskey trade collapsed and why it's on the rise again. The tour also gives you a chance to taste at least three different types of whiskey.

There's also an adults-only premium tour option that includes a fourth whiskey tasting, or you can opt for the whiskey blending experience (6pm and 6.45pm Saturday through Thursday), where you blend your own 30ml bottle at the end of the tour.

DOUGLAS HYDE GALLERY OF MODERN ART GALLERY

Map p238 (www.douglashydegallery.com; Trinity College; ⏱11am-6pm Mon-Wed & Fri, to 7pm Thu, to 4.45pm Sat; 🚌all city centre) FREE One of Dublin's best contemporary art galleries, the Douglas Hyde is tucked away in the Arts & Social Science Building of the Trinity College campus. Its ambitious contemporary program stays firmly in the cutting-edge camp; exhibitions here are often 'enhanced' with film, live music or performance-driven sideshows.

SCIENCE GALLERY MUSEUM

Map p244 (www.sciencegallery.ie; Naughton Gallery, Pearse St; ⏱exhibitions usually noon-8pm Tue-Fri, to 6pm Sat & Sun; 🚌all city centre) FREE Demonstrating that science is fun, engaging and relevant to our everyday lives in more ways than we could even imagine is the mission statement of this immensely popular gallery, which hosts an ever-changing mix of compelling exhibits. Recent shows included an examination of design and violence and a study of the world of secrets. The ground-floor **cafe** (sandwiches €4-8; ⏱8am-8pm Tue-Fri, noon-6pm Sat & Sun) is lovely.

BANK OF IRELAND NOTABLE BUILDING

Map p238 (☎01-671 1488; College Green; ⏱10am-4pm Mon-Wed & Fri, to 5pm Thu; 🚌all city centre) A sweeping Palladian pile occupying one side of College Green, this magnificent building

THE PAGE OF KELLS

The history of the Book of Kells is almost as fascinating as its illuminations. It is thought to have been created around AD 800 by the monks at St Colmcille's Monastery on Iona, a remote island off the coast of Scotland; repeated looting by marauding Vikings forced the monks to flee to Kells, County Meath, along with their masterpiece. It was stolen in 1007, then rediscovered three months later buried underground. The Book of Kells was brought to Trinity College for safekeeping in 1654, and is now housed in the Old Library, with over half a million visitors queueing up to see it annually. The 680-page (340-folio) book was rebound in four calfskin volumes in 1953.

And here the problems begin. Of the 680 pages, only two are on display – one showing an illumination, the other showing text – hence the 'page of Kells' moniker. No getting around that one, though: you can hardly expect the right to thumb through a priceless treasure at random. No, the real problem is its immense popularity, which makes viewing it a rather unsatisfactory pleasure. Punters are herded through the specially constructed viewing room at near lightning pace, making for a quick-look-and-move-along kind of experience.

To really appreciate the book, you can get your own reproduction copy for a mere €22,000. Failing that, the Old Library bookshop stocks a plethora of souvenirs and other memorabilia, including Bernard Meehan's The Book of Kells (€17), which includes plenty of reproductions plus excellent accompanying text.

was the Irish Parliament House until 1801 and was the first purpose-built parliament building in the world. The original building – the central colonnaded section that distinguishes the present-day structure – was designed by Sir Edward Lovett Pearce in 1729 and completed by James Gandon in 1733.

When the parliament voted itself out of existence through the 1801 Act of Union, the building was sold under the condition that the interior would be altered to prevent it ever again being used as a debating chamber. It was a spiteful strike at Irish parliamentary aspirations, but while the central House of Commons was remodelled and offers little hint of its former role, the smaller **House of Lords** (admission free) survived and is much more interesting. It has Irish oak woodwork, a mahogany longcase parliament clock and a late-18th-century Dublin crystal chandelier. Its design was copied for the construction of the original House of Representatives in Washington, DC, now the National Statuary Hall. The House of Lords is open to visitors during banking hours and Dublin historian Sean Ó Laocha does prearranged tours of the chamber on Tuesdays between 10.30am and 12.30pm.

CITY HALL   MUSEUM

Map p242 (www.dublincity.ie/dublincityhall; Dame St; adult/student/child €4/2/1.50; ☉10am-5.15pm Mon-Sat; ▣all city centre) This beautiful Georgian structure was originally built by Thomas Cooley as the Royal Exchange between 1769 and '79, and botched in the mid-19th century when it became the offices of the local government (hence its name). Thankfully, a more recent renovation (2000) restored it to its gleaming Georgian best. The basement has an exhibit on the city's history.

The rotunda and its ambulatory form a breathtaking interior, bathed in natural light from enormous windows to the east. A vast marble statue of former mayor and Catholic emancipator Daniel O'Connell stands here as a reminder of the building's links with Irish nationalism (the funerals of both Charles Stewart Parnell and Michael Collins were held here). Dublin City Council still meets here on the first Monday of the month, gathering to discuss the city's business in the Council Chamber, which was the original building's coffee room.

There was a sordid precursor to City Hall on this spot in the shape of the Lucas Coffee House and the adjoining Eagle Tavern, in which the notorious Hellfire Club was founded by Richard Parsons, Earl of Rosse, in 1735. Although the city abounded with gentlemen's clubs, this particular one gained a reputation for messing about in the arenas of sex and Satan, two topics that were guaranteed to fire the lurid imaginings of the city's gossip-mongers.

Located in the striking vaulted basement, **The Story of the Capital** is a multimedia exhibition that traces the history of the city from its earliest beginnings to its hoped-for future – with ne'er a mention of sex and Satan. More's the pity, as the info is quite overwhelming and the exhibits are a little text-heavy. Still, it's a pretty slick museum with informative audiovisual displays.

MANSION HOUSE   NOTABLE BUILDING

Map p238 (Dawson St; ☉closed to the public; ▣all city centre, ▣St Stephen's Green) Built in 1710 by Joshua Dawson – after whom the street is named – this has been the official residence of Dublin's mayor since 1715, and was the site of the 1919 Declaration of Independence and the meeting of the first parliament. The building's original brick Queen Anne style has all but disappeared behind a stucco facade added in the Victorian era.

NEWMAN HOUSE   NOTABLE BUILDING

Map p242 (☑01-477 9810; www.ucd.ie; 85-86 St Stephen's Green S; ☉closed; ▣all city centre, ▣St Stephen's Green) Among the finest examples of Georgian architecture in Dublin are these two townhouses, founded by Cardinal Newman as the Catholic University of Ireland in 1865, along with an adjoining Victorian hall. The alma mater of James Joyce, Pádraig Pearse and Eamon de Valera is currently closed pending a major restoration that will also see the opening of a new museum dedicated to Irish writers in 2019.

The college was founded as an alternative to the Protestant hegemony of Trinity College, which was then the only option available to those seeking third-level education in Ireland. Newman House is still part of the college, which later decamped to the suburb of Belfield and changed its name to University College Dublin.

The house comprises two exquisitely restored townhouses. No 85, the granite-faced original, was designed by Richard Cassels in 1738 for parliamentarian Hugh Montgomery, who sold it to Richard Chapel Whaley, MP, in 1765. Whaley wanted a grander home, so he commissioned another house next door.

PICKING ON POOR PHILO

Thin Lizzy's Phil Lynott may have been one of the most loved of all Irish rock stars, but the statue dedicated to him has seen its fair share of trouble since its erection in 2005. In 2013 vandals knocked it off its plinth, resulting in its removal for extensive repairs, but no sooner did it reappear than a motorist ran into it, breaking a piece of the bass guitar. Thankfully, the driver stepped forward and took full responsibility but the statue has mysteriously not reappeared, with repairs still 'ongoing'.

Aside from Cassels' wonderful design, the highlight of the building is the plasterwork, perhaps the finest in the city. For No 85, the artists were the Italian stuccodores Paolo and Filippo LaFranchini, whose work is best appreciated in the wonderfully detailed Apollo Room on the ground floor. The plasterwork in No 86 was done by Robert West, but it is not quite up to the high standard of next door. When the newly founded, Jesuit-run Catholic University of Ireland took possession of the house in 1865, alterations were made to some of the more graphic plasterwork, supplying the nude figures with 'modesty vests'.

During Whaley's residency, the house developed a certain notoriety, largely due to the activities of his son, Buck, a notorious gambler and hellraiser who once walked all the way to Jerusalem for a bet and somehow connived to have himself elected to parliament at the tender age of 17. During the university's tenure, however, the residents were a far more temperate lot. The Jesuit priest and wonderful poet Gerard Manley Hopkins lived here during his time as professor of classics, from 1884 until his death in 1889. Hopkins' bedroom is preserved as it would have been during his residence, as is the classroom where the young James Joyce studied while obtaining his Bachelor of Arts degree between 1899 and 1902.

NEWMAN UNIVERSITY CHURCH   CHURCH
Map p242 (☏01-475 9647; www.university church.ie; 87a St Stephen's Green S; ☺8am-6pm; ▣all city centre, ▣St Stephen's Green) FREE Cardinal Newman didn't care too much for the Gothic style of his day, so the 1856 church attached to his Catholic University of Ireland at Newman House is a neo-Byzantine charmer. Its richly decorated interior was mocked at first but has since become the preferred surroundings for fashionable weddings.

ROYAL IRISH ACADEMY   LIBRARY
Map p238 (☏01-676 2570; www.ria.ie; 19 Dawson St; ☺10am-5.30pm Mon-Thu, to 5pm Fri; ▣all city centre, ▣St Stephen's Green) FREE Ireland's preeminent society of letters has an 18th-century library that is home to several important documents, including a collection of ancient manuscripts such as the *Book of Dun Cow*, the *Cathach of St Columba* and the entire collection of 19th-century poet Thomas Moore (1779–1852). To gain access you'll have to register online as a reader and have valid photo ID.

MOLLY MALONE STATUE   STATUE
Map p238 (Suffolk St; ▣all city centre) Dublin's most famous statue is that of fictional fishmonger (and lady of dubious morals) Molly Malone, she of the song alive, alive-o. Pending the ongoing expansion of the Luas tram system, she's been moved from the bottom of Grafton St to Suffolk St, but that doesn't halt the never-ending procession of visitors looking for a selfie with her.

IVEAGH GARDENS   GARDENS
Map p242 (☺dawn-dusk; ▣all city centre, ▣St Stephen's Green) FREE These beautiful gardens may not have the sculpted elegance of the other city parks, but they never get too crowded and the warden won't bark at you if you walk on the grass. They were designed by Ninian Niven in 1863 as the private grounds of Iveagh House (p69) and include a rustic grotto, a cascade, a fountain, a maze and a rosarium. Enter the gardens from Clonmel St, off Harcourt St.

ROYAL COLLEGE OF SURGEONS   UNIVERSITY
Map p242 (www.rcsi.ie; 123 St Stephen's Green W; ☺closed to the public; ▣all city centre) The early 19th-century Royal College of Surgeons has one of the finest facades on St Stephen's Green. During the 1916 Easter Rising, the building was occupied by rebel forces led by the colourful Countess Markievicz (1868–1927), an Irish Nationalist married to a supposed Polish count. The columns are scarred with bullet holes. Today it continues to produce doctors, and is especially popular with students from overseas.

FUSILIERS' ARCH — MONUMENT

Map p238 (St Stephen's Green; ☐all city centre) The main entrance to St Stephen's Green (p64) is beneath Fusiliers' Arch, at the top of Grafton St. Modelled to look like a smaller version of the Arch of Titus in Rome, the arch commemorates the 212 soldiers of the Royal Dublin Fusiliers who were killed fighting in the British Army during the Boer War (1899–1902).

WHITEFRIARS STREET CARMELITE CHURCH — CHURCH

Map p238 (☑01-475 8821; 56 Aungier St; ☺8am-6.30pm Mon & Wed-Fri, to 9.30pm Tue, to 7pm Sat, to 7.30pm Sun; ☐16, 19, 19A, 83, 122 from Trinity College) Inside this nondescript church (more properly known as the Church of Our Lady of Mt Carmel) are some fascinating relics, not least the relics of St Valentine, donated to the Carmelites by Pope Gregory XVI in 1836. A spiral-bound notebook below the shrine is there so anyone struck (or missed) by Cupid's arrow can express their gratitude or hope.

The Carmelites have been here since 1827, when they re-established their former church that had been seized by Henry VIII in the 16th century. In the northeastern corner is a 16th-century Flemish oak statue of the Virgin and Child, believed to be the only wooden statue in Ireland to have escaped the Reformation unscathed.

IRISH-JEWISH MUSEUM — MUSEUM

Map p242 (☑01-453 1797; www.jewishmuseum.ie; 3 Walworth Rd; €5; ☺11am-3pm Sun, Tue & Thu May-Sep, 10.30am-2.30pm Sun Oct-Apr; ☐Harcourt) Housed in an old synagogue, this jam-packed museum tells the story of Ireland's Jewish community over the last 150 years. Amid the old photos and artefacts is memorabilia from WWII, including a Star of David arm patch and the marriage certificate of Ester Steinberg, the only known Irish victim of the Holocaust.

The museum is in the (now) trendy neighbourhood of Portobello, which once had a 5000-strong Jewish community and was known as Little Jerusalem. It was opened in 1985 by the Belfast-born, then-Israeli president, Chaim Herzog.

IVEAGH HOUSE — HISTORIC BUILDING

Map p242 (www.dfa.ie; 80 St Stephen's Green S; ☺closed to the public; ☐all city centre, ☐St Stephen's Green) The headquarters of the Department of Foreign Affairs occupies two splendid Georgian houses that were joined together by Benjamin Guinness when he bought them in 1862 as his city residence. No 80 – the house on the left as you look at the building – was designed by Richard Cassels in 1736. The house was given to the Irish state in 1939 by Benjamin's grandson Rupert.

PHIL LYNOTT STATUE — STATUE

Map p238 (Harry St; ☐all city centre) A bronze statue of Thin Lizzy frontman Phil Lynott by Paul Daly has stood outside Bruxelles pub in Harry St since 2005, but it's been twice damaged (p68) and in 2016 removed for repairs – with no fixed date for its return.

✕ EATING

EATYARD — MARKET €

Map p242 (www.the-eatyard.com; 9-10 South Richmond St; before/after 5pm free/€2; ☺noon-8pm Thu-Sun; ☐14, 15, 44, 65, 140, 142 from city centre, ☐Harcourt) Spend an hour or two eating and drinking your way through a dozen or so of the city's best food vendors. There's always seasonal produce, and plenty of veggie options, as well as craft beer. The vendors rotate every few months and the market can close for a short time to accommodate this – confirm opening times online.

WOW BURGER — BURGERS €

Map p238 (www.wowburger.ie; 8 Wicklow St; burgers €6-7; ☺noon-9.30pm; ☐all city centre) The basement of Mary's Bar (p76) is home to the hottest burger joint in town: hamburgers, cheeseburgers and a sinful bacon cheeseburger come in two sizes (double or single) and with a side of choice – the garlic butter fries are terrific. Order at the bar and eat in the '50s diner–styled room.

ASSASSINATION CUSTARD — CAFE €

Map p242 (19 Kevin St; mains €4-6; ☺8am-3.30pm Mon-Fri; ☐all city centre) It doesn't look like much, but this is one of the tastiest treats in town – how about roasted cauliflower with toasted dukkah, or broccoli with spicy Italian 'nduja pork sausage and Toonsbridge ricotta? And if you're feeling really adventurous, try the tripe sandwich. The name comes from a phrase coined by Samuel Beckett.

GERRY'S — CAFE €

Map p242 (6 Montague St; Irish fry €6.50; ☺8am-2pm Mon-Fri, to 2.30pm Sat; ☐14, 15, 65, 83) A no-nonsense, old-school 'caff' (the British Isles' equivalent of the greasy spoon) is rarer than hen's teeth in the city centre these days, which makes Gerry's something of a treasure. You won't find a more authentic spot to enjoy a traditional Irish fry-up. If you want healthy, it always does porridge, but what's the point?

LITTLE BIRD
CAFE €

(☎085-161 0222; www.little-bird.ie; 82 S Circular Rd; mains €5-8; ☺8am-8pm Mon-Fri, 10am-4pm Sat & Sun; 🚌9, 16, 68, 68A, 122) This cafe started life as an adjunct to the yoga studio upstairs and has since grown into one of Portobello's most desirable coffee spots, which in this neighbourhood of mindful affluence means artisanal Badger & Dodo coffee and a largely vegetarian and organic menu with a particular emphasis on avoiding gluten. Sounds a mite precious but is actually delicious, friendly and welcoming.

PEPPER POT
CAFE €

Map p238 (www.thepepperpot.ie; Powerscourt Townhouse Shopping Centre; mains €5-10; ☺10am-6pm Mon-Wed & Fri, to 8pm Thu, 9am-6pm Sat, noon-6pm Sun; 🚌all city centre) Everything is baked and made daily at the lovely cafe on the 1st-floor balcony of the Powerscourt Townhouse (p81). The salads with homemade brown bread are delicious but the real treat is the soup of the day (€5.50) – the ideal liquid lunch.

MEET ME IN THE MORNING
CAFE €

Map p242 (50 Pleasants St; mains €5-8; ☺8am-5pm Tue-Fri, 10am-5pm Sat & Sun; 🚌14, 15, 65, 83) Scrummy breakfasts (there's eggs done just right, but try the nut eile, a toasted hazelnut and cacao spread on toast with sea salt) and lunches with a Middle Eastern flavour to them (puy lentil tabouli with shaved fennel) make this one of the nicest cafes in town. It's named after a Dylan song.

BROTHER HUBBARD SOUTH
CAFE €

Map p242 (www.brotherhubbard.ie; 46 Harrington St; mains €5-10; ☺7.45am-4.30pm Mon-Fri, 9am-4.30pm Sat & Sun; 🚌15A, 122 from city centre) Tasty breakfasts (the slow-cooked organic porridge is delicious) and fresh sandwiches on ciabatta bread make this the ideal spot to kick off your day and linger a while. It's the sister restaurant to Brother Hubbard (p139) on Capel St.

AUNGIER DANGER
DESSERTS €

Map p243 (☎01-556 2021; www.aungierdanger. ie; 37 Aungier St; doughnuts €3; ☺from 7.30am

Mon-Fri, from 10am Sat & Sun; 🚌all city centre) The Western doughnut craze hit Dublin with a vengeance in 2016, but this little shop stands out as one of the city's best. Don't arrive too late in the day as it closes when sold out – you should be ok if you arrive before 4pm. Try favourites like the Oreo marshmallow or banoffee autopsy.

MURPHY'S ICE CREAM
ICE CREAM €

Map p238 (www.murphysicecream.ie; 27 Wicklow St; scoops €2.50; ☺noon-10pm; 🚌all city centre) Get your sugar hit on with a visit to what might be the best ice-cream shop in the country. Everything is handmade with fresh ingredients from Dingle, home to the first branch of this mini-chain. Flavours rotate but the Dingle Gin ice cream is always popular and the sorbets use distilled Kerry rain.

BUNSEN
BURGERS €

Map p238 (☎01-652 1022; www.bunsen.ie; 3 S Anne St; burgers €7-9; ☺noon-9.30pm Mon-Wed, noon-10.30pm Thu-Sat, 1-9.30pm Sun; 🚌all city centre, 🚇St Stephen's Green) Artisanal burgers that are so popular, the queues go out the door.

BUNSEN
BURGERS €

Map p242 (www.bunsen.ie; 36 Wexford St; burgers €7-9; ☺noon-9.30pm Mon-Wed, noon-10.30pm Thu-Sat, 1-9.30pm Sun; 🚌all city centre) Homemade, succulent artisan burgers so big and tasty, they're almost sinful.

NEON
ASIAN €

Map p242 (☎01-405 2222; www.neon17.ie; 17 Lower Camden St; mains €10-12; ☺noon-10pm; 🚌14, 15, 65, 83) A brilliant spot that specialises in authentic Thai and Vietnamese street food, served in takeaway boxes, which you can eat at home or in the canteen-style dining room. Hardened palates can jump right into the super-spicy *pad ki mow* noodles; more delicate taste buds can live with a delicious massaman curry.

Takeaway is available until 11pm, and it also delivers (from 5pm).

LEMON
CRÊPES €

Map p238 (66 S William St; pancakes from €7; ☺7.30am-7.30pm Mon-Wed & Fri, to 9pm Thu, 8.30am-7.30pm Sat, 9.40am-6.30pm Sun; 🕿; 🚌all city centre) Dublin's best pancake joint has branches on both sides of Grafton St, one on South William and the other on **Dawson St** (61 Dawson St). Each serves up a wide range of sweet and savoury crêpes – those paper-thin ones stuffed with goodies and smothered in toppings – along with super coffee in a buzzy atmosphere.

BOTTEGA TOFFOLI
ITALIAN €

Map p242 (☎01-633 4022; 34 Castle St; pizzas €15, fish dishes market price; ☺open by reservation only; 🚇all city centre) Tucked away on a lane alongside Dublin Castle is this wonderful Italian restaurant with five tables and a maximum of 12 customers. It only opens for reservations, but Carlo's cooking is superb, from his standout pizzas to his careful selection of fish, all fresh and served with a pasta dish. Simple, made to measure and delicious.

LISTONS
SANDWICHES €

Map 242 (www.listonsfoodstore.ie; 25 Lower Camden St; lunch €5-12; ☺9am-6.30pm Mon-Fri, 10am-6pm Sat; 🚇all city centre) They've been making gourmet sandwiches for so long here that it's hard to imagine them getting any better. Besides the delicacies you put between slices of bread, this excellent spot also does roasted-vegetable quiches, rosemary potato cakes and sublime salads. The menu changes daily. On fine days, take your gourmet picnic to the nearby Iveagh Gardens (p68).

SILK ROAD CAFÉ
MIDDLE EASTERN €

Map p242 (Chester Beatty Library, Dublin Castle; mains €12; ☺10am-4.45pm Mon-Fri, 11am-4.45pm Sat & Sun May-Oct, closed Mon Nov-Apr; 🚌50, 51B, 77, 78A, 123) This vaguely Middle Eastern–North African–Mediterranean gem on the ground floor of the Chester Beatty Library (p62) is no ordinary museum cafe. Complementing house specialities including moussaka and spinach lasagne are daily specials such as *djaj mehshi* (chicken stuffed with spices, rice, dried fruit, almonds and pine nuts). All dishes are halal and kosher.

FALLON & BYRNE
DELI €

Map p238 (www.fallonandbyrne.com; Exchequer St; mains €5-10; ☺8am-9pm Mon-Fri, 9am-9pm Sat, 11am-7pm Sun; 🚇all city centre) Dublin's answer to the American Dean and DeLuca chain is this upmarket food hall and wine cellar, which is where discerning Dubliners come to buy their favourite cheeses and imported delicacies, as well as to get a superb takeaway lunch from the deli counter.

Upstairs is an elegant brasserie (p74) that serves Irish-influenced Mediterranean cuisine.

CORNUCOPIA
VEGETARIAN €

Map p238 (www.cornucopia.ie; 19-20 Wicklow St; salads €5.50-11, mains €12.50-14; ☺8.30am-9pm Mon, 8.30am-10pm Tue-Sat, noon-9pm Sun; ✐; 🚇all city centre) Dublin's best-known vegetarian restaurant is this terrific eatery that serves three sizes of wholesome salads, sandwiches and a selection of hot main courses from a daily changing menu. There's live musical accompaniment Thursday to Saturday evenings. The 2nd-floor dining-room windows to the street below are a good spot for people-watching.

HONEST TO GOODNESS
PIZZA €

Map p238 (www.honesttogoodness.ie; 12 Dame St; sandwiches €7, pizzas €10-16; ☺8am-5pm Mon, to 10pm Tue & Wed, to 11pm Thu & Fri, 9am-11pm Sat, 10am-4pm Sun; 🚇all city centre) By day, the downstairs cafe serves wholesome sandwiches, tasty soups and a near-legendary sloppy joe. By night, the upstairs restaurant serves what might be the best pizza in town – authentic enough to earn a Neapolitan's approval. Terrific staff, wonderful atmosphere.

SIMON'S PLACE
CAFE €

Map p238 (George's St Arcade, S Great George's St; sandwiches €5-6; ☺8.30am-5pm Mon-Sat; ✐; 🚇all city centre) Simon's soup-and-sandwich joint is a city stalwart, impervious to the fluctuating fortunes of the world around it, mostly because its doorstep sandwiches and wholesome vegetarian soups are delicious and affordable. As trustworthy cafes go, this is the real deal.

BLAZING SALADS
VEGETARIAN €

Map p238 (42 Drury St; salads €5-10; ☺10am-6pm Mon-Wed, Fri & Sat, to 8pm Thu; ✐; 🚇all city centre) Organic breads (including many special diet varieties), Californian-style salads from a serve-yourself salad bar, smoothies and pizza slices can all be taken away from this delicious deli.

GOVINDA'S
VEGETARIAN €

Map p238 (www.govindas.ie; 4 Aungier St; mains €10.45; ☺noon-9pm Mon-Sat; ✐; 🚇all city centre) An authentic beans-and-pulses place run by the Hare Krishna, with two branches in the city centre. Its cheap, wholesome mix of salads and Indian-influenced hot daily specials is filling and tasty.

★PICHET
FRENCH €€

Map p238 (☎01-677 1060; www.pichetrestaurant.ie; 15 Trinity St; mains €19-27; ☺noon-3pm &

5-10pm Mon-Sat, 11am-4pm & 5-9pm Sun; ▣ all city centre) Head chef Stephen Gibson (formerly of L'Ecrivain) delivers his version of modern French cuisine to this newly refurbished dining room, whose elegance matches the fabulous food and service. Load up on an expertly made cocktail before feasting on as good a meal as you'll find at this price anywhere in the city centre.

HANG DAI
CHINESE €€

Map p242 (🕿01-545 8888; www.hangdaichinese. com; 20 Lower Camden St; mains €16-29; ⊘5pm-midnight Tue-Sat; ▣14, 15, 65, 83) You'll need a reservation to get a seat at the bar or in one of the carriage booths of this super-trendy spot, designed to look like the inside of a railway carriage. The low red lighting and soulful tunes give off the ambience of a '70s porn theatre. The food, however – contemporary versions of Chinese classics – is excellent.

LITTLE JERUSALEM
MIDDLE EASTERN €€

Map p242 (🕿01-424 4001; 77 Lower Camden St; mains €12-17; ⊘noon-midnight; 🕿; ▣14, 15, 65, 83) A candidate for best ethnic cuisine in town, this friendly spot serves up a mix of Lebanese and Palestinian dishes that range from the familiar (hummus, felafel, lamb shwarma) to the exotic – how about *makloubet* (chicken, aubergine, cauliflower, potatoes and onions...served 'upside down')? The extensive menu requires repeat visits. It's strictly BYOB.

777
MEXICAN €€

Map p238 (www.777.ie; 7 Castle House, S Great George's St; mains €15-23, tapas €11-16; ⊘5.30-10pm Mon-Wed, 5.30-11pm Thu, 5pm-midnight Fri & Sat, 2-10pm Sun; ▣ all city centre) You won't eat better, more authentic Mexican cuisine – the tostadas (crispy corn tortillas with various toppings) and taquitos (filled, soft corn tortillas) are great nibbles, and the perfect accompaniment for a tequila fest (it serves 22 different types). The all-dishes-for-€7.77 on Sunday is one of the best deals in town.

PITT BROS BBQ
BARBECUE €€

Map p238 (www.pittbrosbbq.com; Unit 1, Wicklow House, S Great George's St; mains €14-16; ⊘noon-midnight Mon-Fri, 12.30pm-late Sat & Sun; ▣ all city centre) Delicious, Southern-style barbecue – you have a choice of pulled pork, brisket, ribs, sausage or half a chicken – served amid loud music and a hipster-fuelled atmosphere that says Brooklyn, New York, rather than Birmingham, Alabama. For dessert, there's

a DIY ice-cream dispenser. Locals grumble that it's a straight rip-off of Bison Bar, but the happy clientele doesn't care.

FADE STREET SOCIAL
MODERN IRISH €€

Map p238 (🕿01-604 0066; www.fadestreet social.com; 4-6 Fade St; mains €18-32, tapas €5-12; ⊘12.30-10.30pm Mon-Fri, 5-10.30pm Sat & Sun; 🕿; ▣ all city centre) 🍴 Two eateries in one, courtesy of renowned chef Dylan McGrath: at the front, the buzzy tapas bar, which serves up gourmet bites from a beautiful open kitchen. At the back, the more muted restaurant specialises in Irish cuts of meat – from veal to rabbit – served with home-grown, organic vegetables. There's a bar upstairs too. Reservations suggested.

RICHMOND
MODERN IRISH €€

Map p242 (🕿01-478 8783; www.richmondrestaur ant.ie; 43 S Richmond St; mains €16-27; ⊘5.30-9.30pm Wed-Sun, 11am-3pm Sat & Sun; ▣14, 15, 65, 83) At first glance the menu offers nothing particularly novel, just a nice selection of favourites from a burger to a roasted breast of duck. But it's the way it's prepared and presented that makes this place one of the best in town, and proof that expertise in the kitchen trumps everything else. Brunch is a particular favourite.

PORT HOUSE
TAPAS €€

Map p238 (🕿01-677 0298; www.porthouse.ie; 64a South William St; tapas €7-10; ⊘11am-midnight; ▣ all city centre) This dark cavern restaurant is full of flickering candlelight. The extensive, delicious Spanish tapas menu is best enjoyed with the impressive Iberian wines (which the friendly staff can help you navigate). It doesn't take bookings, so if you go at the weekend prepare to wait for a table.

BOW LANE
INTERNATIONAL €€

Map p238 (www.bowlane.ie; 18 Aungier St; mains €19-29; ⊘3pm-late Sun-Thu, 10.30am-late Fri & Sat; ▣ all city centre) It's a '50s-style cocktail bar, but with a standout menu. On offer are dinner mains as diverse as rabbit pie and tandoori chicken, while the excellent brunch menu does it with a twist. Sure, you can order eggs Benedict, but you can also go for 'The Mexicali' – Mexican spiced beans, peppers, cayenne, pulled pork, a fried egg and spicy cheddar.

SUPER MISS SUE
SEAFOOD €€

Map p238 (www.supermisssue.com; 2-3 Drury St; mains €15-28; ⊘noon-9pm Mon-Wed, to 11pm

Thu-Sat, to 4pm Sun; 🚇all city centre) Super Miss Sue is not one restaurant, but three: on the ground floor is a bright cafe-style dining room that serves mostly seafood, including lots of types of oysters and a shellfish platter to die for. Downstairs is **Luna** (open 5pm to 11pm, Wednesday to Saturday), where the focus is Italian and the menu favours meat dishes. There's also **Cerva**, a takeaway fish-and-chip shop.

COPPINGER ROW   MEDITERRANEAN €€

Map p238 (www.coppingerrow.com; Coppinger Row; mains €20-27; ⊙noon-11pm; 🚇all city centre) Virtually all of the Mediterranean basin is represented on the ever-changing, imaginative menu here. Choices include the likes of pan-fried hake with mussels, baby potato and curried broth; or crispy pork belly with mustard mash, caramelised apple and black pudding. A nice touch are the filtered still and sparkling waters (€1): 50% goes to the Movember men's health charity.

GOOD WORLD   CHINESE €€

Map p238 (18 S Great George's St; dim sum €4-6, mains €12-20; ⊙12.30pm-2.30am; 🚇all city centre) To truly appreciate the quality of the southside's best Chinese restaurant, ignore the green Western-style menu and stick to the black-covered one, which is packed with dishes and delicacies that have made it a favourite with Dublin's Chinese community for two decades. It's a great option for a late-night bite if you're looking to avoid fast food.

DADA   MOROCCAN €€

Map p238 (www.dadarestaurant.ie; 45 S William St; mains €14-25; ⊙5-11pm Mon-Thu, 1.30pm-12.30am Fri & Sat, 2.30-11pm Sun; 🚇all city centre) This bustling Moroccan restaurant has an atmospheric, low-lit dining room, spread about lots of alcoves so as to give the feel of a medina, and a substantial menu of North African favourites. The emphasis is on lamb (three separate tagines and a seven-hour roasted lamb shoulder) but there's also fish, chicken and decent vegetarian options.

SOPHIE'S @ THE DEAN   ITALIAN €€

Map p242 (www.sophies.ie; 33 Harcourt St; mains €14-29; ⊙7am-midnight; 🚇10, 11, 13, 14, 15A, 🚆Harcourt) There's perhaps no better setting in all of Dublin – a top-floor glasshouse restaurant with superb views of the city – in which to enjoy this quirky take on Italian cuisine. Delicious pizzas come with nontraditional toppings (pulled pork with

BBQ sauce?) and the 8oz fillet steak is done to perfection. A good spot for breakfast too.

CAMDEN KITCHEN   BISTRO €€

Map p242 (🕿01-476 0125; www.camdenkitchen. ie; 3 Camden Market, Grantham St; mains €16-26; ⊙noon-2.30pm & 5.30-10pm Wed-Fri, 5.30-10pm Tue & Sat; 🚇14, 15, 65, 83) Tucked away off busy Camden St, this inviting little bistro prides itself on its fresh, seasonal menu of changing and beautifully presented dishes like handmade gnocchi with organic spinach and greens and wild mushrooms topped with a free-range egg; or wild Wicklow venison saddle with a pressed potato terrine. The somewhat expensive wine menu complements the reasonably priced food.

PIG'S EAR   MODERN IRISH €€

Map p238 (🕿01-670 3865; www.thepigsear.com; 4 Nassau St; mains €18-28; ⊙noon-2.45pm & 5.30-10pm Mon-Sat; 🚇all city centre) Looking over the playing fields of Trinity College – which counts as a view in Dublin – this fashionably formal restaurant is spread over two floors and is renowned for its exquisite and innovative Irish cuisine, including dishes such as barbecued pork belly, short rib of Irish beef and a superb slow-cooked Lough Erne shepherd's pie.

L'GUEULETON   FRENCH €€

Map p238 (www.lgueuleton.com; 1 Fade St; mains €25-28; ⊙12.30-4pm & 5.30-10pm Mon-Wed, to 10.30pm Thu-Sat, noon-4pm & 5.30-9pm Sun; 🚇all city centre) Despite the tongue-twister name (it means 'gluttonous feast' in French), L'Gueuleton is a firm favourite with locals for its robust (meaty, filling) take on French rustic cuisine – it does a mean onion soup and the steak frites is a big crowd pleaser. It has a no-reservations, leave-your-name-at-the-door policy; just go for a drink and wait for the call.

GREEN HEN   FRENCH €€

Map p238 (🕿01-670 7238; www.thegreenhen.ie; 33 Exchequer St; mains €20-30; ⊙noon-11pm; 🚇all city centre) New York's SoHo meets Parisian brasserie at this stylish eatery, where elegance and economy live side by side. If you don't fancy gorging on oysters or tucking into a divine Irish Hereford rib-eye, you can opt for the *plat du jour* (dish of the day) or avail yourself of the early-bird menus; watch out for its killer cocktails. Reservations recommended for dinner.

DUNNE & CRESCENZI ITALIAN €€

Map p238 (www.dunneandcrescenzi.com; 14-16 S Frederick St; mains €14-19, 3-course evening menu €35; ⊗8am-11pm Mon-Sat, 9.30am-11pm Sun; ▣all city centre) This exceptional Italian eatery delights its regulars with a basic menu of rustic pleasures, such as panini, a single pasta dish and a superb plate of mixed antipasto drizzled in olive oil. It's always full, and the tables are just that little bit too close to one another, but the coffee is perfect and the desserts are sinfully good.

AVOCA CAFE €€

Map p238 (www.avoca.ie; 11-13 Suffolk St; mains €9-16; ⊗9.30am-5.30pm Mon-Wed & Sat, to 7pm Thu & Fri, 11am-6pm Sun; ▣all city centre) This top-floor cafe, part of the marvellous Avoca group, is very popular with discerning shoppers who enjoy a gourmet lunch: how about a Toonsbridge halloumi salad with kale, squash, baba ganoush, pickled onion and dukkah, or felafel with herbed couscous, caramelised onion hummus, beetroot tzatziki and pitta? There's also a takeaway salad bar and hot-food counter in the basement.

EL BAHIA MOROCCAN €€

Map p238 (☏01-677 0213; www.elbahia.com; 1st fl, 37 Wicklow St; tagines €15-18; ⊗5pm-midnight Tue-Fri, noon-midnight Sat, 1-9pm Sun; ▣all city centre) Dark and sultry, this upstairs Moroccan restaurant looks a little like how we imagine a desert harem might. There are some rather fetching geometric designs on the ceilings and walls, and the gimme-gimme food includes the likes of tasty tagines, couscous and *bastile* (pastry stuffed with chicken), while the sweet-and-spicy Moroccan coffee is an unusual treat.

SABA ASIAN €€

Map p238 (☏01-679 2000; www.sabadublin.com; 26-28 Clarendon St; mains lunch €13-19, dinner €24-28; ⊗noon-11pm; ▣all city centre) The name means 'happy meeting place' and this Thai-Vietnamese fusion restaurant is just that. The buzzy atmosphere is all designer cool, the Southeast Asian fare a tad shy of being truly authentic (but still very tasty), and it's a good night out. There's another branch on Baggot St.

YAMAMORI JAPANESE €€

Map p238 (☏01-475 5001; www.yamamorinoodles.ie; 71 S Great George's St; mains €15-28, lunch bentos €10; ⊗12.30-11pm; ☏; ▣all city centre) Yamamori rarely disappoints with its bubbly service and vivacious cooking that swoops from sushi and sashimi to whopping great plates of noodles, with plenty in-between. The lunch bento is one of the best deals in town. There's another branch (p140) north of the river.

DESELBYS MEDITERRANEAN €€

Map p242 (www.deselbys.com; 9 Lower Camden St; mains €12-14; ⊗10am-3.30pm Tue, 10am-3.30pm & 6-10pm Wed-Fri, 11am-3.30pm & 6-11pm Sat, 11am-3.30pm Sun; ▣all city centre) Tasty sandwiches for lunch and classics like burgers, haddock and chips and a *côte de boeuf* (rib steak) for dinner – the menu belies the exotic decor, which is styled like a belle époque cafe in Madrid or Paris. There's also enticing two-for-one deals on cocktails and mimosas for brunch.

DRURY BUILDINGS ITALIAN €€

Map p238 (☏01-960 2095; www.drurybuildings.com; 52-55 Drury St; mains €19-30; ⊗noon-3pm & 5-10.30pm; ▣all city centre) An elegant, 1st-floor restaurant in a converted rag-trade warehouse...sounds like New York's SoHo, and that's exactly what it's trying to emulate. The food – Italian dishes made with local produce and infused with an international twist – is excellent. The ground-floor cocktail bar (p77) has an Italian lunch menu of sandwiches, salads and other titbits.

FALLON & BYRNE RESTAURANT IRISH €€

Map p238 (☏01-472 1000; www.fallonandbyrne.com; Exchequer St; mains €12-17; ⊗noon-3pm & 5.30-9pm Sun-Tue, to 10pm Wed & Thu, to 11pm Fri & Sat; ▣all city centre) An elegant brasserie serving Irish-influenced Mediterranean cuisine. Nothing too imaginative, but it's well-made: good pasta dishes and a fine selection of chicken, beef and fish.

TROCADERO INTERNATIONAL €€

Map p238 (☏01-677 5545; www.trocadero.ie; 3 St Andrew's St; mains €19-32; ⊗4.30pm-midnight Mon-Fri, 4pm-midnight Sat; ▣all city centre) As old school as a Dublin restaurant gets, this art-deco classic has been the social hub of the city's theatrical world for 50 years, a favourite of thespians and other luminaries. It's more of a nostalgia trip now, but the food remains uniformly good – a bunch of classics, solidly made – as does the terrific atmosphere.

★GREENHOUSE SCANDINAVIAN €€€

Map p238 (☏01-676 7015; www.thegreenhouserestaurant.ie; Dawson St; 2-3-course lunch menu €29.50/38, 4-6-course dinner menu €79/95; ⊗noon-2.15pm & 6-9.30pm Tue-Sat; ▣all city centre, ⬚St Stephen's Green) Chef Mickael Viljanen might just be the most exciting chef working in Ireland today thanks to his Scandi-influenced tasting menus, which have made this arguably Dublin's best restaurant. Wine selections are in the capable hands of Julie Dupouy, who in 2017 was voted third-best sommelier in the world, just weeks before the restaurant was awarded a Michelin star. Reservations necessary.

CLIFF TOWNHOUSE   IRISH €€€

Map p238 (☏01-638 3939; www.theclifftownhouse.com; 22 St Stephen's Green N; mains €19-36; ◷7am-2.30pm & 5-11pm; ⬚all city centre, ⬚St Stephen's Green) Sean Smith's menu is a confident expression of the very best of Irish cuisine – Warrenpoint fish pie, organic fillet of pork and a loin of venison share the menu with a masterful fish and chips. The dining room is supremely elegant – lots of white linen, beautiful art on the wall and deep-blue leather booths.

SHANAHAN'S ON THE GREEN   STEAK €€€

Map p242 (☏01-407 0939; www.shanahans.ie; 119 St Stephen's Green W; mains €42-49; ◷6-10pm Sat-Thu, noon-10pm Fri; ⬚all city centre, ⬚St Stephen's Green) You could order seafood or a plate of vegetables, but you'd be missing the point of this supremely elegant steakhouse: the finest cuts of juicy and tender Irish Angus beef you'll find anywhere. The ambience is upscale Americana – the bar downstairs is called the Oval Office and pride of place goes to a rocking chair owned by JFK.

🍷 DRINKING & NIGHTLIFE

★KEHOE'S   PUB

Map p238 (9 S Anne St; ◷10.30am-11.30pm Mon-Thu, to 12.30am Fri & Sat, noon-11pm Sun; ⬚all city centre) This classic bar is the very exemplar of a traditional Dublin pub. The beautiful Victorian bar, wonderful snug and side room have been popular for Dubliners and visitors for generations, so much so that the publican's living quarters upstairs have since been converted into an extension – simply by taking out the furniture and adding a bar.

★GROGAN'S CASTLE LOUNGE   PUB

Map p238 (www.groganspub.ie; 15 S William St; ◷10.30am-11.30pm Mon-Thu, to 12.30am Fri & Sat, 12.30-11pm Sun; ⬚all city centre) This place,

---

THE STAG'S & HOLLYWOOD

The **Stag's Head** is justifiably famous as one of Dublin's most beautiful traditional bars, which has led to it featuring in a couple of Hollywood movies: *Educating Rita* (1983) and *A Man of No Importance* (1994). Not bad on the resumé, but its most loyal patrons are far more thrilled by another, less successful brush with Hollywood: Quentin Tarantino was looking for a pint after the call for last orders had gone out, but he pulled the 'do you know who I am?' card and scuppered his chances of swaying the bartender's sympathies.

---

known simply as Grogan's (after the original owner), is a city-centre institution. It has long been a favourite haunt of Dublin's writers and painters, as well as others from the alternative bohemian set, who enjoy a fine Guinness while they wait for that inevitable moment when they're discovered.

★LONG HALL   PUB

Map p238 (51 S Great George's St; ◷10.30am-11.30pm Mon-Thu, to 12.30am Fri & Sat, noon-11pm Sun; ⬚all city centre) A Victorian classic that is one of the city's most beautiful and best-loved pubs. Check out the ornate carvings in the woodwork behind the bar and the elegant chandeliers. The bartenders are experts at their craft, an increasingly rare attribute in Dublin these days.

STAG'S HEAD   PUB

Map p238 (www.louisfitzgerald.com/stagshead; 1 Dame Ct; ◷10.30am-1am Mon-Sat, to midnight Sun; ⬚all city centre) The Stag's Head was built in 1770, remodelled in 1895 and thankfully not changed a bit since then. It's a superb pub: so picturesque that it often appears in films and also featured in a postage-stamp series on Irish bars. A bloody great pub, no doubt.

MCDAID'S   PUB

Map p238 (☏01-679 4395; 3 Harry St; ◷10.30am-11.30pm Mon-Thu, to 12.30am Fri & Sat, 12.30-11pm Sun; ⬚all city centre) One of Dublin's best-known literary pubs, this classic boozer was popular with the likes of Patrick Kavanagh and Brendan Behan (both of whom were eventually barred) and it still oozes character. The pints are perfect, and best appreciated during the day when it's less busy. Thankfully, there's no music – just conversation and raucous laughter.

CHELSEA DRUG STORE   BAR

Map p238 (25 S Great George's St; ☺4pm-midnight Mon-Fri, noon-1.30am Sat, 4-11pm Sun; ⬚all city centre) It doesn't matter that its name seems plucked out of a trendy focus group and the decor carefully curated to reflect current trends (art-deco elements, old-looking-like-new), this is actually a beautiful bar that, at the time of research, was full of young creatives ordering cocktails with names like The Truth Behind Augustus and Penicillin.

P.MAC'S   BAR

Map p238 (30 Lower Stephen St; ☺noon-midnight Mon-Thu, to 1am Fri & Sat, to 11.30pm Sun; ⬚all city centre) This Brooklyn-style bohemian hangout is full of mismatched vintage furniture, American-style pint glasses and an alternative soundtrack veering towards the '90s. It also has 30-odd taps serving a huge variety of craft beers.

MARY'S BAR   PUB

Map p238 (8 Wicklow St; ☺11am-11.30pm Mon-Wed, to 12.30am Thu, to 1.30am Fri & Sat, noon-11pm Sun; ⬚all city centre) In a twist of irony, the home of the authentic pub has seen the arrival of a classic McPub, complete with pseudo-old hardware shop at the front and oak barrel tables at the back. Utterly artificial but a popular venue; downstairs is the even more popular Wow Burger (p69).

CLEMENT & PEKOE   CAFE

Map p238 (www.clementandpekoe.com; 50 S William St; ☺8am-7pm Mon-Fri, 10am-6pm Sat, noon-6pm Sun; ⬚all city centre) Our favourite cafe in town is this contemporary version of an Edwardian tearoom. Walnut floors, art-deco chandeliers and wall-to-wall displays of handsome tea jars are the perfect setting in which to enjoy the huge range of loose-leaf teas and carefully made coffees, along with a selection of cakes.

ZOZIMUS   BAR

Map p238 (☎01-536 9640; www.zozimusbar.ie; Centenary House, Anne's Lane; ⬚all city centre, ⬚St Stephen's Green) A white marble bar, lots of elegant wood and teal panelling...this handsome bar is undoubtedly eye-catching, and popular for postwork drinks or a good-first-impression date. There's also a decent food menu (mains €10 to €15). It gets its name from Michael Moran (1794–1846), aka-Zozimus, a famous blind balladeer.

PYGMALION   BAR

Map p238 (☎01-674 6712; www.bodytonic music.com; Powerscourt Townhouse Shopping Centre, 59 S William St; ☺10am-midnight; ⬚all city centre) The 'Pyg', with its craft beers, flavoured cocktails, excellent, pounding music and myriad nooks and crannies, is hugely popular with younger drinkers and partygoers. By day, those same revellers work out the previous night's shenanigans over coffee at the covered outside tables.

FARRIER & DRAPER   CLUB

Map p238 (☎01-677 0014; www.farrieranddraper. ie; Powerscourt Townhouse Shopping Centre, S William St; ☺noon-midnight Mon-Thu & Sun, to 2.30am Fri & Sat; ⬚all city centre) This venue in the 18th-century Powerscourt complex (p81) combines Prohibition-era cool (staff in Peaky Blinders hats and sleeve garters) and Georgian decadence (high-vaulted ceilings, lots of paintings on the walls). Upstairs, in what was once Lady Powerscourt's private quarters, is a late-night bar and club; downstairs is the beautiful Epic Bar and, in the basement, an Italian restaurant called La Cucina.

The name is a throwback to the trades that once occupied the courtyard of Powerscourt Townhouse.

NO NAME BAR   BAR

Map p238 (3 Fade St; ☺12.30-11.30pm Sun-Wed, to 1am Thu, to 2.30am Fri & Sat; ⬚all city centre) A low-key entrance just next to the trendy French restaurant L'Gueuleton (p73) leads upstairs to one of the nicest bar spaces in town, consisting of three huge rooms in a restored Victorian townhouse plus a sizeable heated patio area for smokers. There's no sign or a name – folks just refer to it as the No Name Bar.

BERNARD SHAW   BAR

Map p242 (www.bodytonicmusic.com; 11-12 S Richmond St; ☺8am-11.30pm Mon-Thu, to 1am Fri, 10am-1am Sat, 2-11.30pm Sun; ⬚14, 15, 65, 83) This deliberately ramshackle boozer is probably the coolest bar in town for its marvellous mix of music (courtesy of its owners, the Bodytonic production crew) and diverse menu of events such as afternoon car-boot sales, storytelling nights and fun competitions like having a 'tag-off' between a bunch of graffiti artists. They also run the excellent Eatyard (p69).

HOGAN'S — BAR
Map p238 (35 S Great George's St; ⊙1.30pm-11.30am Mon-Wed, to 1am Thu, to 2.30am Fri & Sat, 2-11pm Sun; ⊡all city centre) Midweek this big contemporary bar is a relaxing hang-out for young professionals, and restaurant and bar workers on a night off. But come the weekend the sweat bin downstairs pulls them in for some serious music courtesy of the usually excellent DJs.

SAM'S BAR — BAR
Map p238 (36 Dawson St; ⊙4pm-2am Mon-Thu, 1pm-2.30am Fri-Sun; ⊡all city centre, ⊡St Stephen's Green) A posh Dawson St drinking spot, Sam's has decor that is Middle Eastern (a hangover of its previous incarnation as an Asian-themed bar) meets art-college graffiti. An odd mix, but it doesn't bother the young professional clientele, who come to share tales of success over fancy cocktails.

KAPH — CAFE
Map p238 (31 Drury St; ⊙9am-6pm Mon-Sat, noon-6pm Sun; ⊡all city centre) One of the newer breed of cafes where the barista's creations are considered caffeinated art. Order a flat white and use it to dunk one of the (homemade) madeleines.

DRURY BUILDINGS
COCKTAIL BAR — COCKTAIL BAR
Map p238 (www.drurybuildings.com; 52-55 Drury St; ⊙noon-11.30pm Sun-Thu, to 12.30am Fri & Sat) The ground-floor cocktail bar at the Drury Buildings (p74) is popular for predinner drinks. It also has an Italian lunch menu of sandwiches, salads and other titbits, consumed at the bar or the high tables spread throughout (mains €10 to €12), plus a nice beer garden out back.

WALL AND KEOGH — CAFE
Map p242 (www.wallandkeogh.ie; 45 S Richmond St; ⊙8am-8pm Mon-Fri, 10.30am-7pm Sat & Sun; ⊡all city centre) The Irish love their tea, and this marvellous cafe is the place to enjoy your choice of 150 different types, served in ceramic Japanese teapots with all the care of a traditional tea ceremony. It also serves a fabulous coffee and, for the peckish, sandwiches, baked goods and even sushi.

MERCANTILE — BAR
Map p238 (☑01-670 1700; 28 Dame St; ⊙8am-12.30am Mon-Wed, to 2.30am Thu-Sat, noon-11pm Sun; ⊡all city centre) A big, sprawling bar spread across three floors, the Mercantile's stock-in-trade has been tourists, mostly of the stag-and-hen type, who fill the place at weekends and lend it a party atmosphere which then attracts local lads and lasses looking for a bit of 'fun'. The music is as loud as the atmosphere is boisterous – you know what to expect!

DICEY'S GARDEN — BAR
Map p242 (☑01-478 4066; Russell Court Hotel, 21-25 Harcourt St; ⊙4pm-2.30am; ⊡all city centre, ⊡Harcourt) This massive place is better known as Dicey Reilly's (or just Dicey's) and is one of Dublin's most popular bars, spread across a couple of levels with about three different styles, including old-style pub, modern superbar and European beer garden. Charty music and a fun-lovin' crowd keep it going till the small hours.

INTERNATIONAL BAR — PUB
Map p238 (www.international-bar.com; 23 Wicklow St; ⊙10.30am-11.30pm Mon-Thu, to 12.30am Fri & Sat, noon-11pm Sun; ⊡all city centre) This smallish pub with a huge personality is a top spot for an afternoon pint. It has a long bar, stained-glass windows, red-velour seating and a convivial atmosphere. Some of Ireland's most celebrated comedians stuttered through their first set in the **Comedy Cellar**, which is, of course, upstairs.

KRYSTLE — CLUB
Map p242 (☑01-478 4066; www.krystlenight club.com; Russell Court Hotel, 21-25 Harcourt St; ⊙11pm-3am Fri & Sat; ⊡all city centre, ⊡Harcourt) Chart hits and club classics are the mainstay at this club that for a time fancied itself as the late-night dance floor of choice for the city's VIPs and wannabes, although they'd rarely venture out of the upstairs lounge. These days it operates a more democratic door policy (the beautiful people have moved on).

OPIUM ROOMS — BAR
Map p242 (www.opiumrooms.ie; 26 Wexford St; €5-11; ⊙11pm-2.30am Thu-Sat; ⊡14, 15, 65, 83) Clubbers familiar with the Hakkasan experience – whether in London or in Las Vegas – will recognise that the Opium Rooms is trying to do the same thing, albeit on a less grand scale: the DJs it gets aren't as famous, but the dance floor is just as full and the sound is excellent. Downstairs there's a lovely **restaurant and bar** (☑01-475 8555; www.opium.ie; mains €17-19; ⊙noon-10pm Mon-Wed, noon-2.30am Thu & Fri, 1pm-2.30am Sat, 12.30-9pm Sun).

CAFÉ EN SEINE BAR

Map p238 (☑01-677 4369; 40 Dawson St; ☺noon-midnight Mon & Tue, noon-3am Wed-Sat, noon-11pm Sun; 🚇all city centre) The wildly extravagant art-nouveau style of this huge bar has been a massive hit since it first opened in 1995, and while it may not be the 'in' place it once was, it is still very popular with suburbanites, the after-work crowd and out-of-towners. Maybe it's the glass panelling, or the real 12m-high trees; but most likely it's the beautiful people propping up the wood-and-marble bar.

MARKET BAR BAR

Map p238 (www.marketbar.ie; Fade St; ☺noon-11.30pm Mon-Thu, to 1.30am Fri & Sat, to 11pm Sun; 🚇all city centre) An architectural beauty, this giant red-brick-and-iron-girder room that was once a Victorian sausage factory is now a large, breezy bar that stands as a far more preferable alternative to many of the city's superbars. Unlike virtually every other new pub in town, there's no music. It also does a roaring trade in Spanish-influenced pub grub (tapas €8 to €13).

LILLIE'S BORDELLO CLUB

Map p238 (☑01-679 9204; www.lilliesbordello. ie; 1-2 Adam Ct; €10-20; ☺11pm-3am) The most upmarket club (Twitter: @lilliesdublin) in Dublin makes sure to attract whatever Cristal-swilling superstar is in town. Not that you'll rub shoulders with them, as they'll be safely ensconced in the ultra-VIP Jersey Lil's private members' bar. The hoi polloi make do with bland music and Lillie's Lab, where they can distil their own gin.

GEORGE GAY

Map p238 (www.thegeorge.ie; 89 S Great George's St; weekends after 10pm €5-10, other times free; ☺2pm-2.30am Mon-Fri, 12.30pm-2.30am Sat, 12.30pm-1.30am Sun; 🚇all city centre) The purple mother of Dublin's gay bars is a long-standing institution, having lived through the years when it was the only place in town where the gay crowd could, well, be gay. Shirley's legendary Sunday-night bingo is as popular as ever, while Wednesday's Space N Veda is a terrific night of cabaret and drag.

37 DAWSON STREET BAR

Map p238 (☑01-902 2908; www.37dawsonstreet. ie; 37 Dawson St; ☺10.30am-11.30pm Mon-Thu, to 12.30am Fri & Sat, noon-11pm Sun; 🚇all city centre) Antiques, eye-catching art and elegant bric-a-brac adorn this bar that quickly established itself as a favourite with the trendy crowd. At the back is Whiskey Bar, a '50s-style bar that Don Draper and Co would feel comfortable sipping a fine Scotch at; upstairs is an elegant restaurant that serves a terrific brunch.

COPPER FACE JACKS CLUB

Map p242 (www.copperfacejacks.ie; 29-30 Harcourt St, Jackson Court Hotel; free-€10; ☺10.30pm-3am; 🚇10, 11, 13, 14, 15A, 🚇St Stephen's Green) In rural Ireland you don't go clubbing; you go to 'the disco' for a drink, a dance and – hopefully – 'the shift', a particularly Irish way of describing making out. Coppers (Twitter: @CopperFaceJacks) is a slice of country clubbing in the middle of the capital, and it's all the more popular for it.

PETER'S PUB PUB

Map p238 (☑01-679 3347; www.peterspub.ie; 1 Johnston Pl; ☺11am-11.30pm Mon-Thu, to 12.30am Fri&Sat, 1-11pm Sun; 🚇all city centre) A pub for a chat and a convivial catch-up, this humble and friendly place is more like Peter's Living Room. It's one of the few remaining drinking dens in this area that hasn't changed personality in recent years, and is all the better (and more popular) for it.

DAVY BYRNE'S BAR

Map p238 (☑01-677 5217; www.davybyrnes.com; 21 Duke St; ☺11am-11.30pm Mon-Thu, to 12.30am Fri, 9am-12.30am Sat, 11am-11pm Sun; 🚇all city centre) James Joyce would barely recognise the bar that Leopold Bloom popped into for a gorgonzola sandwich and a glass of burgundy in *Ulysses*. It doesn't stop Davy Byrne's from making the most of its Joycean connections, even though today's version is strictly for out-of-towners and the rugby crowd.

GLOBE BAR

Map p238 (☑01-671 1220; www.theglobe.ie; 11 S Great George's St; ☺5pm-2.30am Mon-Fri, 4pm-2.30am Sat, 4pm-1am Sun; 📶; 🚇all city centre) The grandaddy of the city's contemporary bars celebrated 25 years of groovery in 2017 and has steadfastly stuck to the formula that made it cool in the first place: wooden floors, plain brick walls and a no-attitude atmosphere that you just can't fake. And some pretty good music.

NEARY'S PUB

Map p238 (☑01-677 8596; 1 Chatham St; ☺10.30am-11.30pm Mon-Thu, to 12.30am Fri & Sat, 12.30-11pm Sun; 🚇all city centre) One of a string of off–Grafton St, classic Victorian boozers once patronised by Dublin's legless literati,

Neary's is a perfect stop-off day or night. It combines great service, a bohemian atmosphere and attractively worn furnishings, and is popular with actors from the nearby Gaiety Theatre.

OLD STAND   PUB

Map p238 (✆01-677 7220; 37 Exchequer St; ☺11am-12.30am Mon-Sat, to midnight Sun; 🚇all city centre) Refreshingly unreconstructed, this is one of the oldest pubs in Dublin and it seems to be just sauntering along with scant regard for changing trends. It's named after the old stand at Lansdowne Rd Stadium, and is a favourite with sports fans and reporters.

DAWSON LOUNGE   PUB

Map p238 (25 Dawson St; ☺10.30am-11.30pm Mon-Thu, to 12.30am Fri & Sat, noon-11pm Sun; 🚇all city centre, 🚇St Stephen's Green) To experience *the* smallest bar in Dublin, go through a little doorway, down a narrow flight of steps and into two tiny rooms that always seem to be filled with a couple of bedraggled drunks who look like they're hiding.

BRUXELLES   PUB

Map p238 (7-8 Harry St; ☺9.30am-1.30am Sun-Thu, to 2.30am Fri & Sat; 🚇all city centre) Bruxelles is a raucous music bar split across different areas. It's comparatively trendy on the ground floor, while downstairs is a great, loud and dingy rock bar with live music each weekend.

⭐ ENTERTAINMENT

★DEVITT'S   LIVE MUSIC

Map p242 (✆01-475 3414; www.devittspub.ie; 78 Lower Camden St; ☺from 9pm Thu-Sat; 🚇14, 15, 65, 83) Devitt's – aka the Cusack Stand – is one of the favourite places for the city's talented musicians to display their wares, with sessions as good as any you'll hear in the city centre. Highly recommended.

WHELAN'S   LIVE MUSIC

Map p242 (✆01-478 0766; www.whelanslive.com; 25 Wexford St; 🚇16, 122 from city centre) Perhaps the city's most beloved live-music venue is this midsize room attached to a traditional bar. This is the singer-songwriter's spiritual home: when they're done pouring out the contents of their hearts on stage, you can find them filling up in the bar along with their fans.

NATIONAL CONCERT HALL   LIVE MUSIC

Map p242 (✆01-417 0000; www.nch.ie; Earlsfort Tce; 🚇all city centre) Ireland's premier orchestral hall hosts a variety of concerts year-round, including a series of lunchtime concerts from 1.05pm to 2pm on Tuesdays from June to August.

UKIYO   KARAOKE

Map p238 (✆01-633 4071; www.ukiyobar.com; 7-9 Exchequer St; per hour €30-60; ☺noon-midnight Mon-Wed, to 1am Thu, to 2.30am Sat, 2pm-1.30am Sun; 🚇all city centre) The basement rooms of this trendy sake bar can fit up to 20 people each for a night of singalong fun from the 30,000-odd songs on the menu (in a variety of languages). Bookings recommended, especially for weekend nights.

SAMUEL BECKETT THEATRE   THEATRE

Map p238 (01-677 2941 ✆ext 1239; www.tcd.ie/beckett-theatre; Regent House, Pearse St; 🚇all city centre) The Trinity College Players' Theatre hosts student productions throughout the academic year, as well as the most prestigious plays from the **Dublin Theatre Festival** (www.dublintheatrefestival.com; ☺Oct).

TICKETMASTER   BOOKING SERVICE

Map p238 (✆0818 719 300; www.ticketmaster.ie; Stephen's Green Shopping Centre; 🚇all city centre, 🚇St Stephen's Green) Sells tickets to every genre of big- and medium-sized show – but be aware that it charges between 9% and 12.5% service charge *per ticket*.

GAIETY THEATRE   THEATRE

Map p238 (✆01-677 1717; www.gaietytheatre. com; S King St; ☺7-10pm; 🚇all city centre) The 'Grand Old Lady of South King St' is more than 150 years old and has for much of that time thrived on a diet of fun-for-all-the-family fare: West End hits, musicals, Christmas pantos and classic Irish plays keep the more serious-minded away, leaving more room for those simply looking to be entertained.

BANKER'S COMEDY CLUB   COMEDY

Map p238 (✆01-679 3697; 16 Trinity St; €8; ☺9-11pm Fri & Sat; 🚇all city centre) The basement room of this decent bar hosts two nights of comedy: the Craic Club on Fridays and the usually excellent Stand Up at the Banker's on Saturday nights. There's decent talent on stage – some of whom have made it onto TV.

JJ SMYTH'S   LIVE MUSIC

Map p238 (✆01-475 2565; www.jjsmyths.com; 12 Aungier St; €8-12; ☺8-11.30pm; 🚇all city centre)

There's live music in the upstairs room of this old bar every night, from blues to jazz, performed by some extraordinary players. Check the website for listings.

🛍 SHOPPING

⭐IRISH DESIGN SHOP ARTS & CRAFTS
Map p238 (📞01-679 8871; www.irishdesignshop. com; 41 Drury St; ⏱10am-6pm Mon-Wed, Fri & Sat, to 7pm Thu, 1-5pm Sun; 🚇all city centre) Beautiful, imaginatively crafted items – from jewellery to kitchenware – carefully curated by owners Clare Grennan and Laura Caffrey. If you're looking for a stylish, Irish-made memento or gift, you'll surely find it here.

⭐ARTICLE HOMEWARES
Map p238 (📞01-679 9268; www.articledublin.com; 1st fl, Powerscourt Townhouse Shopping Centre, S William St; ⏱10.30am-6pm Mon-Wed, Fri & Sat, to 7pm Thu, 1-5pm Sun; 🚇all city centre) Beautiful tableware and decorative home accessories all made by Irish designers. Ideal for unique, tasteful gifts that you won't find elsewhere.

⭐AVOCA HANDWEAVERS ARTS & CRAFTS
Map p238 (📞01-677 4215; www.avoca.ie; 11-13 Suffolk St; ⏱9.30am-6pm Mon-Wed & Sat, to 7pm Thu & Fri, 11am-6pm Sun; 🚇all city centre) Combining clothing, homewares, a basement food hall and an excellent top-floor cafe (p74), Avoca promotes a stylish but homey brand of modern Irish life – and is one of the best places to find an original present. Many of the garments are woven, knitted and naturally dyed at its Wicklow factory. There's a terrific kids' section.

⭐BARRY DOYLE DESIGN JEWELLERS JEWELLERY
Map p238 (📞01-671 2838; www.barrydoyledesign. com; 30 George's St Arcade; ⏱10am-6pm Mon-Wed, Fri & Sat, to 7pm Thu; 🚇all city centre) Goldsmith Barry Doyle's upstairs shop is one of the best of its kind in Dublin. The handmade jewellery – using white gold, silver, and some truly gorgeous precious and semiprecious stones – is exceptional in its beauty and simplicity. Most of the pieces have Afro-Celtic influences.

⭐ULYSSES RARE BOOKS BOOKS
Map p238 (📞01-671 8676; www.rarebooks.ie; 10 Duke St; ⏱9.30am-5.45pm Mon-Sat; 🚇all city centre) Our favourite bookshop in the city stocks a rich and remarkable collection of Irish-interest books, with a particular emphasis on 20th-century literature and a large selection of first editions, including rare ones by the big guns: Joyce, Yeats, Beckett and Wilde.

⭐SHERIDAN'S CHEESEMONGERS FOOD
Map p238 (📞01-679 3143; www.sheridanscheese mongers.com; 11 S Anne St; ⏱10am-6pm Mon-Fri, 9.30am-6pm Sat; 🚇all city centre) If heaven were a cheese shop, this would be it. Wooden shelves are laden with rounds of farmhouse cheeses, sourced from around the country by Kevin and Seamus Sheridan, who have almost single-handedly revived cheese-making in Ireland.

SIOPAELLA FASHION & ACCESSORIES
Map p238 (www.siopaella.com; 29 Wicklow St; ⏱10am-6pm Mon-Wed, Fri & Sat, to 7pm Thu, noon-5.30pm Sun; 🚇all city centre) The popular Temple Bar shop (p108) has expanded to a new premises, which gives shoppers even bigger opportunities to nab that secondhand designer handbag at a reasonable price.

LOULERIE JEWELLERY
Map p238 (📞01-672 4024; www.loulerie.com; 14b Chatham St; ⏱10.30am-5.30pm Mon-Tue, to 6pm Wed, to 7pm Thu, 10am-6pm Fri & Sat; 🚇all city centre) Owner Louise Stokes learned her craft in New York, and has since returned with an unerring eye for finding that individual piece of jewellery – rings, necklaces, earrings etc – to suit every mood and occasion.

NOWHERE FASHION & ACCESSORIES
Map p238 (www.nowhere.ie; 65 Aungier St; ⏱noon-7pm Mon-Sat; 🚇all city centre) Men's clothing and accessories by hip designers such as CMMN_SWDN, Christopher Raeburn and A Kind of Guise. It operates an extensive online shop, too.

MOMUSE JEWELLERY
Map p238 (www.momuse.ie; Powerscourt Townhouse Shopping Centre; ⏱10.30am-6pm Mon-Wed, Fri & Sat, to 7pm Thu, 1-5pm Sun; 🚇all city centre) Exquisite jewellery by designer Margaret O'Rourke, with many of the pieces finished in this lovely boutique on the ground floor of Powerscourt Townhouse.

DOLLS STORE TOYS
Map p238 (www.dollstore.ie; Powerscourt Townhouse Shopping Centre; ⏱10am-6pm Mon-Sat; 🚇all city centre) Dolls, doll's houses and toys stock the shelves of this lovely shop on the

2nd floor of the Powerscourt Townhouse, but our favourite bit is the wonderful doll hospital and teddy bear clinic, where children whose dolls or teddies have had the misfortune to fall 'ill' can be treated with a little TLC (and maybe even a stitch).

POWERSCOURT TOWNHOUSE SHOPPING CENTRE
SHOPPING CENTRE

Map p238 (☎01-679 4144; 59 S William St; ⊙10am-6pm Mon-Wed & Fri, to 8pm Thu, 9am-6pm Sat, noon-6pm Sun; ⊒all city centre) This absolutely gorgeous and stylish centre is in a carefully refurbished Georgian townhouse, built between 1741 and 1744. These days it's best known for its cafes and restaurants but it also does a top-end, selective trade in high fashion, art, exquisite handicrafts and other chi-chi sundries.

GEORGE'S STREET ARCADE
MARKET

Map p238 (www.georgesstreetarcade.ie; btwn S Great George's & Drury Sts; ⊙9am-6.30pm Mon-Wed, to 7pm Thu-Sat, noon-6pm Sun; ⊒all city centre) Dublin's best nonfood market is sheltered within an elegant Victorian Gothic arcade. Apart from shops and stalls selling new and old clothes, secondhand books, hats, posters, jewellery and records, there's a fortune teller, some gourmet nibbles, and a fish and chipper that does a roaring trade.

DESIGN CENTRE
CLOTHING

Map p238 (☎01-679 5718; www.designcentre.ie; Powerscourt Townhouse Shopping Centre, S William St; ⊙10am-6pm Mon-Wed, Fri & Sat, to 8pm Thu; ⊒all city centre) Mostly dedicated to Irish designer womenswear, featuring well-made classic suits, evening wear and knitwear. Irish labels include Jill De Burca, Philip Treacy, Aoife Harrison and Erickson Beamon – a favourite with Michelle Obama.

MAGILLS
FOOD

Map p238 (☎01-671 3830; 14 Clarendon St; ⊙9.30am-5.45pm Mon-Sat; ⊒all city centre) With its characterful old facade and tiny dark interior, Magills' has an old-world charm that reminds you of how Clarendon St must have once looked. At this family-run place, you get the distinct feeling that every Irish and French cheese, olive oil, packet of Italian pasta and salami was hand-picked.

WEIR & SON'S
JEWELLERY

Map p238 (☎01-677 9678; www.weirandsons.ie; 96-99 Grafton St; ⊙9am-5.30pm Mon-Wed, Fri

SHOPPING TIPS

Pedestrianised Grafton St was traditionally the shopping street, but the prevalence of the major chain stores has resulted in few surprises. To make the most of the area's retail opportunities, head into the grid of streets surrounding it, especially to the west, where you'll find some of Dublin's most interesting outlets, from bookshops to boutiques, as well as two extraordinary shopping centres. As well as being accessible by all city-centre buses, most places around Grafton St can be accessed from the St Stephen's Luas stop.

& Sat, to 8pm Thu; ⊒all city centre) The largest jeweller in Ireland, this huge shop on Grafton St first opened in 1869 and still has its original wooden cabinets and a workshop on the premises. There's new and antique Irish jewellery (including Celtic designs) and a huge selection of watches, Irish crystal, porcelain, leather and travel goods.

APPLEBY
JEWELLERY

Map p238 (☎01-679 9572; www.appleby.ie; 5-6 Johnson's Ct; ⊙9.30am-5.30pm Mon-Wed & Fri, to 7pm Thu, to 6pm Sat; ⊒all city centre) The best known of the jewellery shops that line narrow Johnson's Ct, Appleby is renowned for the high quality of its gold and silver jewellery, which tends towards more conventional designs. This is the place for serious stuff – diamond rings, sapphire-encrusted cufflinks and Raymond Weil watches.

KILKENNY SHOP
ARTS & CRAFTS

Map p238 (☎01-677 7066; www.kilkennyshop.com; 6 Nassau St; ⊙8.30am-7pm Mon-Wed, Fri & Sat, to 8pm Thu, 10am-6.30pm Sun; ⊒all city centre) A large, long-running repository for contemporary, innovative Irish crafts, including multicoloured, modern Irish knits, designer clothing, Orla Kiely bags and lovely silver jewellery. The glassware and pottery is beautiful and sourced from workshops around the country. Good source for traditional gifts.

LOUIS COPELAND
CLOTHING

Map p238 (☎01-872 1600; www.louiscopeland.com; 19-21 Wicklow St; ⊙9am-5.30pm Mon-Wed, Fri & Sat, to 7.30pm Thu; ⊒all city centre) Dublin's answer to the famed tailors of London's Savile Row, this shop makes fabulous suits to measure, and stocks plenty of ready-to-wear suits by international designers. There's another outlet on Capel St.

STOKES BOOKS
BOOKS

Map p238 (✆01-671 3584; 19 George's St Arcade; ◷11am-6pm Mon-Sat; ⧉all city centre) A small bookshop specialising in Irish history books, both old and new. Other titles, covering a range of subjects, include a number of beautiful, old, leather-bound editions.

COSTUME
CLOTHING

Map p238 (✆01-679 5200; www.costumedublin. ie; 10 Castle Market; ◷10am-6pm Mon-Wed, Fri & Sat, to 7pm Thu; ⧉all city centre) Considered a genuine pacesetter by Dublin's fashionistas; Costume has exclusive contracts with innovative designers such as Vivetta, Isabel Marant, Cedric Charlier and Zadig & Voltaire.

KNOBS & KNOCKERS
ARTS & CRAFTS

Map p238 (✆01-671 0288; 19 Nassau St; ◷9.30am-5.30pm Mon-Sat; ⧉all city centre) Replica Georgian door-knockers are a great souvenir of your Dublin visit, and there are plenty of other souvenir door adornments to look at here too.

MAVEN
FASHION & ACCESSORIES

Map p238 (www.mavenboutique.com; 29 Wicklow St; ◷11am-6pm Tue, Wed & Sat, to 7pm Thu-Fri; ⧉all city centre) This upstairs boutique is pitched at stylishly on-trend women, which really means it stocks labels still cool enough to be worn by fashionistas who are well ahead of the curve. Sounds a mite obnoxious, but this shop is anything but, and the labels – including Irish designers Sian Jacobs and JBK knitwear – are very elegant.

INDUSTRY
HOMEWARES

Map p238 (www.industrydesign.ie; 41 Drury St; ◷10am-6pm Mon-Sat, noon-6pm Sun; ⧉all city centre) High-end homewares and accessories are the stock at this super-cool independently owned design shop, where you can pick up everything from kids' booties to a birch veneer desk. It also has a lunchtime salad bar.

RHINESTONES
JEWELLERY

Map p238 (✆01-679 0759; 18 St Andrew's St; ◷9am-6.30pm Mon-Wed, Fri & Sat, 9am-8pm Thu, noon-6pm Sun; ⧉all city centre) Exceptionally fine antique and quirky costume

jewellery from the 1920s to 1970s, with pieces priced from €25 to €2000. Victorian jet, 1950s enamel, art-deco turquoise, 1930s mother-of-pearl, cut-glass and rhinestone necklaces, bracelets, brooches and rings are displayed in old-fashioned cabinets.

BROWN THOMAS
DEPARTMENT STORE

Map p238 (✆01-605 6666; www.brownthomas. com; 92 Grafton St; ◷9.30am-8pm Mon, Wed & Fri, 10am-8pm Tue, 9.30am-9pm Thu, 9am-8pm Sat, 11am-7pm Sun; ⧉all city centre) Soak up the Jo Malone–laden atmosphere of Dublin's most exclusive shop, where presentation is virtually artistic. Here you'll find fantastic cosmetics, shoes to die for, exotic homewares and a host of fashion labels such as Balenciaga, Lainey Keogh and Philip Treacy. The 3rd-floor Bottom Drawer outlet stocks the finest Irish linen you'll find anywhere.

HOUSE OF NAMES
ARTS & CRAFTS

Map p238 (✆01-679 7287; www.houseofnames. ie; 26 Nassau St; ◷10am-6pm Mon-Wed, Fri & Sat, 10am-8pm Thu, 11am-6pm Sun; ⧉all city centre) Impress your friends by serving them drinks on coasters emblazoned with your family's coat of arms, matching the sweatshirt you're wearing and, of course, the glasses or mugs the drinks are served in. All this and more can be yours from the House of Names, so long as you have a surname with Irish roots.

DUBRAY BOOKS
BOOKS

Map p238 (✆01-677 5568; www.dubraybooks.ie; 36 Grafton St; ◷9am-7pm Mon-Wed & Sat, 9am-9pm Thu & Fri, 11am-6pm Sun; ⧉all city centre) Three floors devoted to bestsellers, recent releases, coffee-table books and a huge travel section make this one of the better bookshops in town. It can't compete with its larger, British-owned rivals on price, but it holds its own with a helpful staff and a lovely atmosphere that encourages you to linger.

ST STEPHEN'S GREEN SHOPPING CENTRE
SHOPPING CENTRE

Map p238 (✆01-478 0888; St Stephen's Green W; ◷9am-7pm Mon-Wed, Fri & Sat, 9am-9pm Thu, 11am-6pm Sun; ⧉all city centre) A 1980s version of a 19th-century shopping arcade; the dramatic, balconied interior and central courtyard are a bit too grand for the nondescript chain stores within. There's Boots,

Benetton and a large Dunnes Store with a supermarket, as well as last-season designer warehouse TK Maxx.

DESIGNYARD   ARTS & CRAFTS
Map p238 (☎01-474 1011; www.designyard.ie; 25 S Frederick St; ☺10am-5.30pm Tue, Wed & Fri, to 8pm Thu, to 6pm Sat; ☐all city centre) A high-end, craft-as-art shop where everything – glass, batik, sculpture, painting – is one-off and handmade in Ireland. It also showcases contemporary jewellery stock from young international designers. Perfect for that bespoke engagement ring or a very special present.

WALTON'S   MUSIC
Map p238 (☎01-475 0661; www.waltons.ie; 69-70 S Great George's St; ☺9am-6pm Mon-Wed, Fri & Sat, to 7pm Thu; ☐all city centre) This is the place to go if you're looking for your very own bodhrán (goat-skin drum) or any other musical instrument associated with Irish traditional music. It also has an excellent selection of sheet music and recorded music.

HODGES FIGGIS   BOOKS
Map p238 (☎01-677 4754; 56-58 Dawson St; ☺9am-7pm Mon-Wed & Fri, to 8pm Thu, to 6pm Sat, noon-6pm Sun; ☐all city centre) The mother of all Dublin bookshops has books on every conceivable subject for every kind of reader spread across three huge floors, including a substantial Irish section on the ground floor.

🏃 SPORTS & ACTIVITIES

★FAB FOOD TRAILS   WALKING
(www.fabfoodtrails.ie; tours €55; ☺10am Sat) Highly recommended 2½-hour tasting walks through the city centre's choicest independent producers. You'll visit up to eight bakeries, cheesemongers, markets and delis, learning about the food culture of each neighbourhood you explore. There is also a Coffee Walk (exploring the best artisanal coffee shops) and a Food & Fashion walk. You meet in the city centre.

★GREEN MILE   WALKING
Map p238 (☎01-661 1000; www.littlemuseum.ie; Little Museum of Dublin, 15 St Stephen's Green N; adult/student €7/5; ☺11am Sat & Sun; ☐all city

centre, ☐St Stephen's Green) Excellent one-hour tour of St Stephen's Green led by local historian Donal Fallon. Along the way you'll hear tales of James Joyce, the park's history and the drafting of the Irish Constitution. Book ahead as tours fill up pretty quickly. The tour also includes admission to and a guided tour of the Little Museum of Dublin (p64).

★HISTORICAL WALKING TOUR   WALKING
Map p238 (☎01-878 0227; www.historicaltours.ie; Trinity College Gate; adult/student/child €12/10/free; ☺11am & 3pm May-Sep, 11am Apr & Oct, 11am Fri-Sun Nov-Mar; ☐all city centre) Trinity College history graduates lead this 'seminar on the street' that explores the Potato Famine, Easter Rising, Civil War and Partition. Sights include Trinity, City Hall, Dublin Castle and Four Courts. In summer, themed tours on architecture, women in Irish history and the birth of the Irish state are also held. Tours depart from the College Green entrance.

SEE DUBLIN BY BIKE   CYCLING
Map p242 (☎01-280 1899; www.seedublinbybike.ie; Daintree Bldg, Pleasants Pl; tours €25; ☐all city centre) Three-hour themed tours that start outside the Daintree Building on Pleasants Pl and take in the city's highlights and not-so-obvious sights. The Taste of Dublin is the main tour, but you can also take a U2's Dublin tour and a Literary Dublin tour. Bikes, helmets and hi-vis vests included.

PAT LIDDY WALKING TOURS   WALKING
Map p238 (☎01-831 1109; www.walkingtours.ie; Visit Dublin Centre, 25 Suffolk St; tours €10-15; ☐all city centre) Local historian Pat Liddy leads a variety of guided walks including Dublin Highlights & Hidden Corners and The Best of Dublin – The Complete Heritage Walking Tour. He is also available for private guided walks. Check the website for timings.

VIKING SPLASH TOURS   TOURS
Map p238 (☎01-707 6000; www.vikingsplash.com; St Stephen's Green N; adult/child Sep-Jun €22/12, Jul-Aug €25/12; ☺every 30-90min 10am-3pm; ☐all city centre, ☐St Stephen's Green) Go on, what's the big deal? You stick a plastic Viking's helmet on your head and yell 'yay' at the urging of your guide, but the upshot is you'll get a 1¼-hour semiamphibious tour that ends up in the Grand Canal Dock. 'Strictly for tourists' seems so...superfluous.

Merrion Square & Around

Neighbourhood Top Five

1 **National Gallery** (p90) Perusing the collection at Ireland's pre-eminent gallery, packed with art from eight centuries of European tradition.

2 **Museum of Natural History** (p92) Visiting this antiquated museum, which has changed little since it was opened in the middle of the 19th century.

3 **National Museum of Ireland – Archaeology** (p86) Uncovering the fascinating treasures of the most important repository of Irish culture, from finely worked gold to prehistoric bodies.

4 **O'Donoghue's** (p97) Enjoying a night of music and beer in the very epitome of an Irish traditional pub.

5 **Fine Dining** (p96) Feasting on the superb cuisine offered by some of Dublin's very best restaurants, including Restaurant Patrick Guilbaud, Ireland's only Michelin two-star.

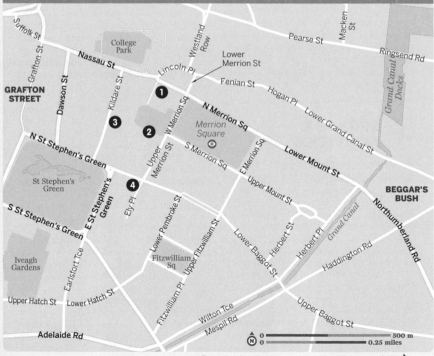

For more detail of this area see Map p244 and p245 ➡

Explore Merrion Square & Around

Ireland's national collections of art, history and natural history are to be found in the imposing neoclassical buildings that line the elegant Georgian streets and parks of the city's best-maintained 18th-century neighbourhood. Depending on your level of interest you'll need to devote as much as half a day to each, or just an hour or two if all you want is an overview.

You'll also want to spend some time looking at the private residences that line Merrion and Fitzwilliam Sqs – the many plaques on these Georgian buildings remind us that it was behind these brightly coloured doors that the likes of Oscar Wilde and William Butler Yeats hung their hats.

These streets also house the offices of some of the country's most important businesses, so when there's even a hint of sunshine, workers pour out into the various parks, or follow the lead of poet Patrick Kavanagh and lounge along the banks of the Grand Canal. When they clock off, these same workers head to the wonderfully atmospheric and historical pubs of Baggot St and Merrion Row for a couple of scoops of chips and some unwinding banter. There are also some smart restaurants, including several of Dublin's best.

Local Life

➡ **High Art** The Jack B Yeats collection in the National Gallery (p90) soothes a Dubliner's troubled soul, while the Royal Hibernian Academy (p94) is an excellent showcase of contemporary art. For something a little more affordable, the weekend art market (p94) along the railings of Merrion Sq displays surprisingly good-quality work.

➡ **Beer Power** Follow the power-brokers, politicians and business crowd as they unwind in some of the city's best traditional boozers: Toner's (p96) and Doheny & Nesbitt's (p97) are established favourites, but O'Donoghue's (p97) of Merrion Row is in a league of its own.

➡ **Fine Dining** The critics regularly praise Restaurant Patrick Guilbaud (p96) as the best in the country; whatever debate there is exists as a result of restaurants like L'Ecrivain (p96), but there's also a bunch of less-exalted spots worth checking out, such as Etto (p95) and the Coburg Brasserie (p95).

Getting There & Away

➡ **Bus** Most cross-city buses will get you here, or close by.

➡ **Train** The most convenient DART stop is Pearse St, with the station entrance on Westland Row.

➡ **On Foot** Merrion Sq is less than 500m from St Stephen's Green (and Grafton St).

Lonely Planet's Top Tip

The Vaughan Collection of watercolours by JMW Turner at the National Gallery is only displayed during the month of January, when the light is just right to appreciate the delicacy and beauty of these masterpieces.

◉ Best Irish Art

➡ Yeats Room, National Gallery (p90)

➡ Treasury, National Museum of Ireland – Archaeology (p86)

➡ Royal Hibernian Academy (RHA) Gallagher Gallery (p94)

For reviews, see p86➡

✕ Best Places to Eat

➡ Restaurant Patrick Guilbaud (p96)

➡ L'Ecrivain (p96)

➡ Coburg Brasserie (p95)

➡ House (p95)

➡ Etto (p95)

For reviews, see p95➡

🍷 Best Places to Drink

➡ O'Donoghue's (p97)

➡ Toner's (p96)

➡ Doheny & Nesbitt's (p97)

➡ House (p97)

➡ Square Ball (p97)

For reviews, see p96➡

MERRION SQUARE & AROUND

FINDS FROM
IRISH WETLANDS

TOP SIGHT
NATIONAL MUSEUM OF IRELAND – ARCHAEOLOGY

This is the mother of all Irish museums and the country's foremost cultural institution. One of four branches, this is the most important, home to Europe's finest selection of Bronze and Iron Age gold artefacts, the most complete collection of medieval Celtic metalwork in the world, and fascinating prehistoric and Viking relics.

Treasury

The Treasury is the most famous part of the collection, and its centrepieces are Ireland's best-known crafted artefacts, the **Ardagh Chalice** and the **Tara Brooch**. The 12th-century Ardagh Chalice is made of gold, silver, bronze, brass, copper and lead; it measures 17.8cm high and 24.2cm in diameter and, put simply, is the finest example of Celtic art ever found. The equally renowned Tara Brooch was crafted around AD 700, primarily in white bronze, but with traces of gold, silver, glass, copper, enamel and wire beading, and was used as a clasp for a cloak. It was discovered on a beach in Bettystown, County Meath, in 1850, but later came into the hands of an art dealer who named it after the hill of Tara, the historic seat of the ancient high kings. It doesn't have quite the same ring to it, but it was the Bettystown Brooch that sparked a revival of interest in Celtic jewellery that hasn't let up to this day. There are many other pieces that testify to Ireland's history as the land of saints and scholars.

Ór-Ireland's Gold

Elsewhere in the Treasury is the *Ór-Ireland's Gold* exhibition, featuring stunning jewellery and decorative objects created by Celtic artisans in the Bronze and Iron Ages. Among them are the **Broighter Hoard**, which includes a 1st-century-BC large gold collar,

DON'T MISS

➡ Tara Brooch
➡ Ardagh Chalice
➡ Loughnasade War Trumpet
➡ *Kingship and Sacrifice* exhibition

PRACTICALITIES

➡ Map p244, A3
➡ www.museum.ie
➡ Kildare St
➡ admission free
➡ ⊙10am-5pm Tue-Sat, 2-5pm Sun
➡ all city centre

unsurpassed anywhere in Europe, and an extraordinarily delicate gold boat. There's also the wonderful **Loughnasade bronze war trumpet**, which also dates from the 1st century BC. It is 1.86m long and made of sheets of bronze, riveted together, with an intricately designed disc at the mouth. It produces a sound similar to the Australian didgeridoo, though you'll have to take our word for it. Running alongside the wall is a **15m log boat**, which was dropped into the water to soften, abandoned and then pulled out 4000 years later, almost perfectly preserved in the peat bog.

Kingship & Sacrifice

One of the museum's biggest showstoppers is the collection of Iron Age 'bog bodies' in the *Kingship and Sacrifice* exhibit – four figures in varying states of preservation dug out of the midland bogs. The bodies' various eerily preserved details – a distinctive tangle of hair, sinewy legs and fingers with fingernails intact – are memorable, but it's the accompanying detail that will make you pause: scholars now believe that all of these bodies were victims of the most horrendous ritualistic torture and sacrifice – the cost of being notable figures in the Celtic world.

Other Exhibits

If you can cope with any more history, upstairs are **Medieval Ireland 1150–1550**, **Viking Age Ireland** – which features exhibits from the excavations at Wood Quay, the area between Christ Church Cathedral and the river – and our own favourite, the aptly named **Clothes from Bogs in Ireland**, a collection of 16th- and 17th-century woollen garments recovered from the bog. Enthralling stuff!

WHAT'S IN A NAME?

Virtually all of the treasures held here are named after the location in which they were found. It's interesting to note that most of them were discovered not by archaeologists' trowels but by bemused farmers out ploughing their fields, cutting peat or, in the case of the Ardagh Chalice, digging for spuds.

If you don't mind groups, the themed guided tours will help you wade through the myriad exhibits. If you want to avoid crowds, the best time to visit is weekday afternoons, when school groups have gone, and never during Irish school holidays.

DID YOU KNOW?

The museum was founded by an act of (British) Parliament on 14 August 1877 as the Museum of Science and Art, Dublin. Its original purview was to house the expanding collection of the Royal Dublin Society, which was duly transferred to state ownership along with important collections owned by Trinity College and the Royal Irish Academy.

National Museum of Ireland

NATIONAL TREASURES

Ireland's most important cultural institution is the National Museum, and its most important branch is the original one, housed in this fine neoclassical (or Victorian Palladian) building designed by Sir Thomas Newenham Deane and finished in 1890. Squeezed in between the rear entrance of Leinster House – the Irish parliament – and a nondescript building from the 1960s, it's easy to pass by the museum. But within its fairly cramped confines you'll find the most extensive collection of Bronze and Iron Age gold artefacts in Europe and the extraordinary collection of the Treasury. This includes the stunning ❶ **Ardagh Chalice** and the delicately crafted ❷ **Tara Brooch**. Amid all the lustre, look out for the ❸ **Broighter Gold Collar** and the impressively crafted ❹ **Loughnashade War Trumpet**, both extraordinary examples of Celtic art. Finally, pay a visit to the exquisite ❺ **Cross of Cong**, which was created after the other pieces but is just as beautiful.

As you visit these treasures – all created after the arrival of Christianity in the 5th century – bear in mind that they were produced with the most rudimentary of instruments.

VIKING DUBLIN

Archaeological excavations in Dublin between 1961 and 1981 unearthed evidence of a Viking town and cemeteries along the banks of the River Liffey. The graves contained weapons such as swords and spears, together with jewellery and personal items. Craftsmen's tools, weights and scales, silver ingots and coins show that the Vikings, as well as marauding and raiding, were also engaged in commercial activities. The Viking artefacts are now part of the National Museum's collection.

First Floor

Ground Floor

Main Entrance

NATIONAL MUSEUM OF IRELAND ©

Cross of Cong

Made in 1123 to encase a fragment of the True Cross that was touring the country at the time, it was kept by the Augustinian monks at their friary in Cong, County Galway. The exquisite gold filigree on both the front and back are testament to the important role the cross was designed to have.

Broighter Gold Collar
The most exquisite element of the larger Broighter Hoard, this beautiful gold neck ornament (called a torc) is decorated in the elaborate curved patterns of high Celtic art, called La Tène style.

Tara Brooch
Designed around AD 700 as a clasp for a cloak, this is the second superstar of the collection – its delicate craftsmanship has become a symbol of the excellence of Irish art.

Loughnashade War Trumpet
One of four bronze trumpets found in a dried-up lake in County Armagh, this magnificent war trumpet is a masterpiece of skilled riveting; the bell-end is beautifully decorated in a lotus-bud motif, and the sound it made terrified all who heard it.

Ardagh Chalice
Made of gold, silver, bronze, brass, copper and lead, the 12th-century Ardagh Chalice is the finest example of Celtic art ever found.

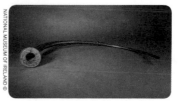

TOP SIGHT
NATIONAL GALLERY

A stunning Caravaggio and a room full of Ireland's pre-eminent artist, Jack B Yeats, are just a couple of highlights from this fine collection. Its original assortment of 125 paintings has grown, mainly through bequests, to over 13,000 artworks, including oils, watercolours, sketches, prints and sculptures.

DON'T MISS

➡ The Yeats Room
➡ *The Taking of Christ* (Caravaggio)
➡ *A Lady Writing a Letter* (Vermeer)
➡ Vaughan Collection

MERRION SQUARE & AROUND NATIONAL GALLERY

The Building
The building itself was designed by Francis Fowke (1823–65), whose architectural credits also include London's Victoria & Albert Museum. The entire building comprises 54 galleries; works are divided by history, school, geography and theme. There are four wings: the original **Dargan Wing**, the **Milltown Wing** (1899–1903), the **Beit Wing** (1964–68) and the **Millennium Wing** (2002). A major refurbishment was completed in 2016.

PRACTICALITIES

➡ Map p244, B2
➡ www.nationalgallery.ie
➡ West Merrion Sq
➡ admission free
➡ ⏰9.15am-5.30pm Mon-Wed, Fri & Sat, to 8.30pm Thu, 11am-5.30pm Sun
➡ 🚌4, 7, 8, 46A from city centre

The Collection
The collection spans works from the 14th to the 20th centuries and includes all the major continental schools.

There is an emphasis on Irish art, and among the works to look out for are William Orpen's *Sunlight,* Roderic O'Conor's *Reclining Nude* and *Young Breton Girl,* and Paul Henry's *The Potato Diggers.* But the highlight, and one you should definitely take time to explore, is the **Yeats Room**, devoted to and containing more than 30 paintings by Jack B Yeats, a uniquely Irish impressionist and arguably the country's greatest artist. Some of his finest moments are *The Liffey Swim, Men of Destiny* and *Above the Fair.*

Caravaggio's The Taking of Christ
The absolute star exhibit from a pupil of the European schools is Caravaggio's sublime *The Taking of Christ,* in which the troubled Italian genius attempts to light the scene figuratively and metaphorically (the artist himself is portrayed holding the lantern on the far right). Fra Angelico, Titian and Tintoretto are all in this neighbourhood. Facing Caravaggio, way down the opposite end of the gallery, is *A Genovese Boy Standing on a Terrace* by Van Dyck. Old Dutch and Flemish masters line up in between, but all defer to Vermeer's *A Lady Writing a Letter,* which is lucky to be here at all, having been stolen by Dublin gangster Martin Cahill in 1992, as featured in the film *The General.*

French Collection
The French section contains Jules Breton's famous 19th-century *The Gleaners,* along with works by Monet, Degas, Pissarro and Delacroix, while Spain chips in with an unusually scruffy *Still Life with Mandolin* by Picasso, as well as paintings by El Greco and Goya, and an early Velázquez. There is a small British collection with works by Reynolds, Hogarth and Gainsborough (*The Cottage Girl* is especially beautiful).

Joseph Turner
One of the most popular exhibitions occurs only in January, when the gallery hosts its annual display of the Vaughan Collection, featuring watercolours by Joseph Turner. The 35 works in the collection are best viewed at this time due to the particular quality of the winter light.

TOP SIGHT
MERRION SQUARE

Elegant Merrion Sq was laid out in 1762 and is to this day the most prestigious of Dublin's squares. Its well-kept lawns and beautifully tended flower beds are flanked on three sides by gorgeous Georgian houses with colourful doors and peacock fanlights, and on the remaining side by the National Gallery, Leinster House and the Museum of Natural History.

DON'T MISS
➡ Oscar Wilde statue
➡ Georgian doorways
➡ Peacock fanlights

PRACTICALITIES
➡ Map p244, C3
➡ ⊙dawn-dusk
➡ 🚌all city centre

Oscar Wilde Statue

Just inside the northwestern corner of the square is a flamboyant **statue of Oscar Wilde**, who grew up across the street at **No 1**. This was the first residence built on the square (1762) and during the Wilde tenancy was renowned for the literary salon hosted by his mother, Lady 'Speranza' Wilde. Alas, you can't visit the restored house (used exclusively by students of the American College Dublin) so you'll have to make do with the statue of Wilde, wearing his customary smoking jacket and reclining on a rock. Wilde may well be sneering at Dublin and his old home, although the expression may have more to do with the artist's attempt to depict the deeply divided nature of the man: from one side he looks to be smiling and happy; from the other, gloomy and preoccupied. Atop one of the plinths, daubed with witty one-liners and Wildean throwaways, is a small green statue of Oscar's pregnant mother.

Other Statuary

Just inside the western side of the square is the **National Memorial** (⊙24hr), a pyramid-shaped sculpture by Brian King. Inside are four bronze figures, representing all elements of the Irish Defense Forces, standing guard over an eternal flame. The middle of the park has the sculpture of a **Jester's Chair**, commissioned in memory of Dermot Morgan, aka Father Ted.

Troubled Times

Despite the air of affluent calm, life around here hasn't always been a well-pruned bed of roses. During the Famine, the lawns of the square teemed with destitute rural refugees who lived off the soup kitchen organised here. After independence, the new Irish Free State government considered it an unwelcome symbol of British rule in Ireland and developed plans to demolish and redevelop the square, but the plans were put aside during WWII and thankfully never pursued. After the killing of 13 civilians on Bloody Sunday in Derry in 1972, an angry crowd of about 20,000 gathered outside the British Embassy at 39 Merrion Sq East and burnt the building out (the embassy then moved to Ballsbridge).

Damage to fine Dublin buildings hasn't always been the prerogative of vandals, terrorists or protesters. East Merrion Sq once continued into Lower Fitzwilliam St in the longest unbroken series of Georgian houses in Europe. Despite this, in 1961 the Electricity Supply Board (ESB) knocked down 16 of them to build an office block – just another in a long list of crimes against architectural aesthetics that plagued the city in the latter half of the 20th century. The Royal Institute of the Architects of Ireland is rather more respectful of its Georgian address and hosts regular exhibitions.

⊙ SIGHTS

NATIONAL MUSEUM OF IRELAND –
ARCHAEOLOGY   MUSEUM
See p86.

NATIONAL GALLERY   MUSEUM
See p90.

MERRION SQUARE   PARK
See p91.

★MUSEUM OF
NATURAL HISTORY   MUSEUM
Map p244 (National Museum of Ireland – Natural History; www.museum.ie; Upper Merrion St; ⊙10am-5pm Tue-Sat, 2-5pm Sun; ⊠7, 44 from city centre) FREE Dusty, weird and utterly compelling, this window into Victorian times has barely changed since Scottish explorer Dr David Livingstone opened it in 1857 – before disappearing into the African jungle for a meeting with Henry Stanley. It is a fine example of Victorian charm and scientific wonderment, and its enormous collection is a testament to the skill of taxidermy.

The **Irish Room** on the ground floor is filled with mammals, sea creatures, birds and butterflies all found in Ireland at some point, including the skeletons of three 10,000-year-old Irish elk that greet you as you enter. The **World Animals Collection**, spread across three levels, has as its centrepiece the skeleton of a 20m-long fin whale found beached in County Sligo. Evolutionists will love the line-up of orang-utan, chimpanzee, gorilla and human skeletons on the 1st floor.

A more recent addition is the **Discovery Zone**, where visitors can do some firsthand exploring of their own, handling taxidermy specimens and opening drawers. Other notables include a Tasmanian tiger (an extinct Australian marsupial, mislabelled as a Tasmanian wolf), a giant panda from China, and several African and Asian rhinoceros. The wonderful **Blaschka Collection** comprises finely detailed glass models of marine creatures whose zoological accuracy is incomparable.

LEINSTER HOUSE   NOTABLE BUILDING
Map p244 (Oireachtas Éireann; ☎01-618 3271; www.oireachtas.ie; Kildare St; ⊙observation galleries 2.30-8.30pm Tue, 10.30am-8.30pm Wed, 10.30am-5.30pm Thu Nov-May; ⊠all city centre) All the big decisions are made at the Oireachtas (parliament). This Palladian mansion was built as a city residence for James Fitzgerald, the Duke

🏃 Neighbourhood Walk
A Georgian Block

START KILDARE ST
END NATIONAL GALLERY
LENGTH 1.7KM; ONE HOUR

Although Dublin is rightfully known as a Georgian city and many of its buildings were built between 1720 and 1814, the style cast such a tall shadow over Dublin design that for more than a century afterwards it was still being copied.

Begin your amble at the bottom (northern) end of ❶**Kildare Street**, opposite the walls of Trinity College Dublin. This street is named after James Fitzgerald, the Duke of Leinster and Earl of Kildare, who broke with 18th-century convention and opted to build his city mansion on the south side of the Liffey, away from the elegant neighbourhoods of the north side where most of his aristocratic peers lived. 'Where I go,' he confidently predicted, 'society will follow.'

He was right, and over the following century the street was lined with impressive buildings. On the left-hand side as you begin is the old Kildare Street Lords Club, a members' club famous for 'aristocracy, claret and whist' that was founded in 1782. In 1860 the original building was replaced by this Byzantine-style construction, designed by Thomas Newenham Deane, where the club remained until 1976. It is now the home of the Alliance Française.

On the same side a little further up is the ❷**National Library** (p94), another one of Deane's designs; immediately after the library, the imposing black gates and police presence protect ❸**Leinster House** (p92), the Palladian city pile that Fitzgerald commissioned Richard Cassels to build for him between 1745 and 1748. It is now the seat of both houses of the Irish parliament. From this side American visitors might think the building looks oddly familiar: the townhouse look is what inspired James Hoban, 1780 winner of the Duke of Leinster's medal for drawings of 'brackets, stairs and roofs', to submit a design that won the competition to build the White House in 1792.

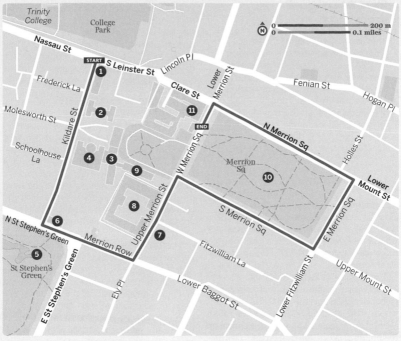

The next building along the street is the **④ National Museum of Ireland – Archaeology** (p86), another Deane building, which opened in 1890 and has since been the repository of the state's most valuable cultural treasures. As you reach the top of the street, the greenery in front of you is that of **⑤ St Stephen's Green** (p64), the city's best-loved public square. Once a common used for punishments and hangings, the green was landscaped with Guinness money in the mid-18th century and quickly became the aristocracy's favourite spot to take a walk.

Turn left onto Merrion Row and walk along the green. You'll pass the **⑥ Shelbourne** (p182), Dublin's most historic hotel. During the Easter Rising of 1916 it treated the injured from both rebel and British sides, and the Irish Constitution of 1922 was framed in Room 112. The hotel even has a tenuous link to Hitler: his half-brother Alois worked as a waiter here. Take another left onto Merrion St. On your right, No 24 in the row of elegant Georgian houses is reputed to be the birthplace of Arthur Wellesley, the Duke of Wellington, who dealt with jibes about being born in Ireland by snippily responding that

'being born in a stable does not make one a horse'. That 'stable' is now part of the city's most elegant hotel, the **⑦ Merrion** (p181).

On your left-hand side you'll pass the **⑧ Government Buildings** (p94), where the current government runs its day-to-day affairs, and just past it, the rear entrance to Leinster House; from here it looks more like a country mansion. The smaller building wedged in between Government Buildings and Leinster House is the **⑨ Museum of Natural History** (p92), opened in 1857.

On your right is **⑩ Merrion Square** (p91), the most elegant of Dublin's public spaces. The park itself is gorgeous, while the houses that surround it are magnificent: their doorways and fanlights are the most photographed of the city's Georgian heritage and a disproportionate number of Dublin's most famous residents lived on it at one point or another.

Walk around or through Merrion Sq, making your way back to West Merrion Sq and the **⑪ National Gallery** (p90), which opened in 1864 and was built by Francis Fowke after a design by Charles Lanyon. For the sake of symmetry, the facade is a copy of that of the Museum of Natural History.

LOCAL KNOWLEDGE

STREET ART

On Sunday, the wrought-iron fences of Merrion Sq convert to gallery walls for the traditional open-air **art market** (Map p244; www.merrionart.com; Merrion Sq; ⊘10am-dusk Sun; 🚋all city centre). At any given time you'll find the work of 150 artists, mostly Sunday-painter types with a penchant for landscapes and still lifes, some of whom are very talented indeed.

of Leinster and Earl of Kildare, by Richard Cassels between 1745 and 1748. Prearranged free **guided tours** (Map p244; www.oireachtas.ie; Kildare St; ⊘10.30am, 11.30am, 2.30pm & 3.30pm Mon-Fri; 🚋all city centre) **FREE** are available when parliament is in session (but not sitting); entry tickets to the observation galleries are available.

The Kildare St facade looks like a townhouse (which inspired Irish architect James Hoban's design for the US White House), whereas the Merrion Sq frontage resembles a country mansion. The obelisk in front of the building is dedicated to Arthur Griffith, Michael Collins and Kevin O'Higgins, the architects of independent Ireland.

The first government of the Irish Free State moved in from 1922, and both the Dáil (lower house) and Seanad (senate, or upper house) still meet here to discuss the affairs of the nation and gossip at the exclusive members bar. The 60-member Seanad meets for fairly low-key sessions in the north-wing saloon, while there are usually more sparks and tantrums when the 166-member Dáil bangs heads in a less-interesting room, formerly a lecture theatre, which was added to the original building in 1897. Parliament sits for 90 days a year.

GOVERNMENT BUILDINGS NOTABLE BUILDING
Map p244 (www.taoiseach.gov.ie; Upper Merrion St; ⊘tours hourly 10.30am-1.30pm Sat; 🚋7, 44 from city centre) **FREE** This gleaming Edwardian pile was the last building (almost) completed by the British before they were evicted; it opened as the Royal College of Science in 1911. When the college vacated in 1989, the then Taoiseach (prime minister) Charles Haughey and his government moved in and spent a fortune refurbishing the complex.

Free 40-minute **tours** visit the Taoiseach's office, the Cabinet Room, the ceremonial

staircase with a stunning stained-glass window – designed by Evie Hone (1894–1955) for the 1939 New York Trade Fair – and many fine examples of modern Irish arts and crafts. Pick up tickets from 9.30am on the day of the tour at the Clare St entrance of the National Gallery.

ROYAL HIBERNIAN ACADEMY (RHA) GALLAGHER GALLERY GALLERY
Map p244 (⊋01-661 2558; www.rhagallery.ie; 15 Ely Pl; ⊘11am-5pm Mon, Tue & Thu-Sat, to 8pm Wed, noon-5pm Sun; 🚋10, 11, 13B, 51X from city centre) **FREE** This large, well-lit gallery at the end of a serene Georgian street has a grand name to fit its exalted reputation as one of the most prestigious exhibition spaces for modern and contemporary art in Ireland. Its exhibitions are usually of a very high quality, and well worth a visit.

The big event is the Annual Exhibition, held in May, which shows the work of those artists deemed worthy enough by the selection committee that is made up of members of the academy (easily identified amid the huge throng that attends the opening by their scholars' gowns). The show is a mix of technically proficient artists, Sunday painters and the odd outstanding talent.

NATIONAL LIBRARY HISTORIC BUILDING
Map p244 (www.nli.ie; Kildare St; ⊘9.30am-7.45pm Mon-Wed, to 4.45pm Thu & Fri, 9.30am-12.45pm Sat; 🚋all city centre) **FREE** Suitably sedate and elegant, the National Library was built from 1884 to 1890 by Sir Thomas Newenham Deane, to a similar design as the National Museum of Ireland – Archaeology. Its extensive collection has many valuable early manuscripts, first editions and maps. Parts of the library are open to the public, including the domed reading room where Stephen Dedalus expounded his views on Shakespeare in James Joyce's *Ulysses*. There's a **Genealogy Advisory Service** (⊋01-603 0256; ⊘9.30am-5pm Mon-Wed, to 4.45pm Thu & Fri) on the 2nd floor.

For those prints that are worth a thousand words, you'll have to head down to Temple Bar to the National Photographic Archive (p103) extension of the library, for which you'll need to pick up a reader's ticket (look for the Readers Ticket Office in the main building).

FITZWILLIAM SQUARE PARK
Map p244 (⊘closed to public; 🚋10, 11, 13B, 46A from city centre) The smallest of Dublin's great

Georgian squares was completed in 1825. William Dargan (1799–1867), the railway pioneer and founder of the National Gallery, lived at No 2, and the artist Jack B Yeats (1871–1957) lived at No 18. In 2017 it began hosting a summer market of more than a dozen vendors.

It's the only one left where the central garden is still the private domain of the square's residents. Look out for the attractive 18th- and 19th-century metal coal-hole covers. The square is now a centre for the medical profession.

HUGUENOT CEMETERY   CEMETERY
Map p244 (St Stephen's Green; ⊘closed to public; 🚇all city centre) This tiny cemetery was established in 1693 by French Protestant refugees. The cemetery is closed but you can see graves through the railings; of the 239 surnames one is Becquett, a relation of the writer Samuel Beckett.

✕ EATING

BRAMBLES   CAFE €
Map p244 (National Museum of Ireland Cafe; National Museum of Ireland, Kildare St; mains around €7; ⊘10am-4pm Mon, 10am-5pm Tue-Sat, noon-5pm Sun; 🚇all city centre) The award-winning cafe of this branch of the National Museum of Ireland serves excellent salads, sandwiches and locally sourced hot dishes such chicken, leek and mushroom pie. It also serves Fairtrade teas and coffees.

★ETTO   ITALIAN €€
Map p244 (☎01-678 8872; www.etto.ie; 18 Merrion Row; mains €18-23; ⊘noon-10pm Mon-Fri, 12.30-10pm Sat; 🚇all city centre) Award-winning restaurant and wine bar that does contemporary versions of classic Italian cuisine. All the ingredients are fresh, the presentation is exquisite and the service is just right. Portions are small, but the food is so rich you won't leave hungry. The only downside is the relatively quick turnover; lingering over the excellent wine would be nice. Book ahead.

★COBURG BRASSERIE   FRENCH €€
Map p244 (☎01-602 8900; www.thecoburgdublin.com; Conrad International, Earlsfort Tce; mains €11-18; 🚇all city centre) The French-inspired, seafood-leaning cuisine at this revamped hotel brasserie puts the emphasis on shellfish: the all-day menu offers oysters, mussels and a range of 'casual' lobster dishes, from lobster rolls to lobster cocktail. The bouillabaisse is chock-full of sea flavours, and you can also get a shrimp burger and a fine plate of Connemara whiskey-cured organic salmon. Top-notch.

HOUSE   MEDITERRANEAN €€
Map p244 (www.housedublin.ie; 27 Lower Leeson St; tapas €9-11, mains €14-26; ⊘8am-midnight Mon-Wed, 8am-3am Thu & Fri, 4pm-3am Sat; 🚇11, 46, 118, 145) This gorgeous bar does a limited selection of main courses, but the real treats are the tapas-style sharing plates, which cover the full Mediterranean spread, from wild mushroom risotto and pulled pork to grilled halloumi and salt and pepper calamari.

MARCEL'S   FRENCH €€
Map p244 (☎01-660 2367; www.marcels.ie; 13 Merrion Row; mains €20-32, 3-course menu €50; ⊘noon-3pm & 5-10pm Sun-Thu, noon-11pm Fri-Sat; 🚇all city centre) An elegant brasserie with Hermès orange-coloured chairs, blue-and-white Churchill china and superb, French-inspired cuisine – just the way they'd eat it in New York. It's owned by the same crowd as the Green Hen (p73), and the similarities are obvious and complementary. To one side is a bar – done in traditional Irish style. Bookings recommended.

MUSASHI HOGAN PLACE   JAPANESE €€
Map p244 (☎01-441 0106; www.musashidublin.com; 48 Hogan Pl; sushi €3-4, maki rolls €7-8, mains €14-16; ⊘noon-10pm Sun-Thu, to 11pm Fri & Sat; 🚇4, 7 from city centre) The third branch of the expanding Musashi empire, serving the same excellent and authentic sushi, sashimi and maki as the original restaurant (p140) on the north side of the Liffey.

XICO   MEXICAN €€
Map p244 (www.xico.ie; 143 Lower Baggot St; mains €10-18; ⊘5pm-midnight Mon-Sat; 🚇all city centre) It's quite the scene at this underground Mexican restaurant, where the music is loud and the food – tacos, tostadas and main courses such as tuna ceviche and a fine chilli bowl – is washed down with margaritas. Yes, it's a restaurant, but you'd better be in the mood for a fiesta.

ELY   MODERN IRISH €€
Map p244 (☎01-676 8986; www.elywinebar.ie; 22 Ely Pl; mains €15-29; ⊘noon-11.30pm Mon-Fri, 5pm-12.30am Sat; 🚇all city centre) 🖉 Scrummy homemade burgers, bangers and mash, and

braised wild mushroom are some of the dishes you can find in this basement restaurant. Meals are prepared with organic and free-range produce from the owner's family farm in County Clare, so you can rest assured of the quality. There's another branch (p149) in the Docklands.

⭐ **RESTAURANT**
PATRICK GUILBAUD   FRENCH €€€
Map p244 (☑01-676 4192; www.restaurantpat rickguilbaud.ie; 21 Upper Merrion St; 2-/3-course set lunch €50/60, dinner menus €90-185; ⊘12.30-2.30pm & 7.30-10.30pm Tue-Sat; ☐7, 46 from city centre) Ireland's only Michelin two-star is understandably considered the best in the country by its devotees, who proclaim Guillaume Lebrun's French haute cuisine the most exalted expression of the culinary arts. If you like formal dining, this is as good as it gets: the lunch menu is an absolute steal, at least in this stratosphere. Innovative and beautifully presented.

The room itself is all contemporary elegance and the service expertly formal yet surprisingly friendly – the staff are meticulously trained and as skilled at answering queries and addressing individual requests as they are at making sure not one breadcrumb lingers too long on the immaculate tablecloths. Owner Patrick Guilbaud usually does the rounds of the tables himself in the evening to salute regular customers and charm first-timers into returning. Reservations are absolutely necessary.

⭐ **L'ECRIVAIN**   FRENCH €€€
Map p244 (☑01-661 1919; www.lecrivain.com; 109a Lower Baggot St; 3-course lunch menus €45, 8-course tasting menus €90, mains €45; ⊘12.30-2pm Wed-Fri, 6.30-10pm Mon-Sat; ☐38, 39 from city centre) Head chef Derry Clarke is considered a gourmet god for the exquisite simplicity of his creations, which put the emphasis on flavour and the best local ingredients – all given the French once over and turned into something that approaches divine dining. The Michelin people like it too and awarded it one of their stars.

UNICORN   ITALIAN €€€
Map p244 (☑01-662 4757; www.theunicorn.restau rant; 12b Merrion Ct, Merrion Row; mains €28-36; ⊘12.30-2.30pm & 5-11pm Mon-Wed, 12.30-11pm Thu-Sat, 1-9pm Sun; ☐all city centre) Saturday lunch at this Italian restaurant in a laneway off Merrion Row is a tradition for Dublin's media types, socialites, politicos and their cronies who guffaw and clink glasses in conspiratorial rapture. The extensive lunchtime antipasto bar is popular, but we still prefer the meaty à la carte menu. There are pasta and fish dishes to cater to all palates.

DAX   FRENCH €€€
Map p244 (☑01-676 1494; www.dax.ie; 23 Upper Pembroke St; mains €26-34; ⊘12.30-2.15pm Tue-Fri, plus 6-10.30pm Tue-Sat; ☐all city centre) Olivier Meisonnave's posh-rustic basement restaurant, named after his hometown north of Biarritz, is popular with serious foodies. They come for the expertly made dishes such as fillet of halibut with a fennel confit, piquillo pepper cream and chickpea fritter and Irish samphire with Irish mussels dressing; or the locally sourced fillet of beef, served with caramelised shallots and fondant potato.

FITZWILLIAM SQUARE MARKET   MARKET
Map p244 (Fitzwilliam Sq; ⊘11.30am-2.30pm Thu May-Sep; ☐10, 11, 13B, 46A from city centre) Over a dozen street-food vendors – from sushi to pizza – take over the middle of the square during the summer. Look out for the excellent Kerala Kitchen and Falafel Bite. There's also music.

🍷 DRINKING & NIGHTLIFE

⭐ **TONER'S**   PUB
Map p244 (☑01-676 3090; www.tonerspub.ie; 139 Lower Baggot St; ⊘10.30am-11.30pm Mon-Thu, to 12.30am Fri & Sat, 11.30am-11pm Sun; ☐7, 46 from city centre) Toner's, with its stone floors and antique snugs, has changed little over the years and is the closest thing you'll get to a country pub in the heart of the city. Next door, Toner's Yard is a comfortable outside space. The shelves and drawers are reminders that it once doubled as a grocery shop.

The writer Oliver St John Gogarty once brought WB Yeats here, after the upper-class poet – who lived just around the corner – decided he wanted to visit a pub. After a silent sherry in the noisy bar, Yeats turned to his friend and said, 'I have seen the pub, now please take me home.' We always suspected he was a little too precious for normal people, and he would probably be horrified by the good-natured business crowd making the racket these days too. His loss.

LITERARY ADDRESSES

Merrion Sq has long been the favoured address of Dublin's affluent intelligentsia. **Oscar Wilde** spent much of his youth at 1 North Merrion Sq, now the campus of the American College Dublin. Grumpy **WB Yeats** (1865–1939) lived at 52 East Merrion Sq and later, from 1922 to 1928, at 82 South Merrion Sq. **George (AE) Russell** (1867–1935), the self-described 'poet, mystic, painter and cooperator', worked at No 84. The great Liberator **Daniel O'Connell** (1775–1847) was a resident of No 58 in his later years. Austrian **Erwin Schrödinger** (1887–1961), he of the alive, dead or simultaneously both cat paradox and co-winner of the 1933 Nobel Prize for Physics, lived at No 65 from 1940 to 1956. Dublin seems to attract writers of horror stories and **Joseph Sheridan Le Fanu** (1814–73), who penned the vampire classic *Camilla,* was a resident of No 70.

★ O'DONOGHUE'S · PUB

Map p244 (www.odonoghues.ie; 15 Merrion Row; ⊗10.30am-11.30pm Mon-Thu, to 12.30am Fri & Sat, noon-11pm Sun; ☐all city centre) The pub where traditional music stalwarts The Dubliners made their name in the 1960s still hosts live music nightly, but the crowds would gather anyway – for the excellent pints and superb ambience, in the old bar or the covered coach yard next to it.

HOUSE · BAR

Map p244 (☑01-905 9090; www.housedublin.ie; 27 Lower Leeson St; ⊗8am-midnight Mon-Wed, 8am-3am Thu & Fri, 4pm-3am Sat; ☐11, 46, 118, 145) Spread across two Georgian townhouses, this could be Dublin's most beautiful modern bar, with gorgeous wood-floored rooms, comfortable couches and even log fires in winter to amp up the cosiness. In the middle there's a lovely glassed-in outdoor space that on a nice day bathes the rest of the bar with beautiful natural light. There's also an excellent menu.

SQUARE BALL · BAR

Map p244 (☑01-662 4473; www.the-square-ball.com; 45 Hogan Pl; ⊗4-11.30pm Mon, noon-11.30pm Tue-Thu, noon-12.30am Fri & Sat, noon-11pm Sun; ☐4, 7 from city centre) This bar is many things to many people: craft beer and cocktail bar in front, sports lounge and barbecue pit in the back and an awesome vintage arcade upstairs. There are also plenty of board games, so bring your competitive spirit.

DOHENY & NESBITT'S · PUB

Map p244 (☑01-676 2945; www.dohenyandnesbitts.ie; 5 Lower Baggot St; ⊗10am-11.30pm Mon-Thu, 10am-2am Fri & Sat, noon-11pm Sun; ☐all city centre) A standout, even in a city of wonderful pubs, Nesbitt's is equipped with antique snugs and is a favourite place for the high-powered gossip of politicians and journalists; Leinster House is only a short stroll away.

HARTIGAN'S · PUB

Map p244 (100 Lower Leeson St; ⊗10.30am-11.30pm Mon-Thu, to 12.30am Fri & Sat, noon-11pm Sun; ☐all city centre) This is about as spartan a bar as you'll find in the city, and the daytime home of some serious drinkers, who appreciate the quiet, no-frills surroundings. In the evening it's popular with students from the medical faculty of University College Dublin.

☆ ENTERTAINMENT

O'DONOGHUE'S · TRADITIONAL MUSIC

Map p244 (☑01-660 7194; www.odonoghues.ie; 15 Merrion Row; ⊗from 7pm; ☐all city centre) There's traditional music nightly in the old bar of this famous boozer. Regular performers include local names such as Tom Foley, Joe McHugh, Joe Foley and Maria O'Connell.

SUGAR CLUB · LIVE MUSIC

Map p244 (☑01-678 7188; www.thesugarclub.com; 8 Lower Leeson St; €7-20; ⊗7pm-late; ☐7, 46 from city centre) There's live jazz, cabaret and soul music on weekends in this comfortable theatre-style venue on the corner of St Stephen's Green.

🛍 SHOPPING

HERALDIC ARTISTS · BOOKS

Map p244 (www.heraldicartists.com; 3 Nassau St; ⊗1-6pm Mon-Sat; ☐all city centre) Hand-painted heraldic plaques and scrolls, as well as an extensive research facility on genealogy, with plenty of books to aid both professional and amateur researchers.

Temple Bar

Neighbourhood Top Five

❶ Temple Bar Food Market (p108) Feasting on organic and exotic nibbles from all over at Dublin's most exciting food market.

❷ Claddagh Records (p108) Shopping for all kinds of Irish traditional and folk music – as well as sounds from around the globe – in this wonderful record shop.

❸ Christ Church Cathedral (p100) Visiting the most impressive – from the outside at least – of Dublin's three cathedrals.

❹ Dublin Musical Pub Crawl (p109) Exploring the pubs of the area to a wonderful traditional soundtrack – sure, isn't this why you came?

❺ Gutter Bookshop (p108) Browsing the shelves of this locally owned bookshop, one of the best in town because it's the kind of place that encourages you to linger.

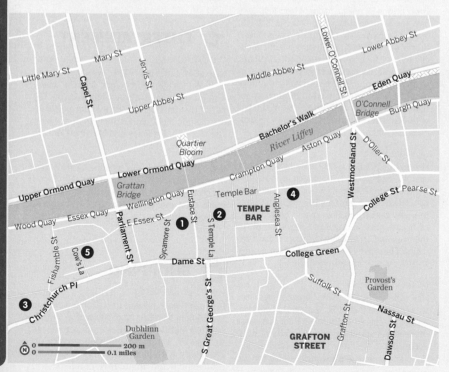

For more detail of this area see Map p236 and p237 ➡

Explore Temple Bar

You can visit all of Temple Bar's attractions in less than half a day, but that's not really the point: this cobbled neighbourhood, for so long the city's most infamous party zone, is really more about ambience than attractions. If you visit during the day, the district's bohemian bent is on display. You can browse for vintage clothes, get your nipples pierced, nibble on Mongolian barbecue, buy organic food, pick up the latest musical releases and buy books on every conceivable subject. You can check out the latest art installations or join in a pulsating drum circle. By night – or at the weekend – it's a different story altogether, as the area's bars are packed to the rafters with revellers looking to tap into their inner Bacchus: it's loud, raucous and usually a lot of fun. Temple Bar is also Dublin's official 'cultural quarter', so you shouldn't ignore its more high-minded offerings like the progressive Project Arts Centre (p107) and the Irish Film Institute (p108).

Local Life

➡Markets The Temple Bar Food Market (p108) is all about gourmet goodies and organic foodstuffs; the Cow's Lane Designer Mart (p109) is a showcase of local art and clothing; while the Book Market (p109) is the place to pick up secondhand novels and CDs.

➡Nightlife A drink in the Liquor Rooms (p106), followed by a gig at the Workman's Club (p107), is always a great night out, and you can really get your grind on at Mother (p107) on a Saturday night.

➡Dining Soaking up the excesses of the night before is a favourite weekend activity, and we recommend the succulent burgers at Bunsen (p105) or the sublime sushi at Banyi (p105), a favourite with the city's Japanese population.

Getting There & Away

➡Bus As Temple Bar is right in the heart of the city, all cross-city buses will deposit you by the cobbled, largely pedestrianised streets, making access – and escape – that bit easier.

➡On Foot Temple Bar is easily accessible on foot from Grafton St to the southeast, Kilmainham to the west and the north side of the river to the north.

Lonely Planet's Top Tip

Unless you're in for a no-holds-barred, knees-up weekend and don't care too much about sleeping, don't overnight in Temple Bar – hotel rooms are generally more cramped and noisier here than elsewhere. Temple Bar's central location and the city's size mean you can get in and out of here with relative ease.

⬤ Best Places to Drink

➡ Vintage Cocktail Club (p106)
➡ Temple Bar (p106)
➡ Liquor Rooms (p106)
➡ Palace Bar (p107)
➡ Street 66 (p106)

For reviews, see p106 ➡

☆ Best Places to be Entertained

➡ Workman's Club (p107)
➡ Project Arts Centre (p107)
➡ Irish Film Institute (p108)
➡ Mother (p107)
➡ Smock Alley Theatre (p107)

For reviews, see p107 ➡

✕ Best Places to Eat

➡ Crackbird (p105)
➡ Bunsen (p105)
➡ Banyi Japanese Dining (p105)
➡ Al Vesuvio (p106)
➡ Cleaver East (p105)

For reviews, see p104 ➡

TEMPLE BAR

TOP SIGHT
CHRIST CHURCH CATHEDRAL

Its hilltop location and eye-catching flying buttresses make this the most photogenic of Dublin's three cathedrals as well as one of the capital's most recognisable symbols.

Early Beginnings

A wooden church was first erected here by Dunán, the first bishop of Dublin, and Sitric, the Viking king, around 1030, at the southern edge of Dublin's Viking settlement. In 1163, however, the secular clergy was replaced by a group of Augustinian monks installed by the patron saint of Dublin, Archbishop Laurence O'Toole. Six years later, the Normans of Richard de Clare, Earl of Pembroke (better known as Strongbow), blew into town and got themselves into the church-building business, arranging with O'Toole (and his successor John Cumin) for the construction of a new stone cathedral that would symbolise Anglo-Norman glory. The new cathedral opened its doors late in the 12th century, by which time Strongbow, O'Toole and Cumin were long dead.

Above ground, the north wall, the transepts and the western part of the choir are almost all that remain from the original. It has been restored several times over the centuries and, despite its apparent uniformity, is a hotchpotch of different styles, ranging from Romanesque to English Gothic.

DON'T MISS

→ Mummified cat and rat in the crypt
→ The Treasury
→ Strongbow monument

PRACTICALITIES

→ Church of the Holy Trinity
→ Map p236, A5
→ www.christchurch cathedral.ie
→ Christ Church Pl
→ adult/student/child €6.50/4/2.50, with Dublinia €14.50/12/7.50
→ ⊙9am-5pm Mon-Sat, 12.30-2.30pm Sun year-round, longer hours Mar-Oct
→ ☐50, 50A, 56A from Aston Quay, 54, 54A from Burgh Quay

Hard Times

From its inception, Christ Church was the State Church of Ireland, and when Henry VIII dissolved the monasteries in the 16th century, the Augustinian priory that managed the church was replaced with a new Anglican clergy, which still runs the church today.

Until the disestablishment of the Church of Ireland in 1869, senior representatives of the Crown all swore their allegiance here. The church's fortunes, however, were not guaranteed. By the turn of the 18th century its popularity waned along with the district itself as the upper echelons of Dublin society fled north, where they attended a new favourite, St Mary's Abbey. Through much of its history, Christ Church vied for supremacy with nearby St Patrick's Cathedral, but both fell on hard times in the 18th and 19th centuries. Christ Church was virtually derelict – the nave had been used as a market and the crypt had earlier housed taverns – by the time restoration took place. Whiskey distiller Henry Roe donated the equivalent of €30 million to save the church, which was substantially rebuilt from 1871 to 1878. Ironically, both of the great Church of Ireland cathedrals are essentially outsiders in a Catholic nation today, dependent on tourist donations for their very survival.

Chapter House & Northern Wall

From the southeastern entrance to the churchyard you walk past ruins of the **chapter house**, which dates from 1230. The **main entrance** to the cathedral is at the southwestern corner, and as you enter, you face the ancient **northern wall**. This survived the collapse of its southern counterpart but has also suffered from subsiding foundations (much of the church was built on a peat bog) and, from its eastern end, it leans visibly.

Strongbow Monument

The southern aisle has a **monument to the legendary Strongbow**. The armoured figure on the tomb is unlikely to be of Strongbow (it's more probably the Earl of Drogheda), but his internal organs may have been buried here. A popular legend relates an especially visceral version of the daddy-didn't-love-me tale: the half-figure beside the tomb is supposed to be Strongbow's son, who was cut in two by his loving father when his bravery in battle was suspect – an act that surely would have saved the kid a fortune in therapist's bills.

DID YOU KNOW?

In March 2012 the heart of St Laurence O'Toole, which had been kept in the church for 890 years, was stolen by a gang linked to the international trade of rhino horns.

The combination ticket that includes Dublinia is good value if you're visiting with kids. The cathedral has a weekly schedule of sung masses, which can be very beautiful; check the website for details.

THE BOY WHO WOULD BE KING

As part of an elaborate attempt to overthrow the Lancastrian Henry VII with a Yorkist, the Earl of Kildare crowned a baker's son called Lambert Simnel as King Edward VI in Christ Church Cathedral on 24 May 1487, to the cheers of gathered Dubliners. The Yorkists were defeated at the Battle of Stoke Field later that year but Simnel was spared and given a job in Henry's kitchens.

CHRIST CHURCH CATHEDRAL

South Transcept

The south transept contains the super baroque **tomb of the 19th Earl of Kildare**, who died in 1734. His grandson, Lord Edward Fitzgerald, was a member of the United Irishmen and died in the abortive 1798 Rising. The entrance to the **Chapel of St Laurence** is off the south transept and contains two effigies, one of them reputed to be of either Strongbow's wife or sister.

Crypt

An entrance by the south transept descends to the unusually large arched **crypt**, which dates back to the original Viking church. Curiosities in the crypt include a glass display case housing a mummified cat in the act of chasing a mummified rat (aka Tom and Jerry), frozen midpursuit inside an organ pipe in the 1860s. Also on display are the stocks from the old 'liberty' of Christ Church, used when church authorities meted out civil punishments to wrongdoers. The **Treasury** exhibit includes rare coins, the Stuart coat of arms and gold given to the church by William of Orange after the Battle of the Boyne. From the main entrance, a **bridge**, part of the 1871–78 restoration, leads to Dublinia (p103).

◉ SIGHTS

CHRIST CHURCH CATHEDRAL CHURCH
See p100.

**DUBLINIA: EXPERIENCE VIKING
& MEDIEVAL DUBLIN** MUSEUM
Map p236 (☏01-679 4611; www.dublinia.ie; Christ Church Pl; adult/student/child €9.50/8.50/6, with Christchurch Cathedral €14.50/12/7.50; ⊙10am-5.30pm Mar-Sep, to 4.30pm Oct-Feb; ⎚50, 50A, 56A from Aston Quay, 54, 54A from Burgh Quay) A must for the kids, the old Synod Hall, added to Christ Church Cathedral (p100) during its late 19th-century restoration, is home to the seemingly perennial Dublinia, a lively and kitschy attempt to bring Viking and medieval Dublin to life. Models, streetscapes and somewhat old-fashioned interactive displays do a fairly decent job of it, at least for kids.

The model of a medieval quayside and a cobbler's shop in **Medieval Dublin** are both excellent, as is the scale model of the medieval city. Up one floor is **Viking Dublin**, which has a large selection of objects recovered from Wood Quay, the world's largest Viking archaeological site. Interactive exhibits tell the story of Dublin's 9th- and 10th-century Scandinavian invaders, but the real treat is exploring life aboard the re-created longboat. A newer section is **History Hunters**, which includes the skeletons of both a Viking warrior and a woman who died in the Middle Ages. You'll also hear the languages of old Dublin. Finally, you can climb neighbouring **St Michael's Tower** and peek through its grubby windows for views over the city to the Dublin hills. There is also a pleasant cafe and the inevitable souvenir shop.

ICON FACTORY ARTS CENTRE
Map p236 (☏086 202 4533; www.iconfactory dublin.ie; 3 Aston Pl; ⊙11am-6pm; ⎚all city centre) FREE This fantastic artists collective in the heart of Temple Bar hosts exhibitions on Ireland's cultural heritage. You'll find colourful, unique souvenirs celebrating the very best in Irish music and literature and every sale goes towards the artists themselves. Take a stroll around their Icon Walk outside and get better acquainted with Irish playwrights, rock stars, sporting heroes and actors.

HA'PENNY BRIDGE BRIDGE
Map p236 (⎚all city centre) Dublin's most famous bridge is the Ha'penny Bridge, built in 1816. One of the world's oldest cast-iron bridges, it was built to replace the seven ferries that plied a busy route between the two banks of the river. Officially known as the Liffey Bridge, it gets its name from the ha'penny toll that was charged until 1919 (for a time the toll was one and a half pence, and so it was called the Penny Ha'penny Bridge).

**ARK CHILDREN'S
CULTURAL CENTRE** CULTURAL CENTRE
(www.ark.ie; 11a Eustace St; ⎚all city centre) Aimed at youngsters between the ages of three and 14, the Ark is a cultural centre that runs a range of age-specific programs, talks and interactive experiences designed to stimulate participants' interest in science, the environment and the arts. The centre also has an open-air stage for summer events.

GALLERY OF PHOTOGRAPHY GALLERY
Map p236 (www.galleryofphotography.ie; Meeting House Sq; ⊙11am-6pm Mon-Sat, 1-6pm Sun; ⎚all city centre) FREE This small gallery devoted to the photograph is set in an airy three-level space overlooking Meeting House Sq. It features a constantly changing menu of local and international work, as well as photography classes. The downstairs shop is well stocked with all manner of photographic tomes and manuals.

**NATIONAL
PHOTOGRAPHIC ARCHIVE** MUSEUM
Map p236 (www.nli.ie; Meeting House Sq; ⊙10am-1pm Tue-Thu, plus 2.30-4.30pm Wed; ⎚all city centre) FREE The archive of photographs taken from the mid-19th century onward are part of the collection of the National Library, and so are open by appointment only and only with a reader's ticket, which can be obtained from the main branch (p94).

MOSAIC HISTORIC SITE
Map p236 (Winetavern St; ⎚all city centre) Fishamble St, Dublin's oldest street, dates back to Viking times. Brass symbols in the pavement direct you towards a mosaic, just northeast of the overpass between Christ Church Cathedral and Dublinia, laid out to show the ground plan of the sort of Viking dwelling excavated here in the early 1980s.

NATIONAL WAX MUSEUM PLUS MUSEUM
Map p236 (www.waxmuseumplus.ie; 22-25 Westmoreland St; adult/child/concession €15/10/13; ⊙10am-10pm; ⎚all city centre) More a mini history museum in wax than Dublin's version

A SAUCY PAST

Purists may cry foul that Temple Bar never lived up to its cultural quarter moniker, but in many ways it's just staying true to its heritage. Imagine yourself back in 1742, for instance, when Handel was conducting the first-ever performance of his *Messiah* in **Handel's Hotel (Neal's Musick Hall)**, while just down the road on Bagnio Slip – now Lower Fownes St – gentlemen were lining up for an altogether different kind of distraction. Bagnio, from the Italian for bath house, had by then become the term for a brothel, and Temple Bar had plenty of them. It seems that pleasures of the flesh and of the mind have never been that far apart!

of Madame Tussauds. It recently moved to a new location, but the quality of the waxworks remains inconsistent – some look like the result of a hastily conceived school project. Still, the Chamber of Horrors (Dracula has a starring role) is pretty good. The 'plus' in the name refers to the interactive use of video and music. Buy tickets online for a 10% discount.

HANDEL'S HOTEL (SITE OF NEAL'S NEW MUSICK HALL)   HISTORIC SITE

Map p236 (16-18 Fishamble St; all city centre) The clue is the name: on the site of this hotel was once Neal's New Musick Hall, where on 13 April 1742, the nearly broke GF Handel conducted the very first performance of his epic work *Messiah*. All that's left now is the original arch, restored to something like its elegant original. Every year the *Messiah* is performed in an open-air concert on Fishamble St – Dublin's oldest street – to commemorate the event.

Ironically, Jonathan Swift – author of *Gulliver's Travels* and dean of St Patrick's Cathedral – suggested the choirs of St Patrick's and Christ Church participate in the original performance, but then he revoked his invitation, vowing to punish vicars who took part for their 'disobedience, rebellion, perfidy and ingratitude'. The concert went ahead nonetheless, in front of an appreciative crowd of roughly 700.

SUNLIGHT CHAMBERS   NOTABLE BUILDING

Map p236 (Parliament St; closed to the public; all city centre) On the southern banks of the Liffey, Sunlight Chambers, designed by Liverpool architect Edward Ould (designer of Port Sunlight in the Wirral, in the UK), stands out among the Georgian and modern architecture for its romantic Italianate style and beautiful art-nouveau frieze-work by German sculptor Conrad Dressler. Sunlight

was a brand of soap made by Lever Brothers and the frieze shows the Lever Brothers' view of the world: men make clothes dirty, women wash them.

CONTEMPORARY MUSIC CENTRE   ARTS CENTRE

Map p236 (CMC, 01-490 1857; www.cmc.ie; 19 Fishamble St; 10am-5.30pm Mon-Fri; all city centre) FREE Anyone with an interest in Irish contemporary music must visit the CMC's national archive where you can hear (and play around with on an electronic organ) 10,000 samples from composers of this and the last century. There's also a good reference library where you can attend courses and meet composers.

⚔ EATING

KLAW   SEAFOOD €

Map p236 (www.klaw.ie; 5a Crown Alley; mains €8-15; noon-10pm Mon-Wed & Sun, to 11pm Thu-Sat; all city centre) There's nothing sophisticated about this crabshack-style place except the food: Irish oysters served naked, dressed or torched; Lambay Island crab claws served with a yuzu aioli; or half a lobster. Whatever you go for it's all delicious; the 'shucksuck' oyster happy hour is a terrific deal with all oysters €1.50.

BISON BAR & BBQ   BARBECUE €

Map p236 (086 056 3144; www.bisonbar.ie; 11 Wellington Quay; mains €14-17; noon-9pm; all city centre) Beer, whiskey sours and finger-lickingly good Texas-style barbecue – served on throwaway plates along with tasty sides such as slaw or mac 'n' cheese – is the fare at this boisterous restaurant. The cowboy theme is taken to the limit with the saddle chairs (yes, actual saddles); this is a place to eat, drink and be merry.

SKINFLINT
PIZZA €

Map p236 (www.joburger.ie; 19 Crane Lane; pizzas €9-15; ⊙noon-10pm Tue-Thu, to 10.30pm Fri & Sat, noon-9pm Sun-Mon; ▣all city centre) Tables made out of old doors and kitchen paper as tablecloths...this is industrial-style pizza brought to you by the people who run Crackbird (p105) around the corner. The pizzas – all with girls' names like Viv, Breda and Philomena – are all super-thin and rectangular, and they use Irish rather than Type 00 Italian flour. The result is OK.

ZAYTOON
MIDDLE EASTERN €

Map p236 (www.zaytoon.ie; 14-15 Parliament St; meals €11; ⊙noon-4am Sun-Thu, to 5am Fri & Sat; ▣all city centre) It's the end of the night and you've got a desperate case of the munchies. Head straight for this terrific kebab joint and gobble the house speciality, the chicken *shish-kebab* meal, complete with chips and a soft drink. You'll feel all the better for it.

BUNSEN
BURGERS €

Map p236 (www.bunsen.ie; 22 Essex St E; burgers €7-10; ⊙noon-9.30pm Mon-Wed, noon-10.30pm Thu-Sat, 1-9.30pm Sun; ▣all city centre) The tag line says Straight Up Burgers, but Bunsen serves only the tastiest, most succulent lumps of prime beef cooked to perfection and served between two halves of a homemade bap. Want fries? You've a choice between skinny, chunky or sweet potato. Order the double at your peril. There are two other branches: on Wexford St (p70) and S Anne St (p70).

QUEEN OF TARTS
CAFE €

Map p236 (☑01-670 7499; www.queenoftarts.ie; 4 Cork Hill; mains €5-10; ⊙8am-8pm Mon-Fri, 8.30am-8pm Sat, 9am-7pm Sun; ▣all city centre) This cute little cake shop does a fine line in tarts, meringues, crumbles, cookies and brownies, not to mention a decent breakfast: the smoked bacon and leek potato cakes with eggs and cherry tomatoes are excellent. There's another, bigger, branch around the corner on **Cow's Lane** (Map p236; 3-4 Cow's Lane; ▣all city centre).

★BANYI JAPANESE DINING
JAPANESE €€

Map p236 (☑01-675 0669; www.banyijapanesedining.com; 3-4 Bedford Row; lunch bento €11, small/large sushi platter €15/27; ⊙noon-11pm; ▣all city centre) This compact restaurant in the heart of Temple Bar has arguably the best Japanese cuisine in Dublin. The rolls are divine, and the sushi as good as any you'll eat at twice the price. If you don't fancy raw fish, the classic Japanese main courses are excellent, as are the lunchtime bento boxes. Dinner reservations are advised, particularly at weekends.

CRACKBIRD
FAST FOOD €€

Map p236 (www.joburger.ie; 60 Dame St; half/full roast chicken €12.50/22; ⊙noon-10pm Mon-Wed, to 11pm Thu-Sat, to 9pm Sun; ☎; ▣all city centre) It's a trendy version of fried chicken in a bucket, but it's oh so tasty. Choose between a half or full portion (half is enough for most) and add some sides – potato salad, chipotle baked beans, couscous or carrot and cranberry salad – for extra flavour and variety.

ELEPHANT & CASTLE
AMERICAN €€

Map p236 (☑01-679 3121; www.elephantandcastle.ie; 18 Temple Bar; mains €12.50-26; ⊙8am-11.30pm Mon-Fri, 10.30am-11.30pm Sat & Sun; ▣all city centre) If it's massive New York–style sandwiches or sticky chicken wings you're after, this bustling upmarket diner – a longtime presence in Temple Bar – is just the joint. Be prepared to queue, though, especially at weekends when the place heaves with the hassled parents of wandering toddlers and 20-somethings looking for a carb cure for the night before.

CHAMELEON
INDONESIAN €€

Map p236 (☑01-671 0362; www.chameleonrestaurant.com; 1 Lower Fownes St; set menus €30-40, tapas €7.50-11; ⊙4-11pm Wed-Sun; ☑; ▣all city centre) Friendly and full of character, Chameleon is draped in exotic fabrics and serves renditions of Indonesian classics such as satay, *gado gado* and *nasi goreng*. Choose from three *rijsttafel* set menus – Java, Sumatra or Vegetarian – or from the selection of smaller tapas-style dishes. The top floor has low seating on cushions, which is perfect for intimate group get-togethers.

CLEAVER EAST
MODERN IRISH €€

Map p236 (☑01-531 3500; www.cleavereast.ie; Clarence, 6-8 Wellington Quay; tasting plates €10-14, main courses €17-26; ⊙12.30-3pm Fri-Sun & 5.30-10.30pm daily; ▣all city centre) Michelin-starred chef Oliver Dunne has brought his cooking chops to bear in Cleaver East, where the decor (think New York brasserie but with cleavers everywhere) is as macho as some of the mains – feast on a succulent 'pornburger' or the excellent mains – the #roadtotipp is 200g of ground Hereford prime rib in a Jameson whiskey glaze. Very tasty.

AL VESUVIO ITALIAN €€
Map p236 (☑01-671 4597; www.alvesuviodublin. com; Meeting House Sq; mains €11-16; ☺5.30-10.30pm Sun-Fri, 1-10.30pm Sat; ▣all city centre) Pizzas – with *(rosse)* or without *(bianche)* cheese – and pastas are the speciality at this vaulted basement restaurant that is like a rustic piece of the Old Boot. Everything is authentic, from the bruschetta starter to the superb tiramisu on the dessert menu, and the Italian wines are *buonissimi*.

LA DOLCE VITA ITALIAN €€
Map p236 (☑01-707 9786; 5 Cow's Lane; mains €9-18; ☺12.30-11pm; ▣all city centre) This easygoing place serves proper Italian antipasti, dished up in sharing plates and named after Fellini movies. You can get mixed cheese platters (Il Viaggio di Mastorna), prosciutto samplers (Amarcord) or a mix of both (La Strada). The pasta dishes are authentic enough to earn Mamma's approval. Wash it all down with a selection of wines by the glass.

🍷 DRINKING & NIGHTLIFE

TEMPLE BAR BAR
Map p236 (☑01-677 3807; 48 Temple Bar; ☺10.30am-1.30am Mon-Wed, to 2.30am Thu-Sat, 11.30am-1am Sun; ▣all city centre) The most photographed pub facade in Dublin, perhaps the world, the Temple Bar (aka Flannery's) is smack bang in the middle of the tourist precinct and is usually chock-a-block with visitors. It's good craic, though, and presses all the right buttons, with traditional musicians, a buzzy atmosphere and even a beer garden.

LIQUOR ROOMS COCKTAIL BAR
Map p236 (☑087 339 3688; www.theliquor rooms.com; 5 Wellington Quay; ☺5pm-2am Mon-Thu & Sun, to 3am Fri & Sat; ▣all city centre) A subterranean cocktail bar decorated in the manner of a Prohibition-era speakeasy. There's lots of rooms – and room – for hip lounge cats to sprawl and imbibe both atmosphere and a well-made, tasty cocktail. There's dancing in the Boom Room, classy cocktails in the Blind Tiger

Room and art-deco elegance in the Mayflower Room.

VINTAGE COCKTAIL CLUB BAR
Map p236 (www.vintagecocktailclub.com; Crown Alley; ☺5pm-1.30am Mon-Fri, 12.30pm-1.30am Sat & Sun; ▣all city centre) The atmosphere behind this inconspicuous, unlit doorway initialled with the letters 'VCC' is that of a Vegas rat pack hang-out or a '60s-style London members' club. It's so popular you'll need to book for one of the 2½-hour evening sittings, which is plenty of time to sample some of the excellent cocktails and finger food.

THE OAK BAR
Map p236 (☑01-670 7220; www.theoak.ie; 1 Parliament St; ☺noon-12.30am Sun-Wed, to 1.30am Thu-Sat; ▣all city centre) Blue velvet chairs, handsome leather booths and walls adorned with prints of Georgian Dublin set a sophisticated tone for this bar, which has a whole shelf devoted to negronis and a cocktail menu straight out of the roaring '20s. A touch of class.

STREET 66 BAR
Map p236 (www.street66.bar; 33 Parliament St; ☺8.30am-midnight Mon-Thu, to 2.30am Fri & Sat, noon-11pm Sun; ▣all city centre) In late 2016 this place replaced the very popular LGBT Front Lounge and promised to be all things to all people: a dog-friendly coffee shop and bar dressed in upcycled chic that is LGBTQ friendly. The front is the Dive Bar, the back the Disco Lounge. Better than most Temple Bar joints.

OLIVER ST JOHN GOGARTY PUB
Map p236 (www.gogartys.ie; 58-59 Fleet St; ☺10.30am-11.30pm Mon-Thu, to 12.30am Fri & Sat, noon-11pm Sun; ▣all city centre) You won't see too many Dubs ordering drinks in this bar, which is almost entirely given over to tourists who come for the carefully manufactured slice of authentic traditionalism...and the knee-slappin', toe-tappin' sessions that run throughout the day. The kitchen serves up Irish cuisine of questionable quality.

FITZSIMONS BAR
Map p236 (☑01-677 9315; www.fitzsimonshotel. com; 21-22 Wellington Quay; ☺10.30am-3am Mon-Sat, noon-2am Sun; ▣all city centre) The epitome of Temple Bar's commitment to a kind of loud and wonderfully unsophisticated nightlife is this sprawling hotel bar (four bars on five floors), which serves booze, sports and

cheesy music to a crowd of pumped revellers. At weekends, it gets so busy the bouncers don't even try to keep the crowd from spilling out onto the cobbled streets.

TURK'S HEAD   BAR
Map p236 (☑01-679 9701; 27-30 Parliament St; ⊘11.30am-3am; 🖳all city centre) This super-pub is decorated in two completely different styles – one really gaudy, the other a recreation of LA c1930 – and is one of the oddest and most interesting in Temple Bar. It pulsates nightly with a young pumped-up crowd of mainly tourists, out to boogie to chart hits. Be mindful of hidden steps all over the place.

AULD DUBLINER   PUB
Map p236 (☑01-677 0527; www.aulddubliner.ie; 24-25 Temple Bar; ⊘10.30am-11.30pm Mon & Tue, 10.30am-2.30am Wed-Sat, 12.30-11pm Sun; 🖳all city centre) Predominantly patronised by tourists, 'the Auld Foreigner', as locals have dubbed it, has a carefully manicured 'old world' charm that has been preserved – or refined – after a couple of renovations. It's a reliable place for a singsong and a laugh, as long as you don't mind taking 15 minutes to get to and from the jax (toilets).

PALACE BAR   PUB
Map p236 (21 Fleet St; ⊘10.30am-11.30pm Mon-Thu, to 12.30am Fri & Sat, noon-11pm Sun; 🖳all city centre) With its mirrors and wooden niches, the Palace (established in 1823) is one of Dublin's great Victorian pubs and a stubborn stalwart against the modernising influences of the last half century. Patrick Kavanagh and Flann O'Brien were once regulars and it was for a long time the unofficial head office of the *Irish Times*.

PORTERHOUSE   BAR
Map p236 (16-18 Parliament St; ⊘11.30am-midnight Mon-Wed & Sun, to 1am Thu, to 2am Fri & Sat; 🖳all city centre) The second-biggest brewery in Dublin, the Porterhouse looks like a cross between a Wild West bar and a Hieronymus Bosch painting. It has lots of its own delicious brews, including its Plain Porter (some say it's the best stout in town) as well as unfamiliar imported beers.

 **ENTERTAINMENT**

SMOCK ALLEY THEATRE   THEATRE
Map p236 (☑01-677 0014; www.smockalley.com; 6-7 Exchange St) One of the city's most diverse

theatres is hidden in this beautifully restored 17th-century building. It boasts a diverse program of events (expect anything from opera to murder mystery nights, puppet shows and Shakespeare) and many events also come with a dinner option.

The theatre was built in 1622 and was the only Theatre Royal to ever be built outside London. It's been reinvented as a warehouse and a Catholic church and was lovingly restored in 2012 to become a creative hub once again.

WORKMAN'S CLUB   LIVE MUSIC
Map p236 (☑01-670 6692; www.theworkmansclub.com; 10 Wellington Quay; free-€20; ⊘5pm-3am; 🖳all city centre) A 300-capacity venue and bar in the former working-men's club of Dublin. The emphasis is on keeping away from the mainstream, which means everything from singer-songwriters to electronic cabaret. When the live music at the Workman's Club (Twitter: @WorkmansClubs) is over, DJs take to the stage, playing rockabilly, hip hop, indie, house and more.

PROJECT ARTS CENTRE   THEATRE
Map p236 (☑1850 260 027; www.projectartscentre.ie; 39 Essex St E; ⊘45min before showtime; 🖳all city centre) The city's most interesting venue for challenging new work – be it drama, dance, live art or film. Three separate spaces allow for maximum versatility. You never know what to expect, which makes it all that more fun: we've seen some awful rubbish here, but we've also seen some of the best shows in town.

OLYMPIA THEATRE   THEATRE
Map p236 (☑01-677 7744; www.olympia.ie; 72 Dame St; tickets €30-60; ⊘shows from 7pm; 🖳all city centre) This lovely Victorian-era theatre specialises in light plays and, at Christmastime, pantomimes. It also hosts some terrific live gigs.

MOTHER   CLUB
Map p236 (www.twitter.com/motherdublin; Copper Alley, Exchange St; €10; ⊘11pm-3.30am Sat; 🖳all city centre) The best club night in the city is ostensibly a gay night, but it does not discriminate: clubbers of every sexual orientation come for the sensational DJs – mostly local but occasionally brought in from abroad – who throw down a mixed bag of disco, modern synth-pop and other danceable styles.

CHAPLINS COMEDY CLUB COMEDY

Map p236 (www.chaplinscomedy.com; Chaplin's Bar, 2 Hawkins St; €10; ☺8-11pm Fri & Sat; ▣all city centre) A regularly changing line-up of up-and-coming and local talent look for laughs at this all-seater club; failing that, there's always pizza and craft beer to guarantee a decent night out. Shows start at 9pm.

BUTTON FACTORY LIVE MUSIC

Map p236 (☏01-670 0533; www.buttonfactory.ie; Curved St; €10-20; ☺7.30-11.30pm Mon-Thu, to 2.30am Fri-Sun; ▣all city centre) A multipurpose venue where one night you might be shaking your glow light to a thumping live set by a top DJ, and the next you'll be shifting from foot to foot as an esoteric Finnish band drag their violin bows over their electric guitar strings. Live gigs are usually followed by club nights.

HA'PENNY BRIDGE INN COMEDY, LIVE MUSIC

Map p236 (☏01-677 0616; www.hapenny bridgeinn.com; 42 Wellington Quay; €6; ☺7.30-11.30pm; ▣all city centre) A traditional old bar that features local comics on the rise upstairs at the Unhinged Comedy Club on Sunday, and Irish music downstairs on Sunday and Wednesday.

NEW THEATRE THEATRE

Map p236 (☏01-670 3361; www.thenewtheatre. com; 43 Essex St E; adult/concession €16/12.50; ☺shows 7.30pm Mon-Fri, 2.30pm & 7.30pm Sat; ▣all city centre) This small theatre's location above a left-wing bookshop should be a guide to the kind of thinking that informs most of the shows taking place on its small stage. It's all about having a social conscience, whether by promoting new work by emerging playwrights or by putting on established works that highlight society's injustices.

IRISH FILM INSTITUTE CINEMA

Map p236 (IFI; ☏01-679 5744; www.ifi.ie; 6 Eustace St; ☺11am-11pm; ▣all city centre) The IFI has a couple of screens and shows classics and new art-house films. The complex also has a bar, a cafe and a bookshop.

🛍 SHOPPING

★GUTTER BOOKSHOP BOOKS

Map p236 (☏01-679 9206; www.gutterbookshop. com; Cow's Lane; ☺10am-6.30pm Mon-Wed, Fri & Sat, to 7pm Thu, 11am-6pm Sun; ▣all city centre) Taking its name from Oscar Wilde's famous line from *Lady Windermere's Fan* – 'We are all in the gutter, but some of us are looking at the stars' – this fabulous place is flying the flag for the downtrodden independent bookshop, stocking a mix of new novels, children's books, travel literature and other assorted titles.

★CLADDAGH RECORDS MUSIC

Map p236 (☏01-677 0262; www.claddaghrecords. com; 2 Cecilia St; ☺10am-6pm Mon-Sat, noon-6pm Sun; ▣all city centre) An excellent collection of good-quality traditional and folk music is the mainstay at this centrally located record shop. The profoundly knowledgable staff should be able to locate even the most elusive recording for you. There's also a decent selection of world music. There's another **branch** (Map p236; ☏01-888 3600; 5 Westmoreland St; ▣all city centre) on Westmoreland St; you can also shop online.

★TEMPLE BAR FOOD MARKET MARKET

Map p236 (www.facebook.com/TempleBarFood Market; Meeting House Sq; ☺10am-5pm Sat; ▣all city centre) From sushi to salsa, this is the city's best open-air food market; pick, prod and poke your way through the organic foods of the world with a compact stroll through gourmet lane. There are tastes of everywhere, from cured Spanish chorizo and paellas to Irish farmhouse cheeses, via handmade chocolates, freshly made crêpes, homemade jams and freshly squeezed juices.

SIOPAELLA DESIGN EXCHANGE VINTAGE

Map p236 (www.siopaella.com; 25 Temple Lane S; ☺noon-6pm Mon-Wed, Fri & Sat, to 7pm Thu; ▣all city centre) A secondhand shop like no other in Dublin: you're as likely to find a vintage Chanel bag priced at €3000 as you are a beautiful preloved shirt for €5. You can exchange clothes for cash, or clothes for other clothes. One of the best shopping experiences in town. There's another branch (p80) on Wicklow St.

LUCY'S LOUNGE VINTAGE

Map p236 (☏01-677 4779; www.lucysloungevin tage.com; 11 Lower Fownes St; ☺noon-6pm; ▣all city centre) Go through the upstairs boutique and you'll find a staircase to an Aladdin's basement of vintage goodies. You can easily while away an hour or two here before re-emerging triumphant with something unique to brighten up your wardrobe. Looking for something specific? The super-friendly staff know where everything is hiding.

FOLKSTER CLOTHING

Map p236 (☎01-675 0917; www.folkster.com; 9 Eustace St; ⏰10.30am-6.30pm Mon-Wed & Sat, to 8pm Thu, to 7pm Fri, to 6pm Sun; 🚇all city centre) This is actually three shops in one, with a surprisingly affordable independent boutique, a funky homewares section and some inspiring vintage clothing. The clothes here are mainly smart casual with sleek lines and minimalist prints selected by owner stylist Blanaid Hennessy.

TAMP & STITCH FASHION & ACCESSORIES

Map p236 (Unit 3, Scarlet Row, Essex St W; ⏰10am-6pm Mon-Sat; 🚇all city centre) The latest midrange fashions and a trendy little cafe doing nearly perfect coffee.

URBAN OUTFITTERS FASHION, MUSIC

Map p236 (☎01-670 6202; www.urbanoutfitters. com; 4 Cecilia St; ⏰10am-7pm Mon-Wed & Sat, 10am-8pm Thu & Fri, noon-6pm Sun; 🚇all city centre) With a blaring techno soundtrack, the Temple Bar branch of this American chain sells ridiculously cool clothes to discerning young buyers. Besides clothing, the shop stocks all kinds of interesting gadgets, accessories and furniture. On the 2nd floor you'll find a hypertrendy record shop (hence the techno).

CONNOLLY BOOKS BOOKS

Map p236 (☎01-670 8707; www.communistpar tyofireland.ie/cbooks; 43 Essex St E; ⏰9.30am-6pm Mon-Sat; 🚇all city centre) Left-wing bookshop beloved of Marxists and radicals.

COW'S LANE DESIGNER MART MARKET

Map p236 (St Michael's & St John's Banquet Hall, Essex St W; ⏰10am-5pm Oct-May; 🚇all city centre) A real market for hipsters, bringing together the best clothing, accessory and craft stalls in town; from June to September it moves just around the corner to Cow's Lane (p109).

COW'S LANE DESIGNER MART MARKET

Map p236 (Cow's Lane; ⏰10am-5pm Sat Jun-Sep; 🚇all city centre) A real market for hipsters, on the steps of Cow's Lane, this market brings together over 60 of the best clothing, accessory and craft stalls in town. It's open June to September; the rest of the year it moves indoors to St Michael's and St John's Banquet Hall, just around the corner.

Buy cutting-edge designer duds from the likes of Drunk Monk, punky T-shirts, retro handbags, costume jewellery by Kink Bijoux and even clubby babywear.

SCOUT CLOTHING

Map p236 (www.scoutdublin.com; 5 Smock Alley Ct, Essex St W; ⏰10.30am-6pm Mon-Wed, Fri & Sat, to 7pm Thu, 1-5pm Sun; 🚇all city centre) Owner Wendy carefully selects every item of vintage clothing, and Irish and international labels including Armor Lux and Manley, plus accessories by Baggu and footwear by Grenson.

FLIP, SHARPSVILLE & HELTER SKELTER FASHION & ACCESSORIES

Map p236 (☎01-671 4299; 4 Upper Fownes St; ⏰10am-6pm Mon-Wed & Fri, 10am-7pm Thu & Sat, 1.30-6pm Sun; 🚇all city centre) Three shops in one all selling the same vintage male fashion moods of the 1950s, from *Rebel Without a Cause*–style leathers to Hawaiian shirts. Downstairs it's newer stuff; upstairs it's really good quality secondhand clothing.

TEMPLE BAR BOOK MARKET MARKET

Map p236 (Temple Bar Sq; ⏰11am-6pm Sat & Sun; 🚇all city centre) Bad secondhand potboilers, sci-fi, picture books and other assorted titles invite you to rummage about on weekend afternoons. If you look hard enough, you're bound to find something worthwhile.

🏃 SPORTS & ACTIVITIES

MELT HEALTH & FITNESS

Map p236 (☎01-679 8786; www.meltonline. com; 2 Temple Lane; full body massages 60/90min €60/100; ⏰9am-7pm Mon-Sat; 🚇all city centre) A full range of massage techniques – from Swedish to shiatsu and many more in-between – are doled out by expert practitioners at Melt, aka the Temple Bar Healing Centre. Also available are a host of other left-of-centre healing techniques, including acupuncture, reiki and polarity therapy. Melt has also set up shop in the Westin (p181).

★ DUBLIN MUSICAL PUB CRAWL WALKING

Map p236 (☎01-478 0193; www.discoverdub lin.ie; 58-59 Fleet St; adult/student €14/12; ⏰7.30pm daily Apr-Oct, 7.30pm Thu-Sat Nov-Mar; 🚇all city centre) The story of Irish traditional music and its influence on contemporary styles is explained and demonstrated by two expert musicians in a number of Temple Bar pubs over 2½ hours. Tours meet upstairs in the Oliver St John Gogarty (p106) pub and are highly recommended.

Kilmainham & the Liberties

Neighbourhood Top Five

1 **Kilmainham Gaol** (p118) Taking a trip through Ireland's troubled history at this foreboding 18th-century prison, which housed many an Irish rebel.

2 **Guinness Storehouse** (p112) Sampling a pint of the black stuff at the factory where it all began in 1759 – and continues to this day.

3 **Teeling Distillery** (p118) Getting familiar with Irish whiskey at the first distillery to open in Dublin for more than a century.

4 **St Patrick's Cathedral** (p115) Visiting Jonathan Swift's tomb in the cathedral where he served as dean for more than 30 years.

5 **Irish Museum of Modern Art** (p118) Admiring modern art in exquisite surroundings at a former hospital for wounded soldiers.

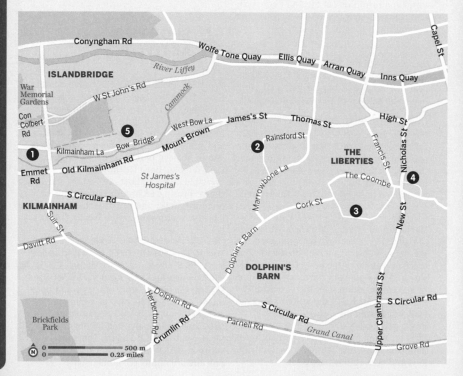

Explore: Kilmainham & the Liberties

Stretching westward along the Liffey from the city centre, you'll need a little bit of planning to get the most out of these two historic neighbourhoods. Coming from the heart of the city centre, you'll first stumble into the Liberties, on the edge of which is St Patrick's Cathedral and, behind the cathedral, the wonderful Marsh's Library. This largely working-class enclave has been beset by myriad social problems in the last couple of centuries, but in recent years the creeping influence of gentrification has turned its fortunes around, as aspiring young Dubs look to combine authenticity with affordable rents. Right in the heart of it is the recently opened Teeling Distillery, next to one of the best food markets in the city.

The Liberties' western edge is where you'll find the Guinness brewery at St James's Gate, even if the only bit you can visit is the old grain storehouse, now the city's most-visited museum. Further west again, just as the Liffey becomes more of a pastoral river in the riverside burg of Kilmainham, you'll come across the country's greatest modern-art museum and Kilmainham Gaol, which has played a key role in the tormented history of a country's slow struggle to gain its freedom. Both are well worth the westward trek (by bus). This is strictly day-trip territory – there's almost nothing in the way of accommodation and just a couple of decent eating options.

Local Life

→**Garden walks** The Italianate garden at the Irish Museum of Modern Art (p118) is beautiful for a gentle amble, but one of the city's best-kept open secrets is the War Memorial Gardens (p119) in Kilmainham, which runs along the Liffey.

→**Markets** The Dublin Food Co-op (p123) in Newmarket is one of the city's best, and an excellent example of socially responsible retailing; it thrives thanks to the dedication of its many customers.

→**Hang-outs** Fumbally (p120) and Legit Coffee Co (p122) are bringing cafe life to the Liberties, while the southern end of Clanbrassil St is where you'll find the excellent Gaillot et Gray (p122) pizzeria.

Getting There & Away

→**Bus** Nos 50, 50A and 56A from Aston Quay and the 55 and 54A serve the cathedrals and the Liberties; for Kilmainham (including Irish Museum of Modern Art) use bus 51, 51D, 51X, 69, 78 or 79 from Aston Quay or the Luas to Heuston, from which it's a short walk.

→**On foot** It's a 1.5km walk to the Guinness Storehouse from the city centre; 3km to IMMA or Kilmainham Gaol.

Lonely Planet's Top Tip

The most convenient way to explore the area is as part of a hop-on, hop-off bus tour, all of which stop at the Guinness Storehouse, Irish Museum of Modern Art and Kilmainham Gaol. This way, you're also free to take a load off in a cafe or restaurant. When your visit is done you can hop back on and get back to the city centre without hassle.

📖 Best Museums to Visit

→ Guinness Storehouse (p112)
→ Kilmainham Gaol (p118)
→ Irish Museum of Modern Art (p118)
→ Marsh's Library (p118)

For reviews, see p112 ➡

✕ Best Places to Eat

→ Fumbally (p120)
→ Union8 (p122)
→ Legit Coffee Co (p122)
→ 1837 Bar & Brasserie (p120)

For reviews, see p120 ➡

☕ Best Places to Drink

→ Fallon's (p122)
→ Old Royal Oak (p122)
→ Arthur's (p123)
→ MVP (p123)

For reviews, see p122 ➡

◉ TOP SIGHT
GUINNESS STOREHOUSE & ST JAMES GATE

More than any beer produced anywhere in the world, Guinness has transcended its own brand and is not just the best-known symbol of the city but a substance with near spiritual qualities, according to its legions of devotees the world over. A visit to the factory museum where it's made is therefore something of a pilgrimage for many of its fans.

Mythology

The mythology around Guinness is remarkably durable: it doesn't travel well; its distinctive flavour comes from Liffey water; it is good for you – not to mention the generally held belief that you will never understand the Irish until you develop a taste for the black stuff. All absolutely true, of course, so it should be no surprise that the Guinness Storehouse, in the heart of the St James's Gate Brewery, is the city's most-visited tourist attraction, an all-singing, all-dancing extravaganza that combines sophisticated exhibits, spectacular design and a thick, creamy head of marketing hype.

The Beginnings of World Domination

In the 1770s, while other Dublin brewers fretted about the popularity of a new English beer known as porter – which was first created when a London brewer accidentally burnt his hops – Arthur Guinness started making his own version. By 1799 he decided to concentrate all his efforts on this single brew. He died four years later, aged 83, but the foundations for world domination were already in place.

At one time a Grand Canal tributary was cut into the brewery to enable special Guinness barges to carry consignments

DON'T MISS
....
➜ A drink of Guinness
➜ Gravity Bar view
➜ 1837 Bar & Brasserie
➜ Advertising exhibit
➜ Connoisseur Experience

PRACTICALITIES
....
➜ Map p247, E3
➜ www.guinness-store-house.com
➜ St James's Gate, South Market St
➜ adult/child €18/16.50, Connoisseur Experience €48
➜ ⊙9.30am-5pm Sep-Jun, to 6pm Jul & Aug
➜ 🖨
➜ 🚌21A, 51B, 78, 78A, 123 from Fleet St, 🚊James's

out onto the Irish canal system or to the Dublin port. When the brewery extensions reached the Liffey in 1872, the fleet of Guinness barges became a familiar sight. Pretty soon Guinness was being exported as far afield as Africa and the West Indies. As the barges chugged their way along the Liffey towards the port, boys used to lean over the wall and shout, 'Bring us back a parrot'. Old-school Dubliners still say the same thing to each other when they're going off on holiday.

The Essential Ingredients

One link with the past that hasn't been broken is the yeast used to make Guinness, essentially the same living organism that has been used since 1770. Another vital ingredient is a hop by the name of fuggles, which used to be grown exclusively around Dublin but is now imported from Britain, the USA and Australia (everyone take a bow).

Guinness Storehouse Museum

The brewery is far more than just a place where beer is manufactured. It is an intrinsic part of Dublin's history and a key element of the city's identity. Accordingly, the quasi-mythical stature of Guinness is the central theme of the brewery's museum, the Guinness Storehouse, which is the only part of the brewery open to visitors.

It occupies the old Fermentation House, built in 1904. As it's a listed building, the designers could only adapt and add to the structure without taking anything away. The result is a stunning central atrium that rises seven storeys and takes the shape of a pint of Guinness. The head is represented by the glassed Gravity Bar, which provides panoramic views of Dublin to savour with your complimentary half-pint.

Before you race up to the top, however, you might want to check out the museum for which you've paid so handsomely. Actually, it's designed as more of an 'experience' than a museum. It has nearly 1.5 hectares of floor space, featuring a dazzling array of audiovisual and interactive exhibits, which cover most aspects of the brewery's story and explain the brewing process in overwhelming detail.

On the ground floor, a copy of Arthur Guinness' original lease lies embedded beneath a pane of glass in the floor. Wandering up through the various exhibits, including 70-odd years of advertising, you can't help feeling that the now wholly foreign-owned company has hijacked the mythology Dubliners attached to the drink, and it has all become more about marketing and manipulation than mingling and magic.

BEST DEAL IN TOWN

When Arthur started brewing in Dublin in 1759, he couldn't have had any idea that his name would become synonymous with Dublin around the world. Or could he? Showing extraordinary foresight, he had just signed a lease for a small disused brewery under the terms that he would pay just £45 annually for the next 9000 years, with the additional condition that he'd never have to pay for the water used.

Real aficionados can opt for the Connoisseur Experience, where you sample the four different kinds of Guinness – Draught, Original, Foreign Extra Stout and Black Lager – while hearing their story from your designated bartender.

DID YOU KNOW

St Patrick's Tower, the large smock windmill on the extensive factory grounds, was originally built as part of the Roe Distillery, which once occupied 7 hectares on the north side of James's St and was Europe's largest producer of whiskey. Arthur Guinness didn't much care for whiskey, branding it the 'curse of the nation' (and his own brew the 'nurse of the nation'). The Roe distillery stopped producing whiskey in 1926 and was taken over by Guinness in 1949.

KILMAINHAM & THE LIBERTIES GUINNESS STOREHOUSE & ST JAMES GATE

Gravity Bar

Whatever reservations you may have, however, can be more than dispelled at the top of the building in the circular Gravity Bar, where you get a complimentary glass of Guinness. The views from the bar are superb, but the Guinness itself is as near-perfect as a beer can be.

1837 Bar & Brasserie

Sitting one floor below the Gravity Bar and blessed with the same views of the city is this surprisingly good lunchtime spot (p120) that would be worth checking out as a stand-alone restaurant, never mind one in a museum. The menu is fairly straightforward – chicken, burgers etc – but everything is exquisitely made.

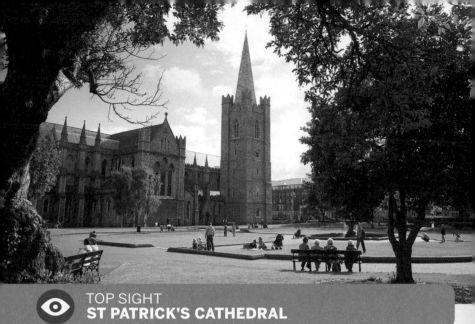

TOP SIGHT
ST PATRICK'S CATHEDRAL

Situated on the very spot that St Paddy supposedly rolled up his sleeves and dunked the heathen Irish into a well and thereby gave them a fair to middling shot at salvation, St Patrick's Cathedral is one of Dublin's earliest Christian sites and a most hallowed chunk of real estate.

History

Although a church has stood here since the 5th century, this building dates from the turn of the 12th century and has been altered several times, most notably in 1864 when it was saved from ruin and, some might say, over-enthusiastically restored. The interior is as calm and soothing as the exterior is sombre. The picturesque St Patrick's Park, adjoining, was a crowded slum until it was cleared in the early 20th century.

It's likely that St Patrick's was intended to replace Christ Church as the city's cathedral, but the older church's stubborn refusal to be usurped resulted in the two cathedrals being virtually a stone's throw from one another. Separated only by the city walls (with St Patrick's outside), each possessed the rights of cathedral of the diocese. While St Pat's isn't as photogenic as its neighbour, it probably surpasses its more attractive rival in historical terms.

Political Interference

Following Henry VIII's 16th-century hissy fit and the dissolution of the monasteries, St Patrick's was ordered to hand over all of its estates, revenues and possessions. The chapter (bureaucratic head of the church) was imprisoned until he 'agreed' to the handover, the cathedral's privileges

DON'T MISS

➡ Swift's Tomb
➡ Stained-glass windows
➡ Boyle Monument

PRACTICALITIES

➡ Map p247, H3
➡ www.stpatrickscathedral.ie
➡ St Patrick's Close
➡ adult/child €6.50/free
➡ ⊙9.30am-5pm Mon-Fri, 9am-6pm Sat, 9-10.30am & 12.30-2.30pm Sun
➡ ⊒50, 50A, 56A from Aston Quay, 54, 54A from Burgh Quay

were revoked and it was demoted to the rank of parish church. It was not restored to its previous position until 1560.

Further indignity followed at the hands of Oliver Cromwell in 1649, when the nave was used as a stable for his horses. In 1666 the Lady Chapel was given to the newly arrived Huguenots and became known as the French Church of St Patrick. It remained in Huguenot hands until 1816. The northern transept was known as the parish church of St Nicholas Without (meaning outside the city), essentially dividing the cathedral into two distinct churches.

Such confusion led to the building falling into disrepair as the influence of the deanery and chapter waned. Although the church's most famous dean, Jonathan Swift (author of *Gulliver's Travels*, who served here from 1713 to 1745), did his utmost to preserve the integrity of the building, by the end of the 18th century it was close to collapse. It was just standing when the benevolent Guinness family stepped in to begin a massive restoration in 1864.

Baptistry & Swift's Tomb

Fittingly, the first Guinness to show an interest in preserving the church, Benjamin, is commemorated with a **statue** at the main entrance. Inside to your left is the oldest part of the building, the **baptistry**, which was probably the entrance to the original building. It contains the original **12th-century floor tiles** and **medieval stone font**, which is still in use. Inside the cathedral proper, you come almost immediately to the **graves of Jonathan Swift and Esther Johnson**, his long-term companion, better known as Stella. The Latin epitaphs are both written by Swift, and assorted Swift memorabilia lies all over the cathedral, including a pulpit and a death mask.

Boyle Monument

You can't miss the huge **Boyle Monument**, erected in 1632 by Richard Boyle, Earl of Cork. It stood briefly beside the altar until, in 1633, Dublin's viceroy, Thomas Wentworth, Earl of Strafford, had it shifted from its prominent position because he felt he shouldn't have to kneel to a Corkman. Boyle took his revenge in later years by orchestrating Wentworth's impeachment and execution. A figure in a niche at the bottom left of the monument is the earl's son Robert, the noted scientist who discovered Boyle's Law, which determined that the pressure and volume of a gas have an inverse relationship at a constant temperature.

ST PATRICK'S CATHEDRAL

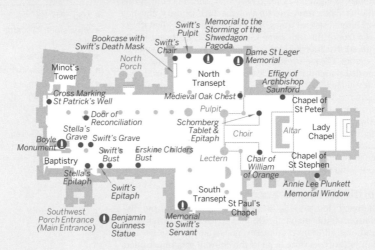

St Patrick's Well

In the opposite corner, there is a cross on a stone slab that once marked the position of **St Patrick's original well**, where (it's said) the patron saint of Ireland rolled up his sleeves and got to baptising the natives.

South Transept & South Aisle

Passing through the south transept, which was once the chapterhouse where the Earl of Kildare chanced his arm, you'll see magnificent **stained-glass windows** above the funerary monuments. The south aisle is lined with memorials to prominent 20th-century Irish Protestants, including Erskine Childers, who was president of Ireland from 1973 to 1974, and whose father was executed by the Free State during the Civil War. The son never spoke of the struggle for Irish independence because, on the eve of his death, his father made him promise never to do anything that might promote bitterness among the Irish people.

Door of Reconciliation

Towards the north transept is a door that has become a symbol of peace and reconciliation since it helped resolve a scrap between the earls of Kildare and Ormond in 1492. After a feud, supporters of the squabbling nobles ended up in a pitched battle inside the cathedral, during which Ormond's nephew – one Black James – barricaded himself in the chapterhouse. Kildare, having calmed down, cut a hole in the door between them and stuck his arm through it to either shake his opponent's hand, or lose a limb in his attempt to smooth things over. James chose mediation over amputation and took his hand. The term 'to chance your arm' entered the English lexicon and everyone lived happily ever after – except Black James, who was murdered by Kildare's son-in-law four years later.

North Transept

The north transept contains various military memorials to Royal Irish Regiments, while the northern choir aisle has a tablet marking the **grave of the Duke of Schomberg**, a prominent casualty of the Battle of the Boyne in 1690. Swift provided the duke's epitaph, caustically noting on it that the duke's own relatives couldn't be bothered to provide a suitable memorial. On the opposite side of the choir is a chair used by William of Orange when he came to give thanks to God for his victory over the Catholic James II during the same battle.

LIVING STONES

On your way around the church, you will also take in the four sections of the permanent exhibition, Living Stones, which explores the cathedral's history and the contribution it has made to the culture of Dublin.

Attend a sung Mass for the best atmosphere – at 11.15am on Sundays throughout the year, or at 9am Monday to Friday during school term only.

TICKETS TIP

Advance tickets are not valid on Sundays between 10.45am and 12.30pm and between 2.45pm and 4.30pm.

Last admission is 30 minutes before closing time.

NATURAL DISASTERS

The cathedral had been built twice by 1254 but succumbed to a series of natural disasters over the following century. Its spire was taken out in a 1316 storm, while the original tower and part of the nave were destroyed by fire in 1362.

⊙ SIGHTS

GUINNESS STOREHOUSE   BREWERY, MUSEUM
See p112.

ST PATRICK'S CATHEDRAL   CATHEDRAL
See p115.

★**MARSH'S LIBRARY**   LIBRARY
Map p247 (www.marshlibrary.ie; St Patrick's Close; adult/child €3/free; ⊙9.30am-5pm Mon & Wed-Fri, 10am-5pm Sat; ⊒50, 50A, 56A from Aston Quay, 54, 54A from Burgh Quay) This magnificently preserved scholars' library, virtually unchanged in three centuries, is one of Dublin's most beautiful open secrets and an absolute highlight of any visit. Atop its ancient stairs are beautiful, dark-oak bookcases, each topped with elaborately carved and gilded gables, and crammed with books, manuscripts and maps dating back to the 15th century.

Founded in 1701 by Archbishop Narcissus Marsh (1638–1713) and opened in 1707, the library was designed by Sir William Robinson, the man also responsible for the Royal Hospital Kilmainham (p118). It's the oldest public library in the country, and contains 25,000 books dating from the 16th to the early 18th century, as well as maps, manuscripts (including one in Latin dating back to 1400) and a collection of incunabula (books printed before 1500).

★**TEELING DISTILLERY**   DISTILLERY
Map p247 (www.teelingwhiskey.com; 13-17 Newmarket; tours €15-30; ⊙9.30am-5.30pm Mon-Fri; ⊒27, 77A & 151 from city centre) FREE The first new distillery in Dublin for 125 years, Teeling only began production in 2015 and it will be several years before any of the distillate can be called whiskey. In the meantime, you can explore the visitor centre and taste (and buy) whiskeys from the family's other distillery on the Cooley Peninsula.

You'll get a taste of whiskey at the end of the tour, but to try the really good stuff you'll have to upgrade to one of the organised tastings, which range from the Teeling Tasting (€15) to the Single Malt Reserve Tasting (€30), where you'll indulge in three special whiskeys, including the exceptional 21-year-old Reserve Single Malt, voted the world's best at the Whiskey Awards in 2014.

There's also an excellent cafe on the premises.

★**KILMAINHAM GAOL**   MUSEUM
Map p247 (⌨01-453 2037; http://kilmainham gaolmuseum.ie; Inchicore Rd; adult/child €8/4; ⊙9.30am-6.45pm Jul & Aug, to 5.30pm rest of year; ⊒69, 79 from Aston Quay, 13, 40 from O'Connell St) If you have *any* desire to understand Irish history – especially the juicy bits about resistance to British rule – then a visit to this former prison is an absolute must. This threatening grey building, built between 1792 and 1795, played a role in virtually every act of Ireland's painful path to independence, and even today, despite closing in 1924, it still has the power to chill.

The uprisings of 1798, 1803, 1848, 1867 and 1916 ended with the leaders' confinement here. Robert Emmet, Thomas Francis Meagher, Charles Stewart Parnell and the 1916 Easter Rising leaders were all visitors, but it was the executions in 1916 that most deeply etched the jail's name into the Irish consciousness. Of the 15 executions that took place between 3 May and 12 May after the revolt, 14 were conducted here. As a finale, prisoners from the Civil War were held here from 1922.

An excellent audiovisual introduction to the building is followed by a thought-provoking tour of the eerie prison, the largest unoccupied building of its kind in Europe. Sitting incongruously outside in the yard is the *Asgard*, the ship that successfully ran the British blockade to deliver arms to Nationalist forces in 1914. The tour finishes in the gloomy yard where the 1916 executions took place. Entrance is via the Kilmainham Courthouse next door.

★**IRISH MUSEUM OF
MODERN ART**   MUSEUM
Map p247 (IMMA; www.imma.ie; Military Rd; ⊙11.30am-5.30pm Tue-Fri, 10am-5.30pm Sat, noon-5.30pm Sun, tours 1.15pm Wed, 2.30pm Sat & Sun; ⊒51, 51D, 51X, 69, 78, 79 from Aston Quay, ⌂Heuston) FREE Ireland's most important collection of modern and contemporary Irish and international art is housed in the elegant, airy expanse of the Royal Hospital Kilmainham, designed by Sir William Robinson and built between 1684 and 1687 as a retirement home for soldiers. It fulfilled this role until 1928, after which it languished for nearly 50 years until a 1980s restoration saw it come back to life as this wonderful repository of art.

The building, which was inspired by Les Invalides in Paris, is a marvellous example of the Anglo-Dutch style that preceded the Georgian Age; at the time of its construction there were mutterings that it was altogether too fine a place for its residents.

Following Irish independence it was briefly considered as a potential home for the new Irish parliament, but it ended up as a storage facility for the National Museum of Ireland. Restorations began on the occasion of its 300th birthday in 1984 and it opened in 1991. A major restoration between 2012 and 2013 gave it an extra bit of sparkle.

The blend of old and new comes together wonderfully, and you'll find such contemporary Irish artists as Louis Le Brocquy, Sean Scully, Barry Flanagan, Kathy Prendergrass and Dorothy Cross featured here, as well as a film installation by Neil Jordan. The permanent exhibition also features paintings from heavy-hitters Pablo Picasso and Joan Miró, and is topped up by regular temporary exhibitions. There's a good cafe and bookshop on the grounds.

There are free guided tours of the museum's exhibits throughout the year.

KILMAINHAM GATE   LANDMARK

Map p247 (🚌69, 79 from Aston Quay, 13, 40 from O'Connell St) Francis Johnston's impressive Georgian gate was designed in 1812 as the Richmond Tower and located on the quays, near the Guinness Brewery. It was moved here in 1846 as it obstructed the increasingly heavy traffic to the new Kingsbridge Station (Heuston Station), which opened in 1844.

PEARSE LYONS DISTILLERY   DISTILLERY

Map p247 (📞01-825 2244; www.pearselyons distillery.com; 121-122 James's St; guided tours €20; 🚌21A, 51B, 78, 78A, 123 from Fleet St) This boutique distillery opened in the former St James's Church in the summer of 2017, distilling small-batch, craft Irish whiskey. On the tour you will explore the distilling process and indulge in a range of Pearse Irish whiskies, including a blend, a sherry cask and a 12-year-old.

The guided tour also includes a history of distilling in the Liberties, as well as the local history of owner Pearse Lyons' family, whose grandfather is buried in the adjacent graveyard.

WAR MEMORIAL GARDENS   PARK

(www.heritageireland.ie; South Circular Rd, Islandbridge; ⏰8am-dusk Mon-Fri, 10am-dusk Sat & Sun; 🚌69, 79 from Aston Quay, 13, 40 from O'Connell St) FREE Hardly anyone ever ventures this far west, but they're missing a lovely bit of landscaping in the shape of the War Memorial Gardens – by our reckoning as pleasant a patch of greenery as any you'll find in the heart of the Georgian centre. Designed by Sir Edwin Lutyens, the memorial commemorates the 49,400 Irish soldiers who died during WWI – their names are inscribed in the two huge granite bookrooms that stand at one end.

ST AUDOEN'S CHURCH OF IRELAND   CHURCH

Map p247 (📞01-677 0088; www.heritageireland. ie; Cornmarket, High St; ⏰9.30am-5.30pm May-Oct; 🚌50, 50A, 56A from Aston Quay, 54, 54A from Burgh Quay) Two churches, side-by-side, each bearing the same name, a tribute to St Audoen, the 7th-century bishop of Rouen (aka Ouen) and patron saint of the Normans. They built the older of the two, the Church of Ireland, between 1181 and 1212, and today it is the only medieval church in Dublin still in use. A free 30-minute guided tour departs every 30 minutes from 9.30am to 4.45pm. Attached to it is the newer, bigger, 19th-century Catholic St Audoen's (p120).

Through the Norman church's heavily moulded Romanesque Norman door, you can touch the 9th-century 'lucky stone' that was believed to bring good luck to business, and check out the 9th-century slab in the porch that suggests it was built on an even older church. As part of the tour you can explore the ruins as well as the present church, which has funerary monuments that were beheaded by Cromwell's purists. Its tower and door date from the 12th century and the aisle from the 15th century, but the church today is mainly a product of a 19th-century restoration.

St Anne's Chapel, the visitor centre, houses a number of tombstones of leading members of Dublin society from the 16th to 18th centuries. At the top of the chapel is the tower, which holds the three oldest bells in Ireland, dating from 1423. Although the church's exhibits are hardly spectacular, the building itself is beautiful and a genuine slice of medieval Dublin.

The church is entered from the south off High St through **St Audoen's Arch**, which was built in 1240 and is the only surviving reminder of the city gates. The adjoining park is pretty but attracts many unsavoury characters, particularly at night.

KILMAINHAM & THE LIBERTIES SIGHTS

ST AUDOEN'S CATHOLIC CHURCH   CHURCH

Map p247 (www.heritageireland.ie; Cornmarket, High St; ⊙9.30am-4.45pm May-Oct; ⊒50, 50A, 56A from Aston Quay, 54, 54A from Burgh Quay) **FREE** Attached to the medieval St Audoen's Church of Ireland (p119) is the bigger, 19th-century Catholic St Audoen's, which since 2006 has been home to the Polish chaplaincy in Ireland.

ST PATRICK'S TOWER   TOWER

Map p247 (Thomas St; ⊙closed to public; ⊒69 from Aston Quay) St Patrick's Tower is Europe's tallest smock windmill (with a revolving top). It was built in 1757 to power the Roe Distillery, which by 1887 covered 17 acres and produced more than two million gallons of whiskey annually, making it Europe's largest distillery. By the mid-1920s, however, the global whiskey market was in decline and the distillery was eventually sold in 1949 to its neighbours, Guinness.

1 THOMAS ST   HISTORIC BUILDING

Map p247 (⊙closed to public; ⊒21A, 51B, 78, 78A, 123 from Fleet St, ⊒James's) The former home of Arthur Guinness at No 1 Thomas St is marked by a plaque.

✗ EATING

★FUMBALLY   CAFE €

Map p247 (☑01-529 8732; www.thefumbally.ie; Fumbally Lane; mains €5-9.50; ⊙8am-5pm Tue-Fri, 10am-5pm Sat, plus 7-9.30pm Wed; ⊒49, 54A from city centre) A bright, airy warehouse cafe that serves healthy breakfasts, salads and sandwiches – while the occasional guitarist strums away in the corner. Its Wednesday dinner (mains €16) is an organic, locally sourced exploration of the cuisines of the world that includes a single dish (and its vegetarian variant) served in a communal dining experience; advance bookings suggested.

★1837 BAR & BRASSERIE   BRASSERIE €

Map p247 (☑01-471 4602; www.guinness-storehouse.com; Guinness Storehouse, St James's Gate; mains €9-14; ⊙noon-3pm; ⊒21A, 51B, 78, 78A, 123 from Fleet St, ⊒James's) This lunchtime brasserie serves up tasty dishes, from really fresh oysters to an insanely good Guinness burger, with skin-on fries and red-onion chutney. The drinks menu features a range of Guinness variants such as West Indian porter and Golden Ale. Highly recommended for lunch if you're visiting the museum.

Neighbourhood Walk
Viking & Medieval Dublin

START ESSEX GATE, PARLIAMENT ST
END DUBLIN CASTLE
LENGTH 2.5KM; TWO HOURS

Begin your walk in Temple Bar, at the corner of Parliament St and Essex Gate, once a main entrance gate to the city. A ❶ **bronze plaque** on a pillar marks the spot where the gate once stood. Further along, you can see the original foundations of the 13th-century ❷ **Isolde's Tower**, once part of the city walls, through a grill in the pavement, in front of the pub of the same name. It is thought the original tower was between 12m and 15m high, but it was demolished in the 17th century to make way for Georgian houses (also now demolished!).

Head west down Essex Gate and West Essex St until you reach Fishamble St; turn right towards the quays and left into Wood Quay. Cross Winetavern St and proceed along Merchant's Quay. To your left you'll see the ❸ **Church of the Immaculate Conception**, otherwise known as Adam & Eve's, after a tavern through which worshippers gained access to a secret chapel during Penal Law times during the 17th and 18th centuries. To make matters even more confusing, it is also known as the Church of St Francis (to whom it was originally dedicated).

Further down Merchant's Quay you'll spot the ❹ **Father Mathew Bridge**, built in 1818 on the spot of the fordable crossing that gave Dublin its Irish name, Baile Átha Cliath (Town of the Hurdle Ford) and named after temperance reformer Theobold Mathew (1790–1856), whose singular contribution to Irish life is 'the Pledge', a commitment to abstain from alcohol that most Irish Catholics took when they were confirmed (around age 12) and then abandoned when they were of age to drink (or earlier). Take a left into Bridge St and stop for said indulgence at Dublin's oldest pub, the ❺ **Brazen Head** (p123), dating from 1198 (although the present building dates from a positively youthful 1668).

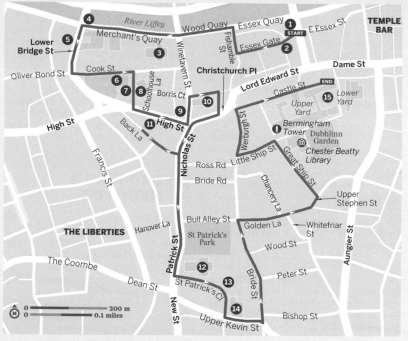

Take the next left onto Cook St, where you'll find ❻ **St Audoen's Arch**, one of the only remaining gates of the 32 that were built into the medieval city walls, dating from 1240. Climb through the arch up to the ramparts to see one of the city's oldest existing churches, ❼ **St Audoen's Church of Ireland** (p119). It was built around 1190, and is the only medieval church in the city that is still in use. Next door is the much newer (and larger) ❽ **St Audoen's Catholic Church** (p120), which was known for the speedy sermons of Father 'Flash' Kavanagh, keen to ensure that he and his parishioners were out in time for the Sunday game of Gaelic football.

Leave the little park, join High St and head east until you reach the first corner. Here on your left is the former Synod Hall, now ❾ **Dublinia** (p103), where medieval Dublin has been interactively recreated. Turn left and walk under the Synod Hall Bridge, which links Dublinia to one of the city's most important landmarks – ❿ **Christ Church Cathedral** (p100) – and, in medieval times, the most important church inside the city walls.

Exit the cathedral onto Christ Church Pl, cross over onto Nicholas St and turn right onto Back Lane. Proceed to ⓫ **Tailors' Hall**, Dublin's oldest surviving guild hall, built between 1703 and 1707 (though it says 1770 on the plaque) for the Tailors Guild. It's now the headquarters of An Taisce, the National Trust for Ireland.

Do an about-turn, head back along the lane and turn right into Nicholas St, which becomes Patrick St. To your left you'll see ⓬ **St Patrick's** (p115), Dublin's most important cathedral, which stood outside the city walls. Along St Patrick's Close, beyond the bend on the left, is the stunningly beautiful ⓭ **Marsh's Library** (p118), named after Archbishop Narcissus Marsh, dean of St Patrick's. Further along again on your left is the ⓮ **Dublin Metropolitan Police** building, once the Episcopal Palace of St Sepulchre.

Finally, follow our route up Bride St, Golden Lane and Great Ship St, and finish up with a long wander around ⓯ **Dublin Castle** (p59). Be sure not to miss the striking powder-blue Bermingham Tower and the nearby Chester Beatty Library, south of the castle, which houses one of the city's most fascinating collections of rare books and manuscripts, and is well worth a visit.

LEGIT COFFEE CO — CAFE €

Map p247 (www.legitcoffeeco.com; 1 Meath Mart, Meath St; mains €4-8; ☺7.30am-5pm Mon-Fri, 9.30am-5pm Sat; 🚇James's) A rare trendy spot in the middle of one of Dublin's most traditional streets, Legit is full of stripped-down wood, speciality teas and strong espressos. A great spot to enjoy a toasted brioche or a filling sandwich.

GAILLOT ET GRAY — PIZZA €

Map p247 (☎01-454 7781; 59 Lower Clanbrassil St; pizzas €8-9; ☺8am-10pm Tue-Sat; 🚌49, 54A from city centre) *Mon dieu*, a French pizzeria? Gilles Gaillot and his wife Emma Gray have combined the forces of Emmental cheese and pizza (biscuit-thin sourdough bases) to create this delicious hybrid. It doesn't taste like classic Italian pizza, which is precisely the point. And it works. It also operates as a bakery.

DUBLIN COOKIE COMPANY — BAKERY €

Map p247 (☎01-473 6566; www.thedublin cookieco.com; 29 Thomas St; cookies from €1; ☺8am-5.30pm Mon-Fri, 10am-4pm Sat; 🚌13, 69 from city centre) Artisanal cookies by Jenny and Elaine, made fresh all day right in front of you. It's always experimenting with new and exciting flavours, and offers strong, aromatic coffee and chocolate or cookie-flavoured milk.

ITSA@IMMA — CAFE €

Map p247 (www.imma.ie; Irish Museum of Modern Art, Military Rd; mains €7-10; ☺11.30am-5.30pm Tue-Fri, 10am-5.30pm Sat, noon-5.30pm Sun; 🚌51, 51D, 51X, 69, 78, 79 from Aston Quay, 🚇Heuston) Freshly made gourmet sandwiches and bagels as well as healthy salads and soups are the mainstay of the museum cafe at the Irish Museum of Modern Art.

UNION8 — MODERN IRISH €€

Map p247 (☎01-677 8707; www.union8.ie; 740 South Circular Rd; mains €18-27; ☺9am-9pm Sun-Tue, to 9.30pm Wed, to 10pm Thu-Sat; 🚌69, 79 from Aston Quay, 13, 40 from O'Connell St) A hub for the local community of Dublin 8 (hence the name), this terrific spot serves tasty breakfasts and contemporary Irish cuisine (beautifully presented fish dishes, succulent lamb, tasty pork belly and the like) for lunch and dinner. Highly recommended if you're in this part of town.

🍷 DRINKING & NIGHTLIFE

★OLD ROYAL OAK — PUB

Map p247 (11 Kilmainham Lane; ☺10.30am-11.30pm Mon-Thu, to 12.30am Fri & Sat, noon-11pm Sun; 🚌68, 79 from city centre) Locals are fiercely protective of this gorgeous traditional pub, which opened in 1845 to serve the patrons and staff of the Royal Hospital (now the Irish Museum of Modern Art). The clientele has changed, but everything else has remained the same, which makes this one of the nicest pubs in the city in which to enjoy a few pints.

FALLON'S — PUB

Map p247 (☎01-454 2801; 129 The Coombe; ☺10.30am-11.30pm Mon-Thu, to 12.30am Fri & Sat, noon-11pm Sun; 🚌123, 206, 51B from city centre) A fabulously old-fashioned bar that has been serving a great pint of Guinness since the end of the 17th century. Prizefighter Dan Donnelly, the only boxer ever to be knighted, was head bartender here in 1818. A local's local.

DISTILLERY CRAZE

The Liberties might be dominated by the world-famous Guinness brewery, but Dublin's most traditional neighbourhood is set to once again become a major centre for the distilling of whiskey. The Teeling Distillery opened up in 2015 after a hiatus of nearly 200 years: the original Teeling Distillery opened in 1782 around the corner on Marrowbone Lane and operated for 40 years. In 2017 the Liberties welcomed the Pearse Lyons Distillery, which began operations in the former St James's Church on James St. Pearse Lyons and his wife Deirdre own a brewery and distillery in Kentucky (as well as the giant animal nutrition company Alltech), but this new project is close to his heart as Lyons' own grandfather is buried in the church's graveyard. And finally (for now, at least) the Dublin Liberties Distillery is scheduled to open in 2018 in a former mill and tannery on Mill St. It seems whiskey is very much back.

MVP
BAR

(☎01-558 2158; http://mvpdublin.com; 29 Upper Clanbrassil St; ⊙4-11.30pm Mon-Thu, to 12.30am Fri & Sat, to 11pm Sun; 🚍49, 54A, 77X from city centre) A small and friendly bar just off the beaten path that is home to potent and inventive cocktails. The menu is pure comfort food; baked and roast potatoes in all varieties are designed to warm your belly.

ARTHUR'S
PUB

Map p247 (☎01-402 0914; www.arthurspub.ie; 28 Thomas St; ⊙noon-11.30pm Mon-Thu, 11am-12.30am Fri & Sat, 11am-11pm Sun; 🚍21A, 51B, 78, 78A, 123 from Fleet St, 🚇James's) Given its location, Arthur's could easily be a cheesy tourist trap, and plenty of Guinness Storehouse (p112) visitors do pass through the doors tempted by another taste of the black stuff. Instead it's a friendly, cosy bar with a menu full of good comfort food. Best visited in the winter so you get the full benefit of the roaring fireplace and soft candlelight.

BRAZEN HEAD
PUB

Map p247 (☎01-679 5186; www.brazenhead.com; 20 Lower Bridge St; ⊙10am-midnight Mon-Thu, 10am-12.30am Fri & Sat, 11am-midnight Sun; 🚍51B, 78A, 123 from city centre) Reputedly Dublin's oldest pub, the Brazen Head has been serving thirsty patrons since 1198 when it set up as a Norman tavern. It's a bit away from the city centre, and the clientele consists of foreign-language students, tourists and some grizzly auld locals.

Though its history is uncertain, the sunken level of the courtyard indicates how much street levels have altered since its construction. Robert Emmet was believed to have been a regular visitor, while in *Ulysses*, James Joyce reckoned 'you get a decent enough do in the Brazen Head'.

 ## ENTERTAINMENT

VICAR STREET
LIVE MUSIC

Map p247 (☎01-454 5533; www.vicarstreet.com; 58-59 Thomas St; tickets €25-60; ⊙7pm-midnight; 🚍13, 49, 54A, 56A from city centre) Vicar Street is a midsized venue with a capacity of around 1000, spread between the table-serviced group-seating downstairs and a theatre-style balcony. It offers a varied program of performers, from comedians to soul, jazz, folk and world music.

TIVOLI THEATRE
THEATRE

Map p247 (☎01-454 4472; www.tivoli.ie; 135-136 Francis St; adult/child & student €20/15; 🚍51B, 51C, 78A, 123 from city centre) This commercial theatre offers a little bit of everything, from a good play with terrific actors to absolute nonsense with questionable comedic value.

🛍 SHOPPING

DUBLIN FOOD CO-OP
MARKET

Map p247 (www.dublinfood.coop; 12 Newmarket; ⊙10am-7pm Wed & Fri, to 8pm Thu, 9.30am-5pm Sat, 11am-5pm Sun; 🚍49, 54A, 77X from city centre) From dog food to detergent, everything in this member-owned co-op is organic and/or ecofriendly. Thursday has a limited selection of local and imported fair-trade products, but Saturday is when it's all on display – Dubliners from all over drop in for their responsible weekly shop. There's an on-the-premises baker and even baby-changing facilities.

MARTIN FENNELLY ANTIQUES
ANTIQUES

Map p247 (www.fennelly.net; 60 Francis St; ⊙9.15am-6pm Mon-Sat, 1.30-4.30pm Sun; 🚍123, 206, 51B from city centre) One of the best-known antiques dealers on Francis St is Martin Fennelly, who specialises in household items ranging from candlesticks and tea caddies to jewellery boxes and French and English porcelain. He also has an excellent collection of exquisite Irish furniture.

O'SULLIVAN ANTIQUES
ANTIQUES

Map p247 (☎01-454 1143; www.osullivanantiques.com; 43-44 Francis St; ⊙10am-6pm Mon-Sat; 🚍123, 206, 51B from city centre) Fine furniture and furnishings from the Georgian, Victorian and Edwardian eras are the speciality of this respected antiques shop (which also has a branch in New York). A rummage might also reveal some distinctive bits of ceramic and crystal, not to mention medals and uniforms from a bygone era that will win you first prize at the costume ball.

FLEURY ANTIQUES
ANTIQUES

Map p247 (☎01-473 0878; 57 Francis St; ⊙9.30am-6pm Mon-Sat; 🚍123, 206, 51B from city centre) This blue-fronted antiques shop does a steady connoisseur's trade in all manner of oil paintings (there's something for virtually every taste), vases, candelabras, silverware, porcelain and decorative pieces from the 18th century right up to the 1930s.

JORDACHE/SHUTTERSTOCK ©

1. The Samuel Beckett Bridge (p148)
Named for the legendary playwright, this bridge over the River Liffey blends Dockland's modern architecture with Dublin's literary heritage.

2. National Museum of Ireland – Decorative Arts & History (p133)
Houses ceramics, silver, weaponry and furniture from another era, as well as an exhibit on the Easter Rising.

3. Phoenix Park (p129)
This 709-hectare park is home to a herd of fallow deer, along with the Irish president, the American ambassador and Europe's oldest zoo.

BIFFBOFBIFF/GETTY IMAGES ©

North of the Liffey

Neighbourhood Top Five

❶ Dublin City Gallery – the Hugh Lane (p128) Nodding sagely at the exquisite collection of modern and contemporary art.

❷ Old Jameson Distillery (p133) Sampling a snifter of the hard stuff after discovering how it's made in this converted distillery museum.

❸ Abbey Theatre (p143) Spending a night at the spiritual home of Irish theatre, being entertained by plays both old and new, by the great dramatists as well as emerging talent.

❹ National Museum of Ireland – Decorative Arts & History (p133) Wandering about the glorious yard of

Collins Barracks, without forgetting the collection itself – which includes fascinating exhibits on Ireland's struggle for independence as well as the history of design.

❺ Tantalising Your Taste Buds (p138) Eating in the northside's new breed of restaurants, like Cotto or Fish Shop.

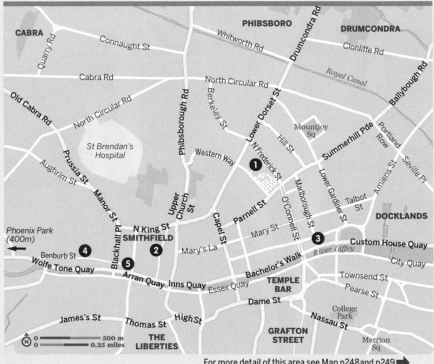

For more detail of this area see Map p248 and p249 ➡

Explore North of the Liffey

With the biggest geographical spread of any of Dublin's neighbourhoods, the area north of the Liffey requires a little planning and a bit of transport in order to be fully explored. O'Connell St and its attractions are pretty straightforward and can be explored with ease on foot, with the biggest demand on your time being the fabulous collection at the Hugh Lane (p128) and the collection at Collins Barracks (p133). The northside's other attractions are to the west, and the best way to get to them is by Luas, which will reduce your journey to mere minutes. The Old Jameson Distillery (p133) and Collins Barracks are within walking distance of each other, on either side of Smithfield, but you'll be under your own steam to explore Europe's largest enclosed city park, Phoenix Park (p129), home to the president, the US ambassador, the zoo and a herd of red deer, not to mention visiting Dubliners when the weather is good.

Beyond the Royal Canal, which encloses the northern edge of the city centre, are a bunch of attractions that are well worth the effort: you could devote the guts of half a day each to visiting the Croke Park museum (p142), Glasnevin cemetery (p142) and the National Botanic Gardens (p142); an excursion to Marino to see the famous Casino (p142) is also worthwhile, and you can get there via the DART suburban train.

Local Life

→**Hang-Out** Go to Brother Hubbard (p139) on Capel St for great coffee and an easy-going atmosphere; equally good is Third Space (p139) in Smithfield.

→**Food** The northside's culinary credentials are elevated by the likes of Oxmantown (p138), Cotto (p138) and Fish Shop (p139) – but don't ignore stalwarts such as 101 Talbot (p140) either!

→**Park Life** Do as Dubliners do on a fine day and take in the massive expanse of Phoenix Park (p129), where you can run, cycle, play, walk or just lie down, depending on your fancy.

Getting There & Away

→**Bus** All city centre buses stop on O'Connell St or the nearby quays. City buses serve Glasnevin and Croke Park, while national bus services, run by Bus Eireann, arrive and depart from the Busáras (p217) depot on Store St.

→**Tram** The Luas runs east – west parallel to the Liffey from The Point to Heuston Station.

→**Train** The DART runs from Connolly Station northeast to Clontarf Rd, which is handy for the Casino at Marino. Mainline trains for the north and northwest go from Connolly Station (p217).

Lonely Planet's Top Tip

The area between Smithfield and Manor St is one of the city's most exciting districts, home to a clutch of new restaurants and shops that have also served to re-invigorate more traditional spots, including a handful of pubs that are among the best in the city.

✖ Best Places to Eat

→ M&L (p138)
→ Chapter One (p141)
→ Oxmantown (p138)
→ Fish Shop (p139)
→ Yarn (p139)

For reviews, see p138 ➡

🍷 Best Places to Drink

→ Walshe's (p141)
→ Dice Bar (p143)
→ Pantibar (p141)
→ Cobblestone (p141)
→ Confession Box (p141)

For reviews, see p140 ➡

🏛 Best Places to Buy Irish

→ Eason's (p144)
→ Winding Stair (p144)
→ Moore Street Market (p144)
→ Louis Copeland (p144)

For reviews, see p144 ➡

NORTH OF THE LIFFEY

TOP SIGHT
DUBLIN CITY GALLERY – THE HUGH LANE

Whatever reputation Dublin may have as a repository of top-class art is in large part due to the collection at this magnificent gallery, home to Impressionist masterpieces, the best of modern Irish work from 1950 onward, and the actual studio of Francis Bacon.

The Gallery

Founded in 1908, the gallery's home since 1933 has been **Charlemont House**, designed by Georgian superstar architect William Chambers in 1763. A modernist extension, which opened in 2006, has seen the addition of 13 bright galleries spread across three floors.

Hugh Lane

The gallery owes its origins to one Sir Hugh Lane (1875–1915). He had a connoisseur's eye and a good nose for the directions of the market, which enabled him to build up a superb collection, particularly strong in Impressionists.

Unfortunately for Ireland, neither his talents nor his collection were much appreciated. Irish rejection led him to rewrite his will and bequeath some of the finest works in his collection to the National Gallery in London. Later he relented and added a rider to his will leaving the collection to Dublin but failed to have it witnessed, thus causing a long legal squabble over which gallery had rightful ownership.

DON'T MISS

➡ The Hugh Lane Bequest 1917 paintings
➡ Francis Bacon Studio
➡ Sean Scully collection

PRACTICALITIES

➡ Map p249, E3
➡ 🖉 01-222 5550
➡ www.hughlane.ie
➡ 22 N Parnell Sq
➡ admission free
➡ ⏱ 9.45am-6pm Tue-Thu, to 5pm Fri & Sat, 11am-5pm Sun
➡ 🚌 7, 11, 13, 16, 38, 40, 46A, 123 from city centre

The Hugh Lane Bequest

The collection (known as the Hugh Lane Bequest 1917) was split in a 1959 settlement that sees the eight masterpieces divided into two groups and alternated between Dublin and London every six years. Currently on show are works by Renoir, Manet, Morisot and Pissarro.

Francis Bacon Studio

Impressionist masterpieces notwithstanding, the gallery's most popular exhibit is the Francis Bacon Studio, which was painstakingly moved, in all its shambolic mess, from 7 Reece Mews, South Kensington, London, where the Dublin-born artist (1909–92) lived for 31 years. The display features some 80,000 items madly strewn about the place, including slashed canvases, the last painting he was working on, tables piled with materials, walls daubed with colour samples, portraits with heads cut out, favourite bits of furniture and many assorted piles of crap. It's a teasing and tantalising, riveting and ridiculous masterpiece that provides the viewer with no real sense of the artist himself. Far more revealing is the 10-minute profile of him with Melvyn Bragg and the immensely sad photographs of Bacon's immaculately tidy bachelor pad, which suggest a deep, personal loneliness.

Elsewhere in the Gallery

Just by the main reception desk is the **Stained Glass gallery**, whose highlight is Harry Clarke's wonderful *The Eve of St Agnes* (1924). His masterpiece is made up of 22 separate panels, each a depiction of a stanza of John Keats' eponymous poem about the doomed love between Madeline and Porphyro, who cannot meet because their families are sworn enemies.

The gallery's newest wing (opened 2006) is a two-storey extension with – on the ground floor – a gallery dedicated to seven abstract paintings by Irish-born **Sean Scully**, probably Ireland's most famous living painter.

TOP SIGHT
PHOENIX PARK

The hugely impressive 709 hectares that comprise Phoenix Park are not just a magnificent playground for all kinds of sport from running to polo, but are also home to the president of Ireland, the American ambassador and a shy herd of fallow deer. It is also where you'll find Europe's oldest zoo. How's that for a place to stretch your legs?

DON'T MISS

➡ Wellington Monument
➡ Tour of Áras an Uachtaráin
➡ Dublin Zoo

Dublin Zoo

Established in 1831, the 28-hectare **Dublin Zoo** (www.dublinzoo.ie; adult/child/family €17.50/13/49; ⊘9.30am-6pm Mar-Sep, to dusk Oct-Feb), just north of the Hollow, is one of the oldest in the world. It is well known for its lion-breeding program, which dates back to 1857 and includes among its offspring the lion that roars at the start of MGM films. You'll see these tough cats, from a distance, on the 'African Savanna', just one of several habitats created since 2005.

PRACTICALITIES

➡ www.phoenixpark.ie
➡ admission free
➡ ⊘24hr
➡ ▣10 from O'Connell St, 25, 26 from Middle Abbey St

The zoo is home to roughly 400 animals from 100 different species, and you can visit all of them across the eight different habitats that range from an Asian jungle to a family farm, where kids get to meet the inhabitants up close and even milk a (model) cow. Sadly, a strain of avian flu in 2017 meant that all of the zoo's birds were moved indoors so as to avoid interaction with native, wild species. There are restaurants, cafes and even a train to get you round.

Áras an Uachtaráin

The residence of the Irish president is a Palladian **lodge** (www.president.ie; Phoenix Park; ⊘guided tours hourly 10.30am-3.30pm Sat; ▣10 from O'Connell St, 25, 26 from Middle Abbey St) FREE that was built in 1751 and enlarged a couple of times since, most recently in 1816. It was home to the British viceroys from 1782 to 1922, and then to the

DID YOU KNOW?

At 709 hectares, Phoenix Park is big – but when it was first developed it was even larger, as it stretched across the Liffey to the south. Part of the original park was on the site of a Viking burial ground (in the Islandbridge/ Kilmainham area) that was the biggest Viking cemetery outside of Scandinavia.

At weekends the football pitches at the Fifteen Acres are used by local league teams that can be fun to watch. Although the park is open 24 hours a day, it is not advised to hang around after dark.

governors general until Ireland cut ties with the British Crown and created the office of president in 1937. Queen Victoria stayed here during her visit in 1849, when she appeared not to even notice the Famine. The candle burning in the window is an old Irish tradition, to guide 'the Irish diaspora' home.

Tickets for the free one-hour Saturday **tours** can be collected from the **Phoenix Park Visitor Centre** (📞01-677 0095; 🕐10am-6pm Apr-Dec, 9.30am-5.30pm Wed-Sun rest of year; 🚌10 from O'Connell St, 25 & 26 from Middle Abbey St) FREE, the converted former stables of the papal nunciate, where you'll see a 10-minute introductory video before being shuttled to the Áras itself to inspect five state rooms and the president's study. If you can't make it on a Saturday, just become elected president of your own country or become a Nobel laureate or something, and then wrangle a personal invite.

The Park

Chesterfield Ave runs northwest through the length of the park from the Parkgate St entrance to the Castleknock Gate. Near the Parkgate St entrance is the 63m-high **Wellington Monument** obelisk, which was completed in 1861. Nearby is the **People's Garden**, dating from 1864, and the **bandstand** in the Hollow. Across Chesterfield Ave from the Áras an Uachtaráin – and easily visible from the road – is the massive **Papal Cross**, which marks the site where Pope John Paul II preached to 1.25 million people in 1979. In the centre of the park the **Phoenix Monument**, erected by Lord Chesterfield in 1747, looks so unlike a phoenix that it's often referred to as the Eagle Monument.

Ashtown Castle

Next door to Áras an Uachtaráin is the restored four-storey Ashtown Castle, a 17th-century tower house 'discovered' inside the 18th-century nuncio's mansion when the latter was demolished in 1986 due to dry rot. You can visit the castle only on a guided tour from the visitor centre.

Farmleigh House

Situated in the northwest corner of Phoenix Park, opulent **Farmleigh House** (📞01-815 5900; www.farmleigh.ie; Phoenix Park, Castleknock; 🕐10am-5pm Sat & Sun, guided tours hourly 10.15am-4.15pm; 🚌37

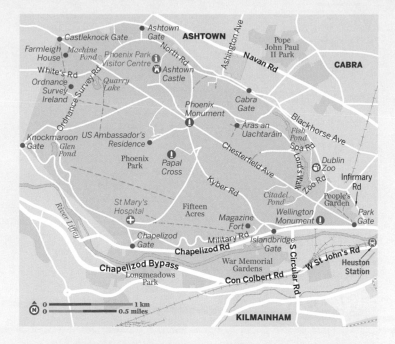

from city centre) **FREE** can only be visited by joining one of the 30-minute house tours. However, the real highlight of the 32-hectare estate is the garden, where regular shows are held. There is also an extensive program of cultural events in summer, ranging from food fairs to classical concerts. The 37m clock tower once housed an 8000L water tank that serviced the estate; views from the top are sensational.

Elsewhere in the Park

The southern part of the park has many **football** and **hurling pitches**; although they actually occupy about 80 hectares (200 acres), the area is known as the **Fifteen Acres**. To the west, the rural-looking **Glen Pond** corner of the park is extremely attractive.

At the northwestern end of the park, near the White's Gate entrance, are the offices of **Ordnance Survey Ireland**, the government mapping department. This building was originally built in 1728 by Luke Gardiner, who was responsible for the architecture in O'Connell St and Mountjoy Sq in north Dublin.

Back towards the Parkgate St entrance is the **Magazine Fort** (see www.phoenix park.ie for tours) on Thomas's Hill. The fort was no quick construction, the process taking from 1734 to 1801. It provided useful target practice during the 1916 Easter Rising, and was raided by the Irish Republican Army (IRA) in 1940 when the entire ammunition reserve of the Irish army was nabbed, but recovered a few weeks later.

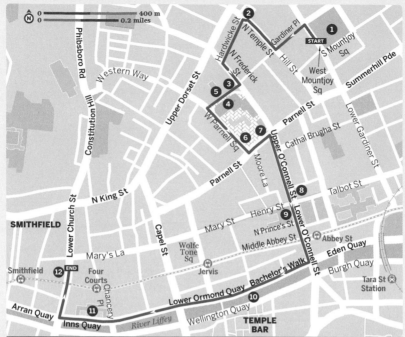

Neighbourhood Walk
A Walk on the Northside

START MOUNTJOY SQ
END ST MICHAN'S CHURCH
LENGTH 2.5KM; TWO HOURS

From **1 Mountjoy Square**, turn left at the northwestern corner and walk down Gardiner Pl, turning right onto North Temple St. Up ahead is the fine but now deconsecrated Georgian **2 St George's Church** (p137), designed by architect Francis Johnston.

Take a left onto Hardwicke St and left again onto North Frederick St. On your right you'll spot the distinctive **3 Abbey Presbyterian Church**, built in 1864.

The northern slice of Parnell Sq houses the **4 Garden of Remembrance** (p137), opened in 1966 for the 50th anniversary of the 1916 Easter Rising. North of the square, is the excellent **5 Dublin City Gallery – the Hugh Lane** (p128), home to some of the best modern art in Europe.

At the southern part of Parnell Sq is the **6 Rotunda Hospital** (p136), a wonderful example of public architecture in the Georgian style and now one of the city's three main maternity hospitals. The southeastern

corner of the square has the **7 Gate Theatre** (p143), one of the city's most important theatres – and where Orson Welles began his acting career in 1931 as a 16-year-old.

Head south down O'Connell St, passing by the 120m-high **8 Spire** (p137). Erected in 2001, it has become an iconic symbol of the city. On the western side of O'Connell St, the stunning neoclassical **9 General Post Office** (p133) towers over the street – this was the operational HQ for the 1916 Easter Rising: you can still see bullet holes in the columns.

When you hit the river, turn right and walk along the boardwalk until you reach the city's most distinctive crossing point, the **10 Ha'Penny Bridge** (p103), named for the charge levied on those who used it.

Continue west along Ormond Quay to one of James Gandon's Georgian masterpieces, the **11 Four Courts** (p135), home to the most important law courts in Ireland. Finally take a right onto Church St to admire **12 St Michan's Church** (p134), a beautiful Georgian construction with grisly vaults populated by the remains of the long departed.

⊙ SIGHTS

**DUBLIN CITY GALLERY –
THE HUGH LANE**   GALLERY
See p128.

PHOENIX PARK   PARK
See p129.

★**OLD JAMESON DISTILLERY**   MUSEUM
Map p249 (www.jamesonwhiskey.com; Bow St; adult/student/child €18/15/9, masterclasses €55; ☺10am-5pm Mon-Sat, 10.30am-5pm Sun; ☐25, 66, 67, 90 from city centre, ☐Smithfield) Smithfield's biggest draw is devoted to *uisce beatha* (ish-kuh ba-ha, 'the water of life'); that's Irish for whiskey. To its more serious devotees, that is precisely what whiskey is, although they may be put off by the slickness of this museum (occupying part of the old distillery that stopped production in 1971), which shepherds visitors through a compulsory tour of the re-created factory (the tasting at the end is a lot of fun) and into the gift shop.

If you're really serious about whiskey, you can deepen your knowledge with the Whiskey Makers or the Whiskey Shakers, two 90-minute masterclasses that deconstruct the creation of Jameson whiskies and teach how to make a range of whiskey-based cocktails. If you're just buying whiskey, go for the stuff you can't buy at home, such as the excellent Red Breast or the superexclusive Midleton, a very limited reserve that is appropriately expensive.

★**NATIONAL MUSEUM
OF IRELAND – DECORATIVE
ARTS & HISTORY**   MUSEUM
Map p249 (www.museum.ie; Benburb St; ☺10am-5pm Tue-Sat, 2-5pm Sun; ☐25, 66, 67, 90 from city centre, ☐Museum) **FREE** Once the world's largest military barracks, this splendid early neoclassical grey-stone building on the Liffey's northern banks was completed in 1704 according to the design of Thomas Burgh (he of Trinity College's Old Library). It is now home to the Decorative Arts & History collection of the National Museum of Ireland, with a range of superb permanent exhibits ranging from a history of the **Easter Rising** to the work of iconic Irish designer **Eileen Gray** (1878–1976).

The building's central square held six entire regiments and is a truly awesome space, surrounded by arcaded colonnades and blocks linked by walking bridges. Following the handover to the new Irish government in 1922, the barracks was renamed to honour Michael Collins, a hero of the struggle for independence, who was killed that year in the Civil War; to this day most Dubliners refer to the museum as the **Collins Barracks**. Indeed, the army coat Collins wore on the day of his death (there's still mud on the sleeve) is part of the **Soldiers and Chiefs** exhibit, which covers the history of Irish soldiery at home and abroad from 1550 to the 21st century.

The museum's exhibits include a treasure trove of artefacts ranging from silver, ceramics and glassware to weaponry, furniture and folk-life displays. The fascinating **Way We Wore** exhibit displays Irish clothing and jewellery from the past 250 years. An intriguing sociocultural study, it highlights the symbolism jewellery and clothing had in bestowing messages of mourning, love and identity. The old Riding School is home to **Proclaiming a Republic: The 1916 Rising**, which opened in 2016 as an enhanced and updated version of the long-standing exhibit dedicated to the rebellion. The exhibit explores the complicated socio-historical background to the Rising and also includes visceral memorabilia such as firsthand accounts of the violence of the Black and Tans and post-Rising hunger strikes, and the handwritten death certificates of the Republican prisoners and their postcards from Holloway prison. Some of the best pieces are gathered in the **Curator's Choice** exhibition, which is a collection of 25 objects hand-picked by different curators and displayed alongside an account of why they were chosen.

GENERAL POST OFFICE   HISTORIC BUILDING
Map p249 (☎01-705 7000; www.anpost.ie; Lower O'Connell St; ☺8am-8pm Mon-Sat; ☐all city centre, ☐Abbey) It's not just the country's main post office, or an eye-catching neoclassical building: the General Post Office is at the heart of Ireland's struggle for independence. The GPO served as command HQ for the rebels during the Easter Rising of 1916 and as a result has become the focal point for all kinds of protests, parades and remembrances, as well as home to an interactive visitor centre.

The building – a neoclassical masterpiece designed by Francis Johnston in 1818 – was burnt out in the siege that resulted from the rising, but that wasn't the end of it. There was bitter fighting in and around the GPO during the Civil War of 1922; you can still see the pockmarks of the struggle in the Doric columns. Since its reopening in 1929 it has lived through quieter times, although its role in Irish history is commemorated inside the visitor centre. For €10, you can take a self-guided tour of an exhibition that brings you through the causes, action and aftermath of the armed rebellion.

JAMES JOYCE
CULTURAL CENTRE   CULTURAL CENTRE
Map p249 (www.jamesjoyce.ie; 35 N Great George's St; adult/student/child €4.50/3.50/free; ☺10am-5pm Tue-Sat, noon-5pm Sun; ☐3, 10, 11, 11A, 13, 16, 16A, 19, 19A, 22 from city centre) Denis Maginni, the exuberant, flamboyant dance instructor and 'confirmed bachelor' immortalised by James Joyce in *Ulysses,* taught the finer points of dance out of this beautifully restored Georgian house, now a centre devoted to promoting and preserving the Joycean heritage. Inside are a handful of exhibits that will pique the interest of a Joyce enthusiast.

The exhibits include some of the furniture from Joyce's Paris apartment; a life-size recreation of a typical Edwardian bedroom (not Joyce's, but one similar to what James and Nora would have used); and the original door of 7 Eccles St, the home of Leopold and Molly Bloom in *Ulysses,* which was demolished in real life to make way for a hospital.

It's not much, but the absence of period stuff is more than made up for by the superb interactive displays, which include three short documentary films on various aspects of Joyce's life and work, and – the highlight of the whole place – computers that allow you to explore the content of *Ulysses* episode by episode and trace Joyce's life year by year. It's enough to demolish the myth that Joyce's works are an impenetrable mystery and render him as he should be to the contemporary reader: a writer of enormous talent who sought to challenge and entertain his audience with his breathtaking wit and use of language.

While here, you can also admire the fine plastered ceilings, some of which are restored originals while others are meticulous reproductions of Dublin stuccodore Michael Stapleton's designs. The street has also been given a facelift and now boasts some of the finest Georgian doorways and fanlights in the city.

JIM LARKIN STATUE   STATUE
Map p249 (Lower O'Connell St; ☐all city centre, ☐Abbey) The most dynamic statue along O'Connell St is that of trade-union leader Jim Larkin (1876–1947) by Oisin Kelly, just south of the General Post Office. Kelly captured him in the middle of one of his eloquent tirades in defence of working people, his arms spread wide. Needless to say, it is one of the most beloved of all Dublin statues.

ST MICHAN'S CHURCH   CHURCH
Map p249 (☐01-872 4154; Lower Church St; adult/child €5/3.50; ☺10am-12.45pm & 2-4.45pm Mon-Fri, 10am-12.45pm Sat; ☐Smithfield) Macabre remains are the main attraction at this church, which was founded by the Danes in 1095 and named after one of their saints. Among the 'attractions' is an 800-year-old Norman crusader who was so tall that his feet were lopped off so he could fit in a coffin. Visits are by guided tour only.

St Michan's was the northside's only church until 1686, a year after it was almost completely rebuilt (it was remodelled in 1825 and again after the Civil War), leaving only the 15th-century battlement tower as its oldest bit. The courtroom-like interior hasn't changed much since the 19th century: still in place is the organ from 1724, which Handel may have played for the first-ever performance of his *Messiah.* The organ case is distinguished by the fine oak carving of 17 entwined musical instruments on its front. A skull on the floor on one side of the altar is said to represent Oliver Cromwell. On the opposite side is the Stool of Repentance, where 'open and notoriously naughty livers' did public penance.

The tours of the underground vaults are the real draw, however. The bodies within are aged between 400 and 800 years, and have been preserved by a combination of methane gas coming from rotting vegetation beneath the church, the magnesium limestone of the masonry (which absorbs moisture from the air) and the perfectly constant temperature. Although there are caskets strewn about the place, the main attractions are 'the big four' – mummified bodies labelled The Unknown (a female about whom nothing is known), The Thief (his hands and feet are missing; some say as punishment for his crimes), The Nun and The Crusader: if he is indeed 800 years old then he may have participated in the piratical free-for-all crusades of the 13th century that resulted in the sack of Constantinople but which weren't sanctioned by the church. Also in the crypt are the bodies of John and Henry Sheares, two brothers executed following the Rising of 1798 and – it is claimed – the remains of Robert Emmett, the fallen leader of the 1803 rebellion. Bram Stoker is said to have visited the crypt, which

O'CONNELL ST STATUARY

O'Connell St is lined with statues of Irish history's good and great. The big daddy of them all is the 'Liberator' himself, **Daniel O'Connell** (Map p249; Lower O'Connell St; ☐all city centre, ☐Abbey) (1775–1847; statue 1880, unveiled 1882), whose massive bronze bulk soars above the street at the bridge end. The four winged figures at his feet represent O'Connell's supposed virtues: patriotism, courage, fidelity and eloquence. Dubs began to refer to the street as O'Connell St soon after the monument was erected; its name was officially changed after independence.

Heading away from the river, past a monument to **William Smith O'Brien** (1803–64), leader of the Young Irelanders, is a statue that easily rivals O'Connell's for drama: just outside the GPO is the spread-armed figure of trade-union leader **Jim Larkin** (p134) (1876–1947). His big moment came when he helped organise the general strike in 1913 – the pose catches him in full flow, urging workers to rise up for their rights.

Next up and hard to miss is the **Spire** (p137), but just below it, on pedestrianised North Earl St, is the detached figure of **James Joyce** (p136), looking on the shiny version of 21st-century O'Connell St with a bemused air. Dubs have lovingly dubbed him the 'prick with the stick' and we're sure Joyce would have loved the vulgar rhyme.

Further on is **Father Theobald Mathew** (1790–1856) the 'apostle of temperance'. There can't have been a tougher gig in Ireland, but he led a spirited campaign against 'the demon drink' in the 1840s and converted hundreds of thousands to teetotalism.

The top of the street is completed by the imposing statue of **Charles Stewart Parnell** (1846–91) the 'uncrowned king of Ireland', who was an advocate of Home Rule and became a political victim of Irish intolerance.

may have inspired him to write a story about a certain vampire who slept in a coffin...

FOUR COURTS
HISTORIC BUILDING

Map p249 (☑01-886 8000; Inns Quay; ⊘9am-5pm Mon-Fri; ☐25, 66, 67, 90 from city centre, ☐Four Courts) FREE This masterpiece by James Gandon (1743–1823) is a mammoth complex stretching 130m along Inns Quay, as fine an example of Georgian public architecture as there is in Dublin. Despite the construction of a brand-new criminal courts building further west along the Liffey, the Four Courts is still the enduring symbol of Irish law going about its daily business. Visitors are allowed to wander through the building, but not to enter courts or other restricted areas.

The Corinthian-columned central block, connected to flanking wings with enclosed quadrangles, was begun in 1786 and not completed until 1802. The original four courts (Exchequer, Common Pleas, King's Bench and Chancery) all branch off the central rotunda. In the lobby of the central rotunda you'll see bewigged barristers conferring and police officers handcuffed to their charges.

ARBOUR HILL CEMETERY
CEMETERY

Map p249 (☑01-821 3021; www.heritageireland.ie; Arbour Hill; ⊘8am-4pm Mon-Fri, 11am-4pm Sat, 9.30am-4pm Sun; ☐25, 25A, 37, 38, 39, 66, 67, 90, 134 from city centre, ☐Museum) FREE This small cemetery is the final resting place of all 14 of the executed leaders of the 1916 Easter Rising. The burial ground is plain, with the 14 names inscribed in stone. Beside the graves is a cenotaph bearing the Easter Proclamation, a focal point for official and national commemorations. There are excellent **guided tours** (Map p249; ⊘2pm Sun mid-Mar–mid-Oct;) FREE during the summer.

The front of the cemetery incongruously, but poignantly, contains the graves of British personnel killed in the War of Independence. Here, in the oldest part of the cemetery, as the gravestones toppled, they were lined up against the boundary walls where they still stand solemnly today.

HENRIETTA STREET
STREET

Map p249 (☐25, 25A, 37, 38, 39, 66, 67, 90, 134 from city centre, ☐Four Courts) Henrietta St dates from the 1720s and was the first project of Dublin's pre-eminent Georgian developer, Luke Gardiner. It was designed as an enclave of prestigious addresses (Gardiner himself lived at No 10), and remained one of Dublin's most fashionable streets until the Act of Union (1801). It's a wonderful insight into the evolution of Georgian residential architecture (p210), and features mansions of varying size and style.

DUBLIN WRITERS MUSEUM MUSEUM

Map p249 (www.writersmuseum.com; 18 N Parnell Sq; adult/child €8/5; ⊗9.45am-4.45pm Mon-Sat, 11am-4.30pm Sun; ⎕3, 7, 10, 11, 13, 16, 19, 46A, 123 from city centre) Memorabilia aplenty and lots of literary ephemera line the walls and display cabinets of this elegant museum devoted to preserving the city's rich literary tradition up to 1970. The building, comprising two 18th-century houses, is worth exploring on its own; Dublin stuccodore Michael Stapleton decorated the upstairs gallery.

However, the curious decision to omit living writers limits its appeal – no account at all is given to contemporary writers, who would arguably be more popular with today's readers.

Although the busts and portraits of the greats in the gallery upstairs warrant more than a cursory peek, the real draws are the ground-floor displays, which include Samuel Beckett's phone (with a button for excluding incoming calls, of course), a letter from the 'tenement aristocrat' Brendan Behan to his brother, and a 1st edition of Bram Stoker's *Dracula*.

The **Gorham Library** next door is worth a visit, and there's also a calming Zen garden. The basement restaurant, Chapter One (p141), is one of the city's best.

While the museum focuses on the dearly departed, the **Irish Writers Centre** (☑01-872 1302; www.irishwriterscentre.ie; 19 N Parnell Sq; ⊗10am-9pm Mon-Thu, to 5pm Fri) next door provides a meeting and working place for their living successors.

NATIONAL LEPRECHAUN MUSEUM MUSEUM

Map p249 (www.leprechaunmuseum.ie; Twilfit House, Jervis St; adult/child €14/10, Darkland Tour €16; ⊗10am-6.30pm, also 7-8.30pm Fri &

Sat May-Jun; ⎕all city centre, ⎕Jervis) Ostensibly designed as a child-friendly museum of Irish folklore, this is really a romper-room for kids sprinkled with bits of fairy tale. Which is no bad thing, even if the picture of the leprechaun painted here is more Lucky Charms and Walt Disney than sinister creature of pre-Christian mythology.

There's the optical illusion tunnel (which makes you appear smaller to those at the other end), the room full of oversized furniture, the wishing wells and, inevitably, the pot of gold; all of which is strictly for the kids. But if Walt Disney himself went on a leprechaun hunt when visiting Ireland during the filming of *Darby O'Gill and the Little People* in 1948, what the hell do we know? They've recently added the summertime Darkland Tour, a night-time storytelling session of dark and haunting tales of folklore.

ROTUNDA HOSPITAL ARCHITECTURE

Map p249 (☑01-873 0700; Parnell Sq; ⊗visiting hours 6-8pm; ⎕3, 10, 11, 13, 16, 19, 22 from city centre) Irish public hospitals aren't usually attractions, but this one – founded in 1748 as the first maternity hospital in the British Isles – makes for an interesting walk-by or an unofficial wander inside if you're interested in Victorian plasterwork. It shares its basic design with Leinster House (p92) because the architect of both, Richard Cassels, used the same floor plan to economise.

LIBERTY HALL LANDMARK

Map p249 (Eden Quay; ⊗closed to the public; ⎕all city centre) Dublin's second-tallest storied building is either a modernist masterpiece or an unconscionable eyesore, depending on how you see modern architecture. It was built between 1961 and 1965 to replace the original Liberty Hall, which had been a hotel before it was taken over by James Connolly's Irish Citizen Army in 1913. Today it's the headquarters of the Services, Industrial, Professional and Technical Union (SIPTU), Ireland's largest trade union, who've long wanted to demolish it and replace it with something new, but so far they've been denied planning permission on account of the building's 'architectural significance'.

JAMES JOYCE STATUE STATUE

Map p249 (N Earl St; ⎕all city centre, ⎕Abbey) Looking about with a bemused air from the corner of pedestrianised North Earl St is a small statue of James Joyce sculpted by US sculptor Marjorie Fitzgibbon. Wagsters

---

❶ STREET SMART

By day, O'Connell St is a bustle of activity, with shoppers, hawkers, walkers and others going about their business. At night, however, it can be a different story, as alcohol and drugs can give the street an air of menace and, sadly, the odd spot of trouble. Dubliners are sick of complaining that the police presence is virtually nonexistent (the police counter by declaring they're sick of their valuable resources constantly being cut), so you'll have to keep your wits about you.

like to refer to it as 'the prick with the stick'. Joyce would have loved the vulgar rhyme.

ST MARY'S PRO-CATHEDRAL   CHURCH

Map p249 (www.procathedral.ie; Marlborough St; ⊙8am-6.30pm; 🚇all city centre, 🚇Abbey) **FREE** Dublin's most important Catholic church is not quite the showcase you'd expect. It's in the wrong place for starters. The large neoclassical building, built between 1816 and 1825, was intended to stand where the GPO is, but Protestant objections resulted in its location on a cramped street that was then at the heart of Monto, the red-light district.

In fact, it's so cramped for space around here that you'd hardly notice the church's six Doric columns, which were modelled on the Temple of Theseus in Athens, much less be able to admire them. The interior is fairly functional, and its few highlights include a carved altar by Peter Turnerelli and the high relief representation of the Ascension by John Smyth. The best time to visit is 11am on Sunday when the Latin Mass is sung by the Palestrina Choir, with whom Ireland's most celebrated tenor, John McCormack, began his career in 1904. If you log on to the website during mass times you'll hear a live stream of the service.

ST GEORGE'S CHURCH   CHURCH

Map p249 (Hardwicke Pl; ⊙closed to the public; 🚇11, 16, 41 from city centre) One of Dublin's most beautiful buildings is this deconsecrated church, built by Francis Johnston between 1802 and 1813 in Greek Ionic style. It is topped by an eye-catching, 60m-high steeple modelled on that of St Martin-in-the-Fields in London. Alas, it has fallen into serious disrepair and has been shrouded in scaffolding for more than a decade.

Although this was one of Johnston's finest works, and the Duke of Wellington was married here, the building's neglect is largely due to the fact that it's Church of Ireland and not Roman Catholic – the Protestant (and largely moneyed) community for whom it was built has shrunk to the point of disappearance. The bells that Leopold Bloom heard in *Ulysses* were removed, the ornate pulpit was carved up and used to decorate a pub, and the spire is in danger of crumbling, which has resulted in the scaffolding.

SPIRE   MONUMENT

Map p249 (O'Connell St; 🚇all city centre, 🚇Abbey) The city's most visible landmark soars over O'Connell St and is an impressive bit of architectural engineering that was erected in 2001: from a base only 3m in diameter, it soars more than 120m into the sky and tapers into a 15cm-wide beam of light...it's tall and shiny and it does the trick rather nicely.

The brainchild of London-based architect Ian Ritchie, it is apparently the highest sculpture in the world, but much like the Parisian reaction to the construction of the Eiffel Tower, Dubliners are divided as to its aesthetic value and have regularly made fun of it. Among other names, we like 'the erection in the intersection', the 'stiletto in the ghetto', and the altogether brilliant 'eyeful tower'.

ST MARY'S CHURCH   CHURCH

Map p249 (Mary St; ⊙closed; 🚇Jervis) Designed by William Robinson in 1697, this is the most important church to survive from that period (although it's no longer in use and is closed to the public). John Wesley, founder of Methodism, delivered his first Irish sermon here in 1747 and it was the preferred church of Dublin's 18th-century social elite. Many famous Dubliners were baptised in its font, and Arthur Guinness was married here in 1793.

BELVEDERE HOUSE   HISTORIC BUILDING

Map p249 (6 Great Denmark St; ⊙closed to public; 🚇3, 10, 11, 13, 16, 19, 22 from city centre) This handsome building has been the home of Jesuit Belvedere College (a secondary school) since 1841. James Joyce studied here between 1893 and 1898 (and described his experiences in *A Portrait of the Artist as a Young Man*), and we can only wonder whether he ever took a moment to admire the magnificent plasterwork by master stuccodore Michael Stapleton in between catechism classes and arithmetic homework?

GARDEN OF REMEMBRANCE   PARK

Map p249 (www.heritageireland.ie; E Parnell Sq; ⊙8.30am-6pm Apr-Sep, 9.30am-4pm Oct-Mar; 🚇3, 10, 11, 13, 16, 19, 22 from city centre) This rather austere little park was opened by President Eamon de Valera in 1966 for the 50th anniversary of the Easter Rising. The most interesting feature in the garden is a bronze statue of the **Children of Lir** by Oisín Kelly; according to Irish legend the children were turned into swans by their wicked stepmother.

KING'S INNS   HISTORIC BUILDING

Map p249 (www.kingsinns.ie; Henrietta St; ⊙closed to the public; 🚇25, 25A, 66, 67, 90, 134 from city centre, 🚇Four Courts) Home to Dublin's legal profession (and where barristers are still trained), King's Inns occupies a classical building constructed by James Gandon between 1795 and 1817 on Constitution Hill, with Francis Johnston chipping in with the cupola. A fine example of Georgian public architecture, the building itself is, alas, only open to members and their guests.

 **EATING**

★ M&L
CHINESE €

Map p249 (☏01-874 8038; www.mlchineseres taurant.com; 13/14 Cathedral St; mains €9-13; ⏱11.30am-10pm Mon-Sat, noon-10pm Sun; 🚌all city centre) Beyond the plain frontage and the cheap-looking decor is Dublin's best Chinese restaurant...by some distance. It's usually full of Chinese customers, who come for the authentic Szechuan-style cuisine – spicier than Cantonese and with none of the concessions usually made to Western palates (no prawn crackers or curry chips).

★ OXMANTOWN
CAFE €

Map p249 (www.oxmantown.com; 16 Mary's Abbey, City Markets; sandwiches €5.50; ⏱7.30am-4pm Mon-Fri; 🚇Four Courts, Jervis) Delicious breakfasts and excellent sandwiches make this cafe one of the standout places for daytime eating on the north side of the Liffey. Locally baked bread, coffee supplied by Cloud Picker (Dublin's only microroastery) and meats sourced from Irish farms are the ingredients, but it's the way it's all put together that makes it so worthwhile.

TRAM CAFE
CAFE €

Map p249 (www.thetramcafe.com; Wolfe Tone Sq; mains €5-8; ⏱7am-6pm Mon-Wed & Fri, to 9pm Thu, 10am-6pm Sat & Sun; 🚇Jervis) The coffee and sandwiches are tasty, but it's the location that's special: a 1902 tram built by Brill in Philadelphia that lay in a field in County Cavan before being restored and transported to Dublin by its two owners. The 1920s musical soundtrack adds a touch of class.

COTTO
MEDITERRANEAN €

Map p249 (www.cotto.ie; 46 Manor St; mains €11-15; ⏱6-10pm Wed-Sun, 11am-3.30pm Sat & Sun; 🚌25, 25A, 66, 67 from city centre) Some of the very best pizzas in town are beautifully prepared in this lovely spot, which is run by the same folks behind Oxman-

town. Ingredients are local, but the end result is straight out of *la cucina Italiana*. Weekend brunches are a nice mix of Irish (sausage rolls, black pudding sandwiches) and Mediterranean (eggs shakshuka with grilled flatbreads and labneh).

BROTHER HUBBARD
CAFE €

Map p249 (☏01-441 6595; www.brotherhubbard. ie; 153 Capel St; dishes €7-11; ⏱8am-4.30pm Mon & Tue, 8am-10pm Wed-Fri, 9am-10pm Sat, 9am-4.30pm Sun; 🚌all city centre, 🚇Jervis) Anchored by its excellent baristas (beans by coffee experts 3FE), this cafe with a small garden at the back also does a nice menu of sandwiches, flatbreads and salads. The evening Mezze and Middle Eastern Feast menus are a sharing experience made up of a variety of small plates (reservations recommended). There's another branch (p70) south of the river.

THIRD SPACE
CAFE €

Map p249 (www.thirdspace.ie; Unit 14, Block C, Smithfield Market; mains €6-9; ⏱7am-6pm Mon-Fri, 9am-3pm Sat & Sun; 🚇Smithfield) One of the most welcoming cafes in town is this wonderful spot in Smithfield, which serves excellent breakfasts and fine sandwiches, as well as a lovely salad for that healthier option. Sit in the window, take out a book and just relax. The staff is fabulous. There's another branch across the Liffey on Aungier St.

SOUP DRAGON
FAST FOOD €

Map p249 (☏01-872 3277; www.soupdragon. com; 168 Capel St; mains €5-7.50; ⏱8am-5pm Mon-Fri; 🍴; 🚌all city centre, 🚇Jervis) Queues are a regular feature outside this fabulous spot which specialises in soups on the go – but it also does excellent stews, sandwiches, bagels and salads. The all-day breakfast options are excellent – we especially like the mini breakfast quiche of sausage, egg and bacon. Bowls come in two sizes and prices include fresh bread and a piece of fruit.

PANEM
CAFE €

Map p249 (www.panem.ie; 21 Lower Ormond Quay; sandwiches €4.80; ⏱8.15am-5.30pm Mon-Fri, 9am-5.30pm Sat, 10am-5.30pm Sun; 🚌all city centre) Not the capital from the *Hunger Games* but a long-standing quayside cafe that serves delicious sandwiches and wickedly sweet and savoury pastries, which are all made on-site. The croissants and brioche – filled with Belgian chocolate, almond cream or hazelnut *amaretti* – are the perfect snack for a holiday stroll. Lunchtimes are chaotic.

TAVERNA   ITALIAN €

Map p249 (⌨01-873 0040; www.wallacewinebars. ie; Quartier Bloom; salads & sandwiches €5-8, mains €8-9; ⊙12.30-10pm; ⌑ all city centre) Right in the heart of Quartier Bloom is this pleasant Italian eatery that serves simple pastas, antipasti and cheeses from the home country. Just a few steps away is its sister spot, the Enoteca Delle Langhe (p141), which mostly specialises in wines and cold cuts.

GOVINDA'S   VEGETARIAN €

Map p249 (83 Middle Abbey St; mains €9-15; ⊙noon-9pm Mon-Sat, to 7pm Sun; ⌕; ⌑ all city centre, ⌑ Abbey) An authentic beans-and-pulses place run by the Hare Krishna, with three branches in the city centre. Its cheap, wholesome mix of salads and Indian-influenced hot daily specials are filling and tasty.

★FISH SHOP   SEAFOOD €€

Map p249 (⌨01-430 8594; www.fish-shop.ie; 6 Queen St; 4-course/tasting menu €39/55; ⊙noon-2.30pm & 5-10pm Wed-Fri, 5-10pm Tue & Sat; ⌑25, 25A, 66, 67 from city centre, ⌑ Smithfield) The menu changes daily at this tiny restaurant (it has only 16 seats) to reflect what's good and fresh, but you'll have to trust them: your only choice is a four-course or tasting menu. One day you might fancy line-caught mackerel with a green sauce, another day slip sole with caper butter. Maybe the best seafood restaurant in town.

YARN   PIZZA €€

Map p249 (www.theyarnpizza.com; 37 Lower Liffey St; pizzas €9-14; ⊙5-10pm; ⌑ all city centre) With a 1st-floor terrace view of the Ha'Penny Bridge, this might be the city's coolest pizza joint. Add that it serves excellent drinks (pizza and Aperol, anyone?) and its credentials are rock solid. Oh, and the pizza – thin base, pomodoro San Marzano and delicious mozzarella – is delicious. It's the sister restaurant to the Woollen Mills (p140) – hence the name.

FISH & CHIP SHOP   FISH & CHIPS €€

Map p249 (⌨01-557 1473; www.fish-shop.ie; 76 Benburb St; mains €12.50-14.50; ⊙noon-1pm Tue-Fri, 4-10pm Sat & Sun; ⌑25, 25A, 66, 67 from city centre, ⌑ Museum) A classic fish-and-chip shop with a gourmet, sit-down twist – not only is the fish the best you'll taste in battered form, but you'll wash it down with a fine wine from

their carefully selected list. It's the original Fish Shop that moved from Queen St, where its fancier sister restaurant is now installed.

L MULLIGAN GROCER   MODERN IRISH €€

Map p249 (⌨01-670 9889; www.lmulligangrocer. com; 18 Stoneybatter; mains €15-29; ⊙4-10pm Mon-Fri, 12.30-10pm Sat & Sun; ⌑25, 25A, 66, 67 from city centre, ⌑ Museum) It's a great traditional pub, but the main reason to come here is for the food, all sourced locally and made by expert hands. The menu includes slow-cooked free-range pork belly and herb-crumbed haddock, as well as a particularly tasty lamb burger. There are about a dozen craft beers on draught and as many again in a bottle.

THUNDERCUT ALLEY   INTERNATIONAL €€

Map p249 (www.facebook.com/ThunderCutAlleyD7; Thundercut Alley; tapas €6-9; ⊙5.30-11pm Mon-Thu, 1-11pm Fri-Sun; ⌑ Smithfield) This tiny, hipper-than-thou joint is a great little spot full of electric-bright '80s decor with a menu of delicious cocktails and mouth-watering nibbles. If you're in the mood for a boozy brunch, it's one of the few venues in the city serving up bottomless mimosas.

LE BON CRUBEEN   IRISH €€

Map p249 (⌨01-704 0126; www.leboncrubeen.ie; 81-82 Talbot St; mains €15-24; ⊙noon-10.30pm; ⌑ Abbey) This is modern Irish cuisine with a subtle French twist, managing to combine hearty comfort food with classic elegance. The saloon-style restaurant is comfortable and cosy, despite its large size, and the menu is top quality, including good vegetarian options.

It's a great pre-theatre option if you're visiting the nearby Abbey Theatre (p143).

101 TALBOT   MODERN IRISH €€

Map p249 (www.101talbot.ie; 100-102 Talbot St; mains €18-24; ⊙noon-3pm & 5-11pm Tue-Sat; ⌑ all city centre) This Dublin classic has expertly resisted every trendy wave and has been a stalwart of good Irish cooking since opening more than two decades ago. Its speciality is traditional meat-and-two-veg dinners, but with Mediterranean influences: chargrilled swordfish with roasted sweet potato and chorizo; pan-roasted duck breast with fondant potato and grilled plums. Superb.

WOOLLEN MILLS   MODERN IRISH €€

Map p249 (www.thewoollenmills.com; 42 Lower Ormond Quay; sandwiches €10-11, mains €18-27;

⊙9am-11pm Mon-Fri, 9am-4pm & 5-11pm Sat, noon-4pm & 5-10.30pm Sun; 🖫all city centre) Styling itself as a modern Irish brasserie, this restaurant spread over two floors serves a spruced-up version of Irish farmhouse cooking, from tasty sandwiches to dishes such as smoked pork belly. For over a century the building was a much-loved knitwear shop (James Joyce worked here for a time), so you're dining in a piece of local history.

MUSASHI NOODLES
& SUSHI BAR   JAPANESE €€
Map p249 (🖉01-532 8057; www.musashidublin. com; 15 Capel St; mains €13-19; ⊙noon-10pm; 🖫all city centre, 🚇Jervis) One of the better Japanese restaurants in town is this low-lit spot that serves freshly crafted sushi and other Japanese specialities for those who don't fancy raw fish. The lunch bento deals are a steal. It's BYOB (corkage charged), and evening bookings are recommended. There is a branch in the IFSC (p148) and another near Merrion Sq (p95).

WINDING STAIR   MODERN IRISH €€
Map p249 (🖉01-873 7320; www.winding-stair.com; 40 Lower Ormond Quay; 2-course lunch €22, mains €22-28; ⊙noon-5pm & 5.30-10.30pm; 🖫all city centre) In a beautiful Georgian building that once housed the city's most beloved bookshop – the ground floor still is one (p144) – the Winding Stair's conversion to elegant restaurant has been faultless. The wonderful Irish menu (creamy fish pie, bacon and organic cabbage, steamed mussels, and Irish farmyard cheeses) coupled with an excellent wine list makes for a memorable meal.

YAMAMORI SUSHI   JAPANESE €€
Map p249 (www.yamamorinoodles.ie; 38-39 Lower Ormond Quay; sushi €4-4.50, mains €17-35; ⊙noon-10.30pm; 🖫all city centre) A sibling of the long-established Yamamori (p74) on South Great George's St, this large restaurant – spread across two converted Georgian houses and including a bamboo garden – does Japanese with great aplomb, serving up all kinds of favourites from steaming bowls of ramen to a delicious *nami moriawase* (sushi platter).

MORRISON GRILL   INTERNATIONAL €€
Map p249 (🖉01-878 2999; www.morrisonhotel.ie; Morrison Hotel, Lower Ormond Quay; mains €18-31; ⊙noon-10pm; 🖫all city centre) The main restaurant at the Morrison Hotel (p185) is really a very fancy grill whose specialities are meats

cooked in Ireland's only Josper indoor barbecue oven. If you don't fancy steaks, burgers or grilled fish, there's a selection of other main courses, but the real treat here is food cooked at over 260°C.

ENOTECA DELLE LANGHE   ITALIAN €€
Map p249 (www.wallacewinebars.ie; Bloom's Lane; mains €14-20; ⊙12.30pm-midnight; 🚇Jervis) Developer, Italophile and, latterly, outspoken parliamentarian Mick Wallace's Italian Quarter – as the lane between Ormond Quay and Great Strand St is known – has a trio of eateries that serve simple pastas, antipasti and cheeses. It also has an excellent selection of Piedmontese wines.

★CHAPTER ONE   MODERN IRISH €€€
Map p249 (🖉01-873 2266; www.chapterone restaurant.com; 18 N Parnell Sq; 2-course lunch €32.50, 4-course dinner €75; ⊙12.30-2pm Tue-Fri, 7.30-10.30pm Tue-Sat; 🖫3, 10, 11, 13, 16, 19, 22 from city centre) Flawless haute cuisine and a relaxed, welcoming atmosphere make this Michelin-starred restaurant in the basement of the Dublin Writers Museum our choice for best dinner experience in town. The food is French-inspired contemporary Irish, the menus change regularly and the service is top-notch. The three-course pre-theatre menu (€39.50) is great if you're going to the Gate (p143) around the corner.

🍸 DRINKING & NIGHTLIFE

★COBBLESTONE   PUB
Map p249 (www.cobblestonepub.ie; N King St; ⊙4.30-11.30pm Mon-Thu, to 12.30am Fri & Sat, 1.30-11.30pm Sun; 🚇Smithfield) It advertises itself as a 'drinking pub with a music problem', which is an apt description for this Smithfield stalwart – although the traditional music sessions that run throughout the week can hardly be described as problematic. Wednesday's Balaclava session (from 7.30pm) is for any musician who is learning an instrument, with musician Síomha Mulligan on hand to teach.

CONFESSION BOX   PUB
Map p249 (🖉01-874 7339; www.c11407968.wix site.com/ryan; 88 Marlborough St; ⊙11am-11pm Mon-Fri, 10am-midnight Sat & Sun; 🚇Abbey) This historic pub is popular with tourists and locals alike. Run by some of the

ONE FOOT IN THE GRAVE

A contender for best pub in Dublin is **John Kavanagh's** (Gravediggers; ☎01-830 7978; 1 Prospect Sq; 🚌13, 19, 19A from O'Connell St) of Glasnevin, more commonly known as the Gravediggers because the employees from the adjacent cemetery had a secret serving hatch so that they could drink on the job. Founded in 1833, it is reputedly Dublin's oldest family-owned pub: the current owners are the sixth generation of Kavanaghs to be in charge. Inside, it's as traditional a boozer as you could hope: stone floors, lacquered wooden wall panels and all. In summer time the green of the square is full of drinkers basking in the sun, while inside the hardened locals ensure that ne'er a hint of sunshine disturbs some of the best Guinness in town. An absolute classic.

friendliest bar staff you're likely to meet, it's also a good spot to brush up on your local history: the pub was a favourite spot of Michael Collins, one of the leaders in the fight for Irish independence.

WALSHE'S   PUB

Map p249 (6 Stoneybatter; ⊙10.30am-11.30pm Mon-Thu, to 12.30am Fri & Sat, noon-11pm Sun; 🚌25, 25A, 66, 67 from city centre, 🚂Museum) If the snug is free, a drink in Walshe's is about as pure a traditional experience as you'll have in any pub in the city; if it isn't, you'll have to make do with the old-fashioned bar, where the friendly staff and brilliant clientele (a mix of locals and trendsetting imports) are a treat. A proper Dublin pub.

PANTIBAR   GAY & LESBIAN

Map p249 (www.pantibar.com; 7-8 Capel St; ⊙5-11.30pm Mon, Wed & Sun, to 2am Tue, to 2.30am Thu-Sat; 🚌all city centre) A raucous, fun gay bar owned by Rory O'Neill, aka Panti, star of 2015's acclaimed documentary *The Queen of Ireland,* about the struggle for equality that climaxes in the historic marriage referendum of May 2015. The bar has since become a place of LGBTQ pilgrimage – and no-holds-barred enjoyment.

DICE BAR   BAR

Map p249 (☎01-633 3936; www.dicebar.com; 79 Queen St; ⊙4pm-midnight Mon-Thu, 3pm-1am Fri & Sat, 3-11.30pm Sun; 🚌25, 25A, 66, 67 from city centre, 🚂Museum) More of a New York dive bar than a traditional Dublin pub, Dice Bar was originally owned by Huey from the Fun Lovin' Criminals. He's since sold his interest, but the look has stayed the same: black-and-red painted interior, dripping candles and stressed seating. Add the rocking DJs and you've got one of the northside's most popular bars.

GRAND SOCIAL   BAR

Map p249 (☎01-874 0076; www.thegrandsocial.ie; 35 Lower Liffey St; ⊙4pm-2.30am Thu-Sat, to 11.30pm Sun-Wed; 🚌all city centre, 🚂Jervis) This multipurpose venue hosts club nights, comedy and live-music gigs, and is a decent bar for a drink. It's spread across three floors, each of which has a different theme: the Parlour downstairs is a cosy, old-fashioned bar; the midlevel Ballroom is where the dancing is; and the upstairs Loft hosts a variety of events.

HUGHES' BAR   PUB

Map p249 (19 Chancery St; ⊙10.30am-11.30pm Mon-Thu, to 12.30am Fri & Sat, noon-11pm Sun; 🚌25, 66, 67, 90 from city centre, 🚂Four Courts) Traditional purists love the music sessions at this pub, which kick off at around 9.30pm nightly Saturday through Tuesday. By day, the pub caters to the sobering conversations of barristers, solicitors and their clients from the nearby Four Courts (p135).

WIGWAM   BAR

Map p249 (www.wigwamdublin.com; 54 Middle Abbey St; ⊙11am-11.30pm Mon-Thu, to 2.30am Fri & Sat; 🚌all city centre, 🚂Abbey) The latest venture by the Bodytonic crew, this excellent new bar serves 50 types of craft beer and 100 different rums on the ground floor and excellent music in the basement bar, where top-notch DJs play regularly. It also does Brazilian-influenced bar grub.

OVAL   PUB

Map p249 (☎01-872 1259; 78 Middle Abbey St; 🚌all city centre, 🚂Abbey) This is a great little pub, where young and old come together in conversation and rich, creamy pints go down a treat. The Tardis effect is evident once you walk through the door: it is much bigger than it looks from the outside, spreading over three floors.

BEYOND THE ROYAL CANAL

The Royal Canal, constructed from 1790, marks the traditional boundary of the city centre's northern edge, and beyond it, amid the semi-detached suburban dwellings, are a handful of sights that are well worth a visit.

Croke Park Experience

The Gaelic Athletic Association (GAA) considers itself not just the governing body of a bunch of Irish games but also the stout defender of a cultural identity that is ingrained in Ireland's sense of self. To get an idea of just how important the GAA is, a visit to the **Croke Park Experience** (www.crokepark.ie; Clonliffe Rd, New Stand, Croke Park; adult/child museum €7/5, museum & tour €14/9; ⊙9.30am-6pm Mon-Sat, 10.30am-5pm Sun Jun-Aug, 9.30am-5pm Mon-Sat, 10.30am-5pm Sun Sep-May; ⌂3, 11, 11A, 16, 16A, 123 from O'Connell St) is a must. The twice-daily tours (except match days) of the impressive Croke Park stadium are excellent, and well worth the extra cost. The stadium's most recent attraction is the **Skyline** (adult/child €20/12; ⊙half-hourly 10.30am-3.30pm Mon-Sat, from 11.30am Sun Jul & Aug, 11.30am & 2.30pm Mon-Fri, half-hourly 10.30am-2.30pm Sat, from 11.30am Sun rest of year), a guided tour around the stadium roof.

Glasnevin Cemetery

The tombstones at Ireland's largest and most historically important **burial site** (Prospect Cemetery; www.glasnevintrust.ie; Finglas Rd; tours €10; ⊙10am-5pm, tours hourly 10.30am-3.30pm; ⌂40, 40A, 40B from Parnell St) FREE read like a 'who's who' of Irish history, as most of the leading names of the last 150 years are buried here.

A modern replica of a round tower acts as a handy landmark for locating the tomb of Daniel O'Connell, who died in 1847. Charles Stewart Parnell's tomb is topped with a large granite rock, on which only his name is inscribed – a remarkably simple tribute to a figure of such historical importance. Other notable people buried here include Sir Roger Casement, Republican leader Michael Collins, docker and trade unionist Jim Larkin, and poet Gerard Manley Hopkins.

The history of the cemetery is told in wonderful, award-winning detail in the **museum** (museum €4.50, museum & tour €10; ⊙10am-6pm Mon-Fri), which tells the social and political story of Ireland through the lives of the people, known and unknown, who are buried here. The best way to visit the cemetery is to take one of the daily tours.

National Botanic Gardens

Founded in 1795, the 19.5-hectare **botanic gardens** (Botanic Rd; ⊙9am-6pm Mon-Sat, 11am-6pm Sun Apr-Oct, 10am-4.30pm Mon-Sat, 11am-4.30pm Sun Nov-Mar; ⌂13, 13A, 19 from O'Connell St, 34, 34A from Middle Abbey St) FREE are home to a series of curvilinear glasshouses, dating from 1843 to 1869, created by Richard Turner. Within these Victorian masterpieces you will find the latest in botanical technology, including a series of computer-controlled climates reproducing environments of different parts of the world. Among the pioneering botanical work conducted here was the first attempt to raise orchids from seed, back in 1844.

Casino at Marino

It's not the roulette-wheel kind of casino but the original Italian kind, the one that means 'summer home', and this particular **casino** (www.casinomarino.ie; Malahide Rd; closed due to essential maintenance work from June 2017, check website for reopening details; ⌂20A, 20B, 27, 27B, 42, 42C, 123 from city centre) is one of the most enchanting constructions in all of Ireland. It was built in the mid-18th century for the Earl of Charlemont, who returned from his grand tour of Europe with more art than he could store in his own home, Marino House. He also came home with a big love of the Palladian style – hence the architecture of this wonderful folly.

The exterior of the building, with a huge entrance doorway, and 12 Tuscan columns forming a templelike facade, creates the expectation that its interior will be a simple single open space. But instead it is an extravagant convoluted maze. A variety of statuary adorns the outside but it's the amusing fakes that are most enjoyable.

SACKVILLE LOUNGE — PUB

Map p249 (Sackville Pl; ⊘11am-11.30pm Mon-Thu, to 12.30am Fri & Sat, noon-11pm Sun; ▣all city centre, ▣Abbey) This tiny 19th-century, one-room, wood-panelled bar lies just off O'Connell St and is popular with actors from the nearby Abbey Theatre, as well as a disproportionate number of elderly drinkers. It's a good pub for a solitary pint.

QUAY 14 — BAR

Map p249 (📞01-878 2999; Morrison Hotel, Lower Ormond Quay; ⊘9am-11pm Sun-Thu, to 12.30am Fri & Sat; ▣all city centre, ▣Jervis) Sleek and contemporary, the main bar at Morrison Hotel (p185) is perfectly adequate if you fancy an evening in a bar that is indistinguishable from a fancy hotel bar found in any city pretty much anywhere.

NEALON'S — PUB

Map p249 (📞01-872 3247; 165 Capel St; ⊘12.30-11.30pm Mon-Thu, to 12.30am Fri & Sat, 1-11pm Sun; ▣all city centre, ▣Jervis) The warm and cosy decor of this traditional pub is matched by the exceptionally friendly staff. There's a pub quiz on Tuesday nights.

 ## ⭐ ENTERTAINMENT

ABBEY THEATRE — THEATRE

Map p249 (📞01-878 7222; www.abbeytheatre.ie; Lower Abbey St; ▣all city centre, ▣Abbey) Ireland's national theatre was founded by WB Yeats in 1904 and was a central player in the development of a consciously native cultural identity. In 2017 it appointed Neil Murray and Graham McLaren of the National Theatre of Scotland as its new directors, and they have promised an exciting new program that will fuse traditional and contemporary fare.

The Abbey's contemporary relevance is a popular subject of debate in the Irish cultural scene, but for visitors it offers the best chance of seeing classic Irish plays (as well as the work of new dramatists) in an established theatrical context.

GATE THEATRE — THEATRE

Map p249 (📞01-874 4045; www.gatetheatre.ie; 1 Cavendish Row; ⊘performances 7.30pm Mon-Sat, 2.30pm Wed; ▣all city centre) The city's most elegant theatre, housed in a late 18th-century building, features a generally unflappable repertory of classic Irish,

American and European plays. Orson Welles and James Mason played here early in their careers. Even today it is the only theatre in town where you might see established international movie stars work on their credibility with a theatre run.

LIGHT HOUSE CINEMA — CINEMA

Map p249 (📞01-872 8006; www.lighthousecinema.ie; Smithfield Plaza; ▣all city centre, ▣Smithfield) The most impressive cinema in town is this snazzy four-screener in a stylish building just off Smithfield Plaza. The menu offers a mix of art-house and mainstream releases, documentaries and Irish films.

ACADEMY — LIVE MUSIC

Map p249 (📞01-877 9999; www.theacademydublin.com; 57 Middle Abbey St; ▣all city centre, ▣Abbey) A terrific midsize venue, the Academy's stage has been graced by an impressive list of performers on the way up – and down – the ladder of success, from Ron Sexsmith to the Wedding Present.

AMBASSADOR THEATRE — THEATRE

Map p249 (📞1890 925 100; www.ambassadordublin.com; S Parnell Sq; ▣all city centre) The Ambassador started life as a theatre and then became a cinema. It's now primarily an exhibition and performance space, hosting everything from contemporary science exhibits to live action performances. Not much has changed inside; if you get the opportunity to do so, it's worth checking out the retro interior.

CINEWORLD MULTIPLEX — CINEMA

Map p249 (📞0818 304 204; www.cineworld.ie; Parnell Centre, Parnell St; ▣all city centre) This 17-screen cinema shows only commercial releases. The seats are comfy, the concession stand is huge and the selection of pick 'n' mix could induce a sugar seizure. It lacks the charm of the older-style cinemas, but we like it anyway.

LAUGHTER LOUNGE — COMEDY

Map p249 (📞01-878 3003; www.laughterlounge.com; 4-8 Eden Quay; from €20; ⊘doors open 7.30pm; ▣all city centre) Dublin's only specially designated comedy theatre is where you'll find those comics too famous for the smaller pub stages but not famous enough to sell out the city's bigger venues. Think comedians on the way up (or on the way down).

SAVOY
CINEMA

Map p249 (☑01-874 6000; Upper O'Connell St; ⊙from 2pm; ▣all city centre) The Savoy is a five-screen, first-run cinema, and has late-night shows at weekends. Savoy Cinema 1 is the largest in the city and its enormous screen is the perfect way to view really spectacular blockbuster movies.

🛍 SHOPPING

WINDING STAIR
BOOKS

Map p249 (☑01-872 6576; www.winding-stair. com; 40 Lower Ormond Quay; ⊙10am-6pm Mon-Wed & Fri, to 7pm Thu & Sat, noon-6pm Sun; ▣all city centre) This handsome old bookshop is in a ground-floor room when once upon a time it occupied the whole building, which is now given over to an excellent restaurant (p140) of the same name. Smaller selection, but still some excellent quality new and old-book perusals.

ARNOTT'S
DEPARTMENT STORE

Map p249 (☑01-805 0400; www.arnotts.ie; 12 Henry St; ⊙10am-6pm Mon-Wed, Fri & Sat, to 7pm Thu, noon-6pm Sun; ▣all city centre) Occupying a huge block with entrances on Henry, Liffey and Abbey Sts, this is our favourite of Dublin's department stores. It stocks virtually everything, from garden furniture to high fashion, and it's all relatively affordable.

LOUIS COPELAND
CLOTHING

Map p249 (☑01-872 1600; www.louiscopeland. com; 39-41 Capel St; ⊙9am-6pm Mon-Wed, Fri & Sat, noon-5pm Sun; ▣all city centre, ▣Jervis) A branch of the fashionable men's designer store. Dublin's answer to Savile Row.

PENNEY'S
DEPARTMENT STORE

Map p249 (☑01-888 0500; www.primark.co.uk; 47 Mary St; ⊙8.30am-8pm Mon-Wed, to 9pm Thu & Fri, to 7pm Sat, 10.30am-7pm Sun; ▣all city centre) Ireland's cheapest department store is a northside favourite, a place to find all kinds of everything without paying a fortune for it – it's the best place in town for men's socks and jocks. True, the stuff you'll find here isn't guaranteed to last, but at prices like these, why quibble over quality?

MOORE STREET MARKET
MARKET

Map p249 (Moore St; ⊙8am-4pm Mon-Sat; ▣all city centre) A shadow of its vibrant former self, this is the most traditional of Dublin street markets. You can get fruit, fish and flowers, while other vendors hawk cheap cigarettes and other products. Don't try to buy just one banana though – if it says 10 for €1, that's what it is.

EASON'S
BOOKS

Map p249 (☑01-873 3811; www.easons.com; 40 Lower O'Connell St; ⊙8am-7pm Mon-Wed & Sat, to 9pm Thu, to 8pm Fri, noon-6pm Sun; ▣all city centre, ▣Abbey) The biggest selection of magazines and foreign newspapers in the whole country can be found on the ground floor of this huge bookshop near the GPO, along with literally dozens of browsers leafing through mags with ne'er a thought of purchasing one.

DUBLIN CITY GALLERY – THE HUGH LANE SHOP
ARTS & CRAFTS

Map p249 (www.hughlane.ie; N Parnell Sq, Charlemont House; ⊙10am-6pm Tue-Thu, to 5pm Fri & Sat, 11am-5pm Sun; ▣7, 11, 13, 16, 38, 40, 46A, 123 from city centre) A cultural playground for adults, where you can dig out cubist fridge magnets, huge po-mo hanging mobiles, masterpiece colour-by-number prints, cloth puppets, unusual wooden toys and beautiful art and pop-culture hardbacks.

JERVIS CENTRE
SHOPPING CENTRE

Map p249 (☑01-878 1323; www.jervis.ie; Jervis St; ⊙9am-6.30pm Mon-Wed, Fri & Sat, to 7pm Thu, 11am-6.30pm Sun; ▣all city centre) This modern, domed mall is a veritable shrine to the British chain store. Boots, Topshop, Debenhams, Argos, Dixons, M&S and Miss Selfridge all get a look-in.

🏃 SPORTS & ACTIVITIES

ADVENTUREROOMS
LIVE CHALLENGE

Map p249 (☑01-872 7243; www.adventure rooms.ie; 6-7 Little Britain St, Campbell's Court; per person €19-33; ⊙10am-8pm; ▣Jervis) This is a good way to test your friendships: you'll be locked into a room and to win your freedom you'll need to work together to solve a series of puzzles. An excellent rainy afternoon activity, it's very popular with stag and hen parties as well as for corporate team-building. All bookings must be made in advance.

Docklands & the Grand Canal

Neighbourhood Top Five

1 **Jeanie Johnston** (p147) Visiting this working replica of a 19th-century 'coffin' ship, as the barques transporting emigrants during the Famine were known.

2 **Famine Memorial** (p147) Contemplating the Famine while walking gently among Rowan Gillespie's thought-provoking bronze statues.

3 **Bord Gáis Energy Theatre** (p149) Attending a gig at this spectacular theatre designed by Daniel Libeskind.

4 Poolbeg Lighthouse (p148) Enjoying stunning views of the bay and city with a late-afternoon stroll down the south wall to this elegant lighthouse.

5 **3 Arena** (p150) Attending a performance at Dublin's largest indoor arena.

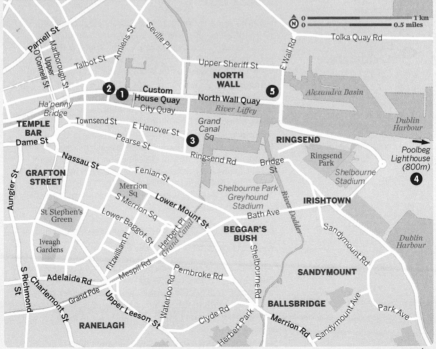

For more detail of this area see Map p252 and p253 ➡

Lonely Planet's Top Tip

Grand Canal Dock has a couple of decent spots for food, but even better ones are to be found southwest at the junction of Haddington Rd, Upper Grand Canal St and Bath Ave, where you'll find a handful of terrific restaurants and popular pubs.

🍷 Best Places to Drink

➡ Slattery's (p149)

➡ John Mulligan's (p149)

For reviews, see p149 ➡

✖ Best Places to Eat

➡ Juniors (p148)

➡ Paulie's Pizza (p148)

➡ Workshop Gastropub (p148)

For reviews, see p148 ➡

◉ Best Architecture

➡ Convention Centre (p148)

➡ Bord Gáis Energy Theatre (p149)

➡ Marker (p186)

For reviews, see p148 ➡

Explore Docklands & the Grand Canal

Although much of the Docklands development that transformed the eastern end of the Liffey towards Dublin Port is given over to office and apartment blocks, there are parts of 'Canary Dwarf' (as it's jokingly named, after London's Canary Wharf) that are worth exploring at ground level. The aesthetic of the area is the 10,000-sq-metre Grand Canal Sq, designed by American landscape architect Martha Schwartz. Flanking its northwestern side is the magnificent 2010 Bord Gáis Energy Theatre (p149), designed by Daniel Libeskind and named after its primary sponsor, one of Ireland's leading energy providers. Stretching across the square from its entrance is a red 'carpet' – a series of red, resin-glass angled sticks that glow – and a green one – made up of polygon-shaped planters filled with marshlike vegetation.

On the north bank of the Liffey, the standout buildings are the snazzy Convention Centre (p148), designed by Kevin Roche; the Custom House (p147), a colossal Georgian building topped by a copper dome; and the city's premier indoor venue, the 3 Arena (p150), which is the main attraction in the Point Village, a development which also includes a cinema and a hotel.

Local Life

➡**Sustenance** For proper Neapolitan-style pizza, Paulie's Pizza (p148) is one of the best in town; just around the corner (and owned by the same two brothers) is the equally popular Juniors (p148), which attracts the trendy crowd with its version of a Brooklyn eatery.

➡**Imbibe** There's a fine choice of public houses in the area, including two traditional gems: Slattery's (p149) and, closer to the city centre, John Mulligan's (p149). The latter is one of the best pubs in the country.

➡**Explore** Irish emigration is a major theme in the Docklands – aboard the Jeanie Johnston (p147); wandering among Rowan Gillespie's haunting statues (p147); exploring the hands-on, interactive exhibits of EPIC The Irish Emigration Museum (p147), devoted to the Irish diaspora; and exploring your own family history at the Irish Family History Centre (p147).

Getting There & Away

➡**Bus** The most convenient public transport option is the bus – Nos 1, 47, 56A and 77A go from Dame St to the edge of Grand Canal Sq. For the northside, bus 151 goes from Bachelor's Walk to the Docklands.

➡**Tram** The Luas Red Line terminus is at the Point Village.

➡**Train** The DART stops at Grand Canal Quay.

SIGHTS

IRISH FAMILY HISTORY CENTRE
CULTURAL CENTRE

Map p252 (☎01-671 0338; www.irishfamily
historycentre.com; CHQ Bldg, Custom House
Quay; €9.50, incl EPIC The Irish Emigration
Museum €22; ⊙10am-5pm; 🚇George's Dock)
Discover your family history with interactive screens where you can track your surname and centuries of Irish emigration.
The ticket price also includes a 15-minute
consultation with a genealogist. You can
visit as part of the EPIC exhibition or buy
a separate ticket.

EPIC THE IRISH EMIGRATION MUSEUM
MUSEUM

Map p252 (☎01-906 0861; www.epicchq.com;
CHQ Bldg, Custom House Quay; adult/child
€14/7; ⊙10am-6.45pm, last entrance 5pm;
🚇George's Dock) This is a high-tech, interactive exploration of emigration and its
effect on Ireland and the 70 million or so
people spread throughout the world who
claim Irish ancestry. Start your visit with
a 'passport' and proceed through 20 interactive – and occasionally moving – galleries examining why they left, where they
went and how they maintained their relationship with their ancestral home.

FAMINE MEMORIAL
MEMORIAL

Map p252 (Custom House Quay; 🚇all city centre) Just east of the Custom House is one
of Dublin's most thought-provoking examples of public art: the set of life-size bronze
figures (1997) by Rowan Gillespie known
simply as *Famine*. Designed to commemorate the ravages of the Great Hunger
(1845–51), their haunted, harrowed look
testifies to a journey that was both hazard-
ous and unwelcome.

The location of the sculptures is also
telling, for it was from this very point in
1846 that one of the first 'coffin ships' (as
they came to be known) set sail for the
USA. Steerage fare on the *Perseverance*
was £3 and 210 passengers made that first
journey, landing in New York on 18 May
1846, with all passengers and crew intact.

In June 2007 a second series of *Famine*
sculptures by Rowan Gillespie was unveiled on the quayside in Toronto's Ireland
Park by Irish president Mary McAleese to
commemorate the arrival of Famine refugees in the New World.

CUSTOM HOUSE
MUSEUM

Map p252 (Custom House Quay; ⊙9am-5pm
Mon-Fri; 🚇all city centre) Georgian genius
James Gandon (1743–1823) announced his
arrival on the Dublin scene with this magnificent building (1781–91), constructed
just past Eden Quay at a wide stretch in
the River Liffey. It's a colossal, neoclassical pile that stretches for 114m topped by
a copper dome, beneath which the **visitor
centre** (Map p252; Custom House Quay; €1.50;
⊙10am-12.30pm Mon-Fri, 2-5pm Sat & Sun mid-
Mar–Oct, closed Mon, Tue & Sat Nov–mid-Mar;
🚇all city centre) features a small museum
on Gandon and the history of the building.
You only get access to a small part of the
building though.

Best appreciated from the south side of
the Liffey, its fine detail deserves closer
inspection. Below the frieze are heads
representing the gods of Ireland's 13 principal rivers; the sole female head, above
the main door, represents the River Liffey.
The cattle heads honour Ireland's beef
trade, and the statues behind the building represent Africa, America, Asia and
Europe. Set into the dome are four clocks
and, above that, a 5m-high statue of Hope.

JEANIE JOHNSTON
MUSEUM

Map p252 (www.jeaniejohnston.ie; Custom House
Quay; adult/student/child/family €10/9/5.50/25;
⊙tours hourly 10am-4pm Apr-Oct, 11am-3pm Nov-
Mar; 🚇all city centre, 🚇George's Dock) One of
the city's most original tourist attractions is
an exact working replica of a 19th-century
'coffin ship', as the sailing boats that transported starving emigrants away from Ireland during the Famine were gruesomely
known. A small on-board museum details
the harrowing plight of a typical journey,
which usually took around 47 days.

This particular ship, a three-masted
barque originally built in Quebec in 1847,
made 16 transatlantic voyages, carrying
more than 2500 people, and never suffered
a single death. The ship also operates as a
Sail Training vessel, with journeys taking
place from May to September. If you are visiting during these times, check the website
for details of when it will be in dock.

GRAND CANAL SQUARE
SQUARE

Map p252 (🚇Grand Canal Dock) The square
was designed by American landscape artist
Martha Schwartz and opened in 2008. Its
most distinctive feature is the red 'carpet'

WORTH A DETOUR

POOLBEG LIGHTHOUSE

One of the city's most rewarding walks is a stroll along the Great South Wall to the **Poolbeg Lighthouse** (South Wall; ⏰24hr; 🚌1, 47, 56A, 77A, 84N from city centre), that red tower visible in the middle of Dublin Bay. The lighthouse dates from 1768, but it was redesigned and rebuilt in 1820. To get there, take the bus to Ringsend from the city centre, and then make your way past the power station to the start of the wall (it's about 1km). It's not an especially long walk out to the lighthouse – about 800m or so – but it will give you a stunning view of the bay and the city behind you, a view best enjoyed just before sunset on a summer's evening.

made of bright red resin-glass paving covered with red glowing angled light sticks.

SAMUEL BECKETT BRIDGE   BRIDGE
Map p252 (🚉Spencer Dock) Spanish architect Santiago Calatrava's second Dublin bridge (his first is the James Joyce Bridge; 2003) is this wishbone-design structure (2007) in the Docklands at Spencer Dock.

CONVENTION CENTRE   LANDMARK
Map p252 (Spencer Dock, North Wall Quay; ⏰closed to the public; 🚌Mayor Square – NCI) The angled, tubelike Convention Centre was designed by Kevin Roche in 2011.

 EATING

CHQ FARMERS' MARKET   MARKET €
Map p252 (www.irishfarmersmarkets.ie; CHQ Bldg; ⏰11am-3pm Fri; 🚌George's Dock) From fresh pastas and sauces to homemade chocolates, this farmers market in the CHQ Building has quality produce from a range of local producers. It is popular with office workers looking for good food and treats on a Friday afternoon.

EDDIE ROCKET'S   DINER €
Map p252 (📞01-524 0152; North Wall Quay; burgers €7-9; ⏰11.30am-10pm Sun-Thu, to 11pm Fri & Sat; 🚌Mayor Square – NCI) Burgers served '50s diner style. There are locations all over the city centre.

★JUNIORS DELI & CAFE   ITALIAN €€
Map p252 (📞01-664 3648; www.juniors.ie; 2 Bath Ave; mains €18-21; ⏰8.30am-2.30pm & 5.30-10pm Mon-Fri, 11am-3pm & 5.30-10.30pm Sat, 11am-3.30pm Sun; 🚌3 from city centre, 🚉Grand Canal Dock) Cramped and easily mistaken for any old cafe, Juniors is anything but ordinary. Designed to imitate a New York

deli, the food (Italian-influenced, all locally sourced produce) is delicious, the atmosphere always buzzing (it's often hard to get a table) and the ethos top-notch, which is down to the two brothers who run the place.

PAULIE'S PIZZA   ITALIAN €€
Map p252 (www.juniors.ie; 58 Upper Grand Canal St; pizzas €12-18; ⏰6-10pm; 👪; 🚌3 from city centre, 🚉Grand Canal Dock) At the heart of this lovely, occasionally boisterous restaurant is a Neapolitan pizza oven, used to create some of the best pizzas in town. Margheritas, *biancas* (no tomato sauce), calzoni and other Neapolitan specialities are the real treat, but there's also room for a classic New York slice and a few local creations.

WORKSHOP GASTROPUB   MODERN IRISH €€
Map p252 (Kennedy's; 📞01-677 0626; www.theworkshopgastropub.com; 10 George's Quay; mains lunch €7-9, dinner €10-24; ⏰noon-3pm Mon-Fri, to 4.45pm Sat & Sun; 📶; 🚌all city centre, 🚉Tara St) Take a traditional pub and introduce a chef with a vision: hey presto, you've got a gastropub (surprisingly one of the few in the city) serving burgers, *moules frites* (mussels served with French fries) and sandwiches, as well as a good range of salads.

MUSASHI IFSC   JAPANESE €€
Map p252 (📞01-555 73 73; www.musashidublin.com; Unit 2, Burton Hall, Custom House Sq; mains €12-18; ⏰noon-10pm Sun-Thu, to 11pm Fri & Sat; 🚌Mayor Square – NCI) Freshly made sushi, sashimi and other Japanese specialities, including a particularly tasty *tatsuta* chicken, served to an appreciative lunchtime and after-work crowd. It is the sister restaurant to Musashi Noodles & Sushi Bar (p140) on Capel St.

ELY BAR & BRASSERIE

ELY BAR & BRASSERIE

ELY BAR & BRASSERIE

ELY BAR & BRASSERIE

ELY BAR & BRASSERIE

ELY BAR & BRASSERIE

ELY BAR & BRASSERIE

ELY BAR & BRASSERIE

ELY BAR & BRASSERIE

ELY BAR & BRASSERIE

ELY BAR & BRASSERIE FUSION €€
Map p252 (01-672 0010; www.elywinebar.ie; Custom House Quay; mains €16-28; noon-11pm Mon-Fri, 4pm-midnight Sat; George's Dock) Scrummy homemade burgers, bangers and mash, and wild smoked salmon salad are some of the meals served in this converted tobacco warehouse in the International Financial Services Centre (IFSC). Dishes are prepared with organic and free-range produce from the owner's family farm in County Clare, so you can be assured of the quality.

HERBSTREET FUSION €€
Map p252 (01-675 3875; www.herbstreet.ie; Hanover Quay; mains €13-19; 8.30am-10pm Mon-Fri, 10am-4pm Sat & Sun; Grand Canal Dock) Low-power hand driers, one-watt LED bulbs, secondhand furniture and strictly European wines: this eatery is taking its green responsibilities seriously. Most of the food is sourced locally, but what really makes this place a hit is the terrific brunch menu – pancakes, Irish breakfasts, Mexican-style eggs...it's all good.

QUAY 16 FUSION €€
Map p252 (01-817 8760; www.mvcillairne.com; MV Cill Airne, North Wall Quay; bar food €4-12, mains €15-28; noon-3pm Mon-Fri, 6-10pm Mon-Sat; Spencer Dock) The MV *Cill Airne*, commissioned in 1961 as a passenger liner tender, is now permanently docked along the north quays, where it serves the public as a bar, a bistro and a fine restaurant. Dishes such as Himalayan-salt-aged fillet steak and pan-roasted sea bass are expertly prepared and served alongside an excellent variety of wines.

DRINKING & NIGHTLIFE

★JOHN MULLIGAN'S PUB
Map p252 (www.mulligans.ie; 8 Poolbeg St; 10.30am-11.30pm Mon-Thu, to 12.30am Fri & Sat, noon-11pm Sun; all city centre) This brilliant old boozer is a cultural institution, established in 1782 and in this location since 1854. A drink (or more) here is like attending liquid services at a most sacred, secular shrine. John F Kennedy paid his respects in 1945, when he joined the cast of regulars that seems barely to have changed since.

SLATTERY'S PUB
Map p252 (01-668 5481; www.slatterysd4.ie; 62 Upper Grand Canal St; 1-11.30pm Mon-Thu, noon-12.30am Fri & Sat, noon-11pm Sun; 4, 7, 8, 120 from city centre) A decent boozer that is a favourite with rugby fans who didn't get tickets to the match – they congregate around the TVs and ebb and flow with each passage of the game. It's also popular on Friday and Saturday nights.

LONG STONE PUB
Map p252 (01-671 8102; 10-11 Townsend St; noon-midnight Sun-Thu, to 1am Fri & Sat; all city centre, Tara St) This is too big a boozer to be an 'old man pub', but it was established in 1754, the flagstone floors are original and the pint it serves is a good one. This is a favourite with students from Trinity College and is usually packed with revellers on a good night out.

☆ ENTERTAINMENT

BORD GÁIS ENERGY THEATRE THEATRE
Map p252 (01-677 7999; www.grandcanaltheatre.ie; Grand Canal Sq; Grand Canal Dock) Forget the uninviting sponsored name: Daniel Libeskind's masterful design is a three-tiered, 2100-capacity auditorium where you're as likely to be entertained by the Bolshoi or a touring state opera as you are to see *Disney on Ice* or Barbra Streisand. It's a magnificent venue – designed for classical, paid for by the classics.

ODEON CINEMA CINEMA
Map p252 (www.odeoncinemas.ie; Point Village; The Point) A six-screen multiplex showing all the latest releases.

SHELBOURNE PARK GREYHOUND STADIUM SPECTATOR SPORT
Map p252 (1890 269 969; www.igb.ie; South Lotts Rd; packages €12-45; 6.30-10.30pm Tue & Thu-Sat; 3, 7, 7A, 8, 45, 84 from city centre) A top-class dog track with terrific vantage points from the glassed-in restaurant, where you can eat, bet and watch without leaving your seat. There's a free **shuttle service** (Map p252; 7pm Fri & Sat) Friday and Saturday only from Burgh Quay.

3 ARENA LIVE MUSIC

Map p252 (☎01-819 8888; www.3arena.ie; East Link Bridge, North Wall Quay; tickets €30-90; ⏲6.30-11pm; ☐The Point) The premier indoor venue in the city has a capacity of 23,000 and plays host to the brightest touring stars in the firmament. Radiohead, Bob Dylan and Take That performed here in 2017.

🔒 SHOPPING

DESIGN TOWER ARTS & CRAFTS

Map p252 (☎01-677 5655; www.thedesigntower. com; Pearse St; ⏲9am-5pm Mon-Fri; ☐Grand Canal Dock) Housed in a 19th-century warehouse that was Dublin's first iron-structured building, this seven-storey design centre houses studios for around 20 local craftspeople, producing everything from Celtic-inspired jewellery to wall hangings and leather bags. Some studios are open by appointment only; check the website for details.

🏃 SPORTS & ACTIVITIES

WAKEDOCK ADVENTURE SPORTS

Map p252 (☎01-664 3883; www.wakedock.ie; Grand Canal Dock; 30min tuition adult/student €60/45; ⏲noon-8pm Tue-Fri, 10am-8pm Sat & Sun; ☐1, 15A, 15B, 56A, 77A from city centre, ☐Grand Canal Dock) Try the relatively new sport of cable wakeboarding – waterskiing by holding on to a fixed overhead cable instead of a motorboat. The sport is shortlisted for the 2020 Olympics. You can also rent wetsuits (€2).

MARKIEVICZ LEISURE CENTRE HEALTH & FITNESS

Map p252 (☎01-672 9121; www.dublincity.ie; Townsend St; adult/child €7/3.50; ⏲7am-9.45pm Mon-Thu, to 8.45pm Fri, 9am-5.45pm Sat, 10am-3.45pm Sun; ☐all city centre, ☐Tara St) This excellent fitness centre has a swimming pool, a workout room (with plenty of gym machines) and a sauna. You can swim for as long as you please, but children are only allowed at off-peak times (10am to 5.30pm Monday to Saturday).

The Southside

Neighbourhood Top Five

❶ Aviva Stadium (p155) Cheering on Leinster or Ireland (in either rugby or football) is one of the more memorable ways to spend a few hours.

❷ Herbert Park (p153) Strolling, sitting or jogging around this glorious stretch of greenery is an ideal way to spend a sunny day in Dublin.

❸ Dinner in Ranelagh (p153) Dining in handsome Ranelagh is always a treat, especially in spots like the Butcher Grill.

❹ National Print Museum (p153) Exploring the surprisingly interesting history of printing in Ireland at this terrific little museum.

❺ Metropolis (p25) Engaging with the superb musicians, artists and speakers at this interdisciplinary festival over three days and six stages.

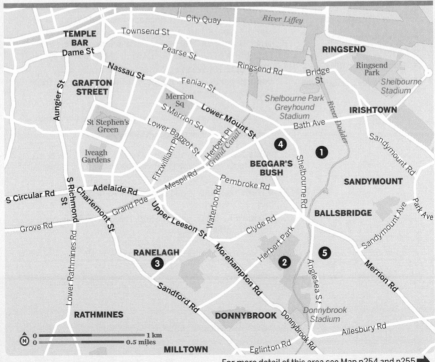

For more detail of this area see Map p254 and p255 ➡

Lonely Planet's Top Tip

Herbert Park (p153) is an excellent spot for a run and can be easily reached on foot from most city-centre hotels.

✕ Best Places to Eat

➡ Farmer Brown's (p153)
➡ Dillinger's (p153)
➡ Butcher Grill (p153)
➡ Chophouse (p153)

For reviews, see p153 ➡

❦ Best Places to Drink

➡ Beggar's Bush (p155)
➡ Taphouse (p155)

For reviews, see p155 ➡

▐ Best Places to Sleep

➡ Aberdeen Lodge (p186)
➡ Dylan (p186)
➡ Ariel House (p186)

For reviews, see p186 ➡

THE SOUTHSIDE

Explore the Southside

Ballsbridge is 2km southeast of St Stephen's Green and so within walking distance; another 2km to the south is Donnybrook, home to the Royal Dublin Society Showground (p155) and Donnybrook Stadium (p155) – the glorious expanse of Herbert Park (p153) is nearby.

Ranelagh is the loveliest of the villages immediately south of the Grand Canal; it's a pleasant, 2km walk south along Camden St and across the bridge; it's also easily accessible on the Luas green line. Rathmines, immediately west of Ranelagh, is accessible by bus 14 or 15 from the city centre, but it's not as pleasant a spot to amble about in. Rathgar, southwest of Rathmines, is the other village in Dublin 6, but it's strictly residential.

Local Life

➡ **Sustenance** Gourmands from all over the city trek to the likes of Butcher Grill (p153) and Dillinger's (p153) in Ranelagh, and Farmer Brown's (p153) on Bath Ave for the relaxed weekend brunch.

➡ **Sleeping** Even Dubliners take a night away from home...in their own city. Luxury B&Bs like Aberdeen Lodge (p186) and Ariel House (p186) are great choices, while for a little glam there's always the Dylan (p186).

➡ **Drinking** Neighbourhood locales like the Taphouse (p155) in Ranelagh and Beggar's Bush (p155) on Haddington Rd are hugely popular with locals and other Dubliners – the latter is especially popular for fans going to and from a match in the Aviva.

➡ **Exercise** Herbert Park (p153) is one of the most popular parks in the city for all kinds of exercise, from running to tennis.

Getting There & Away

➡ **Bus** From the city centre, take bus Nos 5, 7, 7A, 8, 45, 46 to Ballsbridge; for Donnybrook the 10A or 46; and for Rathmines Nos 14 or 15.

➡ **Tram** The Luas green line serves Ranelagh from St Stephen's Green.

➡ **Train** The DART serves Sandymount (for Bath Ave) and Lansdowne Road.

◉ SIGHTS

NATIONAL PRINT MUSEUM   MUSEUM

Map p254 (📞01-660 3770; www.nationalprint
museum.ie; Haddington Rd, Garrison Chapel, Beggar's Bush; adult/concession €3.50/2; ◷9am-5pm
Mon-Fri, 2-5pm Sat & Sun; 🚌4, 7 from city centre,
🚉Grand Canal Dock, Lansdowne Rd) You don't
have to be into printing to enjoy this quirky
little museum, where personalised guided
tours (11.30am daily and 2.30pm Monday,
Tuesday, Thursday and Friday) are offered in
a delightfully casual and compelling way. A
video looks at the history of printing in Ireland and then you wander through the various (still working) antique presses amid the
smell of ink and metal.

The guides are excellent and can tailor the
tours to suit your special interests – for example, anyone interested in history can get
a detailed account of the difficulties encoun-
tered by the rebels of 1916 when they tried
to have the proclamation printed. Upstairs
there are lots of old newspaper pages recording important episodes in Irish history over
the last century.

HERBERT PARK   PARK

Map p254 (Ballsbridge; ◷dawn-dusk; 🚌5, 7, 7A,
8, 45, 46, 🚉Sandymount, Lansdowne Rd) A gorgeous swath of green lawns, ponds and
flower beds near the Royal Dublin Society
Showground (p155). Sandwiched between
prosperous Ballsbridge and Donnybrook, the
park runs along the River Dodder. There's
tennis courts and a playground here too.

✗ EATING

⭐FARMER BROWN'S   INTERNATIONAL €€

Map p254 (📞01-660 2326; www.farmerbrowns.
ie; 25a Bath Ave; brunch €10-12, dinner €14-26;
◷11am-10pm Mon-Fri, 10am-10pm Sat & Sun; 📶;
🚌7, 8 from city centre, 🚉Grand Canal Dock) The
hicky-chic decor and mismatched furniture
won't be to everyone's liking, but there's no
disagreement about the food, which makes
this spot our choice for best brunch in Dublin. From healthy smashed avocado to a stunning Cuban pork sandwich, it has all your
lazy breakfast needs covered. Very much
worth the effort. There's another branch
(p155) in Rathmines.

CHOPHOUSE   GASTROPUB €€

Map p254 (📞01-660 2390; www.thechophouse.
ie; 2 Shelbourne Rd; lunch €12-25, dinner €19-35;

DA NORT'SOYID & THE SOUTHSYDE

It is commonly assumed that the southside is totally posh and the northside
is a derelict slum – it makes the jokes
easier to crack and the prejudices
easier to maintain. But the truth is a
little more complex. The 'southside'
generally refers to Dublin 4 and the
fancy suburbs immediately west and
south – conveniently ignoring the traditionally working-class neighbourhoods
in southwestern Dublin such as Bluebell
and Tallaght. North Dublin is huge, but
the northside tag is usually applied to
the inner suburbs, where incomes are
lower, accents are more pronouncedly
Dublin and – most recently – the influx
of foreign nationals is more in evidence.
All Dubliners are familiar with the posh
twit stereotype born and raised on the
southside, but there's another kind of
Dubliner, usually from the middle-class
districts of northern Dublin, who affects
a salt-of-the-earth accent while talking
about the 'gee-gees' and says things
like 'tis far from sushi we was rared'
while tucking into a *maki* roll.

◷restaurant noon-2.30pm & 6-10pm Mon-Fri,
5-10pm Sat, 1-8pm Sun; 🚌4, 7, 8, 120 from city
centre) This fine sprawling bar is a terrific
gastropub where the focus is on juicy cuts
of steak, but reluctant carnivores also have a
choice of fish, chicken or lamb dishes. It does
an excellent Sunday lunch – the slow-braised
pork belly is delicious. It's a popular watering hole when there's a match on at the Aviva
Stadium (p155).

BUTCHER GRILL   INTERNATIONAL €€

Map p254 (📞01-498 1805; www.thebutchergrill.
ie; 92 Ranelagh Rd; mains €20-28; ◷5.30-9.30pm
Sun-Wed, to 10.30pm Thu-Sat, plus noon-3pm Sat
& Sun; 🚉Ranelagh) No surprise that this terrific spot specialises in meat, which is locally
sourced and cooked to perfection in its wood-
smoked grill. From barbecued baby back ribs
to a superb *côte de boeuf* (rib steak) to share
– there are few spots in town where the meat
sweats are so welcome. Locals will also argue
that the brunch is the best in the city.

DILLINGER'S   AMERICAN €€

Map p254 (📞01-497 8010; www.dillingers.ie;
47 Ranelagh Rd; ◷5.30-9.30pm Mon & Tue, to

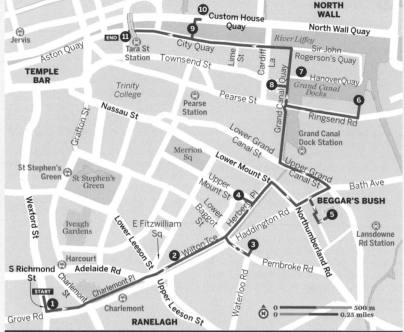

THE SOUTHSIDE

Neighbourhood Walk
Portobello Pub to City Quay

START PORTOBELLO PUB
END WORKSHOP GASTROPUB
LENGTH 5KM; 2½ HOURS

Begin at the ❶ **Portobello Pub** (South Richmond St), a popular watering hole built to service the solid hunger of workers building the canal.

Turn left at the Grand Canal and begin your stroll along the towpath. About 300m past Leeson St Bridge is the statue of ❷ **Patrick Kavanagh**, relaxing on a bench. The Monaghan-born poet is immortalised in the spot he loved most in Dublin – where he couldn't get barred.

When you get to Baggot St Bridge take a right onto Baggot St and refuel at ❸ **Searson's** (42–44 Upper Baggot St), a popular bar. Return to the canal and continue east, diverting left at Upper Mount St for ❹ **St Stephen's Church** (Upper Mount St), a Greek Revival structure known as the 'pepper canister' on account of its curious shape.

Back on the towpath, turn right at Northumberland Rd and left onto Haddington Rd

for one of Dublin's secret little treasures (the vast majority of Dubliners don't even know about it): the ❺ **National Print Museum** (p153). Housed in the old Beggar's Bush barracks, this is a surprisingly interesting museum, especially if you're a fan of old books and the printing process in general.

Turn left onto Upper Grand Canal St, then right into Grand Canal Quay and onto Grand Canal Sq – the heartland of the Docklands. You can try some wakeboarding at ❻ **Wakedock** (p150) if you like, and then sit outside at one of the cafes or restaurants around the dock – ❼ **Herbstreet** (p149) is an excellent choice – and be sure to take in the ❽ **Bord Gáis Energy Theatre** (p149).

Walk north to Sir John Rogerson's Quay and west along City Quay. On the far side of the Liffey, just beyond the ❾ **Samuel Beckett Bridge** (p148), designed by Santiago Calatrava, you'll see the eye-catching ❿ **Convention Centre** (p148). Finally, if you need another spot of sustenance, the ⓫ **Workshop Gastropub** (p148) is the perfect spot to end your tour – with either a beer or food (or both).

10.30pm Wed & Thu, to 11pm Fri, 11am-4pm & 5.30-11pm Sat, 11am-4pm & 5.30-9.30pm Sun; ⌂Ranelagh) This trendy American-style diner is small, so expect a wait if you want to go for the (excellent) weekend brunch. It's worth it just to taste the amazing things they can do with pulled pork, and if you're craving American-style pancakes, this is the place for you.

KINARA
PAKISTANI €€

Map p254 (☎01-406 0066; www.kinarakitchen. ie; 17 Ranelagh Rd; mains €19-30; ⌚5-11pm daily, plus noon-3pm Thu & Fri, 1-5pm Sun; ⌂Ranelagh) Connoisseurs of the various cuisines of South Asia can distinguish between Indian and Pakistani fare; this exceptional restaurant specialising in the latter will soon educate even the most inexperienced palate. Curries like *nehari gosht* (made with beef) are superb, as are fish dishes, including the *machali achari* (fillet of red snapper simmered with pickles).

FARMER BROWN'S
INTERNATIONAL €€

Map p254 (☎086-046 8837; www.farmerbrowns. ie; 170 Lower Rathmines Rd; mains €10-26; ⌚10am-10pm Mon-Sat, to 9pm Sun; ⌂14, 15 from city centre) A second branch of the much-loved restaurant on Bath Ave (p153), offering virtually the same delicious menu. Rathmines' dining scene has improved as a result.

SABA
ASIAN €€

Map p254 (www.sabadublin.com; 22 Upper Baggot St; mains lunch €9-15, dinner €17-26; ⌚noon-10.30pm Mon-Sat, to 9pm Sun; ⌂5, 7, 7A, 8, 18, 45 from city centre) Asian fusion – mostly Thai and Vietnamese – is a popular hit at this thoroughly contemporary restaurant. It's a branch of the original restaurant (p74) on Clarendon St.

DRINKING

BEGGAR'S BUSH
PUB

Map p254 (Jack Ryan's; 115 Haddington Rd; ⌚11am-11pm; ⌂4, 7, 8, 120 from city centre, ⌂Grand Canal Dock) A staunch defender of the traditional pub aesthetic, Ryan's (as it's referred to by its older clientele) has adjusted to the modern age by adding an outside patio for good weather. Everything else, though, has remained the same, which is precisely why it's so popular with flat-capped pensioners and employees from nearby Google.

TAPHOUSE
BAR

Map p254 (☎01-491 3436; www.taphouse.ie; 60 Ranelagh Rd; ⌚12.30pm-12.30am Mon-Sat, to 11pm

Sun; ⌂Ranelagh) Locals refer to it by its original name of Russell's, but that doesn't mean that the regulars aren't delighted with the spruce-up the new owners have brought to a village favourite. What they didn't change was the beloved balcony – the best spot to have a drink on a warm day.

⭐ ENTERTAINMENT

BOWERY
LIVE MUSIC

Map p254 (www.thebowery.ie; 196 Lower Rathmines Rd; ⌚5pm-midnight Sun-Thu, to 12.30am Fri & Sat; ⌂14, 65, 140) With its burnished wood, intricate chandeliers and ship-shaped stage, this music venue is one of the best-looking bars in the city. It features live performances every night of the week, from ska to disco to reggae, and upstairs is an excellent people-watching spot.

AVIVA STADIUM
STADIUM

Map p254 (☎01-238 2300; www.avivastadium.ie; 11-12 Lansdowne Rd; ⌂Lansdowne Rd) Gleaming 50,000-capacity ground with an eye-catching curvilinear stand in the swanky neighbourhood of Donnybrook. Home to Irish rugby and football internationals.

ROYAL DUBLIN SOCIETY SHOWGROUND
SPECTATOR SPORT

Map p254 (☎01-668 9878; Merrion Rd, Ballsbridge; ⌂7 from Trinity College) This impressive, Victorian-era showground is used for various exhibitions throughout the year. The most important annual event here is the late-July **Dublin Horse Show**, which includes an international showjumping contest. Leinster rugby also plays its home matches in the 35,000-capacity arena.

The Royal Dublin Society Showground was founded in 1731 and has had its headquarters in a number of well-known Dublin buildings, including Leinster House from 1814 to 1925. The society was involved in the foundation of the National Museum, National Library, National Gallery and National Botanic Gardens.

DONNYBROOK STADIUM
STADIUM

Map p254 (www.leinsterrugby.ie; Donnybrook Rd; ⌂10, 46A from city centre) This purpose-built, 6000-capacity arena is shared by a bunch of rugby teams, including the Ireland Wolfhounds (the junior national side), the Ireland Women's Team, Leinster 'A' and local club sides Old Wesley and Bective Rangers. Tickets are easily available for virtually all games.

THE SOUTHSIDE DRINKING

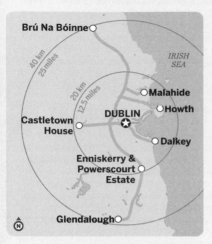

Day Trips from Dublin

Howth 167

A seaside village with terrific restaurants at the foot of a bulbous head with fine walks.

Enniskerry & Powerscourt Estate 170

A Palladian mansion with a stunning garden and even better views of the surrounding countryside.

Castletown House & Around 172

Ireland's largest Palladian home, built for the 18th century's richest man.

Dalkey 173

A picturesque, compact village by the sea with a nice harbour and coastal walks.

Malahide 174

A delightful north Dublin village with a 12th-century castle and 101 hectares of tended gardens.

TOP SIGHT
BRÚ NA BÓINNE

The vast Neolithic necropolis known as Brú na Bóinne (the Boyne Palace) is one of the most extraordinary sites in Europe. A thousand years older than Stonehenge, it's a powerful testament to the mind-boggling achievements of prehistoric humankind.

History

The complex was built to house the remains of those in the top social tier and its tombs were the largest artificial structures in Ireland until the construction of the Anglo-Norman castles 4000 years later. The area consists of many different sites; the three principal ones are Newgrange, Knowth and Dowth.

Over the centuries the tombs decayed, were covered by grass and trees, and were plundered by everybody from Vikings to Victorian treasure hunters, whose carved initials can be seen on the great stones of Newgrange. The countryside around the tombs is home to countless other ancient tumuli (burial mounds) and standing stones.

Brú na Bóinne Visitor Centre

Built in a spiral design echoing Newgrange, this superb interpretive centre houses interactive exhibits on prehistoric Ireland and its passage tombs. It has regional tourism info and an excellent cafe, plus a book and souvenir shop. Upstairs, a glassed-in observation mezzanine looks out over Newgrange.

All visits to Newgrange and/or Knowth depart from here.

DON'T MISS

→ Brú na Bóinne Visitor Centre
→ Newgrange
→ Winter Solstice experience
→ Knowth

PRACTICALITIES

→ 🕿041-988 0300
→ www.heritageireland.ie
→ Donore
→ adult/child visitor centre €4/3, visitor centre & Newgrange €7/4, visitor centre & Knowth €6/4, all 3 sites €13/8
→ ⊙9am-7pm Jun–mid-Sep, 9am-6.30pm May & mid-Sep–early Oct, 9.30am-5.30pm Feb-Apr & early Oct-early Nov, 9am-5pm early Nov-Jan

Brú na Bóinne

All visits start at the **❶ visitor centre**, which has a terrific exhibit that includes a short context-setting film. From here, you board a shuttle bus that takes you to **❷ Newgrange**, where you'll go past the **❸ kerbstone** into the **❹ main passage** and the **❺ burial chamber**. If you're not a lucky lottery winner for the solstice, fear not – there's an artificial illumination ceremony that replicates it. If you're continuing on to tour **❻ Knowth**, you'll need to go back to the visitor centre and get on another bus; otherwise, you can drive directly to **❼ Dowth** and visit, but only from outside (the information panels will tell you what you're looking at).

Newgrange Interior Passage
The passage is lined with 43 orthostats, or standing stones, averaging 1.5m in height: 22 on the left (western) side, 21 on the right (eastern) side.

WIEDITMEDIA/GETTY IMAGES ©

FRANK BACH/SHUTTERSTOCK ©

Knowth
Roughly one third of all megalithic art in Western Europe is contained within the Knowth complex, including more than 200 decorated stones. Alongside typical motifs like spirals, lozenges and concentric circles are rare crescent shapes.

TOP TIP
Best time to visit is early morning mid-week during summer, when there are fewer tourists and no school tours.

LM SPENCER/SHUTTERSTOCK ©

Newgrange Entrance Kerbstone
Newgrange is surrounded by 97 kerbstones (24 of which are still buried), numbered sequentially from K1, the beautifully decorated entrance stone.

Newgrange
Newgrange's passage grave is designed to allow for a solar alignment during the winter solstice

FACT FILE
The winter solstice event is witnessed by a maximum of 50 people selected by lottery and their guests (one each). In 2015, 30,475 people applied.

Dowth
There is no public access to the two passage chambers at Dowth. The crater at the top was due to a clumsy attempt at excavation in 1847.

⑦

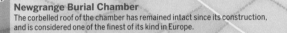

Newgrange Burial Chamber
The corbelled roof of the chamber has remained intact since its construction, and is considered one of the finest of its kind in Europe.

①

Brú na Bóinne Visitor Centre
Opened in 1997, the modern visitor centre was heavily criticised at first as being unsuitable, but then gained plaudits for the way it was integrated into the landscape.

GUIDED TOURS

Brú na Bóinne is one of the most popular tourist attractions in Ireland, and there are plenty of organised tours. Most depart from Dublin. Options include the highly recommended **Mary Gibbons Tours** (✆086 355 1355; www. newgrangetours.com; tour incl entrance fees adult/ child €40/35; ☎).

The **Brú na Bóinne Visitor Centre has a cafe and a picnic area outside (no food or drink is permitted at the monuments themselves). Otherwise, Slane and Drogheda have plenty of options. Drogheda has large supermarkets.**

HERITAGE CARD

If you're planning to visit several archaeological and historic sites, consider investing in a **Heritage Card** (www. heritageireland.ie; adult/ child €40/10), valid for one year and available to buy at the **Battle of the Boyne Site** (www.battle oftheboyne.ie; Drybridge; adult/child €5/2; ☺9am-5pm May-Sep, to 4pm Oct-Apr) ticket office, as well as other participating sites throughout the country. For more information, contact Heritage Ireland (www. heritageireland.ie).

Newgrange

A startling 80m in diameter and 13m high, Newgrange's white round stone walls, topped by a grass dome, look eerily futuristic. Underneath lies the finest Stone Age passage tomb in Ireland – one of the most remarkable prehistoric sites in Europe. Dating from around 3200 BC, it predates Egypt's pyramids by some six centuries.

The tomb's precise alignment with the sun at the time of the winter solstice suggests it was also designed to act as a calendar.

No one is quite sure of its original purpose, however – the most common theories are that it was a burial place for kings or a centre for ritual.

Newgrange's name derives from 'New Granary' (the tomb did in fact serve as a repository for wheat and grain at one stage), although a more popular belief is that it comes from the Irish for 'Cave of Gráinne', a reference to a popular Celtic myth. The Pursuit of Diarmuid and Gráinne tells of the illicit love between the woman betrothed to Fionn McCumhaill (or Finn McCool), leader of the Fianna, and Diarmuid, one of his most trusted lieutenants. When Diarmuid was fatally wounded, his body was brought to Newgrange by the god Aengus in a vain attempt to save him, and the despairing Gráinne followed him into the cave, where she remained long after he died. This suspiciously Arthurian tale (substitute Lancelot and Guinevere for Diarmuid and Gráinne) is undoubtedly a myth, but it's still a pretty good story. Newgrange also plays another role in Celtic mythology as the site where the hero Cúchulainn was conceived.

Over time, Newgrange, like Dowth and Knowth, deteriorated and at one stage was even used as a quarry. The site was extensively restored in 1962 and again in 1975.

A superbly carved **kerbstone** with double and triple spirals guards the tomb's main entrance, but the area has been reconstructed so that visitors don't have to clamber in over it. Above the entrance is a slit, or roof-box, which lets light in. Another beautifully decorated kerbstone stands at the exact opposite side of the mound. Some experts say that a **ring of standing stones** encircled the mound, forming a great circle about 100m in diameter, but only 12 of these stones remain, with traces of others below ground level.

Holding the whole structure together are the 97 boulders of the **kerb ring**, designed to stop the mound from collapsing outwards. Eleven of these are decorated with motifs similar to those on the main entrance stone, although only three have extensive carvings.

The white quartzite that encases the tomb was originally obtained from Wicklow, 70km south – in an age before horse and wheel, it was transported by sea and then up the River Boyne. More than 200,000 tonnes of earth and stone also went into the mound.

You can walk down the narrow 19m passage, lined with 43 stone uprights (some of them engraved), which leads into the tomb chamber about one-third of the way into the colossal mound. The chamber has three recesses, and in these are large basin stones that held cremated human bones. As well as the remains, the basins would have held funeral offerings of beads and pendants, but these were stolen long before the archaeologists arrived.

Above, the massive stones support a 6m-high corbel-vaulted roof. A complex drainage system means that not a drop of water has penetrated the interior in 40 centuries.

Newgrange Winter Solstice

At 8.20am on the winter solstice (between 18 and 23 December), the rising sun's rays shine through the roof-box above the entrance, creep slowly down the long passage and illuminate the tomb chamber for 17 minutes. There is little doubt that this is one of the country's most memorable, even mystical, experiences.

There's a simulated winter sunrise for every group taken into the mound. To be in with a chance of witnessing the real thing on one of six mornings around the solstice, enter the free lottery that's drawn in late September; 50 names are drawn and each winner is allowed to take one guest (be aware, however, that over 30,000 people apply each year). Fill out the form at the Brú na Bóinne Visitor Centre or email brunaboinne@opw.ie.

Knowth

Northwest of Newgrange, the burial mound of Knowth was built around the same time. It has the greatest collection of passage-grave art ever uncovered in Western Europe. Early excavations cleared a passage leading to the central chamber which, at 34m, is much longer than the one at Newgrange. In 1968, a 40m passage was unearthed on the opposite side of the mound.

Excavations continue, and were due to close the site from November 2017 to Easter 2018.

Also in the mound are the remains of six early-Christian souterrains (underground chambers) built into the side. Some 300 carved slabs and 17 satellite graves surround the main mound.

Human activity at Knowth continued for thousands of years after its construction, which accounts for the site's complexity. The Beaker folk, so called because they buried their dead with drinking vessels, occupied the site in the Early Bronze Age (c 1800 BC), as did the Celts in the Iron Age (c 500 BC). Remnants of bronze and iron workings from these periods have been discovered. Around AD 800 to 900, it was turned into a *ráth* (earthen ring fort), a stronghold of the very powerful O'Neill clan. In 965 it was the seat of Cormac MacMaelmithic, later Ireland's high king for nine years, and in the 12th century the Normans built a motte and bailey (a raised mound with a walled keep) here. The site was finally abandoned around 1400.

Visits start only from the visitor centre.

Dowth

The circular mound at Dowth is similar in size to Newgrange – about 63m in diameter – but is slightly taller at 14m high. Due to safety issues, Dowth's tombs are closed to visitors, though you can visit the mound (and its resident grazing sheep) from the L1607 road between Newgrange and Drogheda.

North of the tumulus are the ruins of **Dowth Castle** and **Dowth House**.

TOP SIGHT
GLENDALOUGH

ARNDALE/SHUTTERSTOCK ©

If you've come to Wicklow, chances are that a visit to Glendalough (Gleann dá Loch, meaning 'Valley of the Two Lakes') is one of your main reasons. And you're not wrong, for this is one of the most beautiful corners of the whole country and the epitome of the kind of rugged, romantic Ireland that probably drew you to the island in the first place.

The substantial remains of this important monastic settlement are certainly impressive, but an added draw is the splendid setting: two dark and mysterious lakes tucked into a long, glacial valley fringed in forest. It is, despite its immense popularity, a deeply tranquil and spiritual place, and you will have little difficulty in understanding why those solitude-seeking monks came here in the first place.

History

In AD 498 a young monk named Kevin arrived in the valley looking for somewhere to kick back, meditate and be at one with nature. He pitched up in what had been a Bronze Age tomb on the southern side of the Upper Lake and for the next seven years slept on stones, wore animal skins, maintained a near-starvation diet and – according to the legend – became bosom buddies with the birds and animals. Kevin's ecofriendly lifestyle soon attracted a bunch of disciples, all seemingly unaware of the irony that they were flocking to hang out with a hermit who wanted to live as far away from other people as possible. Over the next couple of centuries his one-man operation mushroomed into a proper settlement and by the 9th century Glendalough rivalled Clonmacnoise as the island's premier monastic city. Thousands of students studied and lived in a thriving community that was spread over a considerable area.

Inevitably Glendalough's success made it a key target for Viking raiders, who sacked the monastery at least four times between 775 and 1071. The final blow came in 1398, when

DON'T MISS

➡ Monastic Site
➡ Reefert Church
➡ St Kevin's Cell
➡ Walking options (p166)
➡ Visitor Centre

PRACTICALITIES

➡ www.glendalough.ie
➡ 25km south of Dublin
➡ admission free
➡ ⊘24hr
➡ P
➡ St Kevin's Bus (www.glendaloughbus.com;one-way/return €9/15)

English forces from Dublin almost destroyed it. Efforts were made to rebuild and some life lingered on here as late as the 17th century when, under renewed repression, the monastery finally died.

Lower Lake

Monastic Site

Nestled between two lakes, haunting Glendalough is one of the most significant monastic sites in Ireland centred on a 1000-year-old **round tower**, a ruined **cathedral** and the tiny church known as **St Kevin's Kitchen**. It was founded in the late 6th century by St Kevin, a bishop who established a monastery on the Upper Lake's southern shore and about whom there is much folklore.

During the Middle Ages, when Ireland was known as 'the island of saints and scholars', Glendalough became a monastic city catering to thousands of students and teachers. The site is entered through the only surviving **monastic gateway** in Ireland.

At the centre of Glendalough's graveyard, to the southwest of the cathedral, is the **Priest's House**. This odd building dates from 1170 but has been heavily reconstructed. It may have been the location of shrines of St Kevin. Later, during penal times, it became a burial site for local priests – hence the name.

St Mary's Church

The 10th-century St Mary's Church, to the southwest of the round tower, stands outside the walls of the monastic site and belonged to local nuns. It has a lovely western doorway.

Deer Stone

At the junction with Green Rd as you cross the river just south of the monastic site is the Deer Stone, set in the middle of a group of rocks. Legend claims that when St Kevin needed milk for two orphaned babies, a doe stood here waiting to be milked. The stone is actually a *bullaun* (a stone used as a mortar for grinding medicines or food).

Many such stones are thought to be prehistoric, and they were widely regarded as having supernatural properties: women who bathed their faces with water from the hollow were supposed to keep their looks forever. The early churchmen brought the stones into their monasteries, perhaps hoping to inherit some of their powers.

Upper Lake

Teampall na Skellig and the Stone Fort

The original site of St Kevin's settlement, Teampall na Skellig is at the base of the cliffs towering over the southern side of the Upper Lake and accessible only

TIME YOUR VISIT

Visitors swarm to Glendalough in summer, so it's best to arrive early and/or stay late, preferably on a weekday, as the site is free and open 24 hours. The lower car park gates are locked when the visitor centre closes.

The National Park Information Office (p166) provides information about Wicklow Mountains National Park, and is the place to pick up maps and leaflets about local hiking trails. It's located by the Upper Lake car park, about 2km west of the Glendalough Visitor Centre (☑0404-45352; www.heritageireland.ie; 9.30am-6pm mid-Mar–mid-Oct, to 5pm mid-Oct–mid-Mar; adult/child €5/3). There's usually someone on hand to help; if you find it closed the staff may be out running guided walks.

LOCAL EATS

Laragh's the place for a bit of grub, as only the **Glendalough Hotel** (☑0404-45135; www.glendaloughhotel.com; r from €69; Ⓟ@🛜♨) serves food near the site.

Glendalough

A WALKING TOUR

A visit to Glendalough is a trip through ancient history and a refreshing hike in the hills. The ancient monastic settlement founded by St Kevin in the 5th century grew to be quite powerful by the 9th century, but it started falling into ruin from 1398 onwards. Still, you won't find more evocative clumps of stones anywhere.

Start at the ❶ **Main Gateway** to the monastic city, where you will find a cluster of important ruins, including the (nearly perfect) 10th-century ❷ **Round Tower**, the ❸ **cathedral** dedicated to Sts Peter and Paul, and ❹ **St Kevin's Kitchen**, which is really a church. Cross the stream past the famous ❺ **Deer Stone**, where Kevin was supposed to have milked a doe, and turn west along the path. It's a 1.5km walk to the ❻ **Upper Lake**. On the lake's southern shore is another cluster of sites, including the ❼ **Reefert Church**, a plain 11th-century Romanesque church where the powerful O'Toole family buried their kin, and ❽ **St Kevin's Cell**, the remains of a beehive hut where Kevin is said to have lived.

ST KEVIN

St Kevin came to the valley as a young monk in AD 498, in search of a peaceful retreat. He was reportedly led by an angel to a Bronze Age tomb now known as St Kevin's Bed. For seven years he slept on stones, wore animal skins, survived on nettles and herbs and – according to legend – developed an affinity with the birds and animals. One legend has it that, when Kevin needed milk for two orphaned babies, a doe stood waiting at the Deer Stone to be milked.

Kevin soon attracted a group of disciples and the monastic settlement grew, until by the 9th century Glendalough rivalled Clonmacnoise as Ireland's premier monastic city. According to legend, Kevin lived to the age of 120. He was canonised in 1903.

Round Tower
Glendalough's most famous landmark is the 33m-high Round Tower, which is exactly as it was when it was built a thousand years ago except for the roof; this was replaced in 1876 after a lightning strike.

OLOS/SHUTTERSTOCK ©

Deer Stone
The spot where St Kevin is said to have truly become one with the animals is really just a large mortar called a *bullaun*, used for grinding food and medicine.

St Kevin's Kitchen
This small church is unusual in that it has a round tower sticking out of the roof – it looks like a chimney, hence the church's nickname.

SIR FRANCIS CANKER PHOTOGRAPHY/GETTY IMAGES ©

St Kevin's Cell
This beehive hut is reputedly where St Kevin would go for prayer and meditation; not to be confused with St Kevin's Bed, a cave where he used to sleep.

Reefert Church
Its name derives from the Irish *righ fearta*, which means 'burial place of the kings'. Seven princes of the powerful O'Toole family are buried in this simple structure.

Upper Lake
The site of St Kevin's original settlement is on the banks of the Upper Lake, one of the two lakes that give Glendalough its name – the 'Valley of the Lakes'.

RAFAL STACHURA/GETTY IMAGES ©

⑧ ⑦ ⑥ ② ③ ①

← NORTH

INFORMATION
At the eastern end of the Upper Lake is the National Park Information Point, which has leaflets and maps on the site, local walks etc. The grassy spot in front of the office is a popular picnic spot in summer.

Cathedral of Sts Peter & Paul
The largest of Glendalough's seven churches, the cathedral was built gradually between the 10th and 13th centuries. The earliest part is the nave, where you can still see the *antae* (slightly projecting column at the end of the wall) used for supporting a wooden roof.

Main Gateway
The only surviving entrance to the ecclesiastical settlement is a double arch; notice that the inner arch rises higher than the outer one in order to compensate for the upward slope of the causeway.

GERARDO BORBOLLA/SHUTTERSTOCK ©

by boat; unfortunately, there's no boat service to the site so you'll have to settle for looking at it from across the lake. The terraced shelf has the reconstructed ruins of a church and early graveyard. Rough wattle huts once stood on the raised ground nearby. Scattered around are some early grave slabs and simple stone crosses. Meanwhile, in the green area behind the Upper Lake car park is a large circular wall thought to be the remains of an early Christian stone fort (caher).

St Kevin's Bed
Just east of Teampall na Skellig, and 10m above the Upper Lake's waters, is the 2m-deep artificial cave called St Kevin's Bed, said to be where Kevin lived. The earliest human habitation of the cave was long before St Kevin's era – there's evidence that people lived in the valley for thousands of years before the monks arrived.

Reefert Church
The considerable remains of Reefert Church sit above the tiny River Poulanass, south of the Upper Lake car park. It's a small, plain, 11th-century Romanesque nave-and-chancel church with some reassembled arches and walls. Traditionally, Reefert (literally 'Royal Burial Place') was the burial site of the chiefs of the local O'Toole family. The surrounding graveyard contains a number of rough stone crosses and slabs, most made of shiny mica schist.

St Kevin's Cell
Climb the steps at the back of the Reefert Churchyard and follow the path to the west and you'll find, at the top of a rise overlooking the Upper Lake, the scant remains of St Kevin's Cell, a small beehive hut.

WALKING IN GLENDALOUGH

The Glendalough Valley is all about walking. There are nine waymarked trails in the valley, the longest of which is about 10km, or about four hours' walking. Before you set off, drop by the **National Park Information Point** (☎0404-45425; www.wicklowmountainsnationalpark.ie; Bolger's Cottage, Upper Lake Car Park; ☺10am-5.30pm May-Sep, to dusk Sat & Sun Oct-Apr) and pick up the relevant leaflet and trail map (around €1). It also has a number of excellent guides for sale – you won't go far wrong with Joss Lynam's *Easy Walks Near Dublin* (€10) or Helen Fairbairn's *Dublin & Wicklow: A Walking Guide* (€15).

A word of warning: don't be fooled by the relative gentleness of the surrounding countryside or the fact that the Wicklow Mountains are really no taller than big hills. The weather can be merciless here, so be sure to take the usual precautions, have the right equipment and tell someone where you're going and when you should be back. For Mountain Rescue call ☎112 or ☎999.

The easiest and most popular walk is the gentle hike along the northern shore of the Upper Lake to the old lead and zinc **mine workings**, which date from 1800. The better route is along the lake shore rather than on the road (which runs 30m in from the shore), a distance of about 2.5km one way from the Glendalough Visitor Centre. Continue up to the head of the valley if you wish.

Alternatively you can walk up the **Spink** (from the Irish for 'pointed hill'; 380m), the steep ridge with vertical cliffs running along the southern flanks of the Upper Lake. You can go part of the way and turn back, or complete a circuit of the Upper Lake by following the top of the cliff, eventually coming down by the mine workings and going back along the northern shore. This circuit is about 6km long and takes about three hours.

The third option is a hike up **Camaderry Mountain** (700m), hidden behind the hills that flank the northern side of the valley. The path (not waymarked) begins opposite the entrance to the Upper Lake car park (near a 'Wicklow Mountains National Park' sign). Head straight up the steep hill to the north and you come out on open mountains with sweeping views in all directions. You can then continue west up the ridge to Camaderry summit. To the top of Camaderry and back is about 7.5km and takes about four hours.

Howth

Explore

Tidily positioned at the foot of a bulbous peninsula, the pretty port village of Howth (the name rhymes with 'both') is a major fishing centre, a yachting harbour and one of the most sought-after addresses in town.

Howth is divided between the upper headland – where the best properties are, discreetly spread atop the gorse-rich hill where there are some fine walks and spectacular views of Dublin Bay – and the busy port town, where all the restaurants are (as well as an excellent weekend farmers market).

The Best...

➡**Sight** Howth Summit
➡**Place to Eat** House (p169)
➡**Place to Drink** Abbey Tavern (p169)

Top Tip

Howth's 'hidden' beach is **Claremont** (☐31, 31A from Beresford Pl, ☐Howth), on the other side of the railway facing Ireland's Eye. To get here, go past the semi-industrial area by the West Pier.

Getting There & Away

DART The 20-minute train ride from Dublin city centre to Howth Village costs €3.25.

Bus Services 31 and 31A from Beresford Pl near Busáras run up to Howth Summit for €2.70.

Need to Know

➡**Area Code** ✆01
➡**Population** 8277
➡**Location** 15km northeast of Dublin

◉ SIGHTS

HOWTH SUMMIT VIEWPOINT
(☐31, 31A from Beresford Pl, ☐Howth) Howth Summit (171m) has excellent views across Dublin Bay right down to County Wicklow. From the top of Howth hill you can walk to

the top of the Ben of Howth, a headland near the village, which has a cairn said to mark a 2000-year-old Celtic **royal grave**. The 1814 **Baily Lighthouse**, at the southeastern corner, is on the site of an old stone fort and can be reached by a dramatic clifftop **walk**.

HOWTH CASTLE CASTLE
(☐31, 31A from Beresford Pl, ☐Howth) FREE
Most of Howth backs onto the extensive grounds of Howth Castle, built in 1564 but much changed over the years, most recently in 1910 when Sir Edwin Lutyens gave it a modernist makeover. Today the castle is divided into four very posh and private residences (the grounds are open to the public). The **castle gardens** (⊙24hr) FREE are worth visiting, as they're noted for their rhododendrons (which bloom in May and June), azaleas and a long, 10m-high beech hedge planted in 1710.

The original estate was acquired in 1177 by the Norman noble Sir Almeric Tristram, who changed his surname to St Lawrence after winning a battle at the behest (or so he believed) of his favourite saint. The family has owned the land ever since, though the unbroken chain of male succession came to an end in 1909.

On the grounds are the ruins of the 16th-century Corr Castle and an ancient dolmen (a tomb chamber or portal tomb made of vertical stones topped by a huge capstone) known as Aideen's Grave. Legend has it that Aideen died of a broken heart after her husband was killed at the Battle of Gavra near Tara in AD 184, but the legend is rubbish because the dolmen is at least 300 years older than that.

Also within the grounds are the ruins of **St Mary's Abbey** (Abbey St) FREE, originally founded in 1042 by the Viking King Sitric, who also founded the original church on the site of Christ Church Cathedral.

DAY TRIPS FROM DUBLIN HOWTH

Howth

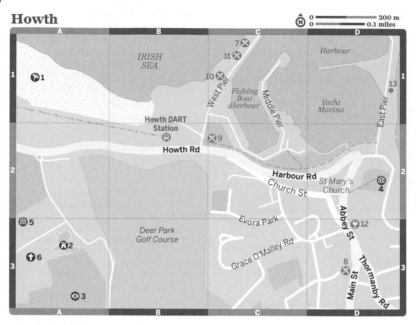

Howth

The abbey was amalgamated with the monastery on Ireland's Eye in 1235. Some parts of the ruins date from that time, but most are from the 15th and 16th centuries. The tomb of Christopher St Lawrence (Lord Howth), in the southeastern corner, dates from around 1470. See the caretaker or read the instructions on the gate for opening times.

**HURDY GURDY MUSEUM
OF VINTAGE RADIO**   MUSEUM
(www.hurdygurdyradiomuseum.wordpress.
com; €4; ⊙11am-4pm daily May-Oct, Sat & Sun only Nov-Apr; ☐31, 31A from Beresford Pl, ℝHowth) Housed in the old Martello tower overlooking the harbour is this museum of wonderful curiosities collected by Pat Herbert. Inside you'll find artefacts related to all forms of communication, from radio to gramophones and early TVs. The name derives from a comment made by former Taoiseach (prime minister) Sean Lemass, who asked a radio controller in the 1950s, 'How's the hurdy-gurdy?' (A hurdy-gurdy is a type of string instrument.)

NATIONAL TRANSPORT MUSEUM MUSEUM
(☑01-832 0427; www.nationaltransportmuseum.
org; Howth Castle; adult €3, child & student €1.50; ⊙2-5pm Sat & Sun; ☐31, 31A from Beresford Pl, ℝHowth) The rather ramshackle National Transport Museum has a range of exhibits including double-decker buses, a bakery van, fire engines and trams – most notably a Hill of Howth electric that operated from 1901 to

1959. To reach the museum, go through the castle gates and turn right just before the castle.

IRELAND'S EYE — BIRD SANCTUARY

(☎01-831 4200) A short distance offshore from Howth is Ireland's Eye, a rocky seabird sanctuary with the ruins of a 6th-century monastery. There's a Martello tower at the northwestern end of the island, where boats from Howth land, while a spectacularly sheer rock face plummets into the sea at the eastern end. It's really only worth exploring if you're interested in birds, although the boat trip out here, with Doyle & Sons, affords some lovely views of Dublin Bay.

As well as the seabirds overhead, you can see young birds on the ground during the nesting season. Seals can also be spotted around the island. Further north from Ireland's Eye is Lambay Island, an important seabird sanctuary that cannot be visited.

EATING

HOWTH MARKET — MARKET €

(☎01-839 4141; www.howthmarket.ie; 3 Harbour Rd, Howth Harbour; ☺9am-6pm Sat, Sun & bank holidays; 🚌31, 31A from Beresford Pl, 🚆Howth) One of the best in greater Dublin, this is the place to come not only for fresh fish (obviously) but also for organic meat and veg, and homemade everything else, including jams, cakes and breads. A great option for Sunday lunch.

★HOUSE — IRISH €€

(☎01-839 6388; www.thehouse-howth.ie; 4 Main St; mains €13-22; ☺8.45am-4pm Mon, to 9.30pm Tue-Fri, 10am-10pm Sat & Sun; 🚌31, 31A from Beresford Pl, 🚆Howth) Wonderful spot on the main street leading away from the harbour where you can feast on dishes such as crunchy Bellingham blue-cheese polenta or wild Wicklow venison stew, as well as a fine selection of fish. The brunch is one of the best you'll find on the north side of the city.

OAR HOUSE — SEAFOOD €€

(☎01-839 4562; www.oarhouse.ie; 8 West Pier; mains €17-29; ☺12.30-10pm; 🚌31, 31A from Beresford Pl, 🚆Howth) A feast-o-fish – of the locally caught variety – is what the menu is all about at this restaurant. Par for the course in a fishing village, but this place stands out both for the way the fish is prepared and because you can get everything on the menu in smaller, tapas-style portions as well as mains.

OCTOPUSSY'S SEAFOOD TAPAS — SEAFOOD €€

(☎01-839 0822; www.octopussys.ie; 7-8 West Pier; tapas €8-16; ☺noon-10pm; 🚌31, 31A from Beresford Pl, 🚆Howth) Best known for its tasty seafood tapas, Octopussy's is a firm local favourite. All of the seafood comes from the fish shop next door, which in turn buys it from the fishing boats that dock right in front. You can't get any fresher than that.

AQUA — SEAFOOD €€€

(☎01-832 0690; www.aqua.ie; 1 West Pier; mains €29-35; ☺12.30-3.30pm & 5.30-10pm Mon-Sat, noon-5pm & 6-8.30pm Sun; 🚌31, 31A from Beresford Pl, 🚆Howth) A contender for best seafood restaurant in Howth, Aqua serves top-quality fish dishes in its elegant dining room overlooking the harbour. The building was once home to the Howth Yacht Club.

DRINKING & NIGHTLIFE

ABBEY TAVERN — PUB

(28 Abbey St; ☺noon-11.30pm Mon-Sat, 12.30-11pm Sun; 🚌31, 31A from Beresford Pl, 🚆Howth) At the front is an old-style tavern frequented by a mix of locals and visitors; at the back is the venue for a nightly **traditional Irish music and dance show** (from 7.30pm), which also includes a four-course meal. A bit of fun, but strictly for tourists!

SPORTS & ACTIVITIES

DOYLE & SONS — BOATING

(☎01-831 4200; www.howth-boats.com; from €15; 🚌31, 31A from Beresford Pl, 🚆Howth) Doyle & Sons takes boats out to Ireland's Eye island (p169) from the East Pier of Howth Harbour. It also conducts half- and full-day angling trips as well as general sightseeing and birdwatching excursions.

Enniskerry & Powerscourt Estate

DAY TRIPS FROM DUBLIN ENNISKERRY & POWERSCOURT ESTATE

Explore

At the top of the '21 Bends', as the steep and winding R117 road from Bray is known, the handsome village of Enniskerry is home to upmarket shops and the kind of all-organic gourmet cafes that would treat you as a criminal if you admitted to eating battery eggs. Such self-regard is a far cry from the village's origins, when Richard Wingfield, earl of nearby Powerscourt, commissioned a row of terraced cottages for his labourers in 1760. These days, you'd need to have laboured pretty successfully to get your hands on one of them.

The Best...

→ **Sight** Powerscourt Estate
→ **Place to Eat** Kennedy's (p171)
→ **Place to Stay** Powerscourt Hotel & Spa (p171)

Getting There & Away

Enniskerry is 18km south of Dublin, just 3km west of the M11 along the R117. From here, getting to Powerscourt House on foot is not a problem (it's 500m from the town).

Bus Éireann (☏01-836 6111; www.buseireann.ie) The no 133 from Dublin to Wicklow town stops in Kilmacanogue (one way/return €4.90, 45 minutes, 10 daily).

The estate is hard to visit via public transport, so a good option is a guided tour. **DoDublin Bus Tour** (www.dodublin.ie; adult/child €21.60/9.60; ⊙10.30am daily Apr-Oct) includes both Powerscourt and Glendalough, and departs from Dublin city centre.

Need to Know

→ **Area Code** ☏01
→ **Population** 1889
→ **Location** 8km south of Dublin

◉ SIGHTS

★**POWERSCOURT ESTATE**　　　　　GARDENS
(☏01-204 6000; www.powerscourt.com; Enniskerry; house free, gardens adult/child €10/5; ⊙9.30am-5.30pm Mar-Oct, to dusk Nov-Feb; P 🚼) Wicklow's most visited attraction is this magnificent 64-sq-km estate, whose main entrance is 500m south of Enniskerry town. At the heart of it is an elegant Palladian mansion, but the real draw is the formal gardens and the stunning views that accompany them. Most of the house is not open to the public, but there's a fine cafe and several gift and homewares shops to be enjoyed, while the grounds are home to two golf courses and the best hotel (p171) in Wicklow.

The estate has existed more or less since 1300, when the LePoer (later anglicised to Power) family built themselves a castle here. The property changed Anglo-Norman hands a few times before coming into the possession of Richard Wingfield, newly appointed Marshall of Ireland, in 1603. His descendants were to live here for the next 350 years. In 1730 the Georgian wunderkind Richard Cassels (or Castle) was given the job of building a 68-room Palladian-style mansion around the core of the old castle. He finished the job in 1741, but an extra storey was added in 1787 and other alterations were made in the 19th century.

The Wingfields left during the 1950s, after which the house had a massive restoration. Then, on the eve of its opening to the public in 1974, a fire gutted the whole building. The estate was eventually bought by the Slazenger sporting-goods family who have overseen a second restoration as well as the addition of all the amenities the estate now has to offer, including the two golf courses and the fabulous hotel, now part of Marriott's Autograph collection.

The star of the show is the 20-hectare **landscaped gardens**, originally laid out in the 1740s but redesigned in the 19th century by gardener Daniel Robinson. Robinson was one of the foremost horticulturalists of his day, and his passion for growing things was matched only by his love of booze: the story goes that by a certain point in the day he was too drunk to stand and so insisted on being wheeled around the estate in a barrow.

Perhaps this influenced his largely informal style, which resulted in a magnificent blend of landscaped gardens, sweeping terraces, statuary, ornamental lakes, secret hollows, rambling walks and walled enclosures replete with more than 200 types of trees and shrubs, all designed to frame the stunning natural backdrop of the Great Sugarloaf Mountain. Tickets come with a map laying out 40-minute and hour-long walks around the gardens. Don't miss the exquisite **Japanese Gardens** or the Pepperpot Tower, modelled on a 3in actual pepper pot owned by Lady Wingfield. Our own favourite, however, is the **animal cemetery**, final resting place of the Wingfield pets and even one of the family's favourite milking cows. Some of the epitaphs are surprisingly personal.

The house itself is every bit as grand as the gardens, but ongoing renovation means there's not much to see beyond the bustle of the ground-floor cafe and gift shop. The sole exception is the **Museum of Childhood** (Tara's Palace; ☑01-274 8090; www.childhoodmuseum.org; adult/child/family €5/3/12; ☺10am-5pm Mon-Sat, noon-5pm Sun; P ♿), full of period miniature dolls and dolls' houses, including Tara's Palace, a 22-room house designed to one-twelfth scale and inspired by the Palladian piles of Castletown House, Leinster House and Carton House. Each of the rooms is decorated in exquisite, handcrafted miniatures.

A 6km drive to a separate part of the estate takes you to the 121m-high **Powerscourt Waterfall** (www.powerscourt.com/waterfall; adult/child €6/3.50; ☺9.30am-7pm May-Aug, 10.30am-5.30pm Mar-Apr, Sep & Oct, to 4.30pm Nov-Feb; P) – walking from house to falls is not recommended, because the route lies on narrow roads with no footpath. It's the highest waterfall in Ireland, and at its most impressive after heavy rain. A nature trail has been laid out around the base of the waterfall, taking you past giant redwoods, ancient oaks, beech, birch and rowan trees. There are plenty of birds in the vicinity, including the chaffinch, cuckoo, chiffchaff, raven and willow warbler.

✖ EATING

KENNEDY'S CAFE €
(www.kennedysofenniskerry.com; Church Hill; mains €5-12; ☺8.30am-5pm; 🛜 ♿) A lovely cafe with old-fashioned furniture in cool pastel shades, this is the place to get excellent breakfasts (it does great poached eggs on sourdough toast) and homemade soups and sandwiches. It also sells delicious artisan bread made by the Bretzel Bakery in Dublin.

POPPIES COUNTRY COOKING CAFE €
(☑01-282 8869; www.facebook.com/poppies ireland; The Square; mains €7-11; ☺8am-6pm) Wholesome salads, filling sandwiches on doorstep-cut bread, and award-winning ice cream will leave you plenty satisfied, even if the service can be a tad slow.

EMILIA'S RISTORANTE ITALIAN €€
(☑01-276 1834; www.emilias.ie; The Square; mains €13-24; ☺5-10.45pm Mon-Sat, noon-9.30pm Sun) A lovely 1st-floor restaurant to satisfy even the most ardent craving for thin-crust pizzas. Emilia's does everything else just right too, from the organic soups and traditional pasta dishes to the perfect steaks and the gorgeous meringue desserts.

JOHNNIE FOX'S SEAFOOD €€
(☑01-295 5647; www.jfp.ie; Glencullen; mains €11-30; ☺food served 12.30-9.30pm; P 🛜 ♿) Busloads of tourists fill this place nightly throughout the summer, mostly for the knees-up, faux-Irish Hooley Show of music and dancing. But there's nothing contrived about the seafood, which is so damn good we'd happily sit through yet another chorus of 'Danny Boy' and even consider joining in the jig. It's 3km northwest of Enniskerry.

🛌 SLEEPING

★**POWERSCOURT HOTEL & SPA** HOTEL €€€
(☑01-274 8888; www.powerscourthotel.com; Powerscourt Estate, Enniskerry; r from €265; P 🛜 ♨) Wicklow's most luxurious hotel is

this 200-room stunner on the grounds of the Powerscourt Estate. Inside this Marriott-managed property all is over-the-top luxury, and the decor is a thoroughly contemporary version of the estate's Georgian style. The rooms are massive. Downstairs there's a decent restaurant and a superb spa.

Castletown House & Around

Explore

Of all of Ireland's Palladian mansions, Castletown House is undoubtedly the grandest. It is a testament to the wealth and ambition of its original owner, William Conolly, who also happened to be the richest man in Ireland during the 18th century. Although parts of the house have been damaged, there's enough on display to give you an intimate look at the extravagant luxuries enjoyed by the Anglo-Irish gentry of the period.

The Best...

➡**Sight** Wonderful Barn (p172)
➡**Place to Stay**
Carton House (✆01-505 2000; www.cartonhouse.com; r from €250; P @ 🛜 ⛵)

Top Tip

The guided tour of the house is informative and full of detail about its construction and larger-than-life occupiers, not least Lady Louisa.

Getting There & Away

➡**Bus** No 67 runs from Dublin to Celbridge (€3.50, one hour, hourly).
➡**Car** Take the N4 to Celbridge.

Need to Know

➡**Area Code** ✆01
➡**Location** 21km west of Dublin
➡**Information** Dublin Discover Ireland Centre

⊙ SIGHTS

★**CASTLETOWN HOUSE**   HISTORIC BUILDING
(✆01-628 8252; www.castletown.ie; Celbridge; adult/child €8/3.50, with guided tour €10/5; ⊙10am-6pm mid-Mar–Oct)   Magnificent Castletown House simply has no peer. It is Ireland's most imposing Georgian estate, and a testament to the vast wealth enjoyed by the Anglo-Irish gentry during the 18th century. Hour-long guided tours begin at noon and 3pm, offering an insight into how the 1% made out in the 18th century; otherwise you can wander at will. Don't miss a stroll down to the river for grand views back to the house. Castletown is signposted from junction 6 on the M4.

The house was built between the years 1722 and 1732 for William Conolly (1662–1729), speaker of the Irish House of Commons and, at the time, Ireland's richest man. Born into relatively humble circumstances in Ballyshannon, County Donegal, Conolly made his fortune through land transactions in the uncertain aftermath of the Battle of the Boyne (1690).

The job of building a palace fit for a prince was entrusted to Sir Edward Lovett Pearce (1699–1733) – hence the colonnades and terminating pavilions. Lovett's design was an extension of a preexisting 16th-century Italian palazzo-style building, created by Italian architect Alessandro Galilei (1691–1737) in 1718, but Conolly wanted something even grander, hence Lovett's appearance on the job in 1724. A highlight of the opulent interior is the Long Gallery, replete with family portraits and exquisite stucco work by the Francini brothers.

Conolly didn't live to see the completion of his wonder-palace. His widow, Katherine, continued to live at the unfinished house after his death in 1729, and instigated many improvements. Her main architectural contribution was the curious 42.6m obelisk, known locally as the Conolly Folly. Her other offering was the Heath Robinson–esque (or Rube Goldberg–esque, if you prefer) **Wonderful Barn** (Leixlip; ⊙dawn-dusk) **FREE**, six teetering storeys wrapped by an exterior spiral staircase, on private property just outside Leixlip.

Castletown House remained in the family's hands until 1965, when it was purchased by Desmond Guinness, who restored the house to its original splendour. His investment was continued from 1979 by the Castletown Foundation. In 1994 Castletown House was transferred to state care and today it is managed by the Heritage Service.

Dalkey

Explore

Dublin's most important medieval port has long since settled into its role as an elegant dormitory village, but there are some revealing vestiges of its illustrious past, most notably the remains of three of the eight castles that once lorded over the area.

Dalkey is small enough that you can get around on foot. Most visitors will be arriving by DART, so start your exploration in the middle of town: the main sights are on Castle St, as are most of the cafes (or on the streets just off it). Coliemore Harbour is where you can get boat trips; overlooking the adjoining Bullock Harbour are the remains of Bullock Castle.

The waters around the island are popular with scuba divers; qualified divers can rent gear in Dun Laoghaire, further north, from Ocean Divers (p174).

The Best...

➡**Festival** Dalkey Book Festival (p205)
➡**Place to Eat** Select Stores (p174)
➡**Place to Drink** Finnegan's (p174)

Top Tip

To the south there are good views from the small park at Sorrento Point and from Killiney Hill. A number of rocky swimming pools are also found along the Dalkey coast.

Getting There & Away

➡**DART** The best way to get to Dalkey is by train from Pearse or Connolly stations – a one-way ticket costs €3.25.

➡**Bus** Service 7 takes a slow route from Mountjoy Sq through Dublin city centre to Dalkey – fare is €3.25.

Need to Know

➡**Area Code** ☑01
➡**Population** 8083
➡**Location** 8km south of Dublin

◉ SIGHTS

DALKEY CASTLE & HERITAGE CENTRE MUSEUM
(☑01-285 8366; www.dalkeycastle.com; Castle St; adult/child €9/7; ◷10am-5.30pm Mon-Fri, 11am-5.30pm Sat & Sun Jun-Aug, closed Tue Sep-May) Spread across Goat Castle and St Begnet's Church, this heritage centre has models, displays and exhibitions on Dalkey's history; a Living History tour in the format of a theatre performance; and a Writers' Gallery, covering the town's rich literary heritage – from Samuel Beckett (who was born here) to Joseph O'Connor (who lives here). The centre also organises **walking tours** (€9; ◷11am & noon Wed & Fri Jun-Aug).

DALKEY ISLAND ISLAND
Dalkey Island's main sight is **St Begnet's Holy Well** (ferry from Coliemore Harbour adult/child €8/5; FREE), but it's also a popular spot for fishing, with shoals of pollock, mackerel and coalfish feeding in its waters. It's also a lovely spot to spend a couple of hours with a picnic – but be sure to take everything off the island with you when you leave. **Ken the Ferryman** (www.kentheferryman.com; Coliemore Harbour; adult/child €8/5; ◷10am-6pm) provides transport to and from the island.

BULLOCK CASTLE RUINS
(Bullock Harbour; ⬛Dalkey) These are the ruins of a castle built by the monks of St Mary's Abbey in Dublin around 1150.

SANDYCOVE

••

Sandycove, just 1km north of Dalkey, has a pretty little beach and a Martello tower – built by British forces as a lookout for signs of a Napoleonic invasion – now home to the **James Joyce Museum** (☑01-280 9265; www.joycetower.ie; Joyce Tower; ◷10am-6pm May-Sep, to 4pm Oct-Apr; ®Sandycove & Glasthule) FREE.

There are really only two things to do here: visit the Martello Tower and, if you're brave enough, get into the water at the adjacent **Forty Foot Pool**.

✖ EATING

★**SELECT STORES**　　　HEALTH FOOD €
(www.selectstores.ie; 1 Railway Rd; mains €4-12; ◷8am-6pm, closed Sun Oct-Apr) This long-established food emporium has been transformed into a one-stop shop for all things good for you: the award-winning kitchen rolls out veggie burgers, fresh juices, salads and, in the mornings, a range of healthy breakfasts. Bono is a fan, apparently.

MAGPIE INN　　　PUB FOOD €€
(☑01-202 3909; www.magpieinn.com; 115-116 Coliemore Rd; mains €12-25; ◷noon-11.30pm) The excellent menu's main strength is, obviously, seafood, including a range of mouth-watering lunch options like fresh Sligo mussels marinière with toasted sourdough bread and more substantial dinner mains like a seafood skillet of pan-fried salmon, cod, langoustine, mussels, tomatoes, potatoes, onions and garlic in a white-wine sauce. Wash it all down with a choice of craft beer.

● DRINKING & ⚲ NIGHTLIFE

FINNEGAN'S　　　PUB
(www.finnegans.ie; 1 Sorrento Rd; ◷noon-11.30pm Mon-Thu, to 12.30am Fri & Sat, noon-11pm Sun) There's a fabulous local atmosphere in this lovely traditional pub, which has been a staple here for over 40 years.

⚡ SPORTS & ACTIVITIES

OCEAN DIVERS　　　DIVING
(www.oceandivers.ie; The Boat Yard, Dun Laoghaire Harbour, Dun Laoghaire; boat dives €35-55; ◷9.30am-5pm Tue-Sat) A PADI diving school operating out of Dun Laoghaire Harbour, Ocean Divers offers boat diving from its RIBs around Dalkey Island, site of two wrecks: the *MV Leinster* (sank in 1918) and the *Bolivar,* which sank in 1947.

Malahide

••

Explore

Malahide (Mullach Íde) was once a small village with its own harbour, a long way from the urban jungle of Dublin. The only thing protecting it from the northwards expansion of Dublin's suburbs is Malahide Demesne, 101 well-tended hectares of parkland dominated by a castle once owned by the powerful Talbot family.

The handsome village remains relatively intact, but the once-quiet marina has been massively developed and is now a bustling centre with a pleasant promenade and plenty of restaurants and shops.

••

The Best...

➡**Sight** Malahide Castle (p175)
➡**Activity** Portmarnock Golf Club (p175)
➡**Place to Eat** Greedy Goose (p175)

••

Top Tip

If travelling by DART, be sure to get on the right train from Dublin city centre as the line splits at Howth Junction.

••

Getting There & Away

➡Malahide is 13km north of Dublin.
➡**Bus** Services 42 and 142 (€3.25) from Talbot St take around 45 minutes.
➡**DART** Stops in Malahide (€3.25).

Need to Know

➡**Area Code** 🖉01
➡**PopulationLocation** 🖉15,846
➡**Location** 🖉18km northeast of Dublin

⊙ SIGHTS

MALAHIDE CASTLE   CASTLE
(🖉01-816 9538; www.malahidecastleandgar
dens.ie; adult/child €12.50/6.50; ⊙9.30am-
5.30pm; 🚌42, 142 from city centre, 🚊Malahide)
The oldest part of this hotchpotch castle,
which was in the hands of the Talbot family from 1185 to 1976, is the three-storey
12th-century tower house. The facade
is flanked by circular towers that were
tacked on in 1765. The castle, now owned
by Fingal County Council, is accessible
via guided tour only (last tour 4.30pm;
3.30pm November to March); the impressive gardens are self-guided.

The castle is packed with furniture and
paintings; highlights are a 16th-century
oak room with decorative carvings, and
the medieval Great Hall, which has family
portraits, a minstrel's gallery and a painting of the Battle of the Boyne. Puck, the
Talbot family ghost, is said to have last appeared in 1975.

✗ EATING

CHEZ SARA   FRENCH €€
(🖉01-845 1882; www.chezsara.ie; 3 Old St;
mains €16-24; ⊙5pm-midnight Tue-Sun; 🚌42,
142 from city centre) Irish lamb, red snapper
and a beautifully cooked steak are just
three of the highlights of this cosy French
restaurant in the middle of the village.

GREEDY GOOSE   INTERNATIONAL €€
(www.greedygoose.ie; 15 Townyard Lane; menus
€24-30; ⊙5-11pm Mon-Fri, 1-11pm Sat & Sun;

🚌42, 142 from city centre) The menu at this
pleasant restaurant overlooking the marina has dishes from all over the globe: take
your pick of barbecued chicken wings,
chana masala, Cajun-style Irish salmon
and others. The food is best enjoyed as
part of three separate menus: pick three
dishes from one and eat portions roughly
equivalent to Spanish *raciones* – bigger
than starters, smaller than mains.

SALE E PEPE   INTERNATIONAL €€
(🖉01-845 4600; www.saleepepe.ie; The Diamond, Main St; mains €17-28; ⊙5-11pm Mon-Sat,
4-11pm Sun; 🚌42, 142 from city centre) Despite
the name, there's only a handful of Italian
dishes on a menu that emphasises well-
prepared steaks, fish and chips, and homemade organic burgers.

☕ DRINKING & NIGHTLIFE

GIBNEY'S   PUB
(6 New St; ⊙10.30am-11.30pm Mon-Wed, to
12.30am Thu-Sat, to 11pm Sun; 🚌42, 142 from
city centre) Malahide's best-known, best-
loved pub is a huge place, spread over a
number of rooms and outdoor areas. At
weekends it's always packed with locals.

☆ SPORTS & ACTIVITIES

★PORTMARNOCK GOLF CLUB   GOLF
(🖉01-846 2968; www.portmarnockgolfclub.ie;
Golf Links Rd, Portmarnock; green fee weekday/
weekend €200/225) Founded in 1894, this
is one of the world's outstanding links
courses and a former long-time host of the
Irish Open. Visitor tee-times are spread
out throughout the day, with 11.30am to
2.30pm reserved exclusively for members.

Sleeping

The surge in tourist numbers and the relative lack of beds means hotel prices are higher than they were during the Celtic Tiger years. There are good midrange options north of the Liffey, but the biggest spread of accommodation is south of the river, from midrange Georgian townhouses to the city's top hotels. Budget travellers rely on the selection of decent hostels.

Accommodation Styles

Top-end and deluxe hotels fall into two categories – period Georgian elegance and cool, minimalist chic. No matter what the decor, you can expect luxurious surrounds, king-sized beds, satellite TV, full room service, wi-fi and discreet, professional pampering. While the luxury of the best places is undeniable, their inevitable affiliation to the world's most celebrated hotel chains has introduced the whiff of corporate homogeneity into the carefully ventilated air.

Dublin's midrange accommodation is more of a mixed bag, ranging from no-nonsense but soulless chains to small B&Bs in old Georgian townhouses. These days, hotel connoisseurs the world over have discovered the intimate, but luxurious, boutique hotel, where the personal touch is maintained through fewer rooms, each of which is given lavish attention. Dublin's townhouses and guesthouses – usually beautiful Georgian homes converted into lodgings – are this city's version of the boutique hotel, and there are some truly outstanding ones to choose from. These are beautifully decked out and extremely comfortable, while at the lower end, rooms are simple, a little worn and often rather overbearingly decorated. Here you can look forward to kitsch knick-knacks, chintzy curtains, lace doilies and clashing floral fabrics so loud they'll burn your retinas. Breakfast can range from home-baked breads, fruit and farmhouse cheeses to a traditional, fat-laden fry-up.

Budget options are few and far between in a city that has undergone a dramatic tourist revolution, so if you want to stay anywhere close to the city centre, you'll have to settle for a hostel. Thankfully, most of these maintain a pretty high standard of hygiene and comfort. Many offer various sleeping arrangements, from a bed in a large dorm to a four-bed room or a double. There are plenty to choose from, but they tend to fill up very quickly and stay full.

There are also central self-catering apartments for groups, families or those on extended stays who may prefer to do their own thing. And there are in excess of 300 rental options in the city, ranging from a basic room in an apartment to fully furnished Georgian homes.

Booking Services

Getting the hotel of your choice without a reservation can be tricky in high season (May to September), so always book your room in advance. You can book through Dublin Tourism's online booking service (www.visitdublin.com). Advance internet bookings are your best bet for deals.

All Dublin Hotels (www.irelandhotels.com/hotels) Decent spread of accommodation in the city centre and suburbs.

Daft.ie (www.daft.ie) If you're looking to rent in Dublin, this is the site to search.

Dublin Hotels (www.dublinhotels.com) Hotels in the city centre and beyond.

Dublin Tourism (www.visitdublin.com) Good selection of rated accommodation.

Hostel Dublin (www.hosteldublin.com) Good resource for hostel accommodation.

Lonely Planet (www.lonelyplanet.com/ireland/dublin/hotels) Recommendations and bookings.

Lonely Planet's Top Choices

Merrion (p181) The city's best hotel.

Conrad Dublin (p182) Exquisite business hotel.

Aberdeen Lodge (p186) Superb B&B in southside suburb.

Merrion Mews (p182) Self-catering in a protected landmark Georgian mews.

Isaacs Hostel (p184) Best bunks in town.

Shelbourne (p182) Historic and very elegant.

Best by Budget

€

Isaacs Hostel (p184) Best bunks in the city.

Generator Hostel (p184) Funky hostel on the north side.

Ariel House (p186) a bit of budget luxury

€€

Radisson Blu Royal Hotel (p179) Swanky spot for business.

Cliff Townhouse (p180) Terrific boutique bolt-hole.

Aberdeen Lodge (p186) Hospitality at its best.

Trinity Lodge (p180) Comfy and central B&B.

€€€

Merrion (p181) Sophisticated, elegant and central.

Fitzwilliam Hotel (p181) Modern and very tasteful.

Conrad Dublin (p182) Superb, modern rooms.

Best Comfy Pillows

Brooks Hotel (p180) Everyone needs a pillow menu.

Merrion (p181) Nestle your head in luxury.

Aberdeen Lodge (p186) Sublime sleeps.

Westin Dublin (p181) The beds are heavenly.

Best Boutique Beds

Cliff Townhouse (p180) Ten magnificent rooms.

Irish Landmark Trust (p184) A unique sleeping experience.

Number 31 (p182) Architect-designed marvel.

NEED TO KNOW

Price Ranges
The following price ranges refer to the cost per night of a standard double room in high season:

€ less than €150

€€ €150–250

€€€ more than €250

Discounted Rates
➡ Keep an eye out for online offers.

➡ Flexibility is a must.

➡ Hotels that cater to business customers offer cheaper weekend rates.

Tipping
It's customary to tip bellhops €1 per bag, and concierges up to €5 for any additional service they provide, like booking restaurants, taxis or advice on what to do or where to go.

Check-In & Check-Out Times
Check-out at most establishments is noon, but some of the smaller guesthouses and B&Bs require that you check out a little earlier, usually around 11am. Check-in is usually between 2pm and 3pm.

SLEEPING

Where to Stay

NEIGHBOURHOOD	FOR	AGAINST
Grafton Street & Around	Close to sights, nightlife and pretty much everything; a good choice of midrange and top-end hotels.	Generally more expensive than elsewhere; not always good value for money and rooms tend to be smaller.
Merrion Square & Around	Lovely neighbourhood, elegant hotels and townhouse accommodation; some of the best restaurants in town are also in the area.	Not a lot of choice; virtually no budget accommodation. Also relatively quiet after dark.
Temple Bar	In the heart of the action; close to everything, especially the party.	Noisy and touristy; not especially good value for money; rooms are very small and often less than pristine.
Kilmainham & the Liberties	Close to the old city and the sights of west Dublin.	No good accommodation; only a small selection of restaurants.
North of the Liffey	Good range of choices; within walking distance of sights and nightlife.	Budget accommodation not always good quality; some locations not especially comfortable after dark.
Docklands & the Grand Canal	Excellent contemporary hotels with good service, including some top-end choices.	Isolated in neighbourhood that doesn't have a lot of life after dark; reliant on taxis or public transport to get to city centre.
The Southside	More bang for your buck; generally bigger rooms and properties with gardens.	If not on the Luas line, bus transfers into town can take up valuable time.

🛏 Grafton Street & Around

Grafton St itself has only one hotel – one of the city's best – but you'll find a host of choices in the area surrounding it. Not surprisingly, being so close to the choicest street in town comes at a premium, but the competition for business is fierce, which ensures quality is top rate.

KELLY'S HOTEL   BOUTIQUE HOTEL €

Map p238 (www.kellysdublin.com; 36 S Great George's St; r from €110; ❄@🛜; 🚇all city centre) A trendy boutique hotel in an original Victorian red-brick. The interiors are thoroughly modern: rooms are small and tastefully decorated with polished wooden floors and elegant minimalist furnishings. It's part of a complex that includes Grafton House (p179), two bars – Hogan's (p77), and the No Name Bar (p76) – and L'Gueuleton (p73) next door. Front-facing rooms can be quite noisy.

CENTRAL HOTEL   HOTEL €

Map p238 (📞01-679 7302; www.centralhoteldublin.com; 1-5 Exchequer St; r from €110; @🛜; 🚇all city centre, 🚇St Stephen's Green) The rooms are a modern – if miniaturised – version of Edwardian luxury. Heavy velvet curtains and custom-made Irish furnishings (including beds with draped backboards) fit a little too snugly into the space afforded them, but they do lend a touch of class. Note that street-facing rooms can get a little noisy. Location-wise, the name says it all.

GRAFTON HOUSE   BOUTIQUE HOTEL €

Map p238 (📞01-648 0010; www.graftonguesthouse.com; 27 S Great George's St; s/d from €90/140; @🛜; 🚇all city centre, 🚇St Stephen's Green) Pine furnishings, pristine white linen and thoroughly modern bathrooms are the defining features of the smallish rooms at this boutique hotel that is a good choice for location and price. Check in at Kelly's Hotel (p179), a couple of doors down; (continental) breakfast is served in L'Gueuleton (p73), just around the corner. Street-facing rooms are noisy, especially at weekends.

AVALON HOUSE   HOSTEL €

Map p238 (📞01-475 0001; www.avalon-house.ie; 55 Aungier St; dm/s/d from €10/34/54; @🛜; 🚇15, 16, 16A, 16C, 19, 19A, 19C, 65, 65B, 83, 122) Pared-back dorms with high ceilings and old-fashioned sinks, metal-framed bunks and shared bathrooms give this an old-school look at odds with newer hostels, but it's popular – because of its location and nice common room. In 2017 the downstairs cafe was taken over by Starbucks. Book well in advance.

GRAFTON CAPITAL HOTEL   HOTEL €

Map p238 (📞01-648 1221; www.graftoncapitalhotel.com; Lower Stephen St; r from €110; P❄@🛜; 🚇all cross-city, 🚇St Stephen's Green) It's hardly recognisable as such today, but this hotel just off Grafton St is actually a couple of converted Georgian townhouses. Its 75 modern rooms are designed along the lines of function before form, ideal for the weekend visitor who wants to bed down somewhere central and still keep some credit-card space for a good night out. Breakfast is included.

DEAN   HOTEL €€

Map p242 (📞01-607 8110; www.deanhoteldublin.ie; 33 Harcourt St; r/ste from €150/370; P@🛜; 🚇10, 11, 13, 14, 15A, 🚇St Stephen's Green) Every room at this newish designer hotel comes with earplugs, vodka, wine and Berocca – so you know what to expect. Take your pick from well-appointed and elegant Mod Pods (single bed on a couch), Punk Bunks (yup, bunk beds) or deluxe doubles (SupeRooms or Hi-Fis) and suites. The more expensive rooms come with Netflix and a turntable.

The hotel deliberately advertises as an upmarket party hotel that borrows its ethos (if not its look) from the Ace Hotel in New York and the Hoxton in London: sandwiched between two of the most popular nightclubs in town the rooms can get very noisy indeed, especially those on the 1st floor. The top floor is home to Sophie's (p73), a brasserie that turns into a popular bar after 11pm.

It has discounted parking arrangements with a car park that is a five-minute walk away.

RADISSON BLU ROYAL HOTEL   HOTEL €€

Map p242 (📞01-898 2900; www.radissonblu.ie/royalhotel-dublin; Golden Lane; r from €200; P❄@🛜; 🚇all city centre, 🚇St Stephen's Green) A business hotel that is an excellent example of how sleek lines and muted colours combine beautifully with luxury, ensuring a memorable night's stay. From hugely impressive public areas to sophisticated bedrooms – each with a flat-screen digital TV embedded in the wall to go along with all the other little touches – this hotel will not disappoint.

TRINITY LODGE GUESTHOUSE €€

Map p238 (☏01-617 0900; www.trinitylodge.com; 12 S Frederick St; r from €170; ☎; ☐all city centre, ☒St Stephen's Green) Martin Sheen's grin greets you upon entering this award-winning guesthouse, which he declared his favourite spot for an Irish stay. Marty's not the only one: this place is so popular they've added a second townhouse across the road, which has also been kitted out to the highest standards. Room 2 of the original house has a lovely bay window.

Discounted parking (€17.50) is available in an adjacent covered car park.

HARRINGTON HALL GUESTHOUSE €€

Map p242 (☏01-475 3497; www.harringtonhall.com; 69-70 Harcourt St; r from €180; @☎; ☒Harcourt) Want to fluff up the pillows in the home of a former Lord Mayor of Dublin? The traditional Georgian style of Timothy Charles Harrington's home – he wore the gold chain from 1901 to 1903 – has thankfully been retained and this smart guesthouse stands out for its understated elegance. The 1st- and 2nd-floor rooms have their original fireplaces and ornamental ceilings.

BROOKS HOTEL HOTEL €€

Map p238 (☏01-670 4000; www.brookshotel.ie; 59-62 Drury St; r from €200; P✳@☎; ☐all cross-city, ☒St Stephen's Green) About 120m west of Grafton St, this small, plush place has an emphasis on familial, friendly service. The decor is nouveau classic with high-veneer-panelled walls, decorative bookcases and old-fashioned sofas, while bedrooms are extremely comfortable and come fitted out in subtly coloured furnishings. The clincher though, is the king- and superking-size beds in all rooms, complete with...a pillow menu.

**O'CALLAGHAN
STEPHEN'S GREEN** HOTEL €€

Map p242 (☏01-607 3600; www.stephensgreenhotel.ie; 1-5 Harcourt St; r from €180; P@☎; ☐all cross-city, ☒St Stephen's Green) Past the glass-fronted lobby are 75 thoroughly modern rooms that make full use of the visual impact of primary colours, most notably red and blue. This is a business hotel par excellence: everything here is what you'd expect from a top international hotel (including a gym and a business centre). There are extraordinary online deals available.

BUSWELL'S HOTEL HOTEL €€

Map p238 (☏01-614 6500; www.buswells.ie; 23-27 Molesworth St; s/d from €165/180; P✳@;

☐all cross-city, ☒St Stephen's Green) This Dublin institution, open since 1882, has a long association with politicians, who wander across the road from Dáil Éireann (Irish Assembly) to wet their beaks at the hotel bar. The 69 bedrooms have all been given the once-over, but have kept their Georgian charm intact.

DAWSON BOUTIQUE HOTEL €€

Map p238 (☏01-612 7900; www.thedawson.ie; 35 Dawson St; r from €160; @☎; ☐all city centre, ☒St Stephen's Green) A boutique hotel with a range of elegant rooms designed in a variety of styles, from classical French to more exotic Moroccan. Crisp white sheets throughout and luxe amenities in the bathrooms. There's also a fancy spa and the trendy Sam's Bar (p77) below.

CLIFF TOWNHOUSE BOUTIQUE HOTEL €€

Map p238 (☏01-638 3939; www.theclifftownhouse.com; 22 St Stephen's Green N; r from €230; @☎; ☐all city centre, ☒St Stephen's Green) As pieds-à-terre go, this is a doozy: there are 10 exquisitely appointed bedrooms spread across a wonderful Georgian property whose best views overlook St Stephen's Green. Downstairs is Sean Smith's superb restaurant Cliff Townhouse (p75).

HILTON HOTEL €€

Map p242 (☏01-402 9988; www.dublin.hilton.com; Charlemont Pl; r from €200; P@☎; ☒Charlemont) Hilton is synonymous with modern, well-appointed rooms with all mod cons, and this canalside property delivers just that. Rooms are bright and comfortable; there's a decent restaurant and a good gym; and the hotel is close to a Luas stop so it's an easy commute into the city centre. As this is a business hotel, rooms are dramatically more expensive midweek.

There are parking arrangements (€15) with a nearby car park.

CAMDEN COURT HOTEL HOTEL €€

Map p242 (☏01-475 9666; www.camdencourthotel.com; Camden St; r from €200; P✳@☎▦; ☐all cross-city, ☒Harcourt) Big and bland ain't such a bad thing this close to St Stephen's Green, especially if the mainstay of your clientele is the business crowd. They like the standardised rooms but *love* the amenities, which include a 16m pool, health club (with jacuzzi, sauna and steam room) and fully equipped gym.

CAMPUS ACCOMMODATION

During the summer months, visitors can opt to stay in campus accommodation, which is both convenient and comfortable.

Trinity College (Map p238; ☑01-896 1177; www.tcd.ie/summeraccommodation; Accommodations Office, Trinity College; s/d from €79/129; ☺May–mid-Sep; P @☎; ☐all cross-city) The extensive range of student accommodation includes modern apartments with all mod cons and older (more atmospheric) rooms with shared bathroom. They're on campus and just off it, on Pearse St.

Dublin City University (DCU; ☑01-700 5736; www.summeraccommodation.dcu.ie; Larkfield Apartments, Campus Residences, Dublin City University; s/d from €80/120; ☺mid-Jun–mid-Sep; ☐11, 11A, 11B, 13, 13A, 19, 19A from city centre) This accommodation is proof that students slum it in relative luxury. The modern rooms have plenty of amenities at hand, including a kitchen, a common room and a fully equipped health centre. The Glasnevin campus is only 15 minutes by bus or car from the city centre.

STAUNTON'S ON THE GREEN　　HOTEL €€

Map p242 (☑01-478 2300; www.stauntonsonthe green.ie; 83 St Stephen's Green S; r from €170; @☎; ☐all cross-city, ☐St Stephen's Green) In a perfect location on St Stephen's Green (next door to the Department of Foreign Affairs), this handsome Georgian house has clean rooms that are just a mite careworn. The front-facing rooms have floor-to-ceiling windows overlooking the Green. Any closer and you're sleeping with the Lord Mayor.

★**FITZWILLIAM HOTEL**　　HOTEL €€€

Map p238 (☑01-478 7000; www.fitzwilliam-hotel. com; St Stephen's Green W; r from €230; P ✳ @☎; ☐all cross-city, ☐Stephen's Green) You couldn't pick a more prestigious spot on the Dublin Monopoly board than this minimalist Terence Conrad–designed number overlooking the Green. Ask for a corner room on the 5th floor (502 or 508), with balmy balcony and a view. The mezzanine-level Citron restaurant serves modern Irish cuisine. It's contemporary elegance at its very best.

WESTBURY HOTEL　　HOTEL €€€

Map p238 (☑01-679 1122; www.doylecollection. com; Grafton St; r/ste from €250/380; P @☎; ☐all city centre, ☐St Stephen's Green) Tucked away just off Grafton St is one of the most elegant hotels in town, although you'll need to upgrade to a suite to really feel the luxury. The standard rooms are perfectly comfortable but not really of the same theme as the luxurious public space – the upstairs lobby is a great spot for afternoon tea or a drink.

WESTIN DUBLIN　　HOTEL €€€

Map p238 (☑01-645 1000; www.thewestindublin. com; Westmoreland St; r from €250; P @☎; ☐all

city centre) Once a fancy bank branch, now a fancier hotel: rooms are decorated in elegant mahogany and soft colours that are reminiscent of the USA's finest. You will sleep on 10 layers of the Westin's own trademark Heavenly Bed, which is damn comfortable indeed. The old bank vault is now the basement bar.

☒ Merrion Square & Around

It's the most sought-after real estate in town, so it's hardly surprising that it's home to the lion's share of the city's top hotels. But although you'll pay for the privilege of bedding down in luxury, there are some excellent deals available at many of these well-located properties, which are within a gentle stroll of the best restaurants, bars and attractions the city has to offer.

DAVENPORT HOTEL　　HOTEL €€

Map p244 (☑01-607 3500; www.davenporthotel. ie; Merrion Sq N; r from €180; P @☎; ☐all city centre) Housed within the old Merrion Hall, which was built in 1863 for the Plymouth Brethren, this is a solid business hotel with large rooms equipped with orthopaedic beds and big bathrooms. It's popular with both business and leisure visitors.

★**MERRION**　　HOTEL €€€

Map p244 (☑01-603 0600; www.merrionhotel. com; Upper Merrion St; r/ste from €400/750; P @☎☒; ☐all city centre) This resplendent five-star hotel, in a terrace of beautifully restored Georgian townhouses, opened in 1988 but looks like it's been around a lot longer.

Try to get a room in the old house (with the largest private art collection in the city), rather than the newer wing, to sample its truly elegant comforts.

Located opposite Government Buildings, its marble corridors are patronised by politicos, visiting dignitaries and the odd celeb. Even if you don't stay, book a table for the superb Art Afternoon Tea (€85 for two), with endless cups of tea served out of silver pots by a raging fire.

★CONRAD DUBLIN   HOTEL €€€

Map p244 (⏺01-602 8900; www.conradhotels. com; Earlsfort Tce; r from €269; ⓟ@🤖; 🖥all city centre) A €13-million refit has transformed this standard business hotel into an exceptional five-star property. The style is contemporary chic – marble bathrooms, wonderfully comfortable beds and a clutter-free aesthetic that doesn't skimp on mod cons (bedside docking stations for iPhones, USB sockets and HD flat-screen TVs) – and it works. The Coburg Brasserie (p95) is exceptional.

The Conrad's one/three/five 'Stay Inspired' concept – where guests can avail of tailored one-, three- and five-hour itineraries based on their interests – is a tad overambitious: it would be miraculous to reach Powerscourt in Wicklow in the 20 minutes allotted in the five-hour itinerary, but the recommendation of Catch 22 in the three-hour itinerary is spot-on.

★NUMBER 31   GUESTHOUSE €€€

Map p244 (⏺01-676 5011; www.number31.ie; 31 Leeson Close; s/d €220/260; ⓟ🤖; 🖥all city centre) The city's most distinctive property is the former home of modernist architect Sam Stephenson, who successfully fused '60s style with 18th-century grace. Its 21 bedrooms are split between the retro coach house, with its coolly modern rooms, and the more elegant Georgian house, where rooms are individually furnished with tasteful French antiques and comfortable beds. Breakfast included.

Gourmet breakfasts with kippers, homemade breads and granola are served in the conservatory.

★MERRION MEWS   GUESTHOUSE €€€

Map p244 (Irish Landmark Trust; www.irishland mark.com; Fitzwilliam Lane; 2 nights from €822; ⓟ🤖; 🖥7, 46A from city centre) This carefully restored Georgian mews dating from 1792 is managed by the Irish Landmark Trust. There are three beautifully appointed double bedrooms that sleep six, a living area and a fully equipped kitchen above a stables – which is still used by the mounted unit of the police. Outside is a garden, one of the few left in the area.

Bookings are for a minimum of two nights and as it's a period home – with thick walls – the wi-fi can be a bit sketchy.

SHELBOURNE   HOTEL €€€

Map p244 (⏺01-676 6471; www.theshelbourne.ie; 27 St Stephen's Green N; r from €385; ⓟ@🤖; 🖥all

HOME AWAY FROM HOME

Self-catering apartments are a good option for visitors staying a few days, for groups of friends, or for families with kids. Apartments range from one-room studios to two-bedroom flats with lounge areas, and include bathrooms and kitchenettes. A decent two-bedroom apartment will cost about €100 to €150 per night. Good, central places include the following:

Premier Suites (Map p244; ⏺01-638 1111; www.premgroup.com; 14-17 Lower Leeson St; s/d from €160/270; ⓟ✳@; 🖥all city centre) Contemporary deluxe studios and suites

Home From Home Apartments (Map p252; ⏺01-678 1166; www.yourhomefromhome. com; The Moorings, Fitzwilliam Quay; apt €130-200; 🚇Grand Canal Dock) There's a two-night minimum stay in high season at these deluxe one- to three-bedroom apartments on the south side.

Latchfords (Map p244; ⏺01-676 0784; www.latchfords.ie; 99-100 Lower Baggot St; studio/2-bedroom apt from €150/190; 🖥all city centre) Elegant Georgian townhouse with studio and two-bedroom apartments.

Oliver St John Gogarty's Penthouse Apartments (Map p236; ⏺01-671 1822; www. gogartys.ie; 18-21 Anglesea St; 2-bed apt €99-199; 🖥all city centre) Self-catering accommodation above the pub of the same name.

city centre, 🚇St Stephen's Green) Dublin's most famous hotel was founded in 1824 and has been the preferred halting post of the powerful and wealthy ever since. Several owners and refurbs later it is now part of Marriott's Renaissance portfolio, and while it has a couple of rivals in the luxury stakes, it cannot be beaten for heritage.

Guests are staying in a slice of history: it was here that the Irish Constitution was drafted in 1921, and this is the hotel in Elizabeth Bowen's eponymous novel. Afternoon tea in the refurbished Lord Mayor's Lounge remains one of the best experiences in town.

🛏 Temple Bar

If you're here for a weekend of wild abandon and can't fathom anything more than a quick stumble into bed, then Temple Bar's choice of hotels and hostels will suit you perfectly. Generally speaking the rooms are small, the prices are large and you must be able to handle the late-night noise of diehard revellers.

PARAMOUNT HOTEL · HOTEL €

Map p236 (📞01-417 9900; www.paramounthotel.ie; cnr Parliament St & Essex Gate; d/tr €115/190; 🅿 @🛜; 🖵all city centre) Behind the Victorian facade, the lobby is a (sort of) re-creation of a 1930s hotel, complete with dark-wood floors, deep-red leather Chesterfield couches and heavy velvet drapes. The 70-odd rooms don't quite bring *The Maltese Falcon* to mind, but they're handsomely furnished and very comfortable. Downstairs is the Turk's Head (p107), one of the area's most popular bars.

ASHFIELD HOUSE · HOSTEL €

Map p236 (📞01-679 7734; www.ashfieldhostel.com; 19-20 D'Olier St; dm/tw from €18/75; @🛜; 🖵all city centre) A stone's throw from Temple Bar and O'Connell Bridge, this modern hostel in a converted church has a selection of tidy four- and six-bed rooms, one large dorm and 25 rooms with private bathroom. It's more like a small hotel, but without the price tag. A continental-style breakfast is included – a rare beast indeed for a hostel. Maximum stay is six nights.

GOGARTY'S TEMPLE BAR HOSTEL · HOSTEL €

Map p236 (📞01-671 1822; www.gogartys.ie/hostel; 58-59 Fleet St; dm/d €16/100; 🅿🛜; 🖵all city centre) Sleeping isn't really the activity of choice for anyone staying in this compact, decent hostel in the middle of Temple Bar, next to the pub of the same name (p106). It tends to get booked up with stag and hen parties so, depending on your mood, bring either your earplugs or your bunny ears. Six self-catering apartments are also available.

BARNACLES · HOSTEL €

Map p236 (📞01-671 6277; www.barnacles.ie; 19 Temple Lane S; dm/d from €20/130; 🅿🛜; 🖵all city centre) If you're here for a good time, not a long time, then this bustling Temple Bar hostel is the ideal spot to meet fellow revellers and tap up the helpful and knowledgable staff for the best places to cause mischief. Rooms are quieter at the back.

KINLAY HOUSE · HOSTEL €

Map p236 (📞01-679 6644; www.kinlaydublin.ie; 2-12 Lord Edward St; dm/d from €20/90; 🛜; 🖵all city centre) This former boarding house for boys has massive, mixed dormitories (for up to 24), and smaller rooms, including doubles. It's in Temple Bar, so it's occasionally raucous. Staff are friendly, and there are cooking facilities and a cafe. Breakfast is included.

DUBLIN CITI HOTEL · HOTEL €

Map p236 (📞01-679 4455; www.dublincitihotel.com; 46-49 Dame St; r from €109; @🛜; 🖵all city centre) An unusual turreted 19th-century building right next to the Central Bank is home to this midrange hotel. Rooms aren't huge, are simply furnished and have fresh white quilts. It's only a stagger (literally) from the heart of Temple Bar, hic.

CLARENCE HOTEL · HOTEL €€

Map p236 (📞01-407 0800; www.theclarence.ie; 6-8 Wellington Quay; r/ste from €150/350; 🅿 @🛜; 🖵all city centre) Bono and the Edge's handsome boutique hotel was once the hottest bed in town, but now it's just another elegant Dublin four-star designed to reflect the aesthetic of a 1930s gentlemen's club, complete with Shaker oak beds draped in Irish linen, an excellent bar and a fine restaurant.

Its owners have been involved in a long-running legal wrangle over plans to demolish part of the building as part of a €150 million expansion, but so far Dublin City Council has proven stubbornly resistant.

MORGAN HOTEL · BOUTIQUE HOTEL €€

Map p236 (📞01-643 7000; www.themorgan.com; 10 Fleet St; r from €200; @🛜; 🖵all city centre) It was built to attract the Spice Girls, now it just caters to girls (and guys) on a spicy

SLEEPING TEMPLE BAR

weekend in Dublin. No bad thing, of course, especially as the hotel has stood up well to the ravages of recession. It's a little less resilient in the face of noise: if you're looking for quiet, you might consider elsewhere.

ELIZA LODGE
GUESTHOUSE €€

Map p236 (☑01-671 8044; www.elizalodge.com; 23-24 Wellington Quay; s/d from €120/200; ✳🏠; 🖳all city centre) It's priced like a hotel, looks like a hotel, but it's still a guesthouse. The 18 rooms are comfortable, spacious and – due to its position right over the Millennium Bridge – come with great views of the Liffey. It has discounted parking rates with a nearby car park.

★IRISH LANDMARK TRUST
HERITAGE HOTEL €€€

Map p236 (☑01-670 4733; www.irishlandmark.com; 25 Eustace St; 2 nights for 7 people €820; 🖳all city centre) This 18th-century heritage house has been gloriously restored to the highest standard by the Irish Landmark Trust. Furnished with tasteful antiques and authentic furniture and fittings (including a grand piano in the drawing room), it sleeps up to seven in its three bedrooms, which must be booked for a minimum of two nights.

The house was built in 1720 and was home to a wealthy wool merchant and later to author and historian Standish O'Grady (1846–1928), whom WB Yeats called the 'Father of the Irish Revival' for works like *The Story of Ireland* (1894; written while he lived in the house), despite being a Protestant and a staunch unionist!

🛏 North of the Liffey

There is a scattering of good midrange options between O'Connell St and Smithfield. Gardiner St, to the east of O'Connell St, was the traditional B&B district of town, but with only a few exceptions it has been rendered largely obsolete by chain hotels elsewhere throughout the city.

★ISAACS HOSTEL
HOSTEL €

Map p249 (☑01-855 6215; www.isaacs.ie; 2-5 Frenchman's Lane; dm/tw from €16/70; @🏠; 🖳all city centre,🚊Connolly) The northside's best hostel – hell, for atmosphere alone it's the best in town – is in a 200-year-old wine vault just around the corner from the main bus station. With summer barbecues, live music in the lounge, internet access,

colourful dorms and even a sauna, this terrific place generates consistently good reviews from backpackers and other travellers.

★GENERATOR HOSTEL
HOSTEL €

Map p249 (☑01-901 0222; www.generatorhostels.com; Smithfield Sq; dm/tw from €16/70; @🏠; 🚊Smithfield) This European chain brings its own brand of funky, fun design to Dublin's hostel scene, with bright colours, comfortable dorms (including women-only) and a lively social scene. It even has a screening room for movies. Good location right on Smithfield Sq, next to the Old Jameson Distillery (p133).

MEC HOSTEL
HOSTEL €

Map p249 (☑01-873 0826; www.mechostel.com; 42 N Great George's St; dm/d from €14/70; 🏠; 🖳36, 36A) A Georgian classic on one of Dublin's most beautiful streets, this popular hostel has a host of dorms and doubles, all with private bathroom. Facilities include a full kitchen, two lounges and a bureau de change. Breakfast is only €2 and there's decent wi-fi throughout.

JACOB'S INN
HOSTEL €

Map p249 (☑01-855 5660; www.jacobsinn.com; 21-28 Talbot Pl; dm/d from €11/70; 🏠; 🖳all city centre, 🚊Connolly) Sister hostel to Isaacs around the corner, this clean and modern hostel offers spacious accommodation with private bathrooms and outstanding facilities, including some wheelchair-accessible rooms, a bureau de change, bike storage and a self-catering kitchen.

CASTLE HOTEL
HOTEL €

Map p249 (☑01-874 6949; www.castle-hotel.ie; 3-4 Great Denmark St; r from €100; P🏠; 🖳all city centre, 🚊Connolly) In business since 1809, the Castle Hotel may be slightly rough around the edges but it's one of the most pleasant hotels this side of the Liffey. The fabulous palazzo-style grand staircase leads to 50-odd bedrooms, whose furnishings are traditional and a tad antiquated, but perfectly good throughout – check out the original Georgian cornicing around the high ceilings.

ABBEY COURT HOSTEL
HOSTEL €

Map p249 (☑01-878 0700; www.abbey-court.com; 29 Bachelor's Walk; dm/d from €16/80; 🏠; 🖳all city centre) Spread over two buildings, this large, well-run hostel has 33 clean dorm beds and good storage. Its excellent facilities include a dining hall, a conservatory and a barbecue area. Doubles with bathrooms are in the newer building where a light breakfast is provided in the adjacent cafe. Not surprisingly, this is a popular spot; reservations are advised.

JURY'S INN PARNELL ST   HOTEL €
Map p249 (☑01-878 4900; www.jurysinns.com; Moore St Plaza, Parnell St; r from €139; ❋@☎; ☒36, 36A) Jury's hotels are nothing if not reliable, and this edition of Ireland's most popular hotel chain is no exception. What do you care that the furnishings were mass-produced and flat-packed and that the decor was created to be utterly inoffensive to everything save good taste? The location – just off Upper O'Connell St – is terrific.

ANCHOR HOUSE   B&B €
Map p249 (☑01-878 6913; www.anchorhousedublin.com; 49 Lower Gardiner St; r from €125; ℗☎; ☒all city centre, ☒Connolly) While most B&Bs round these parts offer pretty much the same stuff – TV, half-decent shower, tea-and coffee-making facilities and wi-fi – the Anchor does all of that with a certain (frayed) elegance, and also has a friendliness the others can't easily match.

ACADEMY PLAZA HOTEL   HOTEL €
Map p249 (☑01-878 0666; www.academyplazahotel.ie; Findlater Pl; r from €120; ℗@☎; ☒all city centre) Only a few steps from O'Connell St, this solidly three-star hotel offers a comfortable, if unmemorable, night's sleep. The deluxe suites come with free wi-fi and flat-screen digital TVs. There's discounted parking (€6) at the covered car park next door.

CLIFDEN GUESTHOUSE   GUESTHOUSE €
Map p249 (☑01-874 6364; www.clifdenhouse.com; 32 Gardiner Pl; r from €100; ℗☎; ☒36, 36A) The Clifden is a very nicely refurbished Georgian house with 14 tastefully decorated rooms. They all come with bathroom, and are immaculately clean and extremely comfortable. It offers a 50% discount on nearby parking as well as exceptional online deals.

MALDRON HOTEL SMITHFIELD   HOTEL €€
Map p249 (☑01-485 0900; www.maldronhotels.com; Smithfield Village; r/ste from €180/220; ☎; ☒25, 25A, 25B, 66, 66A, 66B, 67, 90, 151 to Upper Ormond Quay, ☒Smithfield) With big bedrooms and plenty of earth tones to soften the contemporary edges, this functionally modern hotel is your best bet in this part of town. We love the floor-to-ceiling windows: great for checking out what's going on below in the square.

RIU PLAZA GRESHAM HOTEL   HOTEL €€
Map p249 (☑01-874 6881; www.greshamhotels.com; 23 Upper O'Connell St; r from €200; ℗❋@☎; ☒all city centre) In 2016 the landmark Gresham was purchased by Spanish hotel giants Riu, who so far have not altered a building that has been hosting guests since 1817. Its 323 rooms and 10 suites are spacious and well-serviced. The fabulous open-plan foyer is one of the city's most impressive hotel lobbies.

MORRISON HOTEL   HOTEL €€€
Map p249 (☑01-887 2400; www.morrisonhotel.ie; Lower Ormond Quay; r from €260; ℗@☎; ☒all city centre, ☒Jervis) Space-age funky design is the template at this hip hotel, part of the Hilton Doubletree group. King-size beds (with fancy mattresses), 40in LCD TVs, free wi-fi and deluxe toiletries are just some of the hotel's offerings. Easily the northside's most luxurious address.

🛏 Docklands & the Grand Canal

Staying in the Docklands area means you'll be relying on public transport or taxis to get you in and out of the city centre.

CLAYTON HOTEL CARDIFF LANE   HOTEL €€
Map p252 (☑01-643 9500; www.claytonhotelcardifflane.com; Cardiff Lane; r €230; @☎☒; ☒Grand Canal Dock) A good midrange hotel with excellent amenities (two restaurants, a bar and a fitness centre), this hotel suffers only because of its location, on an isolated street far from the city-centre action. Its saving graces are the nearby Grand Canal Dock, its selection of bars and restaurants, and its swimming pool.

SPENCER HOTEL   HOTEL €€
Map p252 (☑01-433 8800; www.thespencerhotel.com; Custom House Quay; r/ste from €160/230; ℗@☎☒; ☒George's Dock) This swanky business hotel in the heart of the Irish Financial Services Centre has beautiful rooms decorated with contemporary light oak furnishings, designer beds and rainforest power showers. Guests have free use of the health club. Weekend rates are substantially cheaper.

★MARKER   HOTEL €€€
Map p252 (☑01-687 5100; www.themarkerhoteldublin.com; Grand Canal Sq; r/ste from €350/520; ℗@☎; ☒Grand Canal Dock)

Behind the eye-catching chequerboard facade created by Manuel Aires Mateus are 187 swanky rooms and suites decked out in a wintry palette (washed out citruses and cobalts) and starkly elegant furnishings, which give them an atmosphere of cool sophistication. The public areas are a little wilder and the rooftop bar is a summer favourite with the 'in' crowd.

GIBSON HOTEL
HOTEL €€€

Map p252 (☑01-618 5000; www.thegibsonhotel.ie; Point Village; r from €250; P @ ☎; ☐151 from city centre, ☐The Point) Built for business travellers and out-of-towners taking in a gig at the 3 Arena (p150) next door, the Gibson is impressive: 250-odd ultramodern rooms decked out in deluxe beds, flat-screen TVs and internet work stations. You might catch last night's star act having breakfast the next morning in the snazzy restaurant area.

⬛ The Southside

Some of the city's most elegant B&Bs are scattered about these leafy suburbs, including a handful that can rival even the best hotels in town for comfort and service.

⭐ARIEL HOUSE
INN €

Map p254 (☑01-668 5512; www.ariel-house.net; 52 Lansdowne Rd; r from €130; P ☎; ☐4, 7, 8, 84 from city centre) Our favourite lodging in Ballsbridge is this wonderful Victorian-era property that is somewhere between a boutique hotel and a luxury B&B. Its 28 rooms are all individually decorated with period furniture, which lends the place an air of genuine luxury. A far better choice than most hotels.

WATERLOO HOUSE
INN €

Map p254 (☑01-660 1888; www.waterloohouse.ie; 8-10 Waterloo Rd; s/d from €99/119; P ☎; ☐5, 7, 7A, 8, 18, 45 from city centre) Within walking distance of St Stephen's Green, this lovely guesthouse is spread over two ivy-clad Georgian houses off Baggot St. Rooms are tastefully decorated with high-quality furnishings in authentic Farrow & Ball Georgian colours. Home-cooked breakfast is served in the conservatory, or in the garden on sunny days.

⭐ABERDEEN LODGE
GUESTHOUSE €€

Map p254 (☑01-283 8155; www.aberdeen lodgedublin.com; 53-55 Park Ave; r from €160; P @ ☎; ☐2, 3, ℝSydney Parade) Not only is this absolutely one of Dublin's best guesthouses, but it's also a carefully guarded secret, known only to those who dare stay a short train ride away from the city centre. Their reward is a luxurious house with a level of personalised service as good as you'll find in one of the city's top hotels.

Most of the stunning rooms have either a four-poster, a half-tester or a brass bed to complement the authentic Edwardian furniture and tasteful art on the walls. The suites even have fully working Adams fireplaces. As there is one member of staff for every two rooms, the service is exceptional, not to mention totally hands-on and very courteous. An added touch for international guests is the 'meet and greet' service at Dublin Airport, where a driver will collect you and your baggage and escort you to the hotel in a town car (book it in advance).

SCHOOLHOUSE HOTEL
BOUTIQUE HOTEL €€

Map p254 (☑01-667 5014; www.schoolhouse hotel.com; 2-8 Northumberland Rd; r from €170; P ☎ ⬛; ☐5, 7, 7A, 8, 18, 27X, 44 from city centre) A Victorian schoolhouse dating from 1861, this beautiful building has been successfully converted into an exquisite boutique hotel that is (ahem) ahead of its class. Its 31 cosy bedrooms, named after famous Irish people, all have king-sized beds, big white quilts and loudly patterned headboards. The Canteen bar and patio bustles with local businessfolk in summer.

PEMBROKE TOWNHOUSE
INN €€

Map p254 (☑01-660 0277; www.pembroketown house.com; 90 Pembroke Rd; r from €150; P ☎ ⬛; ☐5, 7, 7A, 8, 18, 45 from city centre) This once elegant boutique hotel in a handsome Georgian townhouse has shown signs of age in recent years, and a spruce-up is long overdue. Nevertheless, it is still a comfortable place to stay and its location – on a leafy street near the bustling Baggot St – is excellent.

DYLAN
HOTEL €€€

Map p254 (☑01-660 3001; www.dylan.ie; Eastmoreland Pl; r from €270; ✳ @ ☎; ☐5, 7, 7A, 8, 18, 27X, 44 from city centre) The Dylan's baroque-meets-Scandinavian-sleek designer look has stood the test of time, despite the hotel opening when the Celtic Tiger's brash-is-beautiful attitude was in full voice. These days the Dylan is just a stylishly elegant hotel, with wonderfully appointed rooms adorned in crisp linen and a buzzy bar where the beautiful people still gather in force.

Understand Dublin

Dublin Today

It's a great time to be in Dublin. The austerity blues have been largely chased away, and the city has once again focused its attentions on the business of self-improvement, fun and the turning of a tidy profit. From skyscrapers to food trucks, Dublin is investing once more in itself, although this new wave of prosperity is bringing with it some familiar problems: the city is confronting another crisis of high rents and low availability.

Best on Film

The Commitments (1991) Roddy Doyle's novel about a soul band in Dublin made into a terrific film by Alan Parker.

What Richard Did (2012) The story of what happens when a privileged youth assaults a romantic rival who dies of his injuries; loosely based on real events that occurred in 2000.

The Dead (1987) Stunning rendition of James Joyce's story from *Dubliners* starring Donal McCann and Angelica Huston.

Best in Print

Dubliners (James Joyce; 1914) Fifteen poignant and powerful tales of Dubliners and the moments that define their lives. Even if you never visit, read this book.

Dublin 4 (Maeve Binchy; 1982) Masterful exploration of goings-on in Dublin's most affluent suburb.

The Barrytown Trilogy (Roddy Doyle) *The Commitments* (1987), *The Snapper* (1990) and *The Van* (1991) – yes, they've all been made into films, but the books are still better.

Ain't Nothing Going on but the Rent

The housing and rental market was in crisis in mid-2017. A study revealed that the average rent for a house or one-bed apartment in Dublin city centre was €1690 per month, up 16.2% in the year up to March 2017. On the south side of the city it was €1787 per month – higher than London.

Most experts point the finger at a dearth of supply – the capital needs in excess of 9000 new homes just to keep up with growing demand. Other factors have contributed to what has officially been termed a housing crisis: these include the proliferation of Airbnb, professional landlords setting new market rates, and rental restrictions that gravely penalise new tenants over existing ones.

The property crisis has also impacted on tourism, whose numbers continue to rise. There's a shortage of hotel beds in the city, which means higher hotel rates and a huge spike in the popularity of short-term private letting services such as Airbnb, as landlords eye up the easy cash from visitors over steady rental income from locals.

Light at the End of the Tunnel

In Irish, the word 'luas' means speed, which seems a cruel irony given how long the expansion works of Dublin's light-rail tram network, the Luas, have taken. The city centre from O'Connell St to St Stephen's Green has been dug up for the last few years as workers and engineers laboured to link the existing red and green lines with a new light-rail corridor across the Liffey.

Thankfully, it's all come to an end and the city is once again going about its business without worrying about closed-off streets and unsightly roadworks. The new line is a huge boon to the city, but it won't benefit motor traffic: plans are afoot to make all of College

Green off-limits to all cars except taxis, which is good news for pedestrians and those looking to combat city-centre pollution, but will invariably create bottlenecks elsewhere in the centre as traffic looks for new ways to move across the river.

Brexit & Beyond

Ireland's unique relationship with Britain has made it vulnerable to the vagaries of Brexit, with most government forecasters and private economists adopting the maxim of 'the harder the Brexit, the worse the outcome'.

Bilateral trade flow would be severely impacted – by as much as 20%, experts warn – which is a lot given that Britain is Ireland's main source of imports and its third-largest export market. The other huge issue relates to the border between the Republic and the North: the return of a hard border (effectively the United Kingdom's only land border with the EU) will have a huge impact not just on trade between North and South, but could potentially affect the delicate balance between Unionists and Nationalists.

Dublin's response has been to launch a charm offensive in the hope of offering itself as a viable alternative to London for thousands of financial sector jobs that might seek to relocate following Brexit; an optimistic assessment is that the sector might grow by as much as 50% over the coming years, transforming the city into a major European financial player – and putting even greater pressure on a housing market that is already straining at the seams. Dublin likes its optimism flavoured with a strong dose of fatalism.

Repealing the 8th

2017 saw the reinvigoration of the campaign to repeal the eighth Amendment to the Irish constitution, which effectively bans abortion in all but the most extreme cases. In April, the Citizens' Assembly (a body of 99 citizens convened by the government to discuss constitutional issues) voted overwhelmingly in favour of abortion with 'no restriction as to reasons'. Yet while a majority of the population favours reform of the existing law, polls show two-thirds would reject abortion on request.

Still, the government has indicated that a referendum on the subject will take place in 2018. In the meantime, you may notice some Dubliners sporting a sweatshirt with the word 'Repeal' on it – the most popular variant is 'Repeal the 8th' in cursive script inside a red love heart; designed by Dublin artist Maser.

if Dublin were 100 people

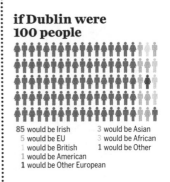

85 would be Irish
5 would be EU
1 would be British
1 would be American
1 would be Other European
3 would be Asian
3 would be African
1 would be Other

age of Dubliners
(% of population)

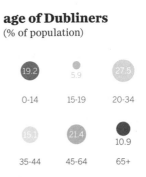

| 19.2 | 5.9 | 27.5 |
| 0-14 | 15-19 | 20-34 |

| 15.1 | 21.4 | 10.9 |
| 35-44 | 45-64 | 65+ |

population per sq km

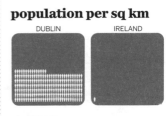

DUBLIN   IRELAND

† ≈ 55 people

History

Until a couple of decades ago, if you'd asked your average Dubliner the key to the city's complex history, they'd most likely give you a version of the past punctuated with '800 years'. This refers to the duration of the English (or British) occupation, the sine qua non of everything that happened to this city. Yet within that narrative is a rich and storied tale of invasion, rebellion and transformation, as Dublin works its way through the various epochs, from Viking to Georgian and beyond.

Early Footprints & Celtic Highways

Stone Age farmers who arrived in Ireland between 10,000 and 8000 BC provided the country's genetic stock and lay the foundations of its agricultural economy. During the following Bronze Age, in addition to discovering and crafting metals to stock the future National Museum, they also found time to refine their farming techniques and raise livestock.

Iron Age warriors from Eastern Europe, who were known as the Celts, arrived in the country around 500 BC and divided Ireland into provinces and myriad districts ruled by chieftains. Roads connecting these provinces converged at a ford over the River Liffey called Átha Cliath (Ford of the Hurdles) – which Ptolemy wrote about in AD 140 as Eblana Civitas – and the town that grew up at this junction during the 9th century was to give Dublin its Irish name, Baile Átha Cliath (Town of the Hurdle Ford).

> Celtic society was ruled by Brehon Law, the tenets of which still form the basis of Ireland's ethical code today.

The Coming of Christianity

St Patrick founded the See of Dublin sometime in the mid-5th century and went about the business of conversion in present-day Wicklow and Malahide, before laying hands on Leoghaire, the King of Ireland, using water from a well next to St Patrick's Cathedral. Or so the story goes. Irrespective of the details, Patrick and his monk buddies were successful because they managed to fuse the strong tradition of druidism and pagan ritual with the new Christian teaching, which created an exciting hybrid known as Celtic, or Insular, Christianity.

TIMELINE

10,000 BC	500 BC	AD 431–432
Human beings arrive in Ireland during the mesolithic era, originally crossing a land bridge between Scotland and Ireland and later the sea in hide-covered boats.	Iron Age warriors from Eastern Europe, known as the Celts, divide Ireland into provinces and myriad districts ruled by chieftains.	Pope Celestine I sends Bishop Palladius to Ireland to minister to those 'already believing in Christ'; St Patrick arrives the following year to continue the mission.

Compared to new hot spots like Clonmacnoise in County Offaly and Glendalough in County Wicklow, Dublin was a rural backwater and didn't really figure in the Golden Age, when Irish Christian scholars excelled in the study of Latin and Greek learning and Christian theology. They studied in the monasteries that were, in essence, Europe's most important universities, producing brilliant students, magnificent illuminated books such as the *Book of Kells* (now housed in Trinity College), ornate jewellery and the many carved stone crosses that dot the island 'of saints and scholars'.

The nature of Christianity in Ireland was one of marked independence from Rome, especially in the areas of monastic rule and penitential practice, which emphasised private confession to a priest followed by penances levied by the priest in reparation – which is the spirit and letter of the practice of confession that exists to this day.

St Patrick showed a remarkable understanding of Celtic power structures by working to convert chieftains rather than ordinary Celts, who inevitably followed their leaders into adopting the new religion.

The Vikings

Raids by marauding Vikings had been a fact of Irish life for quite some time, before a group of them decided to take a break from their hell-raising to build a harbour (or *longphort*, in Irish) on the banks of the Liffey in 837. Although a Celtic army forced them out some 65 years later, they returned in 917 with a massive fleet, established a stronghold by the black pool at Wood Quay, just behind Christ Church Cathedral, and dug their heels in. They went back to plundering the countryside but also laid down guidelines on plot sizes and town boundaries for their town of Dyflinn (derived from the Irish for 'black pool', *dubh linn*), which became the most prominent trading centre in the Viking world.

But their good times came to an end in 1014 when an alliance of Irish clans led by Brian Ború decisively whipped them (and the Irish clans that *didn't* side with Brian Ború) at the Battle of Clontarf, forever breaking the Scandinavian grip on the eastern seaboard. However, rather than abandoning the place in defeat, the Vikings enjoyed Dublin so much that they decided to stay and integrate.

During the 12th century Dublin became a pilgrimage city, in part because it housed the Bacall Íosa (staff of Jesus), St Patrick's legendary crozier.

Strongbow & the Normans

The next wave of invaders came in 1169, when an army of Cambro-Norman knights led by Richard de Clare (better known as Strongbow) landed in Wexford at the urging of Dermot MacMurrough, ousted King of Leinster, who needed help to regain his throne. As a gesture of thanks, MacMurrough made Strongbow his heir and gave him Aoife, his daughter, as a wife. Strongbow and his knights then took Dublin in 1170 and decided to make it their new capital.

917	988	1170	1172
Plundering Vikings establish a new settlement at the mouth of the harbour and call it 'Dyfflin', which soon becomes a centre of economic power.	High King Mael Seachlainn II leads the permanent Irish conquest of Dyfflin, giving the settlement its modern name in Irish – Baile Átha Cliath, meaning 'Town of the Hurdle Ford'.	Strongbow captures Dublin and then takes Aoife, daughter of the High King Dermot MacMurroughs, as his wife before being crowned King of Leinster.	King Henry II of England invades Ireland, forcing the Cambro-Norman warlords and some of the Gaelic Irish kings to accept him as their overlord.

Meanwhile, King Henry II of England, concerned that the Normans might set up a rival power base in Ireland, organised his own invading force, and landed his army in 1171 – with the blessing of Pope Adrian IV, who wanted Henry to make Ireland's renegade monks toe the Roman line.

The Normans declared their fealty to the English throne and set about reconstructing and fortifying their new capital. In 1172 construction began on Christ Church Cathedral, and 20 years later work began on St Patrick's Cathedral, a few hundred metres to the south.

Henry II's son, King John, commissioned the construction of Dublin Castle in 1204 'for the safe custody of our treasure...and the defence of the city'. As capital of the English 'colony' in Ireland, Dublin expanded. Trade was organised and craft guilds developed, although membership was limited to those of 'English name and blood'.

As Dublin grew bigger so did its problems, and over the next few centuries misery seemed to pile upon mishap. In 1317 Ireland's worst famine of the Middle Ages killed off thousands and reduced some to cannibalism. In 1348 the country was decimated by the Black Death; the devastating recurrence over the following century indicates the terrible squalor of medieval Dublin.

In the 15th century the English extended their influence beyond the Pale by throwing their weight behind the dominant Irish lords. The atmosphere was becoming markedly cosier as the Anglo-Norman occupiers began to follow previous invaders by integrating into Irish culture.

The Tudors & The Protestant Ascendancy

Ireland presented a particular challenge to Henry VIII (r 1509–47), in part due to the Anglo-Norman lords' more or less unfettered power over the country, which didn't sit well with Henry's belief in strong monarchical rule. He decreed absolute royal power over Ireland, but the Irish lords weren't going to take it lying down.

In 1534 the most powerful of Leinster's Anglo-Normans, 'Silken' Thomas Fitzgerald, renounced his allegiance to the king, and Henry came at him ferociously: within a year Fitzgerald was dead and all his lands confiscated. Henry ordered the surrender of all lands to the English Crown and, three years later, after his spat with Rome, he dissolved the monasteries and all Church lands passed to the newly constituted Anglican Church. Dublin was declared an Anglican city and relics such as the Bacall Íosa (Staff of Jesus) were destroyed.

Elizabeth I (r 1558–1603) came to the throne with the same uncompromising attitude to Ireland as her father. Ulster was the most hostile to her, with the Irish fighting doggedly under the command of

For all their might, the Anglo-Normans' dominance was limited to a walled area surrounding what today is loosely Greater Dublin, and was then called 'the Pale'. Beyond the Pale – a phrase that entered the English language to mean 'beyond convention' – Ireland remained unbowed and unconquered.

1297	1315	1348	1350–1530
Dublin becomes the main seat of the Parliament of Ireland, comprised of merchants and landowners.	A Scottish army led by Edward de Bruce attacks the city; waning English interest in defending Dublin forces the Earls of Kildare to become the city's main protectors.	Roughly half of the city's population of 30,000 succumbs to the Black Death; victims are buried in mass graves in an area of the Liberties still known as the 'Blackpitts'.	The Anglo-Norman barons establish power bases independent of the English Crown. English control gradually extends to an area around Dublin known as 'the Pale'.

Hugh O'Neill, the Earl of Tyrone, but they too were finally defeated in 1603.

O'Neill's defeat signalled the end of Gaelic Ireland and the renewed colonisation of the country through plantation. Loyal Protestants from England and Scotland were awarded the rich agricultural, confiscated lands of Ulster, sowing the bitter seeds of division that blight the province to this day. Unlike previous arrivals, these new colonists kept very much apart from the native Irish, who were left disenfranchised, landless and reduced to a state of near misery.

All the while, Dublin prospered as the bulwark of English domination and became a bastion of Protestantism. A chasm developed between the 'English' city and the 'Irish' countryside, where there was continuing unrest and growing resentment. After winning the English Civil War (1641–51), Oliver Cromwell came to Ireland to personally reassert English control and, while Protestant Dublin was left untouched (save the use of St Patrick's Cathedral as a stable for English horses), his troops were uncompromising in their dealing with rebellion up and down the eastern coast.

Georgian Dublin & The Golden Age

Following the Restoration of 1660 and the coronation of Charles II (r 1660–85), Dublin embarked upon a century of unparalleled development and essentially waved two fingers at the rest of Ireland, which was being brought to its knees. In 1690 the rest of Ireland backed the losing side when it took up arms for the Catholic king of England, James II (r 1685–88), who was ultimately defeated by the Protestant William of Orange at the Battle of the Boyne, not far from Dublin.

William's victory ushered in the punitive Penal Code, which stripped Catholics of most basic rights in a single, sweeping legislative blow. Again, however, the country's misfortune proved the capital's gain as the city was flooded with landless refugees willing to work for a pittance.

With plenty of cash to go around and an eagerness to live in a city that reflected their new-found wealth, the Protestant nobility overhauled Dublin during the reigns of the four Georges (1714–1830). Speculators bought up swathes of land and commissioned substantial projects of urban renewal, including the creation of new streets, the laying out of city parks and the construction of magnificent new buildings and residences.

It was impossible to build in the heart of the medieval city, so the nouveau riche moved north across the river, creating a new Dublin of stately squares surrounded by fine Georgian mansions. The elegantly

Hugh O'Neill achieved something of a pyrrhic victory in 1603 when he refused to surrender until after he heard of Elizabeth I's death. He and his fellow earls then fled the country in what become known as the Flight of the Earls.

1487	1487	1537	1584
Gerard Mór Fitzgerald, Earl of Kildare, occupies Dublin with help of troops from Burgundy, in direct defiance of King Henry VII.	Fitzgerald supports claims of Yorkist pretender Lambert Simnel, a 10-year-old who is crowned King Edward VI in Christ Church Cathedral.	'Silken' Thomas Fitzgerald, son of the Earl of Kildare, storms Dublin and its English garrisons. The rebellion is squashed; Thomas and his followers are executed.	Mayoress Margaret Ball dies following imprisonment for her Catholic sympathies. Archbishop Dermot O'Hurley is hanged for his support of a rebellion against the English Crown.

made-over Dublin became the second city in the British Empire and the fifth largest in Europe.

Dublin's teeming, mostly Catholic, slums soon spread north in pursuit of the rich, who turned back south to grand new homes around Merrion Sq, St Stephen's Green and Fitzwilliam Sq.

Dublin Declines, Catholicism Rises

Constant migration from the countryside into Dublin meant that, by the end of the 18th century, the capital had a Catholic majority, most of whom lived in terrible conditions in ever-worsening slums. Inspired by the Enlightenment and the principles of the French Revolution of 1789, many leading Irish figures (nearly all of whom were Protestant) began to question the quality and legitimacy of British rule.

Rebellion was in the air by the turn of the century, starting with the abortive French invasion at the urging of Dubliner Wolfe Tone (1763–98) and his United Irishmen in 1798. The 'Year of the French' resulted in defeat for the invaders and the death of Tone, but in 1803 the United Irishmen tried again, this time under the leadership of Robert Emmet (1778–1803), which also resulted in failure and Emmet's execution on Thomas St, near the Guinness brewery.

It was only a matter of time before Dublin's bubble burst, and the pin came in the form of the 1801 Act of Union, which dissolved the Irish parliament (originally established in 1297) and reintroduced direct rule from Westminster. Many of the upper classes fled to London, the dramatic growth that had characterised Dublin in the previous century came to an almost immediate halt, and the city fell into a steady decline.

While Dublin was licking its wounds, a Kerry lawyer called Daniel O'Connell (1775–1847) launched his campaign to recover basic rights for Catholics, achieving much with the Catholic Emancipation Act of 1829. The 'Liberator', as he came to be known, became the first Catholic lord mayor of Dublin, in 1841.

By 1910 it was reckoned that 20,000 Dublin families each occupied a single room.

The end of the 17th century saw an influx of Huguenot weavers, who settled in Dublin after fleeing anti-Protestant legislation in France and established a successful cloth industry, largely in the Liberties, that helped fuel the city's growth.

A Nation's Soup Kitchen

Rural Ireland had become overwhelmingly dependent on the easily grown potato. Blight – a disease that rots tubers – had always been an occasional hazard, but when three successive crops failed between 1845 and 1847, it spelled disaster. The human cost was cataclysmic: up to one million people died from disease and starvation, while more again fled the country for Britain and the United States. The damage

1592	1594–1603	1603	1640s–82
Trinity College is founded on the grounds of a former monastery, on the basis of a charter granted by Elizabeth I to 'stop Ireland being infected by popery'.	Nine Years' War between English and Irish chieftains led by Hugh O'Neill brings English troops to Dublin, who force citizenry to house them.	Hugh O'Neill and the Irish fighting under his command in Ulster are defeated by Elizabeth I's forces. He and his fellow earls flee the country in what is known as the Flight of the Earls.	Dublin's resurgence begins as the city's population grows from 10,000 in the mid-1640s to nearly 60,000 in 1682.

was compounded by the British government's adoption of a laissez-faire economic policy, which opposed food aid for famine occurring within the Empire. In Ireland, landowners refused to countenance any forbearance on rents, all the while exporting crops to foreign markets. Defaulters – starving or not – were penalised with incarceration in workhouses or prison.

The British government's uncompromising stance hardened the steel of opposition. The deaths and mass exodus caused by the Famine had a profound social and cultural effect on Ireland and left a scar on the Irish psyche that cannot be overestimated. Urban Dublin escaped the worst ravages, but desperate migrants flooded into the city looking for relief – soup kitchens were set up all over the city, including in the bucolic Merrion Sq, where presumably its affluent residents bore direct witness to the tragedy.

The horrors of the Famine and its impact on Dublin's centre saw the wealthy abandon the city for a new set of salubrious suburbs south of Dublin along the coast, now accessible via Ireland's first railway line, built in 1834 to connect the city to Kingstown (present-day Dun Laoghaire). The flight from the city continued for the next 70 years and many of the fine Georgian residences became slum dwellings. With such squalor came a host of social ills, including alcohol, which had always been a source of solace but now became a chronic problem.

The Blossoming of National Pride

In the second half of the 19th century, Dublin was staunchly divided along sectarian lines and, although Catholics were still partly second-class citizens, a burgeoning Catholic middle class provided the impetus for Ireland's march towards independence.

It was the dashing figure of Protestant landlord Charles Stewart Parnell (1846–91), from County Wicklow, that first harnessed the broad public support for Home Rule. Elected to Westminster in 1875, the 'Uncrowned King of Ireland' campaigned tirelessly for land reform and a Dublin parliament.

He appeared to have an ally in the British prime minister, William Gladstone, who lightened the burden on tenants by passing Land Acts enabling them to buy property. Gladstone was also converted to the cause of Home Rule, for both principled reasons and practical ones: the granting of some form of self-government would at least have the effect of reconciling Irish nationalism to the British state.

In the twilight of the 19th century there was a move to preserve all things Irish. The Gaelic Athletic Association (GAA) was set up in 1884 to promote Irish sports, while Douglas Hyde and Eoin McNeill formed

In 1745 when James Fitzgerald, the Earl of Kildare, started construction of Leinster House he was mocked for his move into the wilds. 'Where I go society will follow', he confidently predicted. He was right; today Leinster House is the seat of Irish parliament and is in modern Dublin's centre.

British Prime Minister William Gladstone introduced Home Rule bills three times into the House of Commons between 1886 and 1895, but the House of Lords voted them down on each occasion.

1680	1695	1757	1759
The architectural style known as Anglo-Dutch results in the construction of notable buildings such as the Royal Hospital, Kilmainham, now the Irish Museum of Modern Art.	Penal Laws prohibit Catholics from owning a horse, marrying outside their religion and from buying or inheriting property; within 100 years Catholics will own only 5% of Irish land.	The Wide Street Commission is set up to design the framework of a modern city: new parks are laid out, streets widened and new public buildings commissioned.	Arthur Guinness buys a disused brewery on a plot of land opposite St James's Gate. Initially he brews only ale, but in the 1770s turns his expertise to a new beer called porter.

the Gaelic League in 1893 to encourage Irish arts and language. The success of the Gaelic League paved the way for the Celtic Revival Movement, spearheaded by WB Yeats and Lady Gregory, who founded the Abbey Theatre in 1904.

The Struggle for Independence

Charles Stewart Parnell suffered a swift fall from grace after it was made public that he had been having an affair with a married woman, Kitty O'Shea. He was ditched as leader of his own Irish Parliamentary Party in 1890 and died a broken man the following year.

Although Irish culture was thriving at the start of the 20th century, the country's peaceful efforts to free itself from British rule were thwarted at every juncture. Dublin's slums were the worst in Europe, and the emergence of militant trade unionism introduced a socialist agenda to the struggle for self-determination.

In 1905 Arthur Griffith (1871–1922) founded a new political movement called Sinn Féin ('Ourselves Alone'), which sought to achieve Home Rule through passive resistance rather than political lobbying. It urged the Irish to withhold taxes and its MPs to form an Irish government in Dublin.

Meanwhile, trade union leaders Jim Larkin and James Connolly agitated against low wages and corporate greed, culminating in the Dublin Lockout of 1913, where 300 employers 'locked out' 20,000 workers for five months. During this time Connolly established the Irish Citizen Army (ICA) to defend striking workers from the police. Things were heating up.

Home Rule was finally passed by Westminster in 1914, but its provisions were suspended for the duration of WWI. Bowing to pressure from Protestant-dominated Ulster, where 140,000 members of the newly formed Ulster Volunteer Force (UVF) swore to resist any attempts to weaken British rule in Ireland, the bill also made provisions for the 'temporary' exclusion of the North from the workings of the Future act. How temporary was 'temporary' was anybody's guess – and it was in such political fudging that the seeds of trouble were sown. To counter the potential threat from the UVF, Irish nationalists formed the Irish Volunteer Force (IVF), but a stand-off was avoided when the vast majority of them enlisted in the British Army: if Britain was going to war 'in defence of small nations', then loyalty to the Allied cause would help Ireland's long-term aspirations.

The Easter Rising

When WWI ended in 1918, 50,000 Irish citizens had lost their lives.

The more radical factions within Sinn Féin, the IVF and the ICA saw Britain's difficulty as Ireland's opportunity, and planned to rise up against the Crown on Easter Sunday, 1916. In typical fashion, the rhetoric of the rebellion outweighed the quality of the planning. When the head of the IVF, Eoin McNeill, got wind of the plans, he published an

1801	1839	1840	1841
The Act of Union unites Ireland politically with Britain. The Irish Parliament votes itself out of existence following an intensive campaign of bribery.	Following a powerful campaign by Daniel O'Connoll, the 'Liberator', the Catholic Emancipation Act is passed, repealing the remaining Penal Laws.	The Corporation Act allows Catholics to vote in local elections for the first time since the 1690s, giving them a two-to-one majority.	Daniel O'Connell is elected the first Catholic mayor of Dublin in 150 years; one of his first acts is to found a multi-denominational cemetery in Glasnevin.

advertisement in the newspaper cancelling the planned 'manoeuvres'. The leaders rescheduled the revolution for the following day but word never spread beyond the capital, where a motley band of about a thousand rebels assembled and seized strategic buildings. The main garrison was the General Post Office, outside which the poet and school teacher Pádraig Pearse read out the 'Proclamation of the Republic'.

The British Army didn't take the insurgence seriously at first but after a few soldiers were killed, they sent a gunboat down the Liffey to rain shells on the rebels. After six days of fighting the city centre was ravaged and the death toll stood at 300 civilians, 130 British troops (many of whom were Irish) and 60 rebels.

The rebels, prompted by Pearse's fear of further civilian casualties, surrendered and were arrested. Crowds gathered to mock and jeer at them as they were led away. Initially, Dubliners resented them for the damage they had caused with their futile rising, but their attitudes began to change following the executions of the leaders in Kilmainham Gaol. The hostility shown to the rebels turned to outright sympathy and support.

The War of Independence

In the 1918 general election, the more radical Sinn Féin party won three-quarters of the Irish seats. In May 1919 they declared independence and established the first Dáil Éireann (Irish Assembly) in Dublin's Mansion House, led by Éamon de Valera. This was effectively a declaration of war.

Mindful that they could never match the British on the battlefield, Sinn Féin's military wing – made up of Irish Volunteers now renamed the Irish Republican Army (IRA) – began attacking arms dumps and barracks in guerrilla strikes. The British countered by strengthening the Royal Irish Constabulary (RIC) and introducing a tough auxiliary force made up of returning WWI servicemen known as the Black and Tans (after the colour of their uniforms).

They met their match in Michael Collins, the IRA's commander and a master of guerrilla warfare. Although the British knew his name, Collins masterfully concealed his identity and throughout the war was able to freewheel around the city on his bicycle like he didn't have a care in the world.

On 10 November 1920, Collins learned that 14 undercover British intelligence operatives known as the 'Cairo Gang' had just arrived in Dublin. The following morning he had his own crack squad ('the Apostles') assassinate each one of them as they lay in their beds. That afternoon, British troops retaliated by opening fire on the crowd at a hurling

Many Dubliners were appalled at the sentences received by the leaders of the Rising, especially the fate suffered by 18-year-old Willie Pearse, whose main offence was that he was Pádraig's brother. James Connolly was severely injured during the Rising, so was strapped to a chair and shot.

Éamon de Valera, the leader of the first Dáil Éireann (Irish Assembly), was spared the firing squad in 1916 because of his US birth; killing him would have been a public-relations disaster.

HISTORY THE WAR OF INDEPENDENCE

1845–51	1867	1882	1905
A mould called phytophthora ravages the potato harvest. The Great Famine is the single greatest catastrophe in Irish history, with the deaths of up to one million people.	Several thousand supporters of the Irish Republican Brotherhood (IRB) fight the police in Tallaght; they disperse and some 200 agitators are arrested.	An offshoot of the IRB, known as the Invincibles, assassinate the Chief Secretary and his assistant in Phoenix Park.	Journalist Arthur Griffiths founds a new movement whose aim is independence under a dual monarchy; he names the movement Sinn Féin, meaning 'Ourselves Alone'.

match in Croke Park, resulting in the death of 10 spectators and one player, Michael Hogan, whose death was later commemorated when the main stand at the stadium was named after him. The events of 'Bloody Sunday' galvanised both sides in the conflict and served to quash any moral doubts over what was becoming an increasingly brutal struggle.

Brutalities notwithstanding, the war resulted in relatively few casualties – 2014 in total – and by mid-1921 had ground to a kind of stalemate. Both sides were under pressure to end it: the international community was urging Britain to resolve the issue one way or another, while, unbeknown to the British, the IRA was on the verge of collapse. A truce was signed on 11 July 1921.

The 1922 Civil War began when anti-Treaty IRA forces occupied Dublin's Four Courts and were shelled by pro-Treaty forces, led by Michael Collins. Dublin, which escaped any real damage during the War of Independence, became a primary theatre of the Civil War, which cost the lives of 250 Dubliners.

Civil War

The terms of – and the circumstances surrounding – the Treaty that ended the War of Independence make up the single most divisive episode in Irish politics, one that still breeds prejudice, inflames passions and shapes the political landscape in parts of the country.

After months of argument and facing the threat of, in the words of British Prime Minister Lloyd George, an 'immediate and terrible war', the Irish negotiating team, led by Michael Collins, signed the Anglo-Irish Treaty on 6 December 1921. Instead of establishing the Irish Republic for which the IRA had fought, it created an Irish Free State, effectively a British dominion, in which members of the newly constituted parliament would have to swear allegiance to the British Crown before they could participate in government. The six counties comprising Northern Ireland were given the choice of becoming part of the Free State or remaining in the United Kingdom; they chose the latter, sowing the seeds of discontent that would lead to further rounds of the Troubles in the North. Although Collins was dissatisfied with the deal, he hoped it would be the 'first real step' in the journey towards an Irish

BEST BOOKS ON DUBLIN HISTORY

➡ *Dublin: The Making of a Capital City* (2014) David Dickson
➡ *Come Here to Me: Dublin's Other History* (2013) Donal Fallon, Sam McGrath and Ciaran Murray
➡ *Dublin: A Cultural & Literary History* (2005) Siobhán Kilfeather
➡ *Stones of Dublin: A History of Dublin in Ten Buildings* (2014) Lisa Marie Griffith
➡ *A Short History of Dublin* (2010) Richard Killeen

1913	1916	1919–21	1921–22
The largest labour dispute in Irish history sees 20,000 Dublin workers 'locked out' for five months by defiant employers.	Republicans take the GPO in Dublin and announce the formation of an Irish Republic. After less than a week of fighting, the rebels surrender and are summarily executed.	The Irish War of Independence begins in January 1919. Two years (and 2014 casualties) later, the war ends in a truce on 11 July 1921, leading to peace talks.	The Anglo-Irish Treaty is signed on 6 December. It gives 26 counties of Ireland independence and six Ulster counties the choice of opting out. The Irish Free State is founded in 1922.

republic. Nevertheless, he also foresaw trouble and remarked prophetically, 'I've just signed my own death warrant'.

De Valera vehemently opposed the Treaty and the two erstwhile comrades were pitted against one another into pro-Treaty and anti-Treaty camps. Although the Dáil narrowly ratified the Treaty and the electorate accepted it by a large majority, Ireland slid into civil war during June 1922.

Ironically, the Civil War was more brutal than the struggle that preceded it. In 11 months roughly 3000 Irish died – including 77 state executions – but the vindictive nature of the fighting left indelible scars that have yet to be fully healed. The assassination of Michael Collins in his home county of Cork on 22 August 1922 rocked the country; 500,000 people (almost one-fifth of the population) attended his funeral. The last few months of fighting were especially ugly, with both sides engaging in tit-for-tat atrocities. On 24 May 1923, de Valera ordered the anti-Treaty forces to drop their arms.

The Irish Republic

Ireland finally entered a phase of peace. Without an armed struggle to pursue – at least not one pursued by the majority – the IRA became a marginalised force in independent Ireland and Sinn Féin fell apart. In 1926 de Valera created a new party, Fianna Fáil (Soldiers of Destiny), which has been the dominant force in Irish politics ever since. Over the following decades Fianna Fáil gradually eliminated most of the clauses of the Treaty with which it had disagreed (including the oath of allegiance).

In 1932 a freshly painted Dublin hosted the 31st Eucharistic Congress, which drew visitors from around the world. The Catholic Church began to wield disproportionate control over the affairs of the state; contraception was made illegal in the 1930s and the age of consent was raised from 16 to 17.

In 1936, when the IRA refused to disarm, de Valera had it banned. The following year the Civil War–tainted moniker 'Free State' was dropped in favour of Eire as the country's official name in a rewrite of the constitution.

Despite having done much of the groundwork, Fianna Fáil lost out to its rivals Fine Gael, descendants of the original pro-Treaty Free State government, on declaring the 26 counties a republic in 1949.

The Stroll to Modernisation

Sean Lemass succeeded de Valera as Taoiseach (prime minister) in 1959 and set about fixing the Irish economy, which he did so effectively

Author and treaty negotiator Robert Erskine Childers was executed by the government on 24 November 1922. Childers ended up on the anti-Treaty side during the Civil War, but was arrested for possessing a gun given to him by (the now pro-Treaty) Michael Collins and sentenced to death.

HISTORY THE IRISH REPUBLIC

Although Ireland remained neutral during WWII – as a way of pushing its independence – Dublin's North Strand was hit by a 227kg German bomb on 31 May 1941, killing more than 30 and injuring 90.

1948	1960s	1969	1972
Fine Gael, in coalition with the new Republican Clann na Poblachta, wins the 1948 general election and declares the Free State a republic.	A construction boom sees the growth of new suburbs north and south of the city in an effort to re-house Dubliners removed from dangerous city-centre tenements.	Marches in Derry are disrupted by Loyalist attacks and heavy-handed police action, culminating in the 'Battle of the Bogside' (12–14 August). It marks the beginning of the 'Troubles'.	Angry demonstrators burn the British Embassy in Dublin in response to the killing of 13 civilians in Derry by British paratroopers.

that the rate of emigration soon halved. While neighbouring London was swinging in the '60s, Dublin was definitely swaying. Youngsters from rural communities poured into the expanding city and it seemed like the good times were never going to end. But, almost inevitably, the economy slid back into recession.

On the 50th anniversary of the 1916 Easter Rising, Nelson's Pillar on O'Connell St was partially blown up by the IRA and crowds cheered as the remainder was removed the following week. Republicanism was still prevalent and a new round of the 'Troubles' were about to flair up in the North.

Ireland joined the European Economic Community (EEC), a forerunner to the European Union (EU), in 1973 and got a significant leg-up from the organisation's coffers over the following decades. But the tides of change were coming once again. Political instability and an international recession did little to help hopes of economic recovery, and by the early '80s emigration was once again a major issue. But Ireland – and Dublin in particular – was growing increasingly liberal, and was straining at the shackles imposed on its social and moral mores by a largely conservative Catholic Church. Politicians too were seen in a new light as stories of corruption and cronyism became increasingly commonplace.

Dublin was hardly touched by the sectarian tensions that would pull Northern Ireland asunder, although 25 people died after three Loyalist car bombs exploded in the city in 1974.

The visit of Pope John Paul II in 1979 – the first time for a pontiff – saw more than one million people flock to Phoenix Park to hear him say Mass.

From Celtic Tiger...

In the early 1990s European funds helped kick-start economic growth. Huge sums of money were invested in education and physical infrastructure, while the policy of low corporate tax rates coupled with attractive incentives made Ireland very attractive to high-tech businesses looking for a door into EU markets. In less than a decade, Ireland went from being one of the poorest countries in Europe to one of the wealthiest: unemployment fell from 18% to 3.5%, the average industrial wage somersaulted to the top of the European league, and the dramatic rise in GDP meant that the country laid claim to an economic model of success that was the envy of the entire world. Ireland became synonymous with the term 'Celtic Tiger'.

In Dublin, an impressive program of construction began with the Irish Financial Services and then expanded down both sides of the Liffey towards Dublin port; the city's population grew dramatically and suburbs were expanded to accommodate the new arrivals from other parts of Ireland and beyond.

1974	1990s	1993	2008
Simultaneous bombings in Monaghan and Dublin on 17 May leave 33 dead and 300 injured, the biggest loss of life in any single day during the Troubles.	Low corporate tax, decades of investment in higher education, transfer payments from the EU and a low-cost labour market lead to the 'Celtic Tiger' boom.	About 20,000 demonstrators call for an end to IRA violence as a result of the bomb that killed two children in Warrington, England.	The global financial crisis triggers the collapse of the Irish banking system and the property boom; Ireland's economy goes into financial free-fall.

...to Rescue Cat

From 2002 the Irish economy was kept buoyant by a gigantic construction boom that was completely out of step with any measure of responsible growth forecasting. The out-of-control international derivatives market flooded Irish banks with cheap money, and they lent it freely.

Then Lehman Bros and the credit crunch happened. The Irish banks nearly went to the wall, but were bailed out at the last minute, and before Ireland could draw breath, the International Monetary Fund (IMF) and the EU held the chits of the country's mid-term economic future. Ireland found itself yet again confronting the familiar demons of high unemployment and emigration, but a deep-cutting program of austerity saw the corner turned by the end of 2014.

In Dublin, the signs of recovery weren't evident until 2016, when approval was finally given to continue the development of the Docklands; 2017 saw ground broken on what will eventually be the city's tallest building, rising up from Point Sq near the 3Arena.

Taoiseach Leo Varadkar is the eighth Dubliner to become prime minister. He is also the youngest and the first gay man to hold the office.

2009	2011	2015	2017
The publication of the Murphy Report reveals a vast network of secrecy and cover-up of widespread crimes of sexual abuse by serving priests within the Dublin diocese.	Queen Elizabeth II visits Dublin as part of her Irish trip, the first by a British monarch since 1911 and the visit of George V.	The Marriage Equality referendum is passed by a large majority; the results are announced in Dublin Castle and the city centre explodes in celebration.	Dubliner Leo Varadkar, the gay son of an Indian immigrant, becomes Taoiseach. At 38 he is the youngest person to hold the office.

Literary Dublin

Dubliners know a thing or two about the written word. No other city of comparable size can claim four Nobel Prize winners for Literature, but the city's impact on the English-reading world extends far beyond the fab four of Shaw, Yeats, Beckett and Heaney...one name, folks: James Joyce.

Literary Capital

Before Dublin was even a glint in a Viking's eye, Ireland was the land of saints and scholars, thanks to the monastic universities that sprang up around the country to foster the spread of Christianity and the education of Europe's privileged elite. But for our purposes, we need to fast-forward 1000 years to the 18th century and the glory days of Georgian Dublin, when the Irish and English languages began to cross-fertilise. Experimenting with English, using turns of phrase and expressions translated directly from Gaeilge, and combining these with a uniquely Irish perspective on life, Irish writers have dazzled and delighted readers for centuries. British theatre critic Kenneth Tynan summed it up in the *Observer* thus: 'The English hoard words like misers: the Irish spend them like sailors.'

Dublin has as many would-be sailors as Hollywood has frustrated waitresses, and it often seems like a bottomless well of creativity. The section given over to Irish writers is often the largest and busiest in any local bookstore, reflecting not only a rich literary tradition and thriving contemporary scene, but also an appreciative, knowledgeable and hungry local audience that attends readings and poetry recitals like rock fans at a gig.

Indeed, Dublin has produced so many writers, and has been written about so much, that you could easily plan a Dublin literary holiday. *A Literary Guide to Dublin*, by Vivien Igoe, includes detailed route maps, a guide to cemeteries and an eight-page section on literary and historical pubs. A. Norman Jeffares' *O'Brien Pocket History of Irish Writers: From Swift to Heaney* also has detailed and accessible summaries of writers and their work.

Dublin's Nobel Laureates

....

William Butler Yeats (1923)

....

George Bernard Shaw (1925)

....

Samuel Beckett (1969)

....

Seamus Heaney (1995)

Old Literary Dublin

Modern Irish literature begins with Jonathan Swift (1667–1745), the master satirist, social commentator, dean of St Patrick's Cathedral and author of *Gulliver's Travels*. Fast-forward a couple of centuries and you're in the company of acclaimed dramatist Oscar Wilde (1854–1900); *Dracula* creator Bram Stoker (1847–1912) – some have claimed that the name of the count may have come from the Irish *droch fhola* (bad blood); and playwright and essayist George Bernard Shaw (1856–1950), author of *Pygmalion* (which was later turned into *My Fair Lady*), who hailed from Synge St near the Grand Canal.

Towering above all of them – in reputation if not popularity – is James Joyce (1882–1941), whose name and books elicit enormous pride in Ireland. The majority of Joyce's literary output came when he had left Ireland for the artistic hotbed that was Paris, which was also true for another

FIVE BOOKS ABOUT DUBLIN

The Barrytown Trilogy (Roddy Doyle; 1992) Doyle's much-loved trilogy tells the story of the Northside working-class Rabbitte family. The three novels – *The Commitments* (1987), *The Snapper* (1990) and *The Van* (1991) – were published together in 1992.

The Book of Evidence (John Banville; 1989) The true story of a Dublin murder is repurposed by Banville's masterful storytelling into an examination of motive, passion and the mores of middle-class Dublin in the 1980s.

Dublin 4 (Maeve Binchy; 1982) Although written more than three decades ago, Binchy's examination of the tumult that afflicts a group of residents of Dublin's most affluent neighbourhood is just as poignant and relevant today.

Dubliners (James Joyce; 1914) Dublin serves as the unifying bedrock for this classic collection of 15 short stories that chronicle the travails of the capital and its middle-class residents at the turn of the 20th century.

The Illusionist (Jennifer Johnston; 1995) Stella Glover is the protagonist of Johnston's beautiful novel, which tells the story of a mother's attempt to reconnect with her estranged daughter. Using flashbacks, it moves between the past in London and the present in Dublin.

great experimenter of language and style, Samuel Beckett (1906–89). Beckett's work centres on fundamental existential questions about the human condition and the nature of self. He is probably best known for his play *Waiting for Godot,* but his unassailable reputation is based on a series of stark novels and plays.

Of the dozens of 20th-century Irish authors to have achieved published renown, some names to look out for include playwright and novelist Brendan Behan (1923–64), who wove tragedy, wit and a turbulent life into his best works, including *Borstal Boy, The Quare Fellow* and *The Hostage,* before dying young of alcoholism. A collection of his newspaper columns was published under the title *Hold Your Hour and Have Another.*

The Contemporary Scene

The Irish literary scene (largely synonymous with the Dublin scene) is flourishing, in quantity as well as (mostly) quality. Much like the digital revolution that has transformed the music scene, the proliferation of small presses and printing houses has given more authors than ever the chance to see the fruits of their labours in print, and the result has largely been very positive.

Good examples include Sara Baume's *Spill Simmer Falter Wither* (2015), a wonderful exploration of the friendship between a recluse and his one-eyed dog in a small, claustrophobic coastal community. First published by Tramp Press, it was picked up by Houghton Mifflin Harcourt, who afforded Baume a broader platform to showcase her remarkable talent. Tramp was also the first to publish *Solar Bones* (2016) by Mike McCormack, a tour de force tribute to small-town Ireland that consists of a 200-page single sentence narrated by a dead man. This audacious piece of work won the 2016 Goldsmith Prize but was ineligible for the Man Booker only because its original printing was exclusive to Ireland.

Small Towns & Recession

The theme of small-town life is a popular one these days, as many authors explore the changes wrought by the economic crash of 2008. Gone is the nostalgic, repression-infused prose of yesteryear, replaced by a more brazen, often darkly comic style reflective of a new generation of writers

JAMES JOYCE

Uppermost among Dublin writers is James Joyce, author of *Ulysses,* the greatest book of the 20th century – although we've yet to meet five people who've actually finished it. Still, Dubliners are immensely proud of the writer once castigated as a literary pornographer by locals and luminaries alike – even George Bernard Shaw dismissed him as vulgar. Joyce was so unappreciated that he left the city, never to reside in it again, though he continued to live here through his imagination and literature.

His Life

Born in Rathgar in 1882, the young Joyce had three short stories published in an Irish farmers' magazine under the pen name Stephen Dedalus in 1904. The same year he fled town with the love of his life, Nora Barnacle (when Joyce's father heard her name he commented that she would surely stick to him). He spent most of the next 10 years in Trieste, now part of Italy, where he wrote prolifically but struggled to get published. His career was further hampered by recurrent eye problems: he had 25 operations for glaucoma, cataracts and other conditions.

The first major prose he finally had published was *Dubliners* (1914), a collection of short stories set in the city, including the three he had written in Ireland. Publishers began to take notice and his autobiographical *A Portrait of the Artist as a Young Man* (1916) followed. In 1918 the US magazine *Little Review* started to publish extracts from *Ulysses* but notoriety was already pursuing his epic work and the censors prevented publication of further episodes after 1920.

Passing through Paris on a rare visit to Dublin, he was persuaded by Ezra Pound to stay a while in the French capital. What he intended to be a brief visit turned into a 20-year stay. It was a good move for the struggling writer for, in 1922, he met Sylvia Beach of the Paris bookshop Shakespeare & Co, who finally managed to put *Ulysses* (1922) into print. The publicity from its earlier censorship ensured instant success.

Buoyed by the success of the inventive *Ulysses,* Joyce went for broke with *Finnegans Wake* (1939), 'set' in the dreamscape of a Dublin publican. Perhaps not one to read at the airport, the book is a daunting and often obscure tome about eternal recurrence. It is even more complex than *Ulysses* and took the author 17 years to write.

In 1940, WWII drove the Joyce family back to Zürich, Switzerland, where the author died the following year.

Ulysses

Ulysses is the ultimate chronicle of the city in which, Joyce once said, he intended to 'give a picture of Dublin so complete that if the city suddenly one day disappeared from the earth it could be reconstructed out of my book'. It is set here on 16 June 1904 – the day of Joyce's first date with Nora Barnacle – and follows its characters as their journeys around town parallel the voyage of Homer's *Odyssey.*

The experimental literary style makes it difficult to read, but there's much for even the slightly bemused reader to relish. It ends with Molly Bloom's famous stream of consciousness discourse, a chapter of eight huge, unpunctuated paragraphs. Because of its sexual explicitness, the book was banned in the USA and the UK until 1933 and 1937 respectively.

In testament to the book's enduring relevance and extraordinary innovation, it has inspired writers of every generation since. Joyce admirers from around the world descend on Dublin every year on 16 June to celebrate Bloomsday and retrace the steps of *Ulysses'* central character, Leopold Bloom. It is a slightly gimmicky and touristy phenomenon that is aimed at Joyce fanatics and tourists, but it's plenty of fun and a great way to lay the groundwork for actually reading the book.

raised on the optimistic confidence of the Celtic Tiger yet forced to grapple with the frequently harsh realities of post-crash austerity.

This is the meat-and-potato of authors such as Cork-born Lisa McInerney, author of *The Glorious Heresies* (2015), and Colin Barrett, who won the Guardian First Book Award for *Young Skins* (2013). Alan McMonagle's *Ithaca* (2017) treads similar ground, telling the story of a lonely boy's search for his elusive 'Da', and how in hunting for something we've lost, we risk losing sight of what we have. *Multitudes* (2016), by Lucy Caldwell, is a heart-warming debut collection of short stories set almost entirely in Belfast in which a series of young female protagonists go through life's growing pains. Another recession-era novel of note is Donal Ryan's *The Spinning Heart* (2012), in which the effects of the crash on rural Ireland are explored through 21 different voices. The excesses of the Celtic Tiger provide the subject matter for Claire Kilroy's savage satire *The Devil I Know* (2012), the fourth novel by the Dublin author, as is Paul Murray's *The Mark and the Void* (2015), which wasn't as well received as his first novel, *Skippy Dies* (2010), about a group of privileged students at an all-boys secondary school: the Neil Jordan film of the book is in production.

The Big Hitters

Dubliner Colum McCann (1965–) left Ireland in 1986, eventually settling in New York, where his sixth novel, the post–September 11 *Let the Great World Spin* (2009), catapulted him to the top of the literary tree and won him the National Book Award for fiction as well as the International IMPAC Dublin Literary Award. He's added a couple of novels since, and in 2017 published *Letters to A Young Writer: Some Practical and Philosophical Advice*, a tribute to the power of language and an exploration of the trials and tribulations of being a writer. Young readers have been delighted by Shane Hegarty's Darkmouth series, set in a fictional Irish town (Darkmouth), where young Finn is learning about girls and fighting monsters; 2017 saw the third book in the series, *Chaos Descends*.

The *Stinging Fly* (www.stingingfly. org) is one of the best literary magazines for discovering and promoting new authors. It is published quarterly.

Established heavyweights continue to add to the country's literary canon. There's Roddy Doyle (1958–), of course, whose mega-successful Barrytown quartet – *The Commitments, The Snapper, The Van* and *Paddy Clarke, Ha Ha Ha* – have all been made into films; more recently *Dead Man Talking* (2015) is the story of broken friendship, but it's pitched at adults with poor literacy skills.

Sebastian Barry (1955–) has been shortlisted twice for the Man Booker Prize, for his WWI drama *A Long Long Way* (2005) and the absolutely compelling *The Secret Scripture* (2008), about a 100-year-old inmate of a mental hospital who decides to write an autobiography. In 2016 he published the fourth McNulty family novel, *Days Without End*, an award-winning epic set partly in the American Civil War.

LITERARY FESTIVALS

Dublin's literary festivals are a great opportunity to meet Irish and international authors up close. Dublin has a handful of festivals of note:

International Literature Festival Dublin (☏01-969 5259; www.ilfdublin.com; ☺May) The city's biggest literary event is a great showcase of local and international talent.

Dublin Book Festival (www.dublinbookfestival.com; ☺mid-Nov) A three-day festival of literature with readings and talks.

Dalkey Book Festival (www.dalkeybookfestival.org; ☺mid-Jun) A small festival with an impressive line-up.

Mountains to the Sea Dlr Book Festival (www.mountainstosea.ie; ☺mid-Mar) The southside suburb of Dun Laoghaire gets literary.

WOMEN WRITERS

The last few years have seen an important bit of literary revisionism, as scholars and editors seek to redress the imbalance that saw women chronically under-represented in the Irish literary canon. One notable effort has been *The Long Gaze Back* (2015, ed Sinead Gleeson), an anthology of 30 short stories by women writers, including eight by luminaries of the past such as Elizabeth Bowen and Maria Edgeworth, and 22 by contemporary writers such as Anne Enright and Niamh Boyce.

Anne Enright (1962–) did nab the Booker for *The Gathering* (2007), a zeitgeist tale of alcoholism and abuse – she described it as 'the intellectual equivalent of a Hollywood weepie'. Her latest novel, *The Green Road* (2015), also mines the murky waters of the Irish family.

Another Booker Prize winner is heavyweight John Banville (1945–), who won it for *The Sea* (2005); we also recommend either *The Book of Evidence* (1989) or the masterful *roman-à-clef The Untouchable* (1997), based loosely on the secret-agent life of art historian Anthony Blunt. Banville's literary alter ego is Benjamin Black, author of a series of eight hard-boiled detective thrillers set in the 1950s starring a troubled pathologist called Quirke – the latest book is *Wolf on a String* (2017). Another big hitter is Wexford-born Colm Tóibín (1955–), author of nine novels including *Brooklyn* (2009; made into an Oscar-nominated film in 2015 starring Saoirse Ronan) and, most recently, *Nora Webster* (2014), a powerful study of widowhood.

Emma Donoghue (1969–) followed the award-winning *Room* (2010; the 2015 film picked up an Oscar for best actress) with *Frog Music* (2014), about the real-life shooting of cross-dressing *gamine* Jenny Bonnet in late-19th-century San Francisco. And finally, there's John Boyne (1971–), whose Holocaust novel *The Boy in the Striped Pyjamas* (2006; the film version came out in 2008) made him Ireland's most successful author: he's added a few since then, including *The Heart's Invisible Furies* (2017), which charts the life of a gay man from the 1960s to the passage of the marriage equality referendum in 2015.

Modern-Day Poets

Ireland's greatest modern bard was Derry-born-but-Dublin-resident Nobel laureate Seamus Heaney (1939–2013), whose enormous personal warmth and wry humour flow through each of his evocative works. He was, unquestionably, the successor to Yeats and one of the most important contemporary poets of the English language. After winning the Nobel Prize in 1995 he compared the ensuing attention to someone mentioning sex in front of their mammy. *Opened Ground: Poems 1966–1996* (1998) is our favourite of his books.

Dubliner Paul Durcan (1944–) is one of the most reliable chroniclers of changing Dublin. He won the prestigious Whitbread Prize for Poetry in 1990 for *Daddy, Daddy* and is a funny, engaging, tender and savage writer. Poet, playwright and Kerryman Brendan Kennelly (1936–) is an immensely popular character around town. He lectures at Trinity College and writes a unique brand of poetry that is marked by its playfulness, as well as historical and intellectual impact. Eavan Boland (1944–) is a prolific and much-admired writer, best known for her poetry, who combines Irish politics with outspoken feminism; *In a Time of Violence* (1994) and *The Lost Land* (1998) are two of her most celebrated collections.

If you're interested in finding out more about poetry in Ireland in general, visit the website of the excellent Poetry Ireland (www.poetry ireland.ie), which showcases the work of new and established poets.

Musical Dublin

Dublin's literary tradition may have the intellectuals nodding sagely, but it's the city's musical credentials that have the rest of us bopping, for it's no cliché to say that music is as intrinsic to the local lifestyle as a good night out. Even the streets – well, Grafton St and Temple Bar – are alive with the sounds of music, and you can hardly get around without stubbing your toe on the next international superstar busking their way to a record contract.

Traditional & Folk

Irish music – commonly referred to as 'traditional' or simply 'trad' – has retained a vibrancy not found in other traditional European forms. This is probably because, although Irish music has retained many of its traditional aspects, it has itself influenced many forms of music, most notably US country and western – a fusion of Mississippi Delta blues and Irish traditional tunes that, combined with other influences like gospel, is at the root of rock and roll. Other reasons for its current success include the willingness of its exponents to update the way it's played (in ensembles rather than the customary *céilidh* – communal dance – bands) and the popularity of pub sessions.

The pub session is still the best way to hear the music at its rich, lively best – and thanks largely to the tourist demand, there are some terrific sessions in pubs throughout the city. Thankfully, though, the best musicians have also gone into the recording studio. If you want to hear musical skill that will both tear out your heart and restore your faith in humanity, go no further than the fiddle-playing of Tommy Peoples on *The Quiet Glen* (1998), the beauty of Paddy Keenan's uillean pipes on his self-titled 1975 album, or the stunning guitar playing of Andy Irvine on albums such as *Compendium: The Best of Patrick Street* (2000).

The most famous traditional band is The Chieftains, who spend most of their time these days playing in the US, and marked their 50th anniversary in 2012 with the ambitious *Voice of Ages*, a collaboration with the likes of Bon Iver and Paolo Nutini. More folksy than traditional were The Dubliners, founded in O'Donoghue's on Merrion Row the same year as The Chieftains. Most of the original members, including the utterly brilliant Luke Kelly and fellow frontman Ronnie Drew, have died, but the group still plays the odd nostalgia gig. In 2006 it released *Live at Vicar St*, which captures some of its brilliance.

Another band whose career has been stitched into the fabric of Dublin life is The Fureys, comprising four brothers originally from the travelling community (no, not like the Wilburys) along with guitarist Davey Arthur. And if it's rousing renditions of Irish rebel songs you're after, you can't go past The Wolfe Tones. Ireland is packed with traditional talent and we strongly recommend that you spend some time in a specialised traditional shop such as Claddagh Records, which has branches on Cecilia St in Temple Bar and Westmoreland St.

Traditional Playlist
....
Compendium: The Best of Patrick Street (2001)
Patrick Street
....
Old Hag You Have Killed Me (1976)
The Bothy Band
....
Paddy Keenan (1975) Paddy Keenan

LUKE KELLY: THE ORIGINAL DUBLINER

With a halo of wiry ginger hair and a voice like hardened honey, Luke Kelly (1940–84) was perhaps the greatest Irish folk singer of the 20th century, a performer who used his voice in the manner of the American blues singers he admired so much, to express the anguish of being lonely and afraid in a world they never made (to paraphrase AE Housman).

He was a founding member of The Dubliners, along with Ronnie Drew (1934–2008), Barney McKenna (1939–2012) and Ciarán Bourke (1935–88), but he treated Dublin's most famous folk group as more of a temporary cooperative enterprise. He shared the singing duties with Drew, lending his distinctive voice to classic drinking ditties like 'Dirty Old Town' and rousing rebel songs like 'A Nation Once Again', but it was his mastery of the more reflective ballad that made him peerless. His rendition of 'On Raglan Road', from a poem by Patrick Kavanagh that the poet himself insisted he sing, is the most beautiful song about Dublin we've ever heard; but it is his version of Phil Coulter's 'Scorn Not His Simplicity' that grants him his place among the immortals. Coulter wrote the song following the birth of a son with Down syndrome, and even though it became one of Kelly's best-loved songs, he had such respect for it that he only sang it a handful of times, and only in the most respectful of settings.

Luke Kelly: The Collection is recommended listening.

Since the 1970s various bands have tried to blend traditional with more progressive genres with mixed success. The first band to pull it off was Moving Hearts, led by Christy Moore, who went on to become an important folk musician in his own right.

Popular Music

From the 1960s onwards, Dublin became a hotbed of rock and pop; most of the artists have now faded into obscurity. Notable exceptions are Thin Lizzy, led by Phil Lynott (1949–86), and Bob Geldof's new wave Boomtown Rats, who didn't like Mondays or much else either.

But they all paled in comparison to the supernova that is U2, formed in 1976 in North Dublin and by the late 1980s one of the world's most successful rock bands. What else can we say about them that hasn't already been said? After 13 studio albums, 22 Grammy awards and 150 million album sales they have nothing to prove to anyone – and not even their minor faux pas in 2014, when Apple 'gave' copies of their last release, *Songs of Innocence,* to iTunes subscribers whether they wanted it or not, has managed to dampen their popularity. 2017's Joshua Tree Tour, staged to commemorate the 30th anniversary of their groundbreaking album, was a huge commercial and critical success.

Of all the Irish acts that followed in U2's wake during the 1980s and early 1990s, a few managed to comfortably avoid being tarred with 'the next U2' burden. The Pogues' mix of punk and Irish folk kept everyone going for a while, but the real story there was the empathetic songwriting of Shane MacGowan, whose genius has been overshadowed by his heavy drinking – but he still managed to pen Ireland's favourite song, 'A Fairytale of New York', sung with emotional fervour by everyone around Christmas. Sinéad O'Connor thrived by acting like a U2 antidote – whatever they were into she was not – and by having a damn fine voice; the raw emotion on *The Lion and the Cobra* (1987) makes it a great offering. And then there was My Bloody Valentine, the pioneers of late-1980s guitar-distorted shoegazer rock: *Loveless* (1991) is one of the best Dublin albums of all time.

The 1990s were largely dominated by DJs, dance music and a whole new spin on an old notion, the boy band. Behind Ireland's most successful groups (Boyzone and Westlife) is impresario Louis Walsh, whose musical sensibilities seem mired in '60s showband schmaltz. In the last decade, Walsh, who became a judge on *The X Factor* in the UK, unleashed Jedward on the world – identical twins who couldn't sing a note but endeared themselves to everyone with their wacky antics.

The Contemporary Scene

Alternative music has never been in ruder health in Ireland – and Dublin, as the largest city in the country, is where everyone comes to make noise. The up-and-coming bands to look out for include hip-hop artists NEOMADiC and Bad Bones (with the latter also including strong elements of electronica), singer-songwriter Farah Elle and noise-pop band Thumper, whose EP *magnum opuss* has been very well received.

They all hope to join the established names on the scene, including Damien Rice, who spent much of 2017 touring his album *My Favourite Faded Fantasy*; alt-rockers Kodaline, whose second album *Coming Up For Air* (2015) cemented their position as one of the best Irish bands going (they're currently recording their third record); and Bray-born blues-influenced Hozier, whose self-titled debut album in 2015 garnered a huge amount of critical acclaim but inevitably couldn't match the global success of his 2013 single 'Take Me to Church'. Although he spends a lot of his time in New York these days, Glen Hansard (of *Once* fame) is still a major presence in Ireland, and occasionally goes on the road with his old band, The Frames.

Hugely successful Dublin trio The Script have parlayed their melodic brand of pop-rock onto all kinds of TV shows, from *90210* to *Made in Chelsea*. In 2017 they released a single called 'Another War Child', which teased fans as to the more serious content of their new album, which will follow the immensely successful *No Sound Without Silence*, released in 2014. They mightn't sell as many records, but Villagers (which is really just Conor O'Brien and a selection of collaborators) have earned universal acclaim for their brand of indie-folk rock – and in 2016 their last album, *Darling Arithmetic,* won an Ivor Novello award.

But it's not just about musicians with grave intent: if Boyzone and Westlife were big, their success pales in comparison to that of One Direction, another product of 'the X Factory'. We mention them here because one of their members, Niall Horan, is from Mullingar, County Westmeath – about an hour west of Dublin – which inevitably meant that when One Direction played Croke Park in 2015 it was a kind of homecoming. The band has since split, but Niall has launched a successful solo career – 2017 saw the release of his first solo single, 'This Town'.

Dublin Songs

'Lay Me Down' (2001) The Frames

'One' (1991) U2

'Raglan Road' (1972) Luke Kelly and the Dubliners

'Still in Love with You' (1978) Thin Lizzy

Dublin Albums

Boy (1980) U2

I Do Not Want What I Haven't Got (1980) Sinéad O'Connor

Music in Mouth (2003) Bell X1

Loveless (1991) My Bloody Valentine

Becoming a Jackal (2010) Villagers

GABRIELA INSURATELU/SHUTTERSTOCK ©

Architecture

Dublin's skyline is a clue to its age, with visible peaks of its architectural history dating back to the Middle Ages. Of course, Dublin is older still, but there are no traces left of its Viking origins and you'll have to begin your architectural exploration in the 12th century, with the construction of the city's castle and two cathedrals. Its finest buildings, however, date from much later – built during the golden century that came to be known as the Georgian period.

Medieval Dublin

Above: Irish Museum of Modern Art (p118)

Viking Dublin was largely built of not-so-durable wood, of which there's virtually no trace left. The Norman footprint is a little deeper, but even its most impressive structures have been heavily reconstructed. The imposing Dublin Castle – or the complex of buildings that are known as Dublin Castle – bears little resemblance to the fortress that was erected by the Anglo-Normans at the beginning of the 13th century and more to the neoclassical style of the 17th century. However, there are some fascinating glimpses of the lower reaches of the original, which you can visit on a tour.

Although the 12th-century cathedrals of Christ Church and St Patrick's were heavily rebuilt in Victorian times, there are some original features, including the crypt in Christ Church, which has a 12th-century Romanesque door. The older of the two St Audoen's Churches dates from 1190 and it too has a few Norman odds and ends, including a late-12th-century doorway.

Anglo-Dutch Period

After the Restoration of Charles II in 1660, Dublin embarked upon almost a century and a half of unparalleled growth as the city raced to become the second most important in the British Empire. The most impressive examples of the style are the Royal Hospital Kilmainham (1680), designed by William Robinson and now home to the Irish Museum of Modern Art; and the Royal Barracks (now Collins Barracks; 1701) built by Thomas Burgh and now home to a branch of the National Museum of Ireland.

Georgian Dublin

Dublin's architectural apogee can roughly be placed in the period spanning the rule of the four English Georges, between the accession of George I in 1714 and the death of George IV in 1830. The greatest influence on the shape of modern Dublin throughout this period came from the Wide Street Commissioners, appointed in 1757 and responsible for designing civic spaces and the framework of the modern city. Their efforts were complemented by Dublin's Anglo-Irish Protestant gentry who, flush with unprecedented wealth, dedicated themselves wholeheartedly towards improving their city.

Their inspiration was the work of the Italian architect Andrea Palladio (1508–80), who revived the symmetry and harmony of classical architecture. When the Palladian style reached these shores in the 1720s, the architects of the time tweaked it and introduced a number of, let's call them, 'refinements'. Most obvious were the elegant brick exteriors and decorative touches, such as coloured doors, fanlights and ironwork, which broke the sometimes austere uniformity of the fashion. Consequently, Dublin came to be known for its 'Georgian style'.

Sir Edward Lovett Pearce

The architect credited with the introduction of the Georgian style to Dublin's cityscape was Sir Edward Lovett Pearce (1699–1733), who first arrived in Dublin in 1725 and turned heads with the building

Archéire (www. archiseek.com) is a comprehensive website covering all things to do with Irish architecture and design. If you want something in book form, look no further than Christine Casey's superb *The Buildings of Ireland: Dublin* (2005; Yale University Press), which goes through the city literally street by street.

GEORGIAN PLASTERERS

The handsome exteriors of Dublin's finest Georgian houses are often matched by superbly crafted plasterwork within. The fine work of Michael Stapleton (1747–1801) can be seen in Trinity College, Ely House near St Stephen's Green, and Belvedere House in north Dublin. The LaFranchini brothers, Paolo (1695–1776) and Filippo (1702–79), are responsible for the outstanding decoration in Newman House on St Stephen's Green. But perhaps Dublin's most famous plastered surfaces are in the chapel at the heart of the Rotunda Hospital. Although hospitals are never the most pleasant places to visit, it's worth it for the German stuccadore Bartholomew Cramillion's fantastic rococo plasterwork.

The Four Courts (p135)

of Parliament House (now Bank of Ireland; 1728–39). It was the first two-chamber debating house in the world and the main chamber, the House of Commons, is topped by a massive pantheon-style dome.

Pearce also created the blueprint for the city's Georgian town-houses, the most distinguishing architectural feature of Dublin. The local version typically consists of four storeys, including the basement, with symmetrically arranged windows and an imposing, often brightly painted front door. Granite steps lead up to the door, which is often further embellished with a delicate leaded fanlight. The most celebrated examples are on the Southside, particularly around Merrion and Fitzwilliam Sqs, but the Northside also has some magnificent streets, including North Great George's and Henrietta Sts. The latter features two of Pearce's originals (at Nos 9 and 10) and is still Dublin's most unified Georgian street. Mountjoy Sq, the most elegant address in 18th-century Dublin, is currently being renewed after a century of neglect.

Richard Cassels

German architect Richard Cassels (aka Richard Castle; 1690–1751) hit town in 1728. While his most impressive country houses are outside Dublin, he did design Nos 85 and 86 St Stephen's Green (1738), which were combined in the 19th century and renamed Newman House, and No 80 (1736), which was later joined with No 81 to create Iveagh House, now the Department of Foreign Affairs; you can visit the peaceful gardens there still. The Rotunda Hospital (1748), at the top of O'Connell St, is also one of Cassels' works. As splendid as these buildings are, it seems he was only warming up for Leinster House

INGUS KRUKLITIS/SHUTTERSTOCK ©

Grand Canal Square (p147)

(1745–48), the magnificent country residence built on what was then the countryside, but is now the centre of government.

Sir William Chambers

Dublin's boom attracted such notable architects as Swedish-born Sir William Chambers (1723–96), who designed some of Dublin's most impressive buildings, though he never actually bothered to visit the city. It was the north side of the Liffey that benefited most from Chambers' genius: the chaste and elegant Charlemont House (now the Hugh Lane Gallery; 1763) lords over Parnell Sq, while the Casino at Marino (1755–79) is his most stunning and bewitching work.

James Gandon & Thomas Cooley

It was towards the end of the 18th century that Dublin's developers really kicked into gear, when the power and confidence of the Anglo-Irish Ascendancy seemed boundless. Of several great architects of the time, James Gandon (1743–1823) stood out, and he built two of Dublin's most enduring and elegant neoclassical landmarks: the Custom House (1781–91) and the Four Courts (1786–1802). They were both built on the quays to afford plenty of space in which to admire them.

Regency & Victorian

The Act of Union (1801) turned Dublin from glorious capital to Empire backwater, which resulted in precious little construction for much of the 19th century. Exceptions include the General Post Office (GPO; 1814), designed by Francis Johnston (1760–1829), and the stunning series of curvilinear glasshouses in the National Botanic Gardens,

MODERN BRIDGES

Over the last few years the Liffey has been spanned by a handful of new bridges that are all pretty good examples of modern design. Santiago Calatrava's James Joyce Bridge (2003) at Usher's Island gave the city its first piece of design with the imprimatur of a 'starchitect', and he outdid himself again in 2009 with the harp-like Samuel Beckett Bridge at Spencer Dock. In between them is the award-winning pedestrian Sean O'Casey Bridge (2005), designed by Cyril O'Neill, while the latest addition is the Rosie Hackett Bridge, joining Hawkins St and Marlborough St. It opened in 2014 and is the only bridge in Dublin named after a woman; Hackett was a prominent trade unionist and participated in the Easter Rising of 1916.

which were created mid-century by the Dublin ironmaster Richard Turner (1798–1881).

After Catholic Emancipation in 1829, there was a wave of church building, and later the two great Protestant cathedrals of Christ Church and St Patrick's were reconstructed. One especially beautiful example is the splendidly ornate and incongruous Newman University Church (1856), built in a Byzantine style by John Hungerford Pollen (1820–1902) because Cardinal Newman was none too keen on the Gothic style that was all the rage at the time.

Modern Architecture

James Gandon's greatest rival was Thomas Cooley (1740–84), who died too young to reach his full potential. His greatest building, the Royal Exchange (now City Hall; 1779), was butchered to provide office space in the mid-19th century, but returned to its breathtaking splendour in a stunning 2000 restoration.

Without any blank slate like a mass demolition or an architecturally convenient fire (like Chicago suffered in 1871), the architecture of modern Dublin has largely been squeezed in between other periods and has been low on avant-garde examples of international movements.

Exceptions include modernist buildings such as Busáras (1953) and Liberty Hall (1965), which have divided critics; less so Paul Koralek's bold and brazen Berkeley Library (1967) in the grounds of Trinity College.

It wasn't until the explosive growth of the 1990s that the city's modern landscape really began to improve, even if some of the early constructions – such as the Irish Financial Services Centre (IFSC; 1987) and the Waterways Visitor Centre (1994) – don't seem as impressive now as they did when they first opened.

The most stunning makeover has occurred in the Docklands, which has been transformed from quasi-wasteland to a fine example of contemporary urban design. You'll find the best examples on Grand Canal Sq, dominated by Daniel Libeskind's elegant Bord Gáis Energy Theatre (2010) and Manuel Aires Mateus' Marker Hotel (2011), and the plaza itself, designed by American landscape artist Martha Schwartz in 2008, is equally eye-catching.

The crash of 2008 put the kibosh on new construction, but in 2017 ground finally broke for what will be Dublin's tallest office block. The 'Exo' – named in reference to its 'exoskeleton' external supporting structure – will be 74m high, 7m taller than the Montevetro building, Google's HQ on Barrow St. The Exo is expected to be completed by 2019.

Survival Guide

Transport

ARRIVING IN DUBLIN

Ireland's capital and biggest city is the most important point of entry and departure for the country – almost all airlines fly in and out of Dublin Airport. Ferries from the UK arrive at the Dublin Port terminal, while ferries from France arrive in the southern port of Rosslare. Dublin is also the nation's primary rail hub. Flights, cars and tours can be booked online at lonelyplanet.com/bookings.

Dublin Airport

Located 13km north of the city centre, **Dublin Airport** (☑01-814 1111; www.dublinairport.com) has two terminals: most international flights (including most US flights) use Terminal 2; Ryanair and select others use Terminal 1. Both terminals have the usual selection of pubs, res-

taurants, shops, ATMs and car-hire desks.

There are direct flights to Dublin from all major European centres (including a dizzying array of options from the UK) and from Atlanta, Boston, Charlotte, Chicago, Los Angeles, New York, Orlando, Philadelphia, San Francisco and Washington, DC in the USA. Flights from further afield (Australasia or Africa) are usually routed through another European hub such as London; one recently introduced exception is a direct service from Addis Ababa.

Most airlines have walk-up counters at Dublin airport; those that don't have counters have their ticketing handled by other airlines.

There is no train service from the airport to the city centre.

Bus

It takes about 45 minutes to get into the city by bus.

Aircoach (☑01-844 7118; www.aircoach.ie; One way/return €7/12) Private coach service with three routes from the airport to more than 20 destinations throughout the city, including the main streets of the city centre. Coaches run every 10 to 15 minutes between 6am and midnight, then hourly from midnight until 6am.

Airlink Express Coach (☑01-873 4222; www.dublinbus.ie; One way/return €6/10) Bus 747 runs every 10 to 20 minutes from 5.45am to 12.30am between the airport, the central bus station (Busáras) and the Dublin Bus office on Upper O'Connell St. Bus 757 runs every 15 to 30 minutes from 5am to 12.25am between the airport and various stops in the city, including Grand Canal Dock, Merrion Sq and Camden St.

Dublin Bus (Map p249; ☑01-873 4222; www.dublinbus.ie; 59 Upper O'Connell St;

GREENER ARRIVALS

Although the vast majority of visitors will enter and exit Dublin via the airport, you can do your bit for the environment and arrive by boat – and have a bit of an adventure along the way. From Britain it's a cinch: you can buy a combined train-and-ferry ticket (known as Sail & Rail) for under €50 (see www.irishrail.ie for travel from Ireland or www.thetrainline.com for travel from the UK). Or if you're really on a budget, get a bus-and-ferry ticket – from London it won't cost you more than the price of a meal.

You can also arrive at another Irish port. Rosslare in County Wexford has ferry services from France and southwestern Britain, while Larne, a short hop outside Belfast, is served from Stranraer in Scotland. Not only will you get to Dublin easily enough, but you can do some exploring on the way.

CLIMATE CHANGE & TRAVEL

Every form of transport that relies on carbon-based fuel generates CO_2, the main cause of human-induced climate change. Modern travel is dependent on aeroplanes, which might use less fuel per kilometre per person than most cars but travel much greater distances. The altitude at which aircraft emit gases (including CO_2) and particles also contributes to their climate change impact. Many websites offer 'carbon calculators' that allow people to estimate the carbon emissions generated by their journey and, for those who wish to do so, to offset the impact of the greenhouse gases emitted with contributions to portfolios of climate-friendly initiatives throughout the world. Lonely Planet offsets the carbon footprint of all staff and author travel.

⊙8.30am-5.30pm Tue-Fri, to 2pm Sat, 9am-5.30pm Mon; 🚌all city centre) A number of buses serve the airport from various points in Dublin, including buses 16 (Rathfarnham), 41 (Lower Abbey St) and 102 (Sutton/Howth); all cross the city centre on their way to the airport.

Taxi

There is a taxi rank directly outside the arrivals concourse of both terminals. It should take about 25 minutes to get into the city centre by taxi and should cost around €25, including an initial charge of €3.60 (€4 between 10pm and 8am and on Sundays and bank holidays). Make sure the meter is switched on.

Dublin Port Terminal

The **Dublin Port Terminal** (☑01-855 2222; Alexandra Rd; 🚌53 from Talbot St) is 3km northeast of the city centre.

Operators serve the following routes:

Irish Ferries (☑0818 300 400; www.irishferries.com; Ferryport, Terminal Rd South) Holyhead in Wales; €200 return, three hours

P&O Irish Sea (☑01-407 3434; www.poferries.com; Terminal 3) Liverpool; €180 return, 8½ hours or four hours on fast boat

Isle of Man Steam Packet Company/Sea Cat (Map

p252; ☑01-836 4019; www. steam-packet.com; Maritime House, North Wall Quay; 🚌41x, 151 from city centre) Isle of Man; €110 return, 1½ hours

Bus

An express bus transfer to and from Dublin Port is operated by **Morton's** (Map p236; www.mortonscoaches.ie; adult/child €3/1.50; ⊙7.15am, 1.30pm & 7pm), departing from Westmoreland St, timed to coincide with ferry departures. Otherwise, regular bus No 53 serves the port from Talbot St. Inbound ferries are met by timed bus services that serve the city centre.

Busáras Terminal

Dublin's central bus station, **Busáras** (Map p249; ☑01-836 6111; www.buseireann.ie; Store St; 🚇Connolly) is just north of the river behind the Custom House; it has different-sized luggage lockers costing €6 to €10 per day.

It's possible to combine bus and ferry tickets from major UK centres to Dublin on the bus network. The journey between London and Dublin takes about 12 hours and costs from €29 return (€41 for a single!). For details in London, contact **Eurolines** (☑0870 514 3219; www. eurolines.com).

From here, Bus Éireann buses serve the whole national network, including buses to towns and cities in Northern Ireland.

Heuston & Connolly Train Stations

All trains in the Republic are run by **Irish Rail** (Iarnród Éireann; ☑1850 366 222; www.irishrail.ie). Dublin has two main train stations: **Heuston Station** (☑01-836 5421; 🚇Heuston), on the western side of town near the Liffey; and **Connolly Station** (☑01-836 3333; 🚇Connolly, 🚊Connolly Station), a short walk northeast of Busáras, behind the Custom House.

Connolly Station is a stop on the DART line into town; the Luas Red Line serves both Connolly and Heuston stations.

Car & Motorcycle

Road access to and from Dublin is pretty straightforward. A network of motorways radiate outward from the M50 ring road that surrounds Dublin, serving the following towns and cities:

M1 North to Drogheda, Dundalk and Belfast

M3 Northwest to Navan, Cavan and Donegal

M4 West to Galway and Sligo

M7 Southwest to Limerick; also (via M8) to Cork

M9 Southeast to Kilkenny and Waterford

M11 Southeast to Wexford

More Information

There are tolls on limited sections of most motorways, costing between €1.40 and €2.90 for a car and between €1 and €1.50 for a motorcycle. The M50 ring road has a barrier-free toll between junctions 6 and 7 (crossing the Liffey): vehicles not registered with with e-tags are charged €3.10; motorcycles are free.

Many rental cars come equipped with tags that automatically take account of M50 charges and add them to your final bill (a sticker on the rental car will indicate it); otherwise, go to www.eflow. ie and pay the toll before 8pm the following day to avoid penalties.

GETTING AROUND DUBLIN

Bus

The **Dublin Bus Office** (Map p249; ☑01-873 4222; www.dub linbus.ie; 59 Upper O'Connell St; ☺8.30am-5.30pm Tue-Fri, to 2pm Sat, 9am-5.30pm Mon; ☐all city centre) has free single-route timetables for all its services. Buses run from around 6am (some start at 5.30am) to about 11.30pm.

Bus Fares

Fares are calculated according to stages (stops):

Stages	Cash Fare (€)	Leap Card (€)
1-3	2	1.50
4-13	2.70	2.05
over 13	3.30	2.60

A Leap Card (www.leapcard. ie), available from most newsagents, is not just cheaper but also more convenient as you don't have to worry about tendering exact fares (required with cash, otherwise you will get a receipt for reimbursement, which is only possible at the Dublin

Bus main office). Register the card online and top it up with whatever amount you need. When you board a bus, DART, Luas (light rail) or suburban train, just swipe your card and the fare is automatically deducted.

If you're travelling within the College Green Bus Corridor (roughly between Parnell Sq to the north and St Stephen's Green to the south) you can use the €0.50 special City Centre fare.

Fare-Saver Passes

Fare-saver passes include the following:

Freedom of the City (adult/child €33/16) Three-day unlimited travel on all bus services, including Airlink, Dublin Bus Hop-On, Hop-Off tours and entry to the Little Museum of Dublin and a Pat Liddy walking tour.

Luas Flexi Ticket (one/seven/30 days €7/26/100) Unlimited travel on all Luas services.

Rambler Pass (five/30 days €31.50/157.50) Valid for unlimited travel on all Dublin Bus and Airlink services, except Nitelink.

Visitor Leap Card (one/three/seven days €10/19.50/40) Unlimited travel on bus, Luas and DART, including Airlink, Nitelink and Xpresso bus.

Nitelink

Nitelink late-night buses run from the College, Westmoreland and D'Olier Sts triangle. On Fridays and Saturdays, departures are at 12.30am, then every 20 minutes until 4.30am on the more popular routes, and until 3.30am on the less frequented ones; there are no services Sunday to Thursday. Fares are €6.50 (€5.20 with Leap card). See www.dublinbus.ie for routes.

Tram

The Luas (www.luas.ie) light-rail system has two lines: the green line (running every

five to 15 minutes) connects St Stephen's Green with Sandyford in south Dublin via Ranelagh and Dundrum; the red line (every 20 minutes) runs from the Point Village to Tallaght via the north quays and Heuston Station.

There are ticket machines at every stop or you can use a tap-on, tap-off Leap Card, which is available from most newsagents. A typical short-hop fare (around four stops) is €2.30. Services run from 5.30am to 12.30am Monday to Friday, from 6.30am to 12.30am Saturday and from 7am to 11.30pm Sunday.

From 2018, a new cross-city line will connect the green and red lines with a route from St Stephen's Green through Dawson St and around Trinity College and over the river.

Bicycle

Dublin is relatively flat and compact, making it ideal cycling territory. You can zip from one side of the city to the other in double-quick time, and a bike makes the suburbs much more accessible. The city does have a growing network of cycle lanes, especially south of the Liffey, but getting around the centre itself can be a bit of an obstacle course as larger vehicles such as buses and trucks are forced to encroach on lanes nominally reserved for two wheels due to the narrowness of the streets.

There are plenty of spots to lock your bike throughout the city, but be sure to do so thoroughly as bike theft can be a problem – and never leave your bike on the street overnight as even the toughest lock can be broken. Dublin City Cycling (www.cycledub lin.ie) is an excellent online resource.

Bikes are only allowed on suburban trains (not the DART), either stowed in the guard's van or in a special compartment at the end of the train.

Dublinbikes

One of the most popular ways to get around the city is with the blue bikes of Dublinbikes (www.dublinbikes. ie), a public bicycle-rental scheme with more than 100 stations spread across the city centre. Purchase a €10 smart card (as well as pay a credit-card deposit of €150) or a three-day card online or at any station before 'freeing' a bike for use, which is then free of charge for the first 30 minutes and €0.50 for each half-hour thereafter.

Hire, Purchase & Repair

Bike rental has become tougher due to the Dublinbikes scheme. Typical rental for a hybrid or touring bike is around €25 a day or €140 per week.

Cycleways (www.cycleways. com; 185-187 Parnell St; ⊙8.30am-6.30pm Mon-Wed & Fri, to 8pm Thu, 9.30am-6pm Sat; ⊒all city centre) An great bike shop that rents out hybrids and touring bikes during the summer months (May to Sep).

2Wheels (www.2wheels.ie; 57 S William St; ⊙10am-6pm Mon, Tue & Sat, to 8pm Wed, Thu & Fri, noon-6pm Sun; ⊒all city centre) New bikes, all the gear you could possibly need and a decent repair service; but be sure to book an appointment as it is generally quite busy.

MacDonald Cycles (☑01-475 2586; www.macdonaldcycles. ie; 38 Wexford St; ⊙9am-6pm Mon-Fri, 9.30am-6pm Sat; ⊒14, 15, 65, 83) Does repairs, and will have your bike back to you within a day or so (barring serious damage).

Car & Motorcycle

Driving

Traffic in Dublin is a nightmare and parking is an expensive headache. There are no free spots to park anywhere in the city centre during business hours (7am to 7pm Monday to Saturday), but there is plenty of paid parking, priced according to zone: €2.90 per hour in the yellow (central) zone down to €0.60 in the blue (suburban). Supervised and sheltered car parks cost around €4 per hour, with most offering a low-cost evening flat rate.

Clamping of illegally parked cars is thoroughly enforced, and there is an €80 charge for removal. Parking is free after 7pm Monday to Saturday, and all day Sunday, in most metered spots (unless indicated) and on single yellow lines.

Car theft and break-ins are an occasional nuisance, so never leave anything visible or of value in the car. When you're booking accommodation, check on parking facilities.

The **Automobile Association of Ireland** (AA; ☑01-617 9999, breakdown 1800 667 788; www.aaireland.ie; 61 S William St; ⊒all city centre) is located in the city centre.

Hire

All the main agencies are represented in Dublin. Book in advance for the best fares, especially at weekends and during summer months, when demand is highest.

Motorbikes and mopeds are not available for rent. People aged under 21 are not allowed to hire a car; for the majority of rental companies you have to be at least 23 and have had a valid driving licence for a minimum of one year. Many rental agencies will not rent to people over 70 or 75.

The following rental agencies have several branches across the capital and at the airport:

Avis Rent-a-Car (☑01-605 7500; www.avis.ie; 35 Old Kilmainham Rd; ⊙8.30am-5.45pm Mon-Fri, 8.30am-2.30pm Sat & Sun; ⊒23, 25, 25A, 26, 68, 69 from city centre)

Budget Rent-a-Car (☑01-837 9611; www.budget.ie; 151 Lower Drumcondra Rd; ⊙9am-6pm; ⊒41 from O'Connell St)

Europcar (☑01-812 2800; www. europcar.ie; 1 Mark St; ⊙8am-6pm Mon-Fri, 8.30am-3pm Sat & Sun; ⊒all city centre)

Hertz Rent-a-Car (☑01-709 3060; www.hertz.com; 151 South Circular Rd; ⊙8.30am-5.30pm Mon-Fri, 9am-4.30pm Sat, 9am-3.30pm Sun; ⊒9, 16, 77, 79 from city centre)

Thrifty (☑01-844 1944; www. thrifty.ie; 26 Lombard St E; ⊙8am-6pm Mon-Fri, to 3pm Sat & Sun; ⊒all city centre)

Taxi

All taxi fares begin with a flag-fall of €3.60 (€4 from 10pm to 8am), followed by €1.10 per kilometre thereafter (€1.40 from 10pm to 8am). In addition to these, there are a number of extra charges – €1 for each extra passenger and €2 for telephone bookings. There is no charge for luggage.

Taxis can be hailed on the street and found at taxi ranks around the city, including on the corner of Abbey and O'Connell Sts; College Green, in front of Trinity College; and St Stephen's Green at the end of Grafton St.

Numerous taxi companies, such as **National Radio Cabs** (☑01-677 2222; www.nrc.ie), dispatch taxis by radio. Or try MyTaxi (www.mytaxi.com), a taxi app.

Train

The **Dublin Area Rapid Transport** (DART; ☑01-836 6222; www.irishrail.ie) provides quick train access to the coast as far north as Howth (about 30 minutes) and as far south as Greystones in County Wicklow. Pearse Station is convenient for central Dublin south of the Liffey, and Connolly Station for north of the Liffey. There are services every 10 to 20 minutes, sometimes more frequently, from around 6.30am to midnight Monday to Saturday. Services are less frequent on Sunday. A one-way DART ticket from Dublin to Dun Laoghaire or Howth costs €3.25.

There are also suburban rail services north as far as Dundalk, inland to Mullingar and south past Bray.

Train Passes

DART passes include the following:

Adult All Day Rail (one/three days €11.70/27) Valid for unlimited travel on DART and suburban rail travel.

Family All Day Rail (€20) Valid for travel for one day for a family of two adults and two children aged under 16 on rail services.

TOURS

Dublin isn't that big, so a straightforward sightseeing tour is only really necessary if you're looking to cram in the sights or avoid blistered feet. What is worth considering, however, is a specialised guided tour, especially for those of a musical, historical or literary bent. There are bus tours aplenty – Dublin Bus, the city's bus company, runs a variety of tours, all of which can be booked at its **office** (Map p249; ☑01-872 0000; www.dublinsightseeing.ie; 59 Upper O'Connell St; adult €15-28; ☐all city centre, ☐Abbey), or at the Bus Éireann counter at the **Visit Dublin Centre** (Map p238; www.visitdublin.com; 25 Suffolk St; ☺9am-5.30pm Mon-Sat, 10.30am-3pm Sun; ☐all city centre) – and even boat tours, but the best way to get around is on foot, in the company of an expert.

Horse & Carriage

Old-style horse-and-carriage tour operators congregate at the top of Grafton St by St Stephen's Green. Each carriage takes up to five people. A half-hour tour starts at €40, an hour from €70, but different-length trips can be negotiated: fix a price *before* the driver says giddy-up.

Walking

1916 Rebellion Walking Tour (Map p238;☑086 858 3847; www.1916rising.com; 23 Wicklow St; €13; ☺11.30am Mon-Sat, 1pm Sun Mar-Oct; ☐all city centre) Excellent two-hour tours led by Trinity graduates, who give you the lowdown on where, why and how the 1916 Rising took place.

Dublin Literary Pub Crawl

(Map p238;☑01-670 5602; www.dublinpubcrawl.com; 9 Duke St; adult/student €13/11; ☺7.30pm daily Apr-Oct, 7.30pm Thu-Sun Nov-Mar; ☐all city centre) Spend 2½ hours in the company of two actors, who will escort you through a selection of the city's most renowned literary boozers – with plenty of hilarious bits acted out for good measure.

Dublin Musical Pub Crawl (Map p98;☑01-478 0193; www.discoverdublin.ie; 58-59 Fleet St; adult/student €14/12; ☺7.30pm daily Apr-Oct, 7.30pm Thu-Sat Nov-Mar; ☐all city centre) Explore the history of Irish traditional music and its influence on contemporary styles explained and demonstrated by two expert musicians in a number of Temple Bar pubs over 2½ hours. Tours meet upstairs in the Oliver St John Gogarty pub and are highly recommended.

Pat Liddy Walking Tours (Map p238;☑01-831 1109; www.walkingtours.ie; Visit Dublin Centre, 25 Suffolk St; tours €10-15; ☐all city centre) Dublin's best-known tour guide is local historian Pat Liddy, who leads a variety of guided walks including, Dublin Highlights and The Best of Dublin – The Complete Heritage Walking Tour. He is also available for private guided walks (check the website for timings) and has a bunch of podcast walks (www.visitdublin.com/iwalks) available for download.

Dublin Visitor Centre (Map p238; www.visitdublin.com; 25 Suffolk St; ☺9am-5.30pm Mon-Sat, 10.30am-3pm Sun; ☐all city centre) The tourist office has put together an app with four themed walking tours covering Dublin's history over the last 200 years. Each walk takes approximately two hours; the app is available for both iPhone and Android.

Directory A–Z

Customs Regulations

Ireland has a two-tier customs system: one for goods bought duty-free outside the European Union (EU); the other for goods bought in another EU country where tax and duty is paid. There is technically no limit to the amount of goods transportable within the EU, but customs will use certain guidelines to distinguish personal use from commercial purpose.

Duty Free

For duty-free goods from outside the EU, limits include 200 cigarettes, 1L of spirits or 2L of wine, 60mL of perfume and 250mL of *eau de toilette*.

Tax & Duty Paid

Amounts that officially constitute personal use include 3200 cigarettes (or 400 cigarillos, 200 cigars or 3kg of tobacco) and either 10L of spirits, 20L of fortified wine, 60L of sparkling wine, 90L of still wine or 110L of beer.

Discount Cards

Senior citizens are entitled to discounts on public transport and museum fees. Students and under-26s also get discounts with the appropriate student or youth card. Local discount passes include the following:

Dublin Pass (adult/child one-day €52/31, three-day €83/52) For heavy-duty sightseeing, the Dublin Pass will save you a packet. It provides free entry to over 25 attractions (including the Guinness Storehouse), discounts at 20 others and guaranteed fast-track entry to some of the busiest sights. To avail of the free Aircoach transfer to and from the airport, order the card online so you have it when you land. Otherwise, it's available from any Discover Ireland Dublin Tourism Centre.

Heritage Card (adult/child and student €40/10) This card entitles you to free access to all sights in and around Dublin managed by the Office of Public Works (OPW). You can buy it at OPW sites or Dublin Tourism offices.

Electricity

Type G
230V/50Hz

PRACTICALITIES

Newspapers *Irish Independent* (www.independent.ie), *Irish Times* (www.irishtimes.com), *Irish Examiner* (www.examiner.ie), *The Herald* (www.herald.ie).

Radio RTE Radio 1 (88-90MHz), RTE Radio 2 (90-92MHz), Today FM (100-103MHz), Newstalk 106-108 (106-108MHz).

Emergency & Important Numbers

Ambulance, Fire, Police (gardaí), Boat or Coastal Rescue	☎999 or ☎112
Rape Crisis Centre	☎1800 778 888
Country Code	☎+353
International Access Code	☎00

Entry & Exit Formalities

Getting into the country is easy, so long as you have the right documentation. Immigration channels at airports are divided between EU and non-EU passport holders. The former usually results in a cursory glance at your passport, while visitors in the latter category are scrutinised a little more.

Internet Access

Wi-fi and 3G/4G networks are making internet cafes largely redundant (except to gamers); the few that are left will charge around €6 per hour. Most accommodation has wi-fi service, either free or for a daily charge (up to €10 per day).

Legal Matters

The possession of small quantities of marijuana attracts a fine or warning, but harder drugs are treated more seriously. Public drunkenness is illegal but commonplace – the police will usually ignore it unless you're causing trouble. If you need legal assistance, contact the **Legal Aid Board** (☎066-947 1000; www.legalaidboard.ie).

LGBTQ Travellers

Dublin is a pretty good place to be LGBTQ. Being gay or lesbian in the city is completely unremarkable, while in recent years members of the trans community have also found greater acceptance. However, LGBTQ people can still be harassed or worse, so if you do encounter any sort of trouble, call the **Garda LGBTQ Liaison Officer** (☎116006; ⊗24hr) or the **Sexual Assault Unit** (☎01-666 3430; ⊗24hr).

Resources

Gaire (www.gaire.com) Online message board and resource centre.

Gay Men's Health Project (☎01-660 2189; www.hse.ie/go/GMHS) Practical advice on men's health issues.

Gay Switchboard Dublin (☎01-872 1055; www.gay switchboard.ie; ⊗6.30am-4pm Mon-Fri, to 6pm on Sat & Sun) A friendly and useful voluntary service that provides information on matters such as legal issues and where to find accommodation.

National Lesbian & Gay Federation (NLGF; ☎01-675 5025; http://nxf.ie; 2 Upper Exchange St, Temple Bar; ▣all city centre) Publishers of Gay Community News.

Outhouse (☎01-873 4932; www.outhouse.ie; 105 Capel St; ▣all city centre) Top gay, lesbian and bisexual resource centre. Great stop-off point to see what's on, check noticeboards and meet people. It publishes *Ireland's Pink Pages*, a free directory of gay-centric services, which is also accessible on the website.

Money

ATMs are widespread. Credit cards (with PIN) are accepted at most restaurants, hotels and shops.

ATMs

Most banks have ATMs that are linked to international money systems such as Cirrus, Maestro or Plus. Each transaction incurs a currency conversion fee, and credit cards can incur immediate and exorbitant cash-advance interest-rate charges. Also it is strongly recommend that if you're staying in the city centre, you get your money out early on a Friday to avoid the long queues that can form after 8pm.

Changing Money

The best exchange rates are at banks, although bureaux de change and other exchange facilities usually open for more hours. There's a cluster of banks located around College Green opposite Trinity College and all have exchange facilities.

Credit Cards

Visa and MasterCard credit and debit cards are widely accepted in Dublin. Smaller businesses prefer debit cards (and will charge a fee for credit cards). Nearly all credit and debit cards use the chip-and-PIN system, and an increasing number of places will not accept your card if you don't have your pin.

Tipping

You're not obliged to tip if the service or food was unsatisfactory.

Hotels Only for bellhops who carry luggage, then €1 per bag.

Pubs Not expected unless table service is provided, then €1 for a round of drinks.

Restaurants Tip 10% for decent service, up to 15% in more expensive places.

Taxis Tip 10% or round up to the nearest euro.

Toilet attendants Tip €0.50.

Opening Hours

Standard opening hours in relatively late-rising Dublin are as follows:

Banks 10am to 4pm Monday to Friday (to 5pm Thursday).

Offices 9am to 5pm Monday to Friday.

Post offices 9am to 6pm Monday to Friday, 9am to 1pm Saturday.

Restaurants noon to 10pm (or midnight); food service generally ends around 9pm. Top-end restaurants often close between 3pm and 6pm; restaurants serving brunch open around 11am.

Shops 9.30am to 6pm Monday to Saturday (to 8pm Thursday, to 9pm for the bigger shopping centres and supermarkets), noon to 6pm Sunday.

Post

The Irish postal service, An Post, is reliable, efficient and generally on time. Postboxes in Dublin are usually green and have two slots: one for 'Dublin only', the other for 'All Other Places'. There are a couple of post offices in the city centre, including **An Post** (Map p238; ☑01-705 8206; www.anpost.ie; St Andrew's St; ☺8.30am-5pm Mon-Fri; ☐all city centre) and the **General Post Office** (Map p249; ☑01-705 7000; www.anpost.ie; Lower O'Connell St; ☺8am-8pm Mon-Sat; ☐all city centre, ☐Abbey).

Postal Codes

Postal codes on letters and parcels in Dublin (presented as 'Dublin + number') are fairly straightforward. Their main feature is that all odd numbers refer to areas north of the Liffey and all even ones to areas south of the Liffey. They fan out numerically from the city centre, so the city centre to the north of the river is Dublin 1 and its southern equivalent is Dublin 2.

Dubliners are slowly getting used to the new Eircode system that was introduced in 2015. Similar to the UK postcode system, all addresses now have a seven-character alpha-numeric code split into two parts, eg A65 F4E2. And by slowly, we mean slowly: most Dubliners still use the old system.

Public Holidays

Good Friday and Christmas Day are the only two days in the year when all pubs close. Otherwise, the half-dozen or so bank holidays (most of which fall on a Monday) mean just that – the banks are closed, along with about half the shops. St Patrick's Day and St Stephen's Day holidays are taken on the following Monday should they fall on a weekend.

New Year's Day 1 January

St Patrick's Day 17 March

Easter (Good Friday to Easter Monday inclusive) March/April

May Bank Holiday First Monday in May

June Bank Holiday First Monday in June

August Bank Holiday First Monday in August

October Bank Holiday Last Monday in October

Christmas Day 25 December

St Stephen's Day 26 December

Safe Travel

Dublin is a safe city by any standards, except maybe those set by the Swiss. Basically, act as you would at home.

➡ Don't leave anything visible in your car when you park.

➡ Skimming at ATMs is an ongoing problem; be sure to cover the keypad with your hand when you input your PIN.

➡ Take care around the western edge of Thomas St (onto James St), where drug addicts are often present.

➡ The northern end of Gardiner St and the areas northeast of there have crime-related problems.

POLICE STATIONS

Fitzgibbon St (Fitzgibbon St; ☐122 from city centre)

Harcourt Tce (☑01-676 3481; Harcourt Tce; ☺24hr; ☐Harcourt)

Pearse St (☑01-677 8141; Pearse St; ☐all city centre)

Store St (Store St; ☐Connolly)

Taxes & Refunds

A standard VAT rate of 23% is applied to all goods sold in Dublin excluding books, children's clothing and educational items. Non-EU residents can claim the VAT back so long as the store operates either the Cashback or Taxback refund programme. You'll get a voucher with your purchase

ETTIQUETTE

Greetings Shake hands with both men and women when meeting for the first time. Female friends are greeted with a single kiss on the cheek.

Queues Dubliners can be a little lax about proper queuing etiquette, but are not shy about confronting queue-skippers who jump in front of them.

Polite requests Dubliners often use 'Sorry' instead of 'Excuse me' when asking for something; they're not really apologising for anything.

that must be stamped at the last point of exit from the EU.

Telephone

When calling Dublin from abroad, dial your international access code, followed by 353 and 1 (dropping the 0 that precedes it). To make international calls from Dublin, first dial 00, then the country code, followed by the local area code and number.

Country Code	☎+353
City Code	☎01
International Access Code	☎00
Directory Enquiries	☎11811 or 11850
International Directory Enquiries	☎11818

Time

In winter, Dublin (and the rest of Ireland) is on GMT, also known as Universal Time Coordinated (UTC); the same as Britain. In summer, the clock shifts to GMT plus one hour. When it's noon in Dublin in summer, it's 4am in Los Angeles and Vancouver, 7am in New York and Toronto, 1pm in Paris, 7pm in Singapore, and 9pm in Sydney.

Toilets

There are no on-street facilities in Dublin. All shopping centres have public toilets; if you're stranded, go into any bar or hotel.

Tourist Information

A handful of official-looking tourism offices on Grafton and O'Connell Sts are actually privately run enterprises where members pay to be included.

Dublin Visitor Centre (Map p238; www.visitdublin.com; 25 Suffolk St; ⊙9am-5.30pm Mon-Sat, 10.30am-3pm Sun; ⊒all city centre) General visitor information on Dublin and Ireland, as well as accommodation and booking service.

Travellers with Disabilities

Dublin's compact city centre is mostly flat with a few cobblestoned areas and a relatively accessible public transport network, making it an attractive destination for people with a disability. While most DART stations are disabled-friendly, DART and train services require 24 hours' notice before boarding with a wheelchair. All city buses are wheelchair-accessible, but Luas is the way to go for maximum accessibility.

Resources

You can download Lonely Planet's free accessible travel guides from http://lp travel.to/AccessibleTravel.

Ireland.com (www.ireland. com/en-us/accommodation/ articles/accessibility) Informative article with links to accessibility information for transport and tourist attractions.

Mobility Mojo (www.mobili tymojo.com) More than 500 reviews of establishments in a searchable database, mostly in the Dublin and Galway areas but expanding all the time.

Trip-Ability (www.trip-ability. com) Review site which should soon feature a booking facility.

Accessible Ireland (www.ac cessibleireland.com) Reviews,

SMOKING

It is illegal to smoke indoors everywhere except private residences and prisons.

plus short introductions to public transport.

Irish Wheelchair Association (☎01-818 6400; www.iwa.ie; Áras Chúchulain, Blackheath Dr, Clontarf; ⊙9am-5.30pm Mon-Fri) Useful national association.

Visas

If you're an EEA national, you don't need a visa to visit (or work in) the Republic of Ireland. Citizens of Australia, Canada, New Zealand, South Africa and the US can visit Ireland for up to three months without a visa. They are not allowed to work unless sponsored by an employer. To stay longer in the Republic, contact the local *garda* station or the **Garda National Immigration Bureau.** (☎01-666 9100; www.garda.ie; 13-14 Burgh Quay, Dublin; ⊙8am-9pm Mon-Fri; ⊒all city centre)

Although you don't need an onward or return ticket to enter Ireland, it could help if there's any doubt that you have sufficient funds to support yourself while in Dublin.

Women Travellers

Dublin should pose no problems for women travellers. The morning-after pill is available without a prescription from pharmacies.

In the unlikely event of a sexual assault, get in touch with the *gardaí* (police) and the **Rape Crisis Centre** (☎01-661 4911, 24hr 1800 778 888; www.drcc.ie; 70 Lower Leeson St; ⊙8am-7pm Mon-Fri, 9am-4pm Sat; ⊒all city centre).

Behind the Scenes

SEND US YOUR FEEDBACK

We love to hear from travellers – your comments keep us on our toes and help make our books better. Our well-travelled team reads every word on what you loved or loathed about this book. Although we cannot reply individually to your submissions, we always guarantee that your feedback goes straight to the appropriate authors, in time for the next edition. Each person who sends us information is thanked in the next edition – the most useful submissions are rewarded with a selection of digital PDF chapters.

Visit **lonelyplanet.com/contact** to submit your updates and suggestions or to ask for help. Our award-winning website also features inspirational travel stories, news and discussions.

Note: We may edit, reproduce and incorporate your comments in Lonely Planet products such as guidebooks, websites and digital products, so let us know if you don't want your comments reproduced or your name acknowledged. For a copy of our privacy policy visit lonelyplanet.com/privacy.

WRITER THANKS

Fionn Davenport

Thanks to everyone in Dublin who helped with research; to Laura for constantly picking me up from the airport; and to LP editors for indulging my every misstep.

ACKNOWLEDGEMENTS

Cover photograph: Christ Church Cathedral, David Soanes Photography/Getty ©

Illustrations p158-9 by Michael Weldon, p56-7, p164-5 and p88-9 by Javier Zarracina

THIS BOOK

This 11th edition of Lonely Planet's *Dublin* guidebook was researched and written by Fionn Davenport, who also wrote the previous two editions. This guidebook was produced by the following:

Destination Editor James Smart
Product Editor Genna Patterson
Senior Cartographer Mark Griffiths
Book Designer Gwen Cotter
Assisting Editors Imogen Bannister, Michelle Bennett, Nigel Chin, Andrea Dobbin, Helen Koehne, Lauren O'Connell, Chris Pitts, Gabrielle Stefanos, Sam Wheeler
Cover Researcher Naomi Parker
Thanks to Sara Aspey, Viv Baker, Stephen Cluskey, Noelle Daly, Grace Dobell, Sasha Drew, Martin Heng, Sandie Kestell, AnneMarie McCarthy, Sharon Ritchey, Angela Tinson, Tony Wheeler

Index

See also separate subindexes for:

✗ **EATING P228**

🍺 **DRINKING & NIGHTLIFE P229**

☆ **ENTERTAINMENT P230**

🔒 **SHOPPING P230**

🏃 **SPORTS & ACTIVITIES P230**

🛏 **SLEEPING P231**

Dublin Maps

Sights

- Beach
- Bird Sanctuary
- Buddhist
- Castle/Palace
- Christian
- Confucian
- Hindu
- Islamic
- Jain
- Jewish
- Monument
- Museum/Gallery/Historic Building
- Ruin
- Shinto
- Sikh
- Taoist
- Winery/Vineyard
- Zoo/Wildlife Sanctuary
- Other Sight

Activities, Courses & Tours

- Bodysurfing
- Diving
- Canoeing/Kayaking
- Course/Tour
- Sento Hot Baths/Onsen
- Skiing
- Snorkelling
- Surfing
- Swimming/Pool
- Walking
- Windsurfing
- Other Activity

Sleeping

- Sleeping
- Camping
- Hut/Shelter

Eating

- Eating

Drinking & Nightlife

- Drinking & Nightlife
- Cafe

Entertainment

- Entertainment

Shopping

- Shopping

Information

- Bank
- Embassy/Consulate
- Hospital/Medical
- Internet
- Police
- Post Office
- Telephone
- Toilet
- Tourist Information
- Other Information

Geographic

- Beach
- Gate
- Hut/Shelter
- Lighthouse
- Lookout
- Mountain/Volcano
- Oasis
- Park
- Pass
- Picnic Area
- Waterfall

Population

- Capital (National)
- Capital (State/Province)
- City/Large Town
- Town/Village

Transport

- Airport
- Border crossing
- Bus
- Cable car/Funicular
- Cycling
- Ferry
- Metro station
- Monorail
- Parking
- Petrol station
- S-Bahn/Subway station
- Taxi
- T-bane/Tunnelbana station
- Train station/Railway
- Tram
- Tube station
- U-Bahn/Underground station
- Other Transport

Routes

- Tollway
- Freeway
- Primary
- Secondary
- Tertiary
- Lane
- Unsealed road
- Road under construction
- Plaza/Mall
- Steps
- Tunnel
- Pedestrian overpass
- Walking Tour
- Walking Tour detour
- Path/Walking Trail

Boundaries

- International
- State/Province
- Disputed
- Regional/Suburb
- Marine Park
- Cliff
- Wall

Hydrography

- River, Creek
- Intermittent River
- Canal
- Water
- Dry/Salt/Intermittent Lake
- Reef

Areas

- Airport/Runway
- Beach/Desert
- Cemetery (Christian)
- Cemetery (Other)
- Glacier
- Mudflat
- Park/Forest
- Sight (Building)
- Sportsground
- Swamp/Mangrove

Note: Not all symbols displayed above appear on the maps in this book

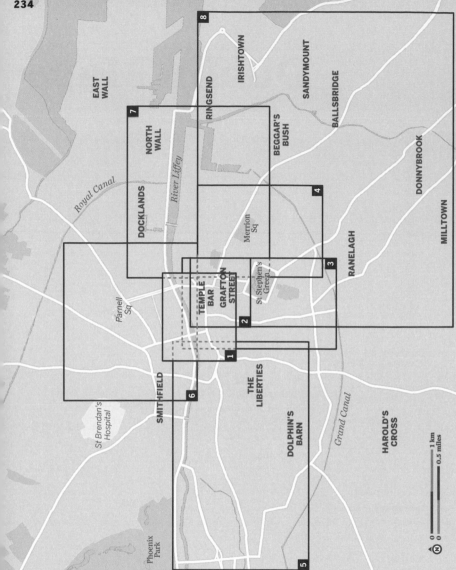

MAP INDEX

TEMPLE BAR *Map on p236*

TEMPLE BAR

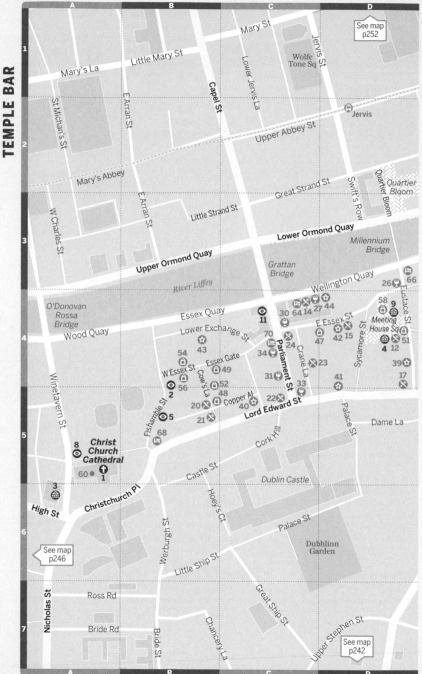

TEMPLE BAR

See map p252

See map p246

See map p242

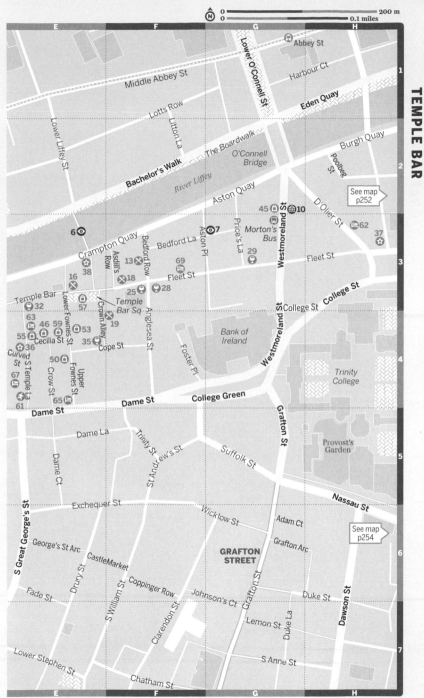

Key on p240

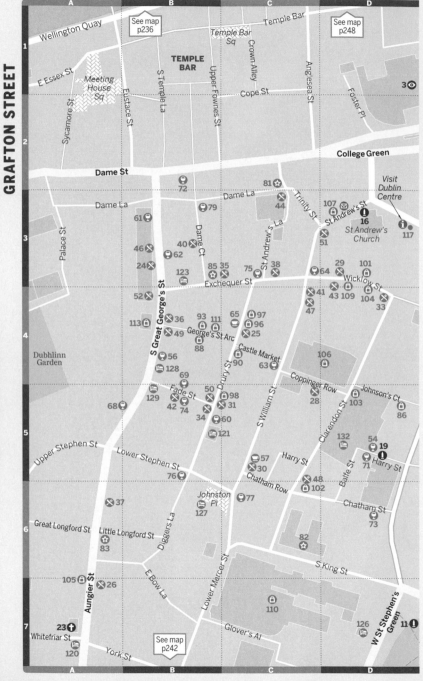

GRAFTON STREET

Wellington Quay

See map p236

Temple Bar

Temple Bar Sq

See map p248

E Essex St

Meeting House Sq

TEMPLE BAR

Crown Alley

Upper Fownes St

Cope St

Anglesea St

Foster Pl

3

Sycamore St

Eustace St

S Temple La

College Green

Dame St

Visit Dublin Centre

Dame La

72

Dame La

81

44

Trinity St

107

St Andrew's St

16

117

Palace St

Dame La

61

79

St Andrew's Church

40

Dame Ct

51

46

62

St Andrew's La

38

29

101

24

123

85 35

75

64

Wicklow St

Exchequer St

41

43 109

104 33

52

47

S Great George's St

113

36

93 111

65

97

106

49

George's St Arc

96

Dubhlinn Garden

56

88

25

Castle Market

128

Drury St

90

63

Coppinger Row

Johnson's Ct

69

28

103

Fade St

50

98

86

129

42 74

31

Clarendon St

68

34

60

132

121

54

19

57

71

Harry St

Upper Stephen St

Lower Stephen St

30

Harry St

Balfe St

76

Chatham Row

48

102

Chatham St

37

Johnston Pl

77

73

127

82

Great Longford St

Little Longford St

Diggers La

83

E Bow La

S King St

105

26

Lower Mercer St

110

Aungier St

23

W St Stephen's Green

126

11

Whitefriar St

120

See map p242

Glover's Al

York St

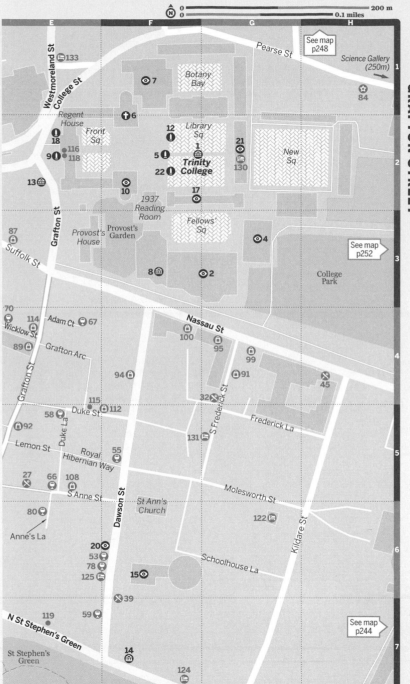

0 200 m
0 0.1 miles

See map
p248

Science Gallery
(250m)

Pearse St

Westmoreland St
College St

133

7

Botany
Bay

84

Regent
House

6

Front
Sq

18

12

Library
Sq

21

1

New
Sq

130

116
118

9

5

Trinity
College

22

13

10

17

Grafton St

1937
Reading
Room

Fellows'
Sq

4

Provost's
House

Provost's
Garden

87

Suffolk St

8

2

College
Park

See map
p252

70

114

Adam Ct

67

Nassau St

100

95

Wicklow St

89

99

Grafton Arc

94

91

45

Grafton St

115

32

58

Duke St

112

S Frederick St

Frederick La

92

Lemon St

Royal
Hibernian Way

55

131

27

66

108

Molesworth St

S Anne St

122

80

Kildare St

Anne's La

20

St Ann's
Church

53

78

Schoolhouse La

125

15

39

119

59

N St Stephen's Green

See map
p244

St Stephen's
Green

14

124

GRAFTON STREET *Map on p238*

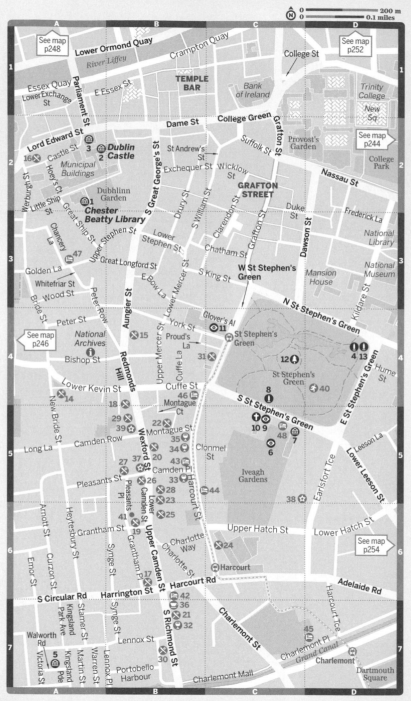

See map p248

Lower Ormond Quay

Crampton Quay

College St

See map p252

River Liffey

Essex Quay

Lower Exchange St

E Essex St

TEMPLE BAR

Bank of Ireland

Trinity College

New Sq

Parliament St

Dame St

College Green

See map p244

College Park

Lord Edward St

Castle St

St Andrew's St

Suffolk St

Provost's Garden

16

Castle St

3

Dublin Castle

Exchequer St

Wicklow St

Nassau St

2

Hoey's Ct

Municipal Buildings

S Great George's St

GRAFTON STREET

Frederick La

Weyburgh St

Little Ship St

Dubhlinn Garden

Drury St

S William St

Clarendon St

Duke St

Dawson St

National Library

Chancery La

Chester Beatty Library

1

Lower Stephen St

Chatham St

Grafton St

National Museum

Golden La

47

Great Longford St

Lower Mercer St

S King St

W St Stephen's Green

Mansion House

3

Whitefriar St

Wood St

E Bow La

Aungier St

York St

Glover's Al

11

N St Stephen's Green

Kildare St

Bride St

Peter Row

Upper Mercer St

Proud's La

St Stephen's Green

Peter St

National Archives

15

31

12

4 13

Hume St

4

Bishop St

Redmonds Hill

Cuffe La

St Stephen's Green

Hume St

14

Lower Kevin St

Cuffe St

8

S St Stephen's Green

New Bride St

18

46

Montague Ct

40

Leeson La

5

29

39

Montague St

10 9

48

7

Lower Leeson St

Long La

Camden Row

22

35

Clonmel St

6

27

37

20

34

43

Iveagh Gardens

Earlsfort Tce

Pleasants St

26

Camden Pl

33

38

Arnott St

Heytesbury St

Pleasants Pl

28

23

Harcourt St

44

Upper Hatch St

Lower Hatch St

6

41

19

Grantham St

25

Upper Camden St

Charlotte Way

24

See map p254

Emor St

Curzon St

Synge St

Grantham Pl

Charlotte St

Harcourt

Adelaide Rd

S Circular Rd

17

Harrington St

Harcourt Rd

Charlemont St

Harcourt Tce

Stamer St

Kingsland Park Ave

Synge St

S Richmond St

42

36

21

32

45

Walworth Rd

5

Victoria St

Kingsland Pde

Martin St

Warren St

Lennox Pl

Lennox St

30

Charlemont Pl

Grand Canal

Charlemont

Dartmouth Square

Portobello Harbour

Charlemont Mall

200 m
0.1 miles

GRAFTON STREET & AROUND

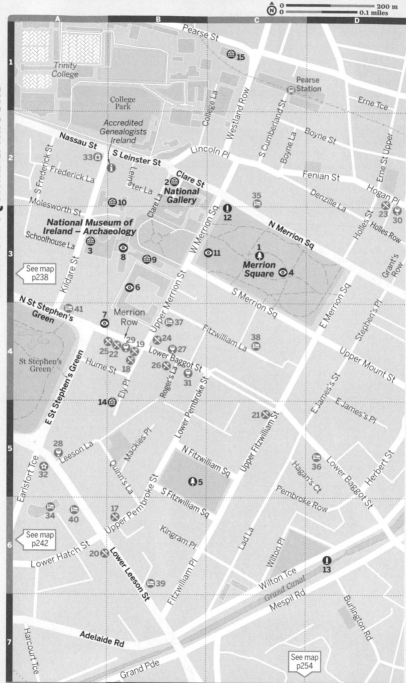

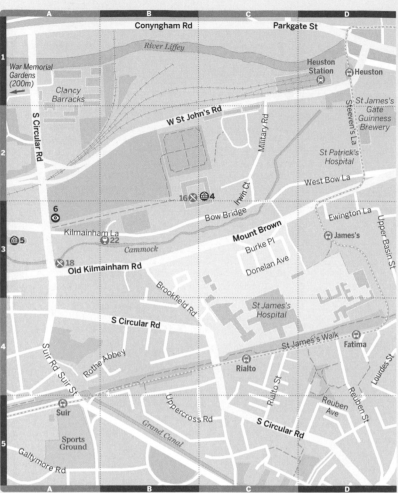

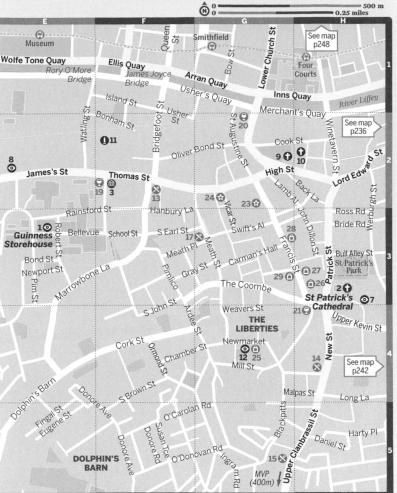

KILMAINHAM & THE LIBERTIES

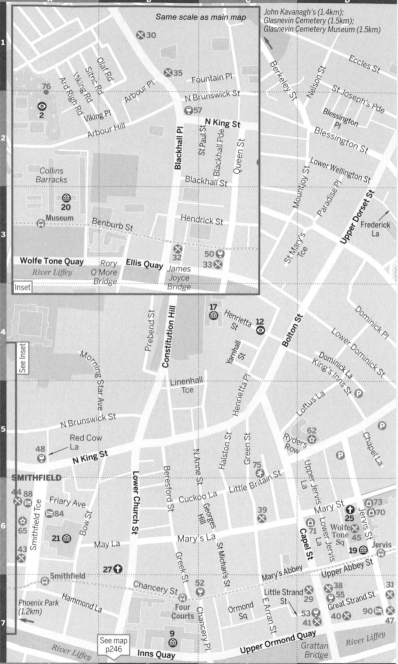

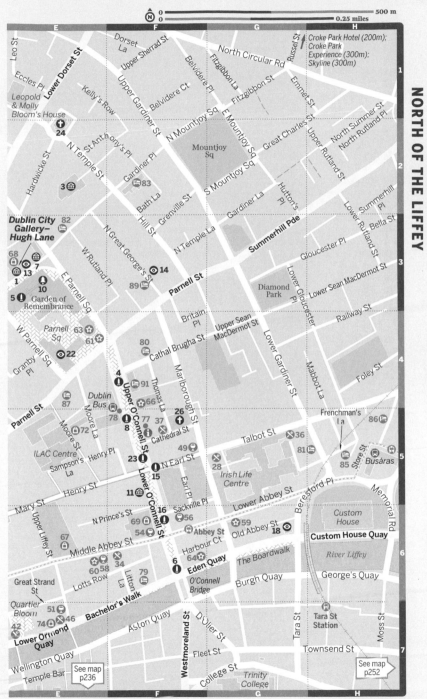

0 ———————— 500 m
0 ———————— 0.25 miles

Croke Park Hotel (200m);
Croke Park
Experience (300m);
Skyline (300m)

See map
p236

See map
p252

NORTH OF THE LIFFEY *Map on p248*

DOCKLANDS

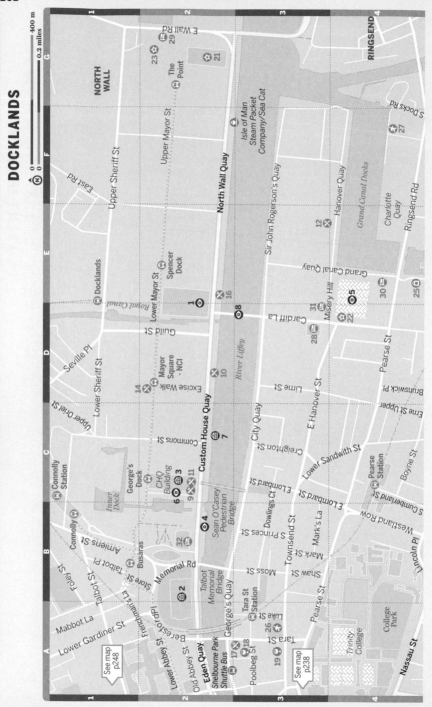

N

0 — 400 m
0 — 0.2 miles

RINGSEND

NORTH WALL

29 E Wall Rd
23
21
The Point
Docklands
Royal Canal
Upper Sheriff St
East Rd
Upper Mayor St
Lower Mayor St
Spencer Dock
Isle of Man Steam Packet Company/Sea Cat
Sir John Rogerson's Quay
Hanover Quay
S Docks Rd
27
Grand Canal Docks
Charlotte Quay
Ringsend Rd
12
Grand Canal Quay
Misery Hill
5
30
25
31
22
28
Cardiff La
North Wall Quay
1
16
8
Guild St
Seville Pl
Lower Sheriff St
Docklands
Mayor Square - NCI
Excise Walk
14
10
River Liffey
Lime St
E Hanover St
Pearse St
Brunswick Pl
Erne St Upper
Upper Oriel St
Commons St
7
Custom House Quay
City Quay
Creighton St
Lower Sandwith St
Pearse Station
Boyne St
George's Dock
CHQ Building
3
6
9
11
4
Sean O'Casey Pedestrian Bridge
E Lombard St
E Lombard St
Dowlings Ct
S Cumberland St
Westland Row
Connolly Station
Inner Dock
Connolly
Amiens St
Busaras
32
Talbot Pl
Store St
Memorial Rd
Talbot Memorial Bridge
George's Quay
S Princes St
Townsend St
Mark's La
Moss St
Shaw St
Mark St
Pearse St
Lincoln Pl
Foley St
Talbot St
Mabbot La
Lower Gardiner St
Lower Abbey St
Old Abbey St
Beresford Pl
Frenchman's La
Eden Quay
Shelbourne Park Shuttle Bus
2
18
17
Poolbeg St
26
Tara St Station
Tara St
Luke St
19
Trinity College
College Park
Nassau St

See map p248

See map p238

DOCKLANDS

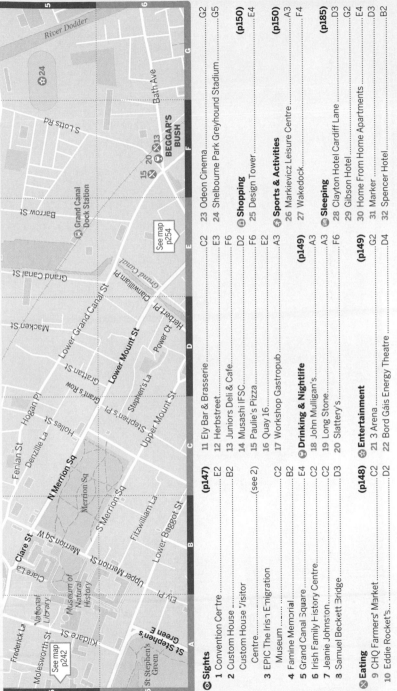

See map p254

See map p242

⊙ Sights (p147)
1 Convention Centre	E2
2 Custom House	B2
Custom House Visitor Centre	(see 2)
3 EPIC The Irish Emigration Museum	C2
4 Famine Memorial	B2
5 Grand Canal Square	E4
6 Irish Family History Centre	C2
7 Jeanie Johnston	C2
8 Samuel Beckett Bridge	D3

⊗ Eating (p148)
9 CHQ Farmers' Market	C2
10 Eddie Rocket's	D2
11 Ely Bar & Brasserie	C2
12 Herbstreet	E3
13 Juniors Deli & Cafe	F6
14 Musashi IFSC	D2
15 Paulie's Pizza	F6
16 Quay 16	E2
17 Workshop Gastropub	A3

⊙ Drinking & Nightlife (p149)
18 John Mulligan's	A3
19 Long Stone	A3
20 Slattery's	F6

⊙ Entertainment (p149)
21 3 Arena	C2
22 Bord Gáis Energy Theatre	D2
23 Odeon Cinema	G2
24 Shelbourne Park Greyhound Stadium	G5

⊙ Shopping (p150)
| 25 Design Tower | E4 |

⊙ Sports & Activities (p150)
| 26 Markievicz Leisure Centre | A3 |
| 27 Wakedock | F4 |

⊙ Sleeping (p185)
28 Clayton Hotel Cardiff Lane	D3
29 Gibson Hotel	G2
30 Home From Home Apartments	E4
31 Marker	D3
32 Spencer Hotel	B2

THE SOUTHSIDE

◎ Sights (p153)
1 Herbert Park.....................D4
2 National Print Museum.....D2

✕ Eating (p153)
3 Butcher Grill.....................B5
4 Chophouse.......................E2
5 Dillinger's.........................B5
6 Farmer Brown's................A5
7 Farmer Brown's................E2

8 Kinara..............................B5
9 Saba.................................C3

◉ Drinking & Nightlife (p155)
10 Beggar's Bush................D2
11 Taphouse.......................B5

✪ Entertainment (p155)
12 Aviva Stadium................E3
13 Bowery...........................A5

14 Donnybrook Stadium......E5
15 Royal Dublin Society Showground......E4

◉ Sleeping (p186)
16 Aberdeen Lodge.............G5
17 Ariel House....................E3
18 Dylan.............................D3
19 Pembroke Townhouse.....D3
20 Schoolhouse Hotel.........D2
21 Waterloo House..............C3

Our Story

A beat-up old car, a few dollars in the pocket and a sense of adventure. In 1972 that's all Tony and Maureen Wheeler needed for the trip of a lifetime – across Europe and Asia overland to Australia. It took several months, and at the end – broke but inspired – they sat at their kitchen table writing and stapling together their first travel guide, *Across Asia on the Cheap.* Within a week they'd sold 1500 copies. Lonely Planet was born.

Today, Lonely Planet has offices in Franklin, London, Melbourne, Oakland, Dublin, Beijing and Delhi, with more than 600 staff and writers. We share Tony's belief that 'a great guidebook should do three things: inform, educate and amuse'.

Our Writers

Fionn Davenport

Irish by birth and conviction, Fionn has spent the last two decades focusing on the country of his birth and his nearest neighbour, England, which he has written about extensively for Lonely Planet and others. In between writing gigs he's lived in Paris and New York, where he was an editor, actor, bartender and whatever else paid the rent; for the last 15 years or so he's also presented a series of radio programmes on Irish radio, most recently as host of Inside Culture on RTE Radio 1. A couple of years ago he moved to the northwest of England where he lives (and commutes from) with his partner Laura and their car Trevor.

Contributing Writers

Neil Wilson wrote the Enniskerry and Glendalough sections of the Day Trips chapter. A Scotsman based in Perthshire, he has been a full-time writer since 1988, working on more than 80 guidebooks for various publishers, including the Lonely Planet guides to Scotland, England, Ireland and Prague.

Catherine Le Nevez wrote the Brú na Bóinne section of the Day Trips chapter. She has traveled to around 60 countries and completed her Doctorate of Creative Arts in Writing, Masters in Professional Writing, and postgrad qualifications in Editing and Publishing along the way. Her work has also appeared in numerous online and print publications.

Published by Lonely Planet Global Limited
CRN 554153
11th edition – March 2018
ISBN 978 1 78657 454 1
© Lonely Planet 2018   Photographs © as indicated 2018
10 9 8 7 6 5 4 3 2 1
Printed in China

Although the authors and Lonely Planet have taken all reasonable care in preparing this book, we make no warranty about the accuracy or completeness of its content and, to the maximum extent permitted, disclaim all liability arising from its use.